The media's watching Vault! Here's a sampling of our coverage.

"For those hoping to climb the ladder of success, [Vault's] insights are priceless."
– *Money*

"The best place on the web to prepare for a job search."
– *Fortune*

"[Vault guides] make for excellent starting points for job hunters and should be purchased by academic libraries for their career sections [and] university career centers."
– *Library Journal*

"The granddaddy of worker sites."
– *U.S. News & World Report*

"A killer app."
– *The New York Times*

One of Forbes' 33 "Favorite Sites."
– *Forbes*

"To get the unvarnished scoop, check out Vault."
– *Smart Money Magazine*

"Vault has a wealth of information about major employers and job-searching strategies as well as comments from workers about their experiences at specific companies."
– *The Washington Post*

"Vault has become the go-to source for career preparation."
– *Crain's New York*

"Vault [provides] the skinny on working conditions at all kinds of companies from current and former employees."
– *USA Today*

VAULT
> the most trusted name in career information™

Enter the real world with a real advantage.

Tyco Electronics is an industry powerhouse driven by an entrepreneurial spirit and an enviable record of innovation. Our emphasis on forward thinking, teamwork and integrity has helped to make us a $13 billion global provider of electronic components, network solutions, undersea telecommunication systems and wireless systems for industries ranging from automotive, appliances and aerospace and defense to telecommunications, computers and consumer electronics.

We have approximately 94,000 dedicated employees around the globe serving customers in 150 countries and we're looking for more top talent to help lead us into the future. Take advantage of our career-making opportunities while working with some of the brightest minds in the business in an atmosphere full of inspiration, empowerment and respect for one another.

Come turn our opportunities into your advantage at Tyco Electronics.

CareersWithAnAdvantage.com

Tyco Electronics is an Affirmative Action/
Equal Opportunity Employer.

Tyco Electronics

Our commitment. Your advantage.

THE VAULT MBA CAREER BIBLE

2009 EDITION

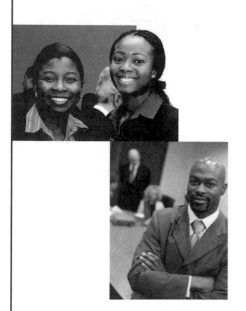

THE VAULT MBA CAREER BIBLE

2009 EDITION

MBA CAREER BIBLE

VAULT EDITORS

For information about permission to reproduce selections from this book, contact Vault.com, Inc.75 Varick Street, 8th Floor,
New York, NY 10013, (212) 366-4212.

Library of Congress CIP Data is available.

ISBN 13: 978-1-58131-624-7
ISBN 10: 1-58131-624-0

Printed in the United States of America

Acknowledgements

We are also extremely grateful to Vault's entire staff for all their help in the editorial, production and marketing processes. Vault also would like to acknowledge the support of our investors, clients, employees, family and friends. Thank you!

Visit Vault at **www.vault.com** for insider company profiles, expert advice, career message boards, expert resume reviews, the Vault Job Board and more.

V\ULT CAREER LIBRARY

vii

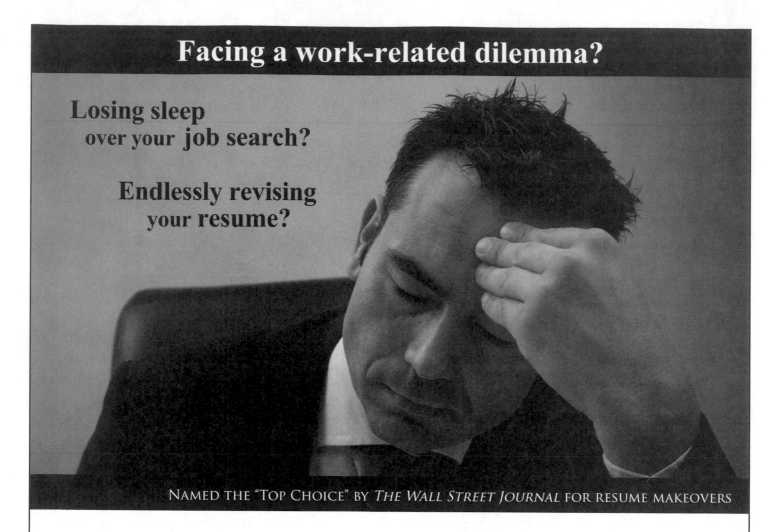

Table of Contents

Visit Vault at **www.vault.com** for insider company profiles, expert advice,
career message boards, expert resume reviews, the Vault Job Board and more.

VAULT CAREER LIBRARY

ix

INDUSTRY OVERVIEWS 43

Visit Vault at **www.vault.com** for insider company profiles, expert advice, career message boards, expert resume reviews, the Vault Job Board and more.

VAULT CAREER LIBRARY   xi

Visit Vault at **www.vault.com** for insider company profiles, expert advice,
career message boards, expert resume reviews, the Vault Job Board and more.

VAULT CAREER LIBRARY   xiii

Introduction

MBA Hiring Overview

So you've spent a few years in business school and (if you're like most B-school grads) a few years in the workforce before that. All of a sudden, you're back on the job market, with a new degree and newer skills, and you want to make sure that they pay off. Déjà vu?

Never fear, Vault is here! Despite the economic downturn, the MBA hiring climate remains strong. The Graduate Management Admission Council (GMAC) reports that even with the global credit crisis, a greater percentage of job seekers had received or accepted offers of employment in 2008 compared with the previous six years. So candidates, get ready: touch up your resumes, press your suits and prepare to interview!

It's not all bad news

Though it's difficult to gauge the full implications of the economic shifts in 2008, one thing is clear: the playing field has dramatically shifted for B-school graduates. Nonetheless, businesses continue to need talented people who can navigate the tumultuous economic environment. GMAC found that though employer hiring projections are less optimistic than in previous years, demand for MBAs holds strong, with 70 percent of companies surveyed planning to hire an MBA in the following year.

Career services steps it up

In the face of tougher times for MBA grads, many schools have amped up their career services to better serve students and alumni. Business schools' career management professionals have been working overtime to open up new avenues of opportunity for current and former students. In an article in *The Wall Street Journal* Patricia Rose, director of career services at the University of Pennsylvania explains, "We are encouraging students to think more broadly." And it's not just for recent alumni, either—*The Wall Street Journal* reports that the not-so-recently graduated are also getting more assistance from their alma maters in the difficult financial climate.

Thinking broadly

Thinking broadly may mean changing one's career path or it may mean just taking a detour. Traditionally, when we think of finance/accounting, consulting and marketing/sales (job functions that claim two-thirds of MBA grads according to the GMAC 2008 *MBA Alumni Perspectives Survey*), we think of the consulting and finance industries. Students and alumni are looking to business jobs in nontraditional sectors, such as energy, health care, technology and consumer goods, as well as boutique and middle-market firms. Considering a job in an industry you previously overlooked may mean the difference between having a job and unemployment. And, rocking that finance job in the energy industry will put you in a better position to move back to finance when something great opens up.

You've come to the right place to explore your options. Vault's *MBA Career Bible* profiles lots of nontraditional industries and describes the opportunities for MBAs within them.

From internships and recruiting to interviews

For many full-time business school students, on-campus recruiting and summer internships following the first year of are the most important methods of finding employment. According to GMAC's 2008 *Global MBA® Graduate Survey*, which surveyed 5,312 graduating MBA students about their experience, 53 percent of MBA students surveyed received their job offers

Visit Vault at **www.vault.com** for insider company profiles, expert advice, career message boards, expert resume reviews, the Vault Job Board and more.

VAULT CAREER LIBRARY

1

through internships or work projects. But landing a great internship isn't the only way to get your foot in the door—far from it. On-campus recruiting is another fast track to employment, and, as mentioned above, it is on the rise. Of the employers polled in GMAC's 2008 *Corporate Recruiters Survey*, 65 percent actively recruit MBAs. Even more encouraging, according to the *Global MBA® Graduate Survey*, more MBA-holders were recruited while still in school. And where recruiters go, interviews will follow—check with career services and fairs for dates. While companies usually make presentations and send representatives to business schools throughout the year, actual on-campus interviewing and recruiting tends to be structured on a predictable schedule. Investment banking and consulting firms, which hire large classes of both summer interns and full-time hires from business schools, tend to interview second-year students for full-time positions in October and November, and first-year students for summer internships in January and February. On-campus interviewing for Fortune 1000 companies traditionally happens later, with interviews in March and April for both full-time and internship hiring.

Shaking hands

One surefire bonus of the MBA degree is high starting salaries. For example, according to GMAC, executives and managers project that in 2008 a typical MBA candidate can expect a starting annual salary of $89,621—nearly 4 percent more than last year's starting annual salary. And that's not even counting other compensation and benefits, which 99 percent of employers tack on. In fact, the average expected total annual salary for a recent MBA graduate in 2008 was $102, 619.

Taking stock

So is the degree worth it? You bet. According to former MBA CSC President Mindy Storrie, "Companies have stepped up recruiting at business schools and MBAs are getting more job offers." The current president of GMAC, David Wilson, agrees: "We have long referred to the MBA as a global currency—a degree that symbolizes value all over the world."

MBA grads concur. According to GMAC's *MBA Alumni Perspectives Survey*, 97 percent of MBA-holders say getting their degree was satisfying on a personal level. Among alumni, 72 percent felt that their MBA education was extremely helpful in landing their current position, and more than half reported being "extremely" or "very" satisfied with their employer and their job. So go ahead, grads—get happy and get hired!

Good luck!

The Team at Vault

THE MBA
JOB SEARCH

MBA

CAREER

BIBLE

Resumes

Ten Seconds

Studies show that regardless of how long you labor over your resume, most employers will spend 10 seconds looking at it. That's it.

Because of the masses of job searchers, most managers and human resource employees receive an enormous number of resumes. Faced with a pile of paper to wade through every morning, employers look for any deficiency possible to reduce the applicant pool to a manageable number. Thus, your resume must present your information quickly, clearly, and in a way that makes your experience relevant to the position in question. That means condensing your information down to its most powerful form.

So distill, distill, distill. Long, dense paragraphs make information hard to find and require too much effort from the over-worked reader. If that reader can't figure out how your experience applies to the available position, your resume is not doing its job.

Solve this problem by creating bulleted, indented, focused statements. Short, powerful lines show the reader, in a glance, exactly why they should keep reading.

Think about how to write up your experience in targeted, clear, bulleted, detail-rich prose. Here are some examples.

Before

Primary Duties: Computer repair and assembly, software troubleshooter, Internet installation and troubleshooting, games.

After

Primary Duties:

- Assembled and repaired Dell, Compaq, Gateway and other PC computers

- Analyzed and fixed software malfunctions for Windows applications

- Installed and debugged Internet systems for businesses such as Rydell's Sports, Apple Foods and Eric Cinemas

Before

Responsibilities included assisting with artist press releases, compiling tracking sheets based on information from reservationists and box office attendants, handling photo and press release mailings to media, assisting in radio copywriting and performing various other duties as assigned.

After

Experience includes:

- Wrote artist press releases that contributed to an increase in sales by 23%

- Compiled and maintained mailing list of 10,000—Cambridge Theater's largest-ever list

- Handled press release mailings to *Anchorage Daily News* and Fox Four Television

- Contributed to copywriting of promotion radio commercials for selected events

Visit Vault at **www.vault.com** for insider company profiles, expert advice, career message boards, expert resume reviews, the Vault Job Board and more.

VAULT CAREER LIBRARY 5

It's What You Did, Not What Your Name Tag Said

Resumes should scream ability, not claim responsibility. Employers should be visualizing you in the new position, not remembering you as "that account assistant from Chase." While some former employers can promote your resume by their mere presence, you don't want to be thought of as a cog from another machine. Instead, your resume should present you as an essential component of a company's success.

Think Broadly

Applicants applying for specific job openings must customize the resume for each position. Many job hunters, particularly those beginning their careers, apply to many different jobs.

A person interested in a career in publishing, for example, might apply for jobs as a writer, proofreader, editor, copywriter, grant proposal writer, fact-checker or research assistant. You may or may not have the experience necessary to apply for any of these jobs. But you may have more skills than you think.

When considering the skills that make you a valuable prospect, think broadly. Anyone who has worked a single day can point to several different skills, because even the most isolated, repetitive jobs offer a range of experience. Highway toll collection, for instance, is a repetitive job with limited variation, but even that career requires multiple job skills. Helping lost highway drivers read a map means "Offering customer service in a prompt, detail-oriented environment." Making change for riders translates as "Financial transactions in a high-pressure, fast-paced setting." But unless these toll-booth workers emphasize these skills to prospective employers, it'll be the highway life for them.

Selected History

A lot of things happen in everyone's day, but when someone asks, "How was your day?" you don't start with your first cough and your lost slippers. You edit. Resumes require that same type of disciplined, succinct editing. The better you are at controlling the information you create, the stronger the resume will be.

When editing your history to fit the resume format, ask yourself, "How does this particular information contribute towards my overall attractiveness to this employer?" If something doesn't help, drop it. Make more space to elaborate on the experiences most relevant to the job for which you are applying.

Similarly, if information lurks in your past that would harm your chances of getting the job, omit it. In resume writing, omitting is not lying. If some jobs make you overqualified for a position, eliminate those positions from your resume. If you're overeducated, don't mention the degree that makes you so. If you're significantly undereducated, there's no need to mention education at all. If the 10 jobs you've had in the last five years make you look like a real-life Walter Mitty, reduce your resume's references to the most relevant positions while making sure there are no gaps in the years of your employment.

Sample MBA Resume

EUGENE H. HUANG

5050 S. Lake Shore Dr., Apt. 1407
Chicago, IL 60615
(773) 555-1234
ehuang@uchicago.edu

EDUCATION

MIDWAY SCHOOL OF BUSINESS   Chicago, IL
Master of Business Administration – Finance and Strategic Management   June 2008

- Dean's Honor List
- Active member of Management Consulting, Corporate Management and Strategy, and High Tech Clubs

ANDERSEN COLLEGE   Boston, MA
Bachelor of Arts in Physics (Cum Laude)   June 2003

- Andersen College Scholarship for academic distinction; Dean's List all semesters
- Violinist in Andersen College Symphony
- Physics tutor for Bureau of Study Counsel; active participant in Habitat for Humanity
- Completed dissertation in the field of condensed matter theory

EXPERIENCE

SMART BROTHERS   New York, NY
Technology Project Manager – Investment Banking   June 2004 – July 2006

- Managed project teams to develop profit and loss systems for proprietary trading group
- Promoted to project leadership role in two years, well ahead of department average of four
- Developed an original mathematical algorithm for trading processing module, improving performance by 1,200%
- Led team of six analysts in firmwide project to re-engineer loan syndicate trading flows in firm's largest technology project of 2004. Recommendations established new firmwide standard for real-time trade processing
- Appointed lead developer of interest accrual team after just three months in department. Initiated and designed project to create customized, improved interest accrual and P&L applications for fixed-income controllers
- Selected to work on high-profile project to re-engineer corporate bond trading P&L system. Reduced overnight processing time from six hours to 20 minutes and improved desktop application speed by 350%
- Devoted 20 to 25 hours a month to instructing junior members of the team in interest accrual and trading

FINANCIAL TECHNOLOGY GROUP   New York, NY
Analyst   June 2003 – May 2004

- Developed cutting-edge analytic software for use by Wall Street traders
- Worked on a daily basis with clients to create and implement customized strategic software solution for equity traders. Helped create and deliver extensive training program for clients
- Initiated, created and documented new firmwide standard for software module development

OTHER

- Winner of Mastermaster.com stock trading competition in November 2004. Won first place out of over 1,600 entrants worldwide with one-month return of 43.3%
- Other interests include violin, soccer and the harmonica
- Recent travel to Yemen, Egypt and Venezuela

Visit Vault at www.vault.com for insider company profiles, expert advice, career message boards, expert resume reviews, the Vault Job Board and more.

VAULT CAREER LIBRARY   7

Cover Letters

The Cover Letter Template

Your Name
Your Street Address, Apartment #
Your City, State Zip
Your Email Address
Your Home Phone Number
Your Fax Number

Contact's Name
Contact's Title
Contact's Department
Contact's Name
Contact's Street Address, Suite #
Company City, State Zip
Company Phone Number
Company Fax Number

Date

Dear Ms./Mr. Contact:

The first paragraph tells why you're contacting the person, then either mentions your connection with that person or reveals where you read about the job. It also quickly states who you are. Next it wows them with your sincere, researched knowledge of their company. The goal: Demonstrating that you are a worthy applicant, and enticing them to read further.

The second and optional third paragraph tell more about yourself, particularly why you're an ideal match for the job by summarizing why you're what they're looking for. You may also clarify anything unclear on your resume.

The last paragraph is your goodbye: you thank the reader for his or her time. Include that you look forward to their reply or give them a time when you'll be getting in contact by phone.

Sincerely,

Sign Here

Visit Vault at **www.vault.com** for insider company profiles, expert advice, career message boards, expert resume reviews, the Vault Job Board and more.

VAULT CAREER LIBRARY 9

Date

Placement of the date, whether left justified, centered or aligned to the right, is up to your discretion, but take the time to write out the entry. If you choose to list the day, list it first, followed by the month, date and year, as follows: Tuesday, July 9, 2007. (Europeans commonly list the day before month, so writing a date only in numbers can be confusing. Does a letter written on 4/7/07 date from April 7th, or July 4th?)

Name and address

Your name and address on the cover letter should be the same as the one on your resume. Uniformity in this case applies not only to the address given, but the way the information is written. If you listed your street as Ave. instead of Avenue on your resume, do so on your cover letter, too.

Your header can be displayed centrally, just like the resume header—including your name in a larger and/or bolded font. But in most cases, the heading is either left justified or left justified and indented to the far right-hand side of the page.

If you choose to list your phone number, make sure that you don't list it somewhere else on the page.

Next comes the address of the person you are writing. In many circumstances, you'll have the complete information on the person you're trying to contact, in which case you should list it in this order:

• Name of contact

• Title of contact

• Company name

• Company address

• Phone number

• Fax number

However, in many cases, you have less than complete information to go on. This is particularly true when responding to an advertisement. If you have an address or phone or fax number but no company name, try a reverse directory, such as Superpages (www.superpages.com), which lets you trace a business by either its address or phone number.

When you're trying to get a name of a contact person, calling the company and asking the receptionist for the name of the recipient (normally, though not always, head of HR) may work. But usually, companies don't list this information because they don't want you calling at all. So if you call, be polite, be persistent, ask for a contact name, say thank you and hang up. Don't identify yourself. If you have questions, wait until the interview.

If you don't get all of the info, don't worry. There are several salutations to use to finesse the fact that you've got no idea who you're addressing. Some solutions are:

To whom it may concern: A bit frosty, but effective.

Dear Sir or Madam: Formal and fusty, but it works.

Sirs: Since the workforce is full of women, avoid this outdated greeting.

Omitting the salutation altogether: Effective, but may look too informal.

Good morning: A sensible approach that is gaining popularity.

Format

Unlike the resume, the cover letter offers the writer significant room for flexibility. Successful cover letters have come in various different forms, and sometimes cover letters that break rules achieve success by attracting attention. But most don't. Here are some basic guidelines on what information the body of a cover letter should deliver.

First paragraph

To be successful, this first paragraph should contain:

• A first line that tells the reader why you're contacting them, and how you came to know about the position. This statement should be quick, simple and catchy. Ultimately, what you're trying to create is a descriptive line by which people can categorize you. This means no transcendental speeches about "the real you" or long-winded treatises on your career and philosophy of life.

• Text indicating your respect for the firm's accomplishments, history, status, products or leaders.

• A last line that gives a very brief synopsis of who you are and why you want the position. The best way to do this, if you don't already have a more personal connection with the person you're contacting, is to lay it out like this:

I am a (your identifying characteristic)

+

I am a (your profession)

+

I have (your years of experience or education)

+

I have worked in (your area of expertise)

+

I am interested in (what position you're looking for)

And thus a killer first paragraph is born.

Middle paragraph(s)

The middle paragraph allows you to move beyond your initial declarative sentences, and into more expansive and revealing statements about who you are and what skills you bring to the job. This is another opportunity to explicitly summarize key facts of your job history. The middle paragraph also offers you the opportunity to mention any connection or prior experience that you may have with the company.

Tell the employer in this paragraph how, based on concrete references to your previous performances, you will perform in your desired position. This does not mean making general, unqualified statements about your greatness, such as "I'm going to be the best you've ever had" or my "My energetic multitasking will be the ultimate asset to your company."

Comments should be backed up by specific references. Try something along the lines of "My post-graduate degree in marketing, combined with my four years of retail bicycle sales would make me a strong addition to Gwinn Cycles' marketing team."

Or, "Meeting the demands of a full-time undergraduate education, a position as student government accountant, and a 20-hour-a-week internship with Davidson Management provided me with the multitasking experience needed to excel as a financial analyst at Whittier Finance."

Visit Vault at **www.vault.com** for insider company profiles, expert advice, career message boards, expert resume reviews, the Vault Job Board and more.

VAULT CAREER LIBRARY   11

Many advertisements ask you to name your salary requirements. Some avoid the problem altogether by ignoring this requirement, and this may be the safest route—any number you give might price you out of a job (before you have the chance to negotiate face-to-face at an interview). Alternatively, you might be pegged at a lower salary than you might otherwise have been offered. If you must give a salary requirement, be as general as possible. The safest bet is to offer as general a range as possible ("in the $30,000s"). Put the salary requirement at the end of the paragraph, not in your first sentence.

Some cover letter writers use another paragraph to describe their accomplishments. This makes sense if, for example, your experience lies in two distinct areas, or you need to explain something that is not evident on your resume, such as "I decided to leave law school to pursue an exciting venture capital opportunity" or "I plan to relocate to Wisconsin shortly." Do not get overly personal—"I dropped out of business school to care for my sick mother" is touching, but will not necessarily impress employers.

Final paragraph

The final paragraph is your fond farewell, your summation, a testament to your elegance and social grace. This should be the shortest paragraph of the letter. Here, tell your readers you're pleased they got so far down the page. Tell them you look forward to hearing from them. Tell them how you can be reached. Here's some sample sentences for your conclusion.

Thank you sentences:

Thank you for your time.

Thank you for reviewing my qualifications.

Thank you for your consideration.

Thank you for your review of my qualifications.

Way too much:

It would be more than an honor to meet with you.

A note of confidence in a callback:

I look forward to your reply.

I look forward to hearing from you.

I look forward to your response.

I look forward to your call.

Over the top:

Call me tomorrow, please.

MBA Summer Internship Cover Letter

February 1, 2009

Kimberly Sharpe, Recruiting Manager
Hexagonal Consulting
666 Avenue of the Americas
13th Floor
New York, NY 10010

Dear Ms. Sharpe,

I am a first-year MBA student at State Business School. I was extremely impressed with Hexagonal Consulting's approach to management consulting after attending the presentation given by your firm earlier this year. I also learned more about your firm by talking with William Field and several other summer interns. My discussions with them confirmed my interest in Hexagonal Consulting, and I am now writing to request an invitation to interview for a summer associate consulting position.

After graduating from Northern College with a degree in accounting, I worked as an associate in the finance department of AutoCo, a well-known automotive manufacturer. I gained solid analytical and problem-solving skills there. I was responsible for identifying and resolving financial reporting issues, as well as generating innovative methods to improve our processes. I also fine-tuned my communication and consensus building skills, as I often needed to present and market my work to middle and upper management. Finally, during my last year of employment, I took on a team leadership role, managing the daily work of five junior members of our team and taking an active role in our training for new hires.

I am excited by the strong potential fit I see with Hexagonal Consulting. I feel that the analytical, leadership and teamwork abilities gained through my employment and academic experience have provided me with the tools and skills necessary to perform well in a consulting career, and will allow me to make a significant contribution at your firm. I am particularly intrigued by the shareholder value focus of Hexagonal Consulting's methodology, since it fits well with my experience in finance.

I have enclosed my resume for your review. I welcome the opportunity to meet with you when you recruit at SBS for summer internships later this month, and I would greatly appreciate being included on your invitational list.

Thank you for your time and consideration. I look forward to hearing from you.

Sincerely,

Laura Haley
314 Broadway, Apt. 15
New York, NY 10007
lbethhaley@hotmail.com

Visit Vault at **www.vault.com** for insider company profiles, expert advice, career message boards, expert resume reviews, the Vault Job Board and more.

VAULT CAREER LIBRARY   13

MBA Full-Time Cover Letter

Ms. Margaret Jones, Recruiting Manager
Mainstream Consulting Group
123 21st Street
Boston, Massachusetts 02145

November 19, 2008

Dear Ms. Jones:

It was a pleasure to meet you in person last week at the Mainstream Consulting invitational lunch on the Boston Business School campus. Having spoken with your colleagues at the event, I believe that Mainstream would be an exciting and challenging firm in which to build my career.

My background fits well with a position in strategy consulting. As a Midway University physics undergraduate, I developed an analytic, creative mind geared towards solving complex problems. I applied and enhanced my problem-solving skills as a technology project leader at Smart Brothers Investment Bank, where I focused on making business processes faster, more effective and more efficient. Creating these results for traders, financial analysts and senior management taught me how to effectively partner with clients throughout the various phases of business transformation. In addition, I gained valuable team leadership experience at Smart Brothers, guiding many project teams through the successful design and implementation of cutting-edge technology strategies.

As a telecommunications strategy intern at Global Consulting Associates this summer, I confirmed that strategy consulting is indeed the right career for me. Our project team helped a major telecommunications provider formulate a wireless data services strategy. I led the industry analysis and market opportunity assessment. This experience showed me that I am an effective contributor in a consulting environment, where industry knowledge, creative problem-solving skills, fact-based analysis and client focus are rewarded.

Mainstream appeals to me over other firms because of its focus on pure strategy projects, small firm atmosphere and accelerated career growth opportunities. Please consider me for your invitational campus interviews this fall. I am particularly interested in positions in the San Francisco and Chicago offices, and I have enclosed my resume for your review.

Thank you for your time, and I look forward to hearing from you soon.

Sincerely,

Michael A. Thomas
100 Wellany Way
Boston, MA 02111
michaelt3@bostonu.edu

Interviews

Interviewing during on-campus MBA recruiting can be a harrowing process for several reasons. First, there is the sheer volume of interviewing: some students interview with a dozen or more companies within a few week period, all while maintaining a busy class schedule.

At each interview, students work to convince interviewers that they represent a good "fit" with the company. Part of being a good fit, of course, means that students have specific interest and knowledge of the companies with which they are interviewing. This crucial element of interview performance requires students to research the employers as thoroughly as possible in order to make their cases convincingly to many companies, a feat made more difficult by the large number of companies with which many students interview. To help students prepare for their interviews with specific companies, Vault publishes 50-page employer profiles of major MBA employers, as well as "snapshots" of thousands of other major employers online at www.vault.com.

Interviewers use a variety of techniques to test students. According to the Graduate Management Admission Council's (GMAC) Corporate Recruiters Survey survey of more than 1,000 MBA employers, behavior-based interviews (during which candidates describe specific examples of skills such as leading a team or managing a difficult employee) are used by 79 percent of recruiters, and are the most common technique used by MBA recruiters. More than half of the recruiters surveyed (53 percent) use "case" or situational interviews in which the interviewers describe a hypothetical or real business situation and ask the job seeker to work through a course of action out loud. And more than one-third (36 percent) use question that measure position-specific knowledge (such as the ability to price a bond for a fixed-income finance position).

Case interviews and technical finance interviews can be particularly stress-inducing, as students cannot as easily predict questions and prepare answers for these types of interviews as they can for behavior-based interviews. (In fact, some interviewers, most notoriously in the investment banking industry, choose to deliberately make interviews stressful in order to assess how business school students respond to stressful situations.) To help students prepare for these types of interviews, we discuss case and finance interviews in detail in the next two sections.

Case Interviews

What is a case interview?

Simply put, a case interview is the analysis of a business question. Unlike most other interview questions, it is an interactive process. Your interviewer will present you with a business problem and ask you for your opinion. Your job is to ask the interviewer logical questions that will permit you to make a detailed recommendation. The majority of case interviewers don't have a specific answer that you, the candidate, are expected to give. What the interviewer is looking for is a thought process that is both analytical and creative (what consultants love to call "out-of-the-box" thinking). Specific knowledge of the industry covered by the case question is a bonus but not necessary. Business school students and candidates with significant business world experience receive case questions that require a deeper understanding of business models and processes.

The interview with a consulting company normally lasts about half an hour. Of this time, about five to 10 minutes is taken up with preliminary chat and behavioral questions and five minutes of you asking questions about the company. This leaves five to 15 minutes for your case interview question or questions. Make them count!

Why the case?

Your impressive resume may get you an interview with a consulting firm, but it won't get you the job. Consultants know that a resume, at its very best, is only a two-dimensional representation of a multifaceted, dynamic person.

Visit Vault at **www.vault.com** for insider company profiles, expert advice,
career message boards, expert resume reviews, the Vault Job Board and more.

VAULT CAREER LIBRARY   15

And because consulting firms depend on employing those multi-faceted, dynamic people, the firms rely heavily on the case interview to screen candidates. The interview process is especially pertinent in the consulting industry, since consulting professionals spend the lion's share of their business day interacting with clients and colleagues and must themselves constantly interview client employees and executives.

Consultants must have a select set of personality and leadership traits in order to be successful. The consultant's work environment is extremely turbulent. There are nonstop co-worker changes, hostile client environments, countless political machinations, and near-perpetual travel. These factors mandate that an individual be cool under pressure, be influential without being condescending, be highly analytical, have the ability to understand the smallest aspects of a problem (while simultaneously seeing the big picture), and have the ability to maintain a balance between the personal and professional.

Consultants are often staffed in small groups in far-flung areas. As a result, the individual must be able to function, and function well, without many of the traditional workplace standards: a permanent working space, the ability to return home each night, easily accessed services such as administrative assistance, faxing and photocopying, and the camaraderie that develops among co-workers assigned to the same business unit.

All these factors necessitate a unique interview structure focused on assessing a candidate's ability to manage these particular circumstances with professionalism and excellence. The case interview has evolved as a method for evaluating these characteristics.

Types of case interviews

What case interviews are not designed to do is to explore educational, professional or experiential qualifications. If you've reached the case interview stage, take a deep breath—the consulting firm has already weighed your background, GPA and experience, and found you worthy of a deeper skill assessment. This means that the case interview is yours to lose. Triumph over your case interviews and chances are that a slot at the firm will open for you.

Case interviews vary widely, but in general they fall into three groups: business cases, guesstimates and brainteasers.

Business case

Case interviews vary somewhat in their format. The classic and most common type of case interview is the business case, in which you're presented with a business scenario and asked to analyze it and make recommendations. Most cases are presented in oral form, though some involve handouts or slides, and a few (like Monitor Company's) are entirely written. (In a written case, the interviewer will not contribute any other information besides what's on the handout.) Another variation on the case interview is the group case interview, where three to six candidates are grouped together and told to solve a case cooperatively. Consultants from the firm watch as silent observers. Though you should certainly be prepared for these variations on case interviews, you are most likely to come across the traditional, mano-a-mano case interview.

Guesstimates

Whether freestanding or as part of a case, learning how to make "back-of-the-envelope" calculations (rough, yet basically accurate) is an essential part of the case interview. As part of a guesstimate, you might be asked to estimate how many watermelons are sold in the United States each year, or what the market size for a new computer program that organizes your wardrobe might be. (For example, you might need to figure out the market size for the wardrobe software as a first step in determining how to enter the European market.) You will not be expected to get the exact number, but you should come close—hence the guesstimate. Non-business school students and others who appear to be weak quantitatively may get standalone guesstimates—guesstimates given independently of a case.

Brainteasers

Brainteasers are normally logic puzzles or riddles. They may be timed. Often, brainteasers are meant to test both analytic and "out-of-the-box" thinking, as well as grace under pressure.

Skills assessed in the case interview

Following your case interview, your consulting interviewer will complete a written evaluation form. The evaluation forms often include a list of qualities, traits and abilities, and ask the interviewer to assess the candidate against the list. Following is a list of these special traits that, according to consulting insiders, interviewers will be keeping an eye out for as you work through the case interview:

Leadership skills

You'll hear this from every consulting firm out there—they want leaders. Why, you might ask, would a consulting firm need a leader? After all, many beginning consultants are consigned to independent number-crunching and research. The fact is, however, that consultants are often called upon to work independently, shape projects with very little direction and direct others. You should demonstrate your leadership skills by taking charge of the case interview. Ask your questions confidently. Inquire whether the case interview relates to the interviewer's own experience. While your resume and previous leadership experience will probably most strongly convey your leadership ability, your demeanor in the case interview can help.

Analytical skills

The core competency of consulting is analysis—breaking down data, formulating it into a pattern that makes sense, and deriving a sensible conclusion or recommendation. You should display this skill through your efficient, on-target and accurate questions while wrestling your case to a solution.

Presentation skills

Presenting your analysis is an essential part of consulting. Once consultants have analyzed their case engagement and decided on the proper course of action, they must present their findings and recommendations to their case team and to their clients. Interviewers will be watching you closely to see if you stumble over words, use inadvisable fillers like "um" or "like" frequently, or appear jittery under close questioning. Remember: When you're speaking, slow down and smile. If asked a question that temporarily stumps you, take a deep breath and pause. It's always better to pause than babble. Ask the interviewer to restate information if necessary.

Energy

Even the most qualified and analytical hire won't be much good if she quits at 5 p.m. during a long and arduous engagement. Interviewers look for zest and energy—firm handshake, sincere and warm smile, bright eyes. Remember that consulting firms expect you to take a long flight and show up at work the next day alert, perky and ready to go. If you must, drink lots of coffee and use eyedrops—just be energized.

Attention to detail/organization

Consultants must be as painstaking as scientists in their attention to detail. And consultants who juggle two or more flights a week and engagements all over the world must be extremely organized. You can display this skill through a disciplined, logical approach to your case solution and by showing up for your interview prepared. You'll want to take notes, so bring a pad of paper and a pen. Interviewers notice when candidates must ask for these materials. You must arrive on time.

Visit Vault at **www.vault.com** for insider company profiles, expert advice, career message boards, expert resume reviews, the Vault Job Board and more.

V\ULT CAREER LIBRARY   17

Quantitative skills

Those spreadsheets you'll be working with as a management consultant need numbers to fill them. Consulting interviews will inevitably test your grasp of numbers and your ability to manipulate them. Many interviewers will assess your quantitative skills by giving you a "guesstimate," either within the case question or separately.

Flexibility

Consultants may have to arrive at the office one day and be packed off to Winnipeg for six months the next. This kind of flexibility of schedule is mirrored in tests for mental flexibility. To test your grasp of a case interview, the interviewer may suddenly introduce a new piece of information ("OK, let's say the factories must be opened either in Canada or China") or flip the terms of the case interview ("What if this labor contract is not guaranteed, as I said earlier?") and then watch how quickly you're able to alter your thinking.

Maturity

Consultants must often work with executives and company officials decades older than they are. (This is why consultants are taught the right way to answer the question, "How old are you?") Eliminate giggling, fidgeting and references to awesome fraternity events you may have attended, even if the interviewer seems receptive.

Intelligence, a/k/a/ "mental horsepower"

Rather straightforward—consulting interviewers are looking for quickness of analysis and depth of insight. Don't be afraid to ask questions for fear of looking stupid—smart people learn by asking questions and assimilating new information. At the same time, asking your interviewer to repeat an elementary (or irrelevant) concept 20 times will not do you any favors.

What kind of case will I get?

While there's no way to tell for sure what case question you'll get, there are some things that can tip you off to the kind of case you'll receive.

For a business school student or graduate, the case question will probably be less open-ended and drive toward an actual solution. Your interviewer may posit something from her own experience—knowing what course of action the consultancy actually ended up recommending. This doesn't mean you have to make the same recommendation—but you'd better be able to back up your reasoning! Alternatively, one thing case interviewers love to do is look at your resume and give you a case question that relates to your past experience. "For example," says one consultant, "if you were on the advertising staff for the school newspaper, you might be given a question about investing in advertising agencies." For this reason, advise consultants, "it makes sense to follow up on your field in *The Wall Street Journal* because you may be asked about recent developments in it. If you know what's going on you'll be that much more impressive." Some guesstimates, like figuring out the total worldwide revenue of *Tarzan*, are broad enough so that most people can make a reasonable assumption of numbers.

Sample Case

You are advising a credit card company that wants to market a prepaid phone card to its customers. Is this a good idea?

Whoa! Better find out more about this prepaid phone card first before you even begin to think about recommending it.

You: What is the role of our company? Do we simply market the card or must we create them ourselves? Are we expected to provide the telephone services?

Interviewer: This card will be co-marketed with an outside phone company. We do not need to perform telecommunications functions.

You: What are our expenses connected with the card?

Interviewer: We must pay 15 cents for every minute we sell. We also have to pay $1 as a startup cost for the card and card systems.

You: What are our marketing expenses?

Interviewer: We normally use slips of paper that are attached to the backs of our credit card payment envelopes. We sometimes also send customers a direct mailing in a separate envelope. Or we can have telemarketers call selected customers.

You: What's the cost of each of these marketing techniques, and what is their response rate?

Interviewer: Telemarketers have a 2 percent response rate and cost $1 per call. Direct mailings cost us 41 cents per mailing and have a 0.50 percent rate of response. Our payment attachments have a 0.25 percent rate of response, but only cost us 5 cents each.

You: I'm going to assume we will sell one-hour phone cards. That will cost us $9 for the minutes and a dollar per card—so each card costs us $10.

Interviewer: OK, that sounds reasonable.

You: And what is our expected revenue on a one-hour phone card? What is the current market rate for a 60-minute phone card?

Interviewer: Assume it's 50 cents a minute.

You: So if we sell the cards for $30, we have a $20 profit, minus our expenditures on marketing.

Interviewer: What's our cost structure look like?

You: OK, let's figure this out. To sell 1,000 cards through telemarketing, we would need to contact 50,000 people. That would cost us $50,000. To use direct mail, we would have to contact 200,000 thousand people, which, at 40 cents per mailing, costs us $80,000. Since the envelope inserts aren't very reliable, we will need to contact 800,000 people using that method. But at 5 cents each, it costs only $20,000 to sell 1,000 cards.

We make $20 profit on each card. But even using the cheapest promotional vehicle, at $20 profit, we would only break even, because our profit on 1,000 cards would be $20,000. We shouldn't market this card, unless we can further cut our marketing costs or increase the price of the card. If we could slice the cost of the envelope attachments a penny or so, or sell the card for $35, or convince our co-marketer to reduce our costs, it might be worth selling.

Interviewer: What are some other issues you might want to consider? (Notice how the interviewer is nudging you to add to your analysis.)

You: We should also consider the competitive landscape for this business. Is the per-minute rate for calling card minutes expected to fall? If so, and our costs are held constant, we may lose money. Of course, we can learn more from marketing these cards. It could be that the people likely to buy these cards might be frequent travelers and could be targeted for other promotions

Sample Guesstimate

How many square feet of pizza are eaten in the United States each month?

Take your figure of 300 million people in America. How many people eat pizza? Let's say 200 million. Now let's say the average pizza-eating person eats pizza twice a month, and eats two slices at a time. That's four slices a month. If the average slice of pizza is perhaps six inches at the base and 10 inches long, then the slice is 30 square inches of pizza. So four

Visit Vault at **www.vault.com** for insider company profiles, expert advice, career message boards, expert resume reviews, the Vault Job Board and more.

VAULT CAREER LIBRARY

19

pizza slices would be 120 square inches. Therefore, there are a billion square feet of pizza eaten every month. To summarize:

- There are 300 million people in America.
- Perhaps 200 million eat pizza.
- The average slice of pizza is six inches at the base and 10 inches long = 30 square inches (height x half the base).
- The average American eats four slices of pizza a month.
- Four pieces x 30 square inches = 120 square inches (one square foot is 144 inches), so let's assume one square foot per person.
- Your total: 200 million square feet a month.

Finance Interviews

An overview of finance interviews

Investment banking positions and other finance positions are some of the more stressful and demanding positions on the planet, and this is reflected in the interview. In fact, insiders say that occasionally, an interviewer will yell at an applicant to see how he or she will react. Interviews normally go three or four rounds (sometimes as many as six or more rounds), and these rounds can have up to six interviews each, especially in the later rounds. Investment banking and finance interviews are also known for being deliberately stressful (as opposed to the attendant nervousness that goes with any interview). Some firms may ask you specific and detailed questions about your grades in college or business school, even if your school policy prohibits such questions. At other firms, interview rounds may be interspersed with seemingly casual and friendly dinners. Don't let down your guard! While these dinners are a good opportunity to meet your prospective co-workers, your seemingly genial hosts are scrutinizing you as well. (Hint: Don't drink too much.)

There are generally two parts to the finance hiring process: the fit part and the technical part. In asking technical questions, the interviewer wants to judge your analytical and technical skills. If you don't know the basic concepts of finance and accounting, your interviewers will believe (rightly) that you are either (1) not interested in the position, (2) not competent enough to handle the job. An important part of the interview is what is called "fit." As you go through recruiting in finance interviews, understand that you compete with yourself. Most firms are flexible enough to hire people that are a good fit.

The fit interview

They call it the O'Hare airport test, the Atlanta airport test, or the whatever-city-you-happen-to-be-applying-in airport test. They also call it the fit interview or the behavioral interview. It means: "Could you stand to be stranded in an airport for eight hours with this person?" Although bankers may have reputations for being aggressive individuals, don't act that way in your interview.

And while your performance in the fit interview partly depends—as the airport test suggests—on how well you gel with your interviewer, it also depends on your ability to portray yourself as a good fit as an investment banker, asset manager, etc. In other words, interviewers will try to figure out what your attitude towards work is like, how interested you are in a career in the industry, and how interested you are in the job for which you are applying.

I'm a hard worker

As a general rule, you should emphasize how hard you have worked in the past, giving evidence of your ability to take on a lot of work and pain. You don't have to make things up or pretend that there's nothing you'd want more than to work 100-hour weeks. In fact, interviewers are sure to see through such blatant lying. Says one I-banking interviewer, "If somebody acted too enthusiastic about the hours, that'd be weird." If you ask investment bankers and others in finance what they dislike most about their jobs, they will most likely talk about the long hours. Be honest about this unpleasant part of the job, and convince your interviewer that you can handle it well. For example, if you were in crew and had to wake up at 5 a.m. every morning in the freezing cold, by all means, talk about it. And if you put yourself through school by working two jobs, mention that, too.

Got safe hands?

As with all job interviews, those for finance positions will largely be about figuring out whether you can handle the responsibility required of the position. (In many cases with finance positions, that responsibility will mean making decisions with millions or billions of dollars at stake.)

An interviewer will try and figure out if you've got safe hands and won't be dropping the ball. "This is a critical I-banking concept," says one banker about safe hands. "The idea is: 'Can I give this person this analysis to do and feel comfortable that they will execute it promptly and correctly?' The people with safe hands are the ones who advance in the company. They are not necessarily the hardest workers but they are the most competent." Make sure you bring up examples of taking responsibility.

A mind to pick things apart

The world of finance is largely about number crunching and analytical ability. While this doesn't mean you have to be a world-class mathematician, it does mean that you have to have an analytic mind if you are to succeed. Explains one insider at a numbers-heavy Wall Street firm, "You can't be any old English major. You've got to have a really logical, mathematical head." Make sure you have examples of your problem-solving and analytic strengths.

T-E-A-M! Go team!

Teamwork is the buzzword of these days not just for the investment banking industry, but for every employer. Every finance position (except, perhaps, for research) requires that an employee work closely with others—whether this be in the form of investment banking deal teams, or finance officials working with marketers at a corporation. Interviewers will ask questions to make sure that you have experience, and have excelled, in team situations. Yeah, you can break out those glory days stories about the winning touchdown pass, but lots of other situations can also help describe your teamwork ability—previous work experience, volunteer activities, etc.

Preparing for finance interviews

When you review career options, don't discount the amount of time it takes to prepare for finance interviews. First of all, you should evaluate whether you actually want to be in investment banking, commercial banking, venture capital, etc. In short, you should know what you're getting into. Not only should you know this for your own sake (this is your future, after all), but your interviewers want to know that you understand the position and industry.

You should use the opportunity of nonevaluative settings (i.e., not an interview) to get answers to these questions. These are questions to which we strongly suggest you have answers before interviewing. Make a point to attend recruiting presentations by firms. Your informational interviews with alumni and (for those in business school) second-years are also good ways to get answers to some of your questions.

As for written materials, you can start with general business publications like *The Wall Street Journal*, *The Economist*, *BusinessWeek* and *The Financial Times*. From there, you can move on to trade publications that will give more industry-specific news and analysis. *American Banker*, *Institutional Investor*, *Investment Dealers' Digest* and *The Daily Deal* are some examples.

Your interaction with alumni can have direct results. The results can be good if you prepare properly before contacting them. You can also assure yourself a ding if you don't handle a meeting or phone conversation correctly.

Here are some questions about finance positions you should ask before you have your first interview:

Visit Vault at **www.vault.com** for insider company profiles, expert advice, career message boards, expert resume reviews, the Vault Job Board and more.

V∧ULT CAREER LIBRARY

21

• What is a typical day like?

• What are the hours in the industry really like? Are they 100 hours every week or every other week? Is it the same for every firm?

• How do people cope with the lifestyle issues in the industry?

• What kind of money do people make in the industry?

• What are the things I-bankers (or commercial bankers, venture capitalists, etc.) like about their jobs? What would they like to change?

• What is the future of the industry for the next few years? How will the industry change? How will the margins change? The return on equity?

• What is the career track in the industry? What skills are required at what stage?

• What is so exciting about this job?

• What is the culture of an I-banking firm as compared to a Fortune 500 company? Compared to a startup?

• What are the exit opportunities after 10 years in the industry? After two years?

Research individual firms

Once you've answered questions about the industry, you should begin to narrow your research to specific firms—both to know which firms to target, and to be knowledgeable for your interviews. Good sources for research are easily accessible publications like *The Wall Street Journal*, *BusinessWeek* and *Fortune*. If you have the resources (perhaps at a school library), you can also read through recent issues of trade publications like *Investment Dealers' Digest*.

Insiders at business school who have gone through the recruiting process suggest that you form research and interview practice teams. There is a lot of material to cover, and it is not possible to do it all by yourself. Form teams for researching industries and firms. Later, you can use the same teams to practice interviews. If you are in business school, your school will undoubtedly have such a club, or you may want to team up with other students who are looking into finance careers. Teams of four to six work quite well for this research process.

Practice your interviews

You should prepare answers to common questions given at finance interviews—whether they be fit questions, technical questions or brainteasers. While this may be easiest for technical questions and brainteasers (after all, we can help you to nail those questions with the right answers), it is also important to prepare for fit questions even if there are no right or wrong answers. We can steer you onto the right path with these questions, but you'll need to fill in the blanks. What's the hardest thing you've ever had to do? Can you give me an example of a time when you came up with a creative solution? You don't want to be cursing yourself after an interview, thinking about what you should have said, or examples you could have brought up.

One of the best ways to prepare answers to these questions is to use mock/practice interviews. You can practice by role-playing with your friends and classmates, or by taking advantage of interview training offered by your school. Many MBA career centers offer students the opportunity to perform mock interviews, which are normally videotaped. These practice sessions are conducted either by professional career counselors or by second-year students. The mock interviewees are given the videotape of their critique to watch at home (again and again). Students may choose what kind of interview they'd like to receive: finance, consulting, etc.

What mistakes are commonly unearthed by the videotaped interview? One business school career counselor says that he finds that "most MBAs don't have their story down. They can't elaborate why they came to business school, and why they want to work in the industry." The best candidates are able to describe their background and career history, and make a pitch about why they are interested in a firm, all in a minute or less, career counselors say. Another problem is that many students apparently "can't elaborate their strengths. They have them, but can't sell them. They are too modest." While there's no use demurring when explicating your good points, career center professionals warn that "there is also a danger of tooting your horn too much"—so make sure you're not making any claims for competency you can't back up with relevant experience.

To take full advantage of their mock interviews, career counselors say, students should take them as seriously as possible. Dress professionally "to get into the interviewing mindset." Afterwards, the interviewer will go over the session, assessing the candidate's strengths and weaknesses. It's a good idea to take notes on this feedback.

Mock interviewers also coach students on appropriate answers. "For example," explains one mock interviewer, "many candidates are asked to name their top three weaknesses. Answering with your actual weaknesses is not a good idea. So when I identify a student's weaker point—maybe they are weak on real teamwork experience—we strategize on an appropriate answer. It's better to say something like 'I wouldn't call them weaknesses, but there are three areas in which I still have room to grow,' and then choose three areas that are not deal-breakers."

Do interviewers thus end up hearing the same canned answers over and over again? "I do hear from some interviewers at certain schools—not mine!—that they do hear identical answers to certain questions," says one insider. "My advice to students is to always put answers into their own words."

Prepare questions

Finally, don't forget that finance interviewers often ask candidates whether they have any questions. Don't get caught looking like a job applicant who hasn't done research and is not curious about the opportunities. Read about the firms, read about the industries, and prepare some intelligent questions.

Sample Finance Interview Questions

What happens to each of the three primary financial statements when you change (a) gross margin; (b) capital expenditures; (c) other.

This problem tests your understanding of the interconnection between all three statements.

(a) If gross margin were to say, decrease, then your income statement would first be affected. You would pay lower taxes, but if nothing else changed, you would have lower net income. This would translate to the cash flow statement on the top line. If everything else remained the same, you would have less cash. Going to the balance sheet, you would not only have less cash, but to balance that effect, you would have lower shareholder's equity.

(b) If capital expenditure were to say, decrease, then first, the level of capital expenditures would decrease on the Statement of Cash Flows. This would increase the level of cash on the balance sheet, but decrease the level of property, plant and equipment, so total assets stay the same. On the income statement, the depreciation expense would be lower in subsequent years, so net income would be higher, which would increase cash and shareholder's equity in the future.

(c) Just be sure you understand the interplay between the three sheets. Remember that changing one sheet has ramifications on all the other statements both today and in the future.

How do you calculate the terminal value of a company?

The value of the terminal year cash flows (usually calculated for 10 years in the future) is calculated by calculating the present value of cash flows from the terminal year (in our case, Year 10) continuing forever with the following formula:

$$\text{TY FCF} = \frac{FCF_{10}\,(1 + g)}{(r_d - g)}$$

Visit Vault at www.vault.com for insider company profiles, expert advice, career message boards, expert resume reviews, the Vault Job Board and more.

VAULT CAREER LIBRARY 23

Here "g" is an assumed growth rate and r_d is the discount rate. Remember that you could also calculate the terminal value of a company by taking a multiple of terminal year cash flows, and discounting that back to the present to arrive at an answer. This alternative method might be used in some instances because it is less dependent on the assumed growth rate (g).

If you add a risky stock into a portfolio that is already risky, how is the overall portfolio risk affected?

a. It becomes riskier

b. It becomes less risky

c. Overall risk is unaffected

d. It depends on the stock

Answer: D. It depends on the stock. In modern portfolio theory, if you add a risky stock into a portfolio that is already risky, the resulting portfolio may be more or less risky than before.

A portfolio's overall risk is determined not just by the riskiness of its individual positions, but also by how those positions are correlated with each other. For example, a portfolio with two high-tech stocks might at first glance be considered risky, but if those two stocks tends to move in opposite directions, then the riskiness of the portfolio overall could be significantly lower. So the risk effect of adding a new stock to an existing portfolio depends on how that stock correlates with the other stocks in the portfolio.

When should a company issue stock rather than debt to fund its operations?

There are several reasons for a company to issue stock rather than debt. If the company believes its stock price is inflated it can raise money (on very good terms) by issuing stock. The second is when the projects for which the money is being raised may not generate predictable cash flows in the immediate future. A simple example of this is a startup company. The owners of startups generally will issue stock rather than take on debt because their ventures will probably not generate predictable cash flows, which is needed to make regular debt payments, and also so that the risk of the venture is diffused among the company's shareholders. A third reason for a company to raise money by selling equity is if it wants to change its debt-to-equity ratio. This ratio in part determines a company's bond rating. If a company's bond rating is poor because it is struggling with large debts, they may decide to issue equity to pay down the debt.

If inflation rates in the U.S. falls relative to the inflation rate in Russia, what will happen to the exchange rate between the dollar and the ruble?

The dollar will strengthen relative to the ruble.

This section was excerpted from the *Vault Guide to Finance Interviews* and the *Vault Guide to the Case Interview*. Get the inside scoop on consulting and finance interviews:

- **Vault Guides:** *Vault Guide to the Case Interview, Vault Case Interviews Practice Guide, Vault Guide to Finance Interviews, Vault Finance Interviews Practice Guide, Vault Guide to Advanced and Quantitative Finance Interviews*
- **Career Services:** One-on-One Finance Interview Prep, One-on-One Case Interview Prep
- **Vault Employee Surveys:** See what employees say about their interviews at top finance and consulting firms

Go to www.vault.com/finance
or
www.vault.com/consulting
or ask your bookstore or librarian for other Vault titles.

Visit Vault at **www.vault.com** for insider company profiles, expert advice,
career message boards, expert resume reviews, the Vault Job Board and more.

VAULT CAREER LIBRARY

25

DIVERSITY

1st Annual

Asian MBA Leadership Conference & Career Expo

- Jacob Javits Convention Center
  New York City
- September 10-12, 2009

★ For more information, please visit **www.AsianMBA.net**

Asian Diversity Inc. (ADI) is privileged to present the first **Asian MBA Leadership Conference & Career Expo in 2009.** This will be the first time present and future Asian leaders from corporate, government, and the community sectors convene in such a scale. following the enormous successes of **The National Black MBA Association and National Socirty of Hispanic MBA conferences**, we hope our efforts will unite and inspire Asian leaders to take further strides not only in the corporate sector, but in the global community as well.

The Importance of Mentors

What makes the difference between a career that thrives and one that stalls? For many women and minorities, the narrow gap between failure and success is bridged by mentorships. Mentors are people who share their general business knowledge, as well as their knowledge of a specific company, with lucky mentees (someone who is mentored). Here is some advice on how to make these valuable relationships work for you.

Mentors can keep you with an employer

After several years at the prestigious consulting firm Booz Allen Hamilton, Cathy Mhatre had her first child. Mhatre credits her mentors at Booz Allen with keeping her at the firm. "I've now been at Booz Allen for six years, which is unusual for any consultant. One of the main reasons I am still here is because there were people who wanted to keep me here." Mhatre estimates that she has "four to six" mentors at the firm, and advises, "Because women mentors are scarce in general, find enlightened men."

Have many mentors for many reasons

Do you need help on balancing your family life and career without sacrificing your career viability? You could probably use some help from a mentor who's done just that at your company. Your work/life balance mentor, however, may not be the same person who can help you polish your presentation skills and confidence. If you seek someone who will be your advocate at performance and promotion reviews, look for someone at least two levels above you (or with four or more years of experience at the company).

Find out if your employer assigns you a mentor—then keep looking

Increasingly, employers assign mentors to incoming associates—a practice that has been common at law firms for some time and is spreading rapidly to other industries as well. Some consulting firms have entire mentor family trees—with a "founder" mentor, his or her mentees, their mentees, and so on. Make sure to take advantage of these mentors, who have specifically volunteered to serve as resources.

At the same time, the most valuable mentors are normally the ones that evolve from everyday working relationships. If someone appears willing to share their experience and skills with you and takes an interest in your career, it is likely that they would like to mentor you in some way.

Don't expect your mentor to share your background

While it's terrific to have mentors that share your ethnicity or gender, it's no sure thing. Some of the MBAs we spoke to indicate that the old "succeed and close the door behind you" ethos is still in existence. "When I was working," says Lanchi Venator, a NYU Stern MBA graduate, "it seemed that most successful women were not open to helping other women out. It was almost as if they were saying, 'I made it when it was tough on me. Why should I soften it for you?'"

Be careful of having only one mentor

One-on-one mentorship has its pitfalls. Corporate historians may recall the case of Mary Cunningham and William Agee at Bendix Corp. After rising rapidly through the ranks of Bendix, Cunningham, a 1979 graduate of Harvard Business School, was accused of sleeping with her mentor. Cunningham eventually left the firm. Even when the shadow of romance doesn't

Visit Vault at **www.vault.com** for insider company profiles, expert advice, career message boards, expert resume reviews, the Vault Job Board and more.

VAULT CAREER LIBRARY 29

Grow with Us!

Robert Half, the leader in specialized staffing services since 1948, invites you to learn more about exciting career opportunities as a member of our internal business development management team.

Our people are the core of our business. We are seeking Account Executives with accounting, finance, technology, legal, marketing or administrative backgrounds to work within one of our multiple lines of business. If you are interested in learning more about career opportunities worldwide, please login to our corporate website, **www.rhi.com** and visit our "Careers" section to submit your resume. **Please reference where you heard about us.**

Robert Half®

Celebrating 60 Years of Excellence

enter a close mentorship, mentees with only one advisor run the risk of being seen as an appendage or sidekick, not a full professional. Whenever possible, seek mentorship from a wide variety of people.

Tips for Mentees

It's not enough to find a good mentor—it's just as important to use them correctly. Here are a few tips to make the most of your mentor relationship.

- **Find mentors at all levels of the company.** The classic mentor is someone a few levels above you in an organization—close enough to your experience to guide you upwards in the ranks, experienced enough to have some pull. But you can also gain experience from mentors at your level and at other companies as well. Your business school professors are another invaluable set of potential mentors.

- **Don't approach someone and formally ask them to be your mentor.** This kind of artificiality is akin to handing your business card to someone and asking them to be your contact—it's too artificial to take root. If someone wants to be your mentor, they will indicate that fact through the interest they take in you.

- **Keep in touch with your mentors.** Mentorship is a relationship, and relationships are built from frequent, informal contact. This is important even when your mentor is assigned to you by your company. If you move on from a company, stay in touch with your mentor there.

- **Establish trust.** Everything you discuss with your mentor is between the two of you.

- **Have realistic expectations.** Your mentor is an advisor and advocate—not someone to do your career networking for you, or someone to cover your errors.

- **Find your own mentees.** Mentorship is a two-way street. As soon as possible, start finding people who are willing to learn from you. You never know when the mentee will become the mentor!

- **Don't pass up the opportunity to have a mentor.** Having a mentor can make a major difference in your career path and your self-confidence.

Vault Diversity Q&A: Pipasu Soni, Financial Analyst, Honeywell

Pipasu Soni is a graduate of the Johnson School of Management at Cornell University. A former engineer of Indian descent, he previously worked at Ingersoll-Rand before getting an MBA. He currently works in Minneapolis as a financial analyst with Honeywell's Automation and Control Solutions (ACS) division, an $8 billion division encompassing seven different strategic business units including environmental controls, fire solutions, security systems and more.   He took time out to talk to Vault a bit about being a minority MBA and working at Honeywell.

Vault: How did you end up in your current position? Did you go to business school knowing you wanted to do finance?

Soni: Actually, I was initially interested in going into marketing, but after the very first semester, my focus shifted to finance. Previously I worked in new product development for Ingersoll-Rand. There's always some tension between the engineering and marketing side during new product introduction, and I was interested in exploring the marketing/product management aspect, to get more of a general management perspective.

But as an engineer, I enjoyed the technical side of finance and the role it played within an organization. When it came to recruiting, I really liked the Finance Pathways Program and the fact that the finance group at Honeywell is one of the keys to implementing the strategic vision of the organization.

Vault: Did you intern at Honeywell?

Visit Vault at **www.vault.com** for insider company profiles, expert advice,
career message boards, expert resume reviews, the Vault Job Board and more.

VAULT CAREER LIBRARY

31

Soni: No actually, I interned with a consulting firm. I wanted to find out more about the consulting field, and decided it wasn't for me. I enjoyed being part of the day-to-day operations of an organization where I could influence the performance and visibly see the product. I knew Honeywell would be a great place to leverage my past experience with Ingersoll-Rand.

Vault: What sort of program were you hired into?

Soni: I was hired into Honeywell's Finance Pathways Program. It's one of their career development programs for MBA graduates. The program consists of two 18-month assignments across different Honeywell businesses. I'm in my first rotation, which ends this December. My current assignment consists of working in the corporate finance group supporting the annual operating plan, strategic plan, corporate initiatives, and other functional areas—Six Sigma and Technology. At the end of the assignment I'll move into an operational finance role at a business unit level.

Vault: Is there a formal mentorship program with the Pathways program?

Soni: No, not "formal." Mentoring takes several forms at Honeywell. All employees are encouraged to seek out mentors as well as offer to mentor others. My particular businesses assisted me in identifying a formal mentor at the beginning of my assignment. The main focus of my mentor is to provide a contact that can give me insight and advice as I move throughout my career.

In addition, you receive mentoring through working with managers on assignments. Also, your supervisor gives you regular feedback on performance and instructs you on training you should pursue.

Vault: Are there diversity organizations for you at Honeywell?

Soni: Yes, there's an Indian and Asian Association that meets on a regular basis. These groups usually meet once a month for a networking hour or a guest speaker presentation. Honeywell also has several other minority employee groups throughout the company, like the Hispanic Network and the Black Employees Network.

Vault: Did you get the feeling during recruiting that Honeywell targets minorities and women for diversity hiring purposes?

Soni: No, I don't think Honeywell specifically targets minorities, but focuses on recruiting individuals that are the right fit with the company. Honeywell defines diversity more as individual uniqueness. I don't think it's just gender, race and ethnic background, but also things such as educational and cultural background and work experience.

With that said, Honeywell's incoming Pathways class is a diverse group similar to what you would find in a typical MBA class.

Vault: What attracted you to Honeywell?

Soni: The things that attracted me the most were the people and the job assignments. For me, having a first assignment in financial planning and analysis at the corporate level allowed me to understand the strategic vision of the organization before moving into a business unit role.

Other things unique to Honeywell included the ability to work across several functions, mandatory green-belt training and certification for all incoming MBAs, and ability to switch roles—from finance to marketing if desired. I spoke with several Cornell alumni and other Pathway program members before joining and it seems that our perspective of Honeywell is very similar.

Vault: What aspects of your MBA education do you think have proved most helpful in your experience so far at Honeywell?

Soni: In my current assignment, finance, accounting and leadership classes have been the most helpful. The classes in accounting and finance have been invaluable in reviewing business unit results. The classes in leading, communicating and team building have been also valuable in day-to-day communication getting people to meet deadlines and goals.

You learn about metrics in business school and using metrics to drive performance, but you don't realize the significance until you actually use it. It's been a great experience, and I feel like I'm going to the next level in my ability to lead teams and drive results.

Vault Diversity Q&A: Ann Silverman, M&T Bank

A graduate of the Wharton School at the University of Pennsylvania, Ann Silverman was a project manager and exhibition developer at the Smithsonian Institution in New York prior to business school. She decided to get an MBA in order to have a greater impact on the community in which she lives and ended up choosing to join the executive associate program at M&T Bank in the Washington, D.C. metro area after graduation. She took time out to talk with Vault about her choice of regional banking and about being a woman professional in finance.

Vault: Going into business school, did you know that you wanted to go into finance and commercial banking?

Silverman: I knew that I wanted to go into finance, but I suppose coming from such a different background, I didn't know what individual buckets [in finance] there were. Once I got into business school and understood more, I knew that commercial banking in particular was what I wanted, and that I wanted a regional bank.

Vault: What in particular about regional banks and commercial banking appeals to you?

Silverman: At the Smithsonian, one of the things I loved most was the community impact of the job, but I felt that I wasn't going to have a real impact until I had a profession that hits people's wallets. When I looked at the landscape out there I thought, "Wow, commercial banking is really a wonderful area that contributes to the businesses in the community and the community at large."

Vault: Why did you choose M&T?

Silverman: Looking at all of the mergers and acquisitions activity that have gone on in the banking industry, I really wanted to find a place where I would have opportunities for business development and client interaction earlier rather than later and a smaller, regional bank seemed the best place to get this experience and the chance to contribute in meaningful ways. And M&T's mission emphasizes being really involved in the community, and I take that very seriously.

Vault: Can you describe the program that you were hired into? Is it a rotational program?

Silverman: M&T has what's called the executive associate program. It's not really a formal rotation program; you're hired into a functional position. I was hired into commercial lending as knew I wanted to be a lender. In my case, my title is relationship manager. "Executive associate" is more of a hiring title.

Vault: How long are you in the executive associate program?

Silverman: The first year is the more defined part of the program, though the bank does track us as executive associates throughout our career.

The first year has really been a mix of both project work, which gives you exposure to people throughout the bank, and learning the skills to being a lender, everything from the financial and industry analysis and the business development skills to integrating yourself into the community.

Vault: Are there training sessions for executive associates outside of on-the-job training?

Silverman: In the first year, we have seminars. Almost once a month, all the MBAs are brought together at the bank's headquarters in Buffalo. Each time, there's a lunch with one of the members of the executive committee, and bookending that in the morning and afternoon are presentations from departments throughout the bank. This way, you get a chance to meet the other EAs that you've been hired with and the managers and staff that work across the bank.

Vault: How many executive associates were there in your class?

Silverman: I believe there were 21 that were hired in my class.

Visit Vault at **www.vault.com** for insider company profiles, expert advice, career message boards, expert resume reviews, the Vault Job Board and more.

VAULT CAREER LIBRARY

33

Vault: Did you have any concerns about going into finance, which is notoriously male-dominated? And do you find, in comparing notes with your business school classmates, that commercial banking is any better than other areas of finance, such as investment banking or investment management?

Silverman: I would agree that finance is an area where women are underrepresented. I knew that that would be part of the world that I would enter regardless of where I went into finance. I don't feel that there's a difference between investment banking and commercial banking.

With the issue of representation of women in finance, it's only going to change as more of us come into the field. There are a lot of women who have certainly gone before me, and we need to keep that momentum. Taking my peer group at Wharton as an example, many of the women that I was friends with are going into finance, so there's continued progress.

Vault: How many women are there in your executive associate class at M&T?

Silverman: There were three of us. I know them quite well—we speak frequently and try to foster close relationships with each other.

One thing that was important to me about M&T is that it has a diversity council. It's a bank-wide initiative that's headed up by a gentleman on the senior committee of the bank. Particularly as the bank has grown in the last three years, it has made an effort to takes issues of diversity seriously, as evidenced by the formation of this group. The idea that you've really got to grow and nurture that, it doesn't happen overnight.

Vault: What types of companies and organizations are you working with as a lender?

Silverman: We service middle market companies, which are companies that have revenues above $10 million. The economy in D.C. is incredibly diverse. There are lots of life sciences and biotechnology companies, there are government related contractors, high technology companies. Just everything under the sun.

Vault: And how do you go about developing business with these organizations?

Silverman: One of the ways that we get a lot of business is through referrals. And one of the ways to do that is to make sure you're really well networked with accountants and lawyers in the region and others that work with businesses. People in the bank are very generous about making sure you get the external introductions you need. There are many business organizations in the county that have breakfasts, lunches, dinners, etc. Let's just say that my evenings are quite full.

Vault: Do you work with professional groups for women with respect to business development initiatives?

Silverman: Oh, yes. In the D.C. region, there's a group called Women in Bio, there's one called Women in Information Technology—there are a lot of those groups, and those are definitely resources I tap into.

Diversity Employer Directory

Bristol-Myers Squibb Co.

P.O. Box 4000
Princeton, NJ 08543-4000
Phone: (609) 252-4000
www.bms.com/career

Bristol-Myers Squibb
Hope, Triumph and the Miracle of Medicine™

BMS offers opportunities for MBA students and graduates to join summer and full-time associate programs in the following areas: marketing, finance, information management, and technical operations.

Different perspectives make it possible. At Bristol-Myers Squibb, we're a diverse team of talented and creative people—each with a different perspective. We value each person's unique contributions and inspire each other to develop the innovative solutions that extend and enhance the lives of our patients around the world.

Flexibility makes it possible. At Bristol-Myers Squibb, our people find fulfillment in their work, extending and enhancing the lives of patients around the world. And they have fulfilling lives at home too. Bristol-Myers Squibb offers a flexible range of work/life programs that help our employees at each stage of their lives. We're proud to be ranked in the top 100 of *Working Mother* magazine's Best Companies for Working Mothers.

Opportunities make your growth possible. Ask yourself—how far do you want to go? At Bristol-Myers Squibb, we're determined to be the company where our employees can achieve their career goals. We offer a range of opportunities to help you get there. It's simple. Your growth helps us to better extend and enhance the lives of patients around the world.

Business schools Bristol-Myers Squibb recruits from: Columbia, Cornell, Dartmouth, Duke, NYU, U. Michigan, North Carolina, Thunderbird.

Credit Suisse

11 Madison Avenue
New York, NY 10010
www.credit-suisse.com/careers

CREDIT SUISSE

Fostering an inclusive workplace is an integral part of Credit Suisse's business strategy. Diversity and Inclusion promotes a culture of team work which respects, values and leverages employee's differences. Diverse perspectives lead to innovative solutions for our clients. It also allows us to attract and retain top talent in a highly competitive industry. This is Credit Suisse's competitive advantage.

Global Diversity and Inclusion helps the Bank win new business, advises clients on Credit Suisse's diversity strategy and strengthens relationships our clients.

In the past year, Credit Suisse received a dozen awards from independent organizations recognizing us as a premier diversity employer.

Visit Vault at **www.vault.com** for insider company profiles, expert advice, career message boards, expert resume reviews, the Vault Job Board and more.

VAULT CAREER LIBRARY 35

Mattel, Inc.

333 Continental Blvd.
El Segundo, CA 90245
Phone: (310) 252-2000

Recruiting E-mail:

MBAIntern@Mattel.com
UndergradIntern@Mattel.com

At Mattel, we have a vision to be The World's Premier Toy Brands - Today and Tomorrow. We understand that a culture rich in diversity is a key to business success. It allows us to better understand the business opportunities in various markets around the world, and develop products that resonate with consumers in diverse cultures. As the worldwide leader in the design, manufacture and marketing of toys and family products, including Barbie®, Hot Wheels®, American Girl® and Fisher-Price®, Mattel is not only one of the best places to work, it's also a lot of fun.

Osram Sylvania

100 Endicott Street
Danvers, MA 01923
Phone: (978) 977-1900
Leah Weinberg
Manager, Diversity Inclusion
www.sylvania.com/AboutUs/Diversity/

Recruiting E-mail:

Diversity.recruiter@sylvania.com
www.sylvania.com/AboutUs/Careers

OSRAM SYLVANIA is honored to have received "2007 and 2008 Best Diversity Company" recognition. We are committed to developing an increasingly diverse workforce with fair and open access to career opportunities. We believe that variety of opinion, approach, perspective, and talent are the cornerstones of a strong, flexible, and competitive company. Affinity groups, a mentoring program, and strategic relationships with professional organizations and colleges all support OSRAM SYLVANIA's commitment to an inclusive environment where every talented individual can be proud to work.

ROTATIONAL PROGRAMS

MBA Rotations

The internship after the first year of business school is a great opportunity for MBA students to experiment a bit and get a taste of a specific job or company. What if you're now in your second year and looking for your first position after business school, but still would like to try your hand at a variety of positions?

Some major employers provide rotational MBA hiring programs for new business school graduates that provide just this opportunity. MBAs who join rotational programs are hired into a specific function such as finance or marketing, but then can rotate through different specialties within the broader function (for example, treasury vs. risk management in finance). Rotations also allow for new MBA hires to gain experience with different business units at a large organization.

The following Vault Q&As will help give you a sense of how some of these rotational programs work.

Vault Q&A: Federico Sercovich, Citigroup

Upon graduating from the University of Maryland's Robert H. Smith School of Business, Federico Sercovich, joined Citigroup's rotational MBA Management Associate program with the company's North American credit card division. The program consists of two one-year rotations. Now finishing up his second rotation, he spoke with Vault about why he chose a rotational program and his experience with it.

Vault: Tell me a little bit about your pre-business school background.

Sercovich: I'm originally from Argentina. I spent four years doing marketing in Chile, in a variety of industries and functions within marketing. First I worked with the country's largest global advertising firm, BBDO, then at L'Oreal in brand management, then with B2B marketing for a smaller regional telecom.

Vault: Did you want to do a career change from marketing when you went to get your MBA?

Sercovich: Overall, the idea of doing the MBA was the opportunity to expand my skill set and move on to a more general management-oriented career path.

The management associate program at Citigroup allowed me—in a rather "safe environment"—to gain more experience in different business functions. While marketing is still my passion, I've expanded my skill base to achieve my long-term aspirations.

Vault: What do you mean by a "safe environment?"

Sercovich: You know it's a one-year term job, and so you get to learn a lot and to add value at the same time. However it's not something you will be doing for more than 12 months, it has a defined term, which allows you to go beyond your professional comfort zone

For example, during my current rotation which I'm finishing up this week, I'm in a CFO role supporting a new product function clearly outside my comfort zone. I was encouraged to take the risk and I've seen other people doing it and succeeding at it. The program gives you the opportunity to go ahead and do these kinds of things.

Vault: So tell me a little bit about the program and the rotations that you've done.

Sercovich: It's a two-year program, with two one-year rotations in different areas. My first rotation was in a marketing/strategy role in our merchant acquiring business. With that group, the customer is not the cardholder—unlike the rest of the North America Cards, it's merchants who want to take credit cards as payment instruments. During said rotation, I had the opportunity to leverage my B2B skills, and it provided me with a broad view of the payment landscape and the consumer's behavior at the point of sale.

Visit Vault at **www.vault.com** for insider company profiles, expert advice, career message boards, expert resume reviews, the Vault Job Board and more.

VAULT CAREER LIBRARY

39

Vault: Did you know that you were going to that type of position when you joined the management associates program?

Sercovich: I was actually first a summer associate during the summer between my first and second years of business school. I was in the e-business department, working with the strategic alliances team with various partners on different cross-sell initiatives.

At the end of the summer, at the end of my performance evaluation I was offered a position in the MA Program, which I happily accepted. The way it works—you know you have a job, but you initially don't know in which business you're going to be working. When it's closer to the point of joining, you start an interview process. You meet with different managers and network. I think it's pretty cool because you are completely in charge of your career choices—you get to decide for which opportunities you want to interview.

Vault: So what about your second rotation, your current role.

Sercovich: It's a CFO role in an area called cross-sell. I provide financial planning and analysis support for a new set of products under the umbrella of the alternate lending franchise. The products are unsecured personal loans.

These are new products, and this is a function I haven't been exposed to in my past. In this role, I do financial forecasting and profitability analyses, I have been solely in charge of the development of the 2006 financial plan for these products.

Vault: As a role outside of your "comfort zone" how have you found this experience?

Sercovich: Well, it's definitely stressful, but very exciting. The numbers I report roll up all the way to the CEO of Citi Cards and that's a big responsibility. The value I contribute to the business is clear and tangible.

Vault: So what are you drawing on to do your job, given that your background is in marketing?

Sercovich: It's part business school theory, part on-the-job training, and a lot of common sense. It's not rocket science—the math is fairly straightforward—but it was definitely a good challenge. I was able to put together from scratch the forecasting models for the business, which are now used every month.

Vault: Is there a formal mentorship program component to the program?

Sercovich: Last year, we joined the overall Citi Cards mentorship program, through which the MAs are paired up with a mentor who has been in the company for a while. But I think there is a huge component that is totally informal. As an MA, many doors are open, many times you can just call up a senior member of the organization and ask them for some time in their calendar. They are open to help you, and they give you wise career advice. It's sort of weird sometimes to be talking with these senior leaders who are dedicating part of their valuable time to giving career advice to a management associate.

Vault: So what will you be doing once you finish this rotation?

Sercovich: I have accepted a role in Citigroup International Cards, I will be working on strategic initiatives with different regions—global competitor analysis, different practices and products, taking a look at what's been successful in North America which could be rolled out elsewhere.

Vault Q&A: Rebecca Preston, Chevron

After graduating with her MBA from the University of Michigan Business School, Rebecca Preston joined Chevron's finance MBA development program, one of several MBA hiring programs maintained by the company. After stints in London and Houston in a variety of roles, Preston returned to the company's corporate headquarters in California to oversee the program. She talked to us about the program, which has been around for close to 60 years.

Vault: How many MBAs does Chevron hire a year?

Preston: For the finance program, we just increased the target this year. Historically it's been six to eight and it's now eight to 10. The HR program does about four, the marketing program hires about four, supply and trading out of Houston hires about three, global gas is considering starting and MBA program, and procurement hires in the neighborhood of four. Every group has MBA summer interns. Finance has also increased its intern target, from six to eight; the other programs do between two and four.

Vault: How long has the finance MBA program been running?

Preston: The program started in 1946. We'll be 60 years old next year. The other programs are more recent.

Vault: I'd imagine that would mean that a lot of the company's leaders have come through the program.

Preston: Yes. The former chairman came through the program. The current vice chairman is off the program, our head of international upstream (exploration and production), vice president of government and public affairs, and our CFO are all program alumni. The finance heads for major strategic business units are off the program; the comptroller, the treasurer, they're all from the program.

Vault: Is there any crossover between the various MBA programs in terms of rotations?

Preston: Not in terms of rotations. Functionally the programs are quite different. However, we do some joint events. Typically these would be around general industry or company knowledge. For example, we bring in external instructors— last week we had a geophysics professor, Dr. Hines from University of Tulsa, lecture about topics from how the earth was formed and how oil was created through to drilling and production of resources. It's a very complex industry, so getting fluency outside of your discipline is important.

Vault: In what types of roles and locations are incoming MBA hires for the finance program placed?

Preston: I've got eight people coming in this year. Six are starting here in California, two are overseas...

Vault: You're already sending them overseas for their first positions?

Preston: These two are returning interns. If they've had an internship at HQ and so grounding with us, we're comfortable in sending them overseas right off the bat. One's in Aberdeen [Scotland] in the North Sea, and another's in Singapore with our treasury function. The international component is increasingly important.

Vault: How long is the program and how many rotations do employees do?

Preston: It's a two-year program. They do three or four rotations. Domestic rotations are typically six months long. Sometimes the international assignments will be longer, and someone may elect to do three rotations with a longer, more in-depth experience overseas. This is particularly true of people who have interned here. Other people might feel strongly they need to see four different areas while on the program.

We always try to maximize the diversity of experience with different business units, and different finance functions. I get contacted from Chevron businesses all over the world looking for the talent. Every month I send out an update that shows where everyone in the program is in the company, and what opportunities have come in.

Visit Vault at www.vault.com for insider company profiles, expert advice, career message boards, expert resume reviews, the Vault Job Board and more.

VAULT CAREER LIBRARY

41

We encourage people to do a rotation outside of the finance discipline, too, and we have had many people cross over in past years.

Vault: What sort of rotations would they do outside of finance?

Preston: Typically people cross over into two areas: planning and business development. The planning roles are corporate strategy roles within the business units—developing the business plan, the strategic plan for the organization, within overall corporate strategy. The business development roles might be supporting commercial teams looking for new opportunities. For example, you might be supporting a team that's negotiating for new opportunities in Russia.

Vault: With the program having been in place for so long, there must be a lot of alumni from the program.

Preston: Yes. There are about 150 alumni and we've got a very active alumni network for the program. As the program manager I maintain all that information. We have two to three events a year that pull in all the alumni. We do a "family picnic" every year. We have a summer cocktail, where people meet the interns and the new hires. This year, the CFO was there, the head of investor relations was there, and other senior people. And every year we do the holiday luncheon and that pulls in all the alumni as well. These are typically in the Bay Area.

About a quarter of the alumni are international now. There are alumni in Moscow, Kuwait, London, Singapore, Scotland, Barbados, Beijing, Bogotá, Angola, Venezuela…

Vault: Is there any resentment among other finance professionals toward what might be thought of as an elite group?

Preston: There's definitely the risk of it becoming sort of an elitist group, and if that were to happen, the program would lose much of its effectiveness. But that hasn't happened because we're highly selective in who we bring in. Our industry is enormously complex, so you have to be humble and learn from the experienced people around you. You also have to be very capable so that you can take these learnings and produce superior results in a short period of time (six months or less for the rotations). Fit is very important—we have a highly collaborative and cooperative culture at Chevron.

Bringing in people with strong teamwork orientation, combined with demonstrated performance, means that rather than resentment, there's a lot of respect for the program and its members. They're able to perform at a high level quickly so people are clamoring for program members to work on their teams.

There's brisk, brisk demand for program graduates once their 24 months on the program is over. A big part of my job is matching the right opportunity with a program member's individual interests and development goals. It's quite common to move every 18 months to three years after you're off the program, because you're building up a broad base of experience.

Vault: Do most of the people who join the program have energy industry experience?

Preston: Not necessarily. I'd say it's less than a quarter that have direct industry experience, although a lot of them have technical backgrounds, such as engineering or geosciences. A lot of people have finance backgrounds or economics backgrounds.

Vault: But when interviewing, you're trying to make sure they are interested in the industry.

Preston: That's very important. In the first round for full-time hires, I spend almost all of the time trying to understand fit and motivation—is energy something they're passionate about? Will they thrive in our culture or clash with it? I then use the second round to push on the technical skills. Can they do the job? We're looking for every hire to be a career hire. We have 90 percent retention over 10 years. Fit and motivation is what's going to sustain you over the long run.

Vault: Is there a formal mentoring program?

Preston: We do not do a formal mentor matching in the finance program, but some of the other programs do. Instead, our alumni are very receptive to program members. I facilitate connections and our members find diverse and successful mentoring relationships that way. For interns we do match them with a "buddy," someone who's currently on the program and can help them evaluate us as a full-time employer.

INDUSTRY OVERVIEWS

Aerospace and Defense

Industry Overview

The Wright stuff

The aerospace industry consists of companies which produce aircraft, spaceships and the jets, engines and rockets that propel them. The defense industry produces a complementary group of goods, including satellites, ships and submarines, tanks and armored vehicles, and guns, bullets, explosives and other weapons. These industries are closely allied, with companies frequently participating in both spheres.

The aerospace industry makes most of its money by supplying individuals and commercial airlines with planes for business or pleasure. The commercial airline industry is notoriously cyclical, operating at the mercy of the business cycle; factors like the price of airline tickets and terrorism (or the threat thereof) also affect the number of people who travel by air, and hence the rate at which airline companies purchase new planes.

The lucrative nature of defense contracts shouldn't be underestimated, either: the U.S. government budgeted a whopping $480 billion for defense in 2008, give or take the odd hundred million allotted for special items during the year. Since making fighter jets and cargo planes require largely similar skill sets, and defense contracts are a generally recession-proof form of revenue, many aerospace and defense companies have arms that handle both commercial and military production. Major manufacturers of engines for planes include Pratt & Whitney, a subsidiary of United Technologies, Westinghouse and GE, Rolls Royce, and Daimler-Benz, which put the "vroom" in more than just cars.

Take it to the skies

The commercial aircraft market is dominated by archrivals Boeing and Airbus, who also have interests in defense contracts—Boeing derived nearly half its revenue from government contracts in 2007, while archrival Airbus is partly owned by EADS, the European Aeronautic Defense and Space Company. Smaller players, like Textron (which owns Cessna), Embraer and Bombardier also have interests in both commercial and military aircraft and technology. Other major defense contractors include contract leader Lockheed Martin, ship- and submarine-builder Northrop Grumman, General Dynamics, Raytheon, BAE Systems and United Technologies.

Plane dealing

The biggest rivalry in the industry is between U.S.-based Boeing and European-owned Airbus. These companies are the two largest suppliers of large jets to airlines, and the summer of 2007 saw them battling it out with their newest offerings. Airbus hoped to tempt buyers from the airlines that ferry large numbers of people between major airports with its A380, a double-decker plane of Brobdingnagian proportions. It seats 500 passengers, give or take, but has been plagued by problems with its assembly and wiring, which delayed its release by two years, and drove Airbus into the red—and its customers to Boeing's offerings, like the proven 747, which seats about 400. Boeing's newest offering, the 787 Dreamliner, was introduced in July 2007, but encountered its own fleet of production setbacks and delays. (There were also problems with its flight-test program, delivery schedule and its subcontracted and outsourced elements.) It's now expected to formally debut during 2009, by different accounts either "early" in the year or at the end of the third quarter.

The 787 has been designed to transport comparatively smaller numbers of passengers—only about half as many as the A380—but its carbon-composite construction offers several advantages. The plane is lighter, and hence more fuel efficient; the construction also mean that the plane requires less maintenance and isn't as prone to metal fatigue—a boon to airlines, whose margins have been falling as customers become more savvy about comparison-shopping for tickets. The composite

Visit Vault at www.vault.com for insider company profiles, expert advice, career message boards, expert resume reviews, the Vault Job Board and more.

VAULT CAREER LIBRARY 45

structure also means passenger-pleasing features like larger windows and higher cabin pressure and humidity. As of January 2008, Boeing had received 817 orders for the new model, making the plane the fastest-selling commercial airliner ever.

A new player enters the game

Boeing and Airbus may face a third competitor, however. China is reveling in its newfound industrial might, and plans to launch its own aircraft manufacturer. China Aviation Industry Corporation (AVIC) has already produced the ARJ-21, a short-haul plane tailored to the vagaries of air travel in China that can carry about 80 people; it is scheduled to enter service in 2009. The Chinese government is loath to see its rapidly growing market for air transport—which is expected to create a demand for 1,500 planes by 2010—farmed out to foreign companies, however, and AVIC has its sights set on producing large jets for the international market.

DE-fence!

Speaking of international relations, the defense portion of the industry has been affected by a wave of large mergers, as well as other factors. The industry inked deals worth some $31 billion in 2007 (including GE's $4.8 billion acquisition of Smiths Aerospace); almost half of the 43 transactions outside the U.S. involved the BRIC countries (Brazil, Russia, India, China). During the 2008 presidential election, industry watchers waited to see the impact on aerospace. While some pundits saw a democratic president as bad for the industry, others thought that spending levels would be consistent through 2010 or so, and then funding for war-related expenditures would simply slide under the Homeland Security umbrella. Almost all the experts believe the rapid pace of industry consolidation will continue.

And aside from all that getting and spending, the defense industry has had to cope over the past few years with changes in the methods of warfare. Modern battles are unlikely to be fought on a traditional battlefield against a professional army fielded by a government, and to be more like the agonizing and protracted conflict going on in Iraq and Afghanistan. Of course, this means that enormous tanks are out—and smaller, faster and lighter equipment is in. Automation is also a growing trend. Machines, unlike humans, never need to sleep or eat, are always paying attention and can be easily repaired or replaced in the event they are damaged.

Industry innovations show up in a variety of different guises. In 2007, Honeywell's MAV (Micro Air Vehicle) was sent to Iraq in order to help troops identify and defuse bombs and other threats. The device, which is about the size of a breadbox, consists of a fan in a cylindrical housing (which provides lift) as well as a small payload of wireless cameras and other sensors. The MAV can hover inches above a suspected bomb, allowing it to be more closely examined, or climb to about 10,000 feet for surveillance of a larger area. Remotely operated sensors are also the latest trend in border surveillance. Also in 2007, Boeing set up its first 27-mile stretch of monitored border between the U.S. and Mexico. Aimed at preventing smuggling and illegal immigration, the border security consists of a series of towers outfitted with radar, cameras, loudspeakers and data links. The towers are tall enough to see over trees and other obstacles, and allow rangers to monitor the movements of people as far away as several miles.

Spatial relations

Then, of course, there's space, the final frontier, which is soon to become as crammed with tourists as Times Square the weekend before Christmas. After Richard Branson, scion of the Virgin Group, announced that he would be offering space tours via Virgin Galactic in 2004, EADS Astrium, the space wing of the European defense giant, announced in 2007 that it would be offering 1.5 minute stints in a weightless environment on a space ship for €200,000. The spacecraft, which has yet to be built, would take off like an ordinary jet before lighting its rocket.

More prosaically, most effort in the space division of aerospace is devoted to the design, launching and maintenance of satellites for GPS devices, communications, weather prediction and research, and television and radio broadcast. Specialized leaders in this field include Alcatel Space, Astrium, Orbital Sciences and Arianespace, a division of EADS. Government and military demand for satellite bandwidth is expected to quadruple in the next decade—and, as such, companies in this group (which can't seem to launch satellites fast enough) have been attaching their tech to civilian birds. Major aerospace and defense companies continue to build space activities into their long-term investment plans, even though shooting for the stars won't turn cash flow positive in any time frame outside of a science fiction novel.

Working in the Indusry

Who, how, and how many

According to the AIA (Aerospace Industries Association), as of 2008, about 650,000 people were employed in the aerospace industry, and about two-thirds of those jobs were in aircraft and parts manufacturing. According to the Bureau of Labor Statistics, the industry has a higher-than-average number of people with advanced degrees in subjects like mechanical and electrical engineering. Besides engineers, defense industry employers are perennially seeking employees with security clearances. In order to obtain one, an employee must be a U.S. citizen, submit to a thorough investigation of his background, and be sponsored, either by a corporation or the government.

Giving the kids their wings

Companies are trying to recruit the latest crop of young'uns, as a quarter of their workforce will be retirement-ready by 2010. In order to woo their newest hires, major aerospace firms like Boeing and Lockheed Martin are getting all Web 2.0. Boeing lured in potential job seekers with the promise of a shot at winning an IPod, as well as sponsoring a Facebook group for former interns. Lockheed, on the other hand, allows potential job seekers to IM recruiters, while Rolls Royce's engine department instituted a fast-track management program that will promote new hires into management positions after a few years.

Roger, niner

So you've electronically networked your way into an interview. Now what? Insiders report that questions include behavioral questions—"Tell me about a time when you were working in a group and something when wrong. What went wrong? What was your role in the situation? What was the outcome?" Some engineers likewise report they're being given technical questions to test their expertise: "Have you ever had to resolve a complex technical challenge without all of the necessary information? If so, how did you find out what you needed to know?" Companies can give as little as one interview, or as many as three and these vary from an informal chat on the phone with a recruiter to a panel interview. Another common question relates to the interviewee's eligibility for security clearance, a necessary attribute when working in many defense sectors. Only U.S. citizens can be granted security clearances, and must submit to having their backgrounds thoroughly searched in order to obtain it.

Looking up

In the long term, both the aerospace and defense industries are poised to grow. Worldwide, passenger air traffic is forecast to increase by 5 percent a year through 2027 to 9 billion passengers—well over twice the number that fly the skies today, and someone's got to build all those planes. Growth in this sector might be depressed by lower consumer spending, brought about by rising prices, in the U.S. or Europe (which still account for the majority of airline customers), but it will be tempered by expansion in Asia.

Visit Vault at **www.vault.com** for insider company profiles, expert advice, career message boards, expert resume reviews, the Vault Job Board and more.

V/\ULT CAREER LIBRARY   47

In addition, with the debacles in Afghanistan and Iraq, not to mention the increase in religious fanaticism in general, terrorism is a continuing concern, so the defense industry looks as if it's got its hands full for the time being. The U.S. defense budget is up about 60 percent over its 2001 levels, and politicians are unlikely to reduce it lest they appear to be neglecting domestic security.

Employer Directory

AAR Corp.
1100 North Wood Dale Road
Wood Dale, IL 60191
Phone: (630) 227-2000
Fax: (630) 227-2039
Toll free: (800) 422-2213
www.aarcorp.com

Alliant Techsystems Inc.
7480 Flying Cloud Drive
Minneapolis, MN 55344
Phone: (952) 351-3000
Fax: (952) 351-3009
www.atk.com

BAE Systems
6 Carlton Gardens
London, SW1Y 5AD
United Kingdom
Phone: +44-12-52-37-32-32
Fax: +44-12-52-38-30-00
www.baesystems.com

Ball Aerospace & Technologies Corporation
1600 Commerce Street
Boulder, CO 80301
Phone: (303) 939-4000
Fax: (303) 939-5100
www.ballaerospace.com

The Boeing Company
100 North Riverside Plaza
Chicago, IL 60606
Phone: (312) 544-2000
Fax: (312) 544-2082
www.boeing.com

C&D Zodiac, Inc.
5701 Bolsa Avenue
Huntington Beach, CA 92647
Phone: (714) 934-0000
Fax: (714) 934-0088
www.cdzodiac.com

Cessna Aircraft Company
1 Cessna Boulevard
Wichita, KS 67215
Phone: (316) 517-6000
Fax: (316) 517-5669
Toll free: (800) 423-7762
www.cessna.com

Cubic Corporation
9333 Balboa Avenue
San Diego, CA 92123
Phone: (858) 277-6780
Fax: (858) 277-1878
www.cubic.com

Curtiss-Wright Corporation
4 Becker Farm Road, 3rd Floor
Roseland, NJ 07068
Phone: (973) 597-4700
Fax: (973) 597-4799
www.curtisswright.com

DRS Technologies, Inc.
5 Sylvan Way
Parsippany, NJ 07054
Phone: (973) 898-1500
Fax: (973) 898-4730

DynCorp International Ino.
3190 Fairview Park Drive, Suite 700
Falls Church, VA 22042
Phone: (571) 722-0210
Fax: (571) 722-0252
www.dyn-intl.com

Esterline Technologies Corporation
City Center Bellevue
500 108th Avenue NE, Suite 1500
Bellevue, WA 98004
Phone: (425) 453-9400
Fax: (425) 453-2916
www.esterline.com

GenCorp, Inc.
Highway 50 and Aerojet Road
Rancho Cordova, CA 95742
Phone: (916) 355-4000
Fax: (916) 351-8668
www.gencorp.com

General Dynamics Corporation
2941 Fairview Park Drive, Suite 100
Falls Church, VA 22042-4513
Phone: (703) 876-3000
Fax: (703) 876-3125
www.gendyn.com

General Electric Company
3135 Easton Turnpike
Fairfield, CT 06828-0001
Phone: (203) 373-2211
Fax: (203) 373-3131
www.ge.com

Goodrich Corporation
4 Coliseum Centre
2730 West Tyvola Road
Charlotte, NC 28217
Phone: (704) 423-7000
Fax: (704) 423-5540
www.goodrich.com

Hamilton Sundstrand Corporation
1 Hamilton Road
Windsor Locks, CT 06095
Phone: (860) 654-6000
www.hamiltonsundstrand.com

Honeywell International Inc.
101 Columbia Road
Morristown, NJ 07962
Phone: (973) 455-2000
Fax: (973) 455-4807
Toll-Free: (800) 601-3099
www.honeywell.com

ITT Corporation
4 West Oak Lane
White Plains, NY 10604
Phone: (914) 641-2000
Fax: (914) 696-2950
www.itt.com

Jacobs Technology Inc.
600 William Northern Boulevard
Tullahoma, TN 37388
Phone: (931) 455-6400
Fax: (931) 393-6389
www.jacobstechnology.com

Visit Vault at www.vault.com for insider company profiles, expert advice, career message boards, expert resume reviews, the Vault Job Board and more.

VAULT CAREER LIBRARY

49

Employer Directory, cont.

L-3 Communications Holdings
600 3rd Avenue
New York, NY 10016
Phone: (212) 697-1111
Fax: (212) 805-5477
www.L-3Com.com

Lockheed Martin
6801 Rockledge Drive
Bethesda, MD 20817-1877
Phone: (301) 897-6000
Fax: (301) 897-6704
www.lockheedmartin.com

Moog Inc.
Plant 4, Jamison Road
East Aurora, NY 14052
Phone: (716) 687-4567
Fax: (716) 687-5969
www.moog.com

Northrop Grumman Corporation
1840 Century Park East
Los Angeles, CA 90067-2199
Phone: (310) 553-6262
Fax: (310) 553-2076
www.northropgrumman.com

Orbital Sciences Corporation
21839 Atlantic Boulevard
Dulles, VA 20166
Phone: (703) 406-5000
Fax: (703) 406-3502
www.orbital.com

Parker Hannifin Corporation
6035 Parkland Boulevard
Cleveland, OH 44124-4141
Phone: (216) 896-3000
Fax: (216) 896-4000
www.parker.com

Pratt & Whitney
400 Main Street
East Hartford, CT 06108
Phone: (860) 565-4321
Fax: (860) 565 5442
www.pratt-whitney.com

Raytheon Company
870 Winter Street
Waltham, MA 02451-1449
Phone: (781) 522-3000
Fax: (781) 522-3001
www.raytheon.com

Rockwell Collins, Inc.
400 Collins Road NE
Cedar Rapids, IA 52498
Phone: (319) 295-1000
Fax: (319) 295-1523
www.rockwellcollins.com

Rolls-Royce Corporation
2001 South Tibbs Avenue
Indianapolis, TN 46206
Phone: (317) 230-2000
Fax: (317) 230-4020
www.rolls-royce.com

Sequa Corporation
200 Park Avenue
New York, NY 10166
Phone: (212) 986-5500
Fax: (212) 370-1969
www.sequa.com

Teledyne Technologies Incorporated
1049 Camino Dos Rios
Thousand Oaks, CA 91360
Phone: (805) 373-4545
Fax: (805) 373-4775
www.teledyne.com

Textron Inc.
40 Westminster Street
Providence, RI 02903-2596
Phone: (401) 421-2800
Fax: (401) 457-2220
www.textron.com

Triumph Group, Inc.
1550 Liberty Ridge Drive, Suite 100
Wayne, PA 19087
Phone: (610) 251-1000
Fax: (610) 251-1555
www.triumphgroup.com

United Space Alliance
1150 Gemini Street
Houston, TX 77058
Phone: (281) 212-6200
Fax: (281) 212-6177
www.unitedspacealliance.com

United Technologies Corporation
1 Financial Plaza
Hartford, CT 06103
Phone: (860) 728-7000
Fax: (860) 565-5400
www.utc.com

Wyman-Gordon Company
16801 Greenspoint Park Drive
Suite 355
Houston, TX 77060
Phone: (281) 856-9900
Fax: (281) 856-3601
www.wyman-gordon.com

Agriculture

Industry Overview

Feed me

The agriculture industry's broad scope includes everyone from farmers and ranchers to scientists who devise new and better foods and the businesspeople who keep it all running. The various disciplines within the industry seek ways to more efficiently feed Earth's ever-growing population while improving profit margins for food-related businesses. Allied industries provide the infrastructure that makes this possible, including rail and road transportation, pesticides and fertilizers, and processors that transform raw products into comestibles.

Looking at the numbers, the agriculture industry is a massive undertaking. In 2008, more than 87 million acres of land—an area slightly larger than that of Germany—were devoted to planting corn, with wheat production taking up 60 million acres and soybeans another 75 million acres. Soybean production is up 17 percent over 2007's harvest, while corn production is down nearly 10 percent, which will still produce the second-largest harvest in U.S. history (the largest crop was produced in 2007, the largest since 1944). To feed the protein-ravenous masses, more than 100,000 cattle and 378,000 hogs are slaughtered every day in the U.S. Agriculture's not just about edibles, though; rather it covers everything that is grown or raised for consumption. Cotton and wool are agricultural products, as are animal byproducts, ornamental plants, tobacco, lumber and the various fruits and grains used to produce alcohol. The industry, unsurprisingly, is huge, accounting for 1 percent of U.S. gross domestic product (GDP). That might seem like small potatoes, but 1 percent of the 2007 GDP—$13,843,825,000,000, according to the International Monetary Fund—is a hefty chunk of change.

The farmer's dilemma

Despite its significant contribution to the GDP, agriculture is very risky and often unprofitable. Profit margins, especially for crops such as soybeans, wheat and corn, are very low, so these plants are frequently grown on large, industrial farms, as tiny returns per acre make small-scale farming economically unfeasible. Fruits and vegetables offer higher returns on lower acreage, but the investment in plants, soil preparation and the necessary labor-intensive harvesting makes the likelihood of farmers breaking even in the first few years unlikely.

Farmers are also at the mercy of pests, plant diseases and weather, the king of all X-factors. While insecticides and pest- and disease-resistant strains of plants can mitigate these risks, they of course cannot be entirely controlled. Heat, drought, flooding, storms and other "acts of God" wreak havoc on yields and, in extreme circumstances, can even lead to famine. The weather doesn't even have to be especially dramatic to drive up prices: the per-bushel cost of 2006 corn went gone up 28 percent, a two-year high, due to a hot, dry spell in the Midwest in July of that year. The flooding of during the summer of 2008 destroyed about 10 percent of the harvest.

Further complicating matters is the fact that commodities such as corn, soybeans, and wheat are subject to market forces. To wit: a good harvest suppresses the price of a commodity and lowers profits, while a poor one raises prices but causes shortages. This inverse relationship between productivity and profit has plagued agribusiness for decades. Government subsidies for corn, wheat, milk, cotton and a number of other farm products also affect the equation. Designed to hedge risks and lessen farmers' financial burden, these subsidies keep agricultural commodity prices artificially low in domestic markets and around the world.

All of the issues detailed above have forced the consolidation of farms and processing firms. Today, the real players in the industry are all big companies such as Cargill, Archer Daniels Midland, Tyson, Perdue, Bunge and Pilgrim's Pride. ConAgra, at one time a major farming firm, is currently divesting its agricultural business to focus on branded and value-added

Visit Vault at **www.vault.com** for insider company profiles, expert advice, career message boards, expert resume reviews, the Vault Job Board and more.

VAULT CAREER LIBRARY

51

packaged foods. Meanwhile, Bayer, Dow and DuPont all have a stake in biotech, fungicides and pesticides, each with its own crop sciences division. Monsanto, meanwhile, is a leader in the genetic engineering field.

Little. Yellow. Different.

When you think of corn, what initially comes to mind is probably something edible: creamy corn on the cob dripping with golden butter, or crisp, salty corn chips or sweet sodas. It's unlikely that you would consider postage stamps, aspirin or imitation silk, but all of these goods are manufactured using corn byproducts. Archer Daniels Midland is one of the largest agricultural processors in the world, turning oilseeds (like soybeans), corn, wheat and nuts into food products like flour, sweeteners and emulsifiers, as well as plant-derived wood preservatives, industrial starches (which become everything from wallboard to glue) and ethanol. Bunge is the world's largest processor of oilseeds, turning them into such products as biofuels, livestock meal and mayonnaise, while Cargill is a highly diversified agricultural products processor, making such items as soy waxes, vitamins, pharmaceutical coatings, flavoring agents, dairy and meat products.

Fueling a greener future

Demand for biofuel has made the past few years a boom time for corn producers like Archer Daniels Midland. Ethanol—the alcohol-based fuel produced from fermenting corn, beets, wheat, or any other sugar-bearing feedstock—has quickly become the poster child for America's solution to gas shortages and the greenhouse effect. Mixed with gasoline to create E85 (85 percent ethanol, 15 percent gasoline), ethanol promises to replace America's reliance on foreign oil with a renewable, homegrown resource. The flurry of activity around the hot new fuel has caused corn prices to spike and corn production to swell—farmers planted 92.9 million acres of corn in 2007, a high not reached since 1944, when 95.5 million acres of corn were planted to supply depleted allies in Europe.

Another biofuel seeing growth is biodiesel, which can be produced from vegetable oils, animal fat and even leftover, artery-clogging grease used in restaurants. In its purest form, biodiesel releases 75 percent less carbon dioxide than petroleum diesel. Additionally, there's no conversion or new technology involved to scare off new consumers—as long as it runs on diesel, it'll run on biodiesel. The growing popularity of biodiesel has increased demand for soybeans (whose oil is commonly used for biodiesel), as production of the fuel tripled from 2004 to 2005 and doubled between 2006 and 2007; about 900 million gallons are produced annually.

Bean there, done that

Biodiesel aside, soybeans have taken a bit of a beating as of late, due to the sudden and resounding condemnation of trans fats in American foods. The process of hydrogenation that soybean oil undergoes to lengthen its shelf-life (and that of the products it's used in, including some brands of crackers, cookies and fish sticks) produces the much-loathed trans fats, which are believed to clog arteries and raise cholesterol levels when consumed in excess. Fast food restaurants and junk food manufacturers are cutting trans fats out of their products in response to growing consumer concern and outright bans—like New York's December 2006 decision to cut trans fats from its restaurants. Soybean farmers are being pressured to grow beans low in linolenic acid (a substance that causes soybean oil to go rancid), thereby eliminating the need for hydrogenation while keeping the soybean oil flavor intact. However, the conversion to low-linolenic soybeans isn't far enough along to replace the traditional, high-linolenic beans, although production of the coveted bean is expected to triple in 2008.

Not exactly American Pastoral

You're in for a shock if "agriculture" brings to mind amber waves of grain and fruited plains. Rather, agribusiness is as tech-focused and cutting-edge as every other industry these days. Steroids, hormones and antibiotics, for example, are routinely administered to U.S. meat and dairy animals. Steroids up the rate at which meat animals transform feed into muscle, while hormones, when administered through slow-release pellets implanted in the animal's ear, cause it to gain weight and, in cows, improve milk production. Hormones are also applied to fruits and vegetables. In order to ship fruit long distances, it must be picked before it is fully ripe to withstand the journey. Once it reaches its destination, it is treated with ethylene, the chemical which, in nature, causes fruits to ripen.

Antibiotics are given to animals to cure illnesses—a frequent occurrence when stock is kept in close conditions and fed an unnatural diet. Modern poultry flocks, for instance, are so large that sick animals frequently cannot be isolated, so producers treat all the birds that may have come into contact with the infected individual by adding antibiotics to the animals' drinking water. Feed lot-fattened, corn-fed cattle must be given antibiotics too; the feedlot diet of corn can distress their digestive tracts and lead to fatal infections. Antibiotics are more widely used in subtherapeutic doses, or doses not large enough to cure an infection, a practice that encourages the proliferation of antibiotic-resistant bacteria (much as with a human who takes antibiotics at the first sign of every sniffle). Without competition, resistant bacteria can spread rapidly throughout a population and subsequently be transferred to people who eat raw or undercooked meat.

Begun, this clone war has

Beyond antibiotics and hormones, recent biotech advances have become major issues in the agriculture industry. While farmers have been selecting crops for higher yield, greater disease resistance, better flavor and other desirable qualities for the last 12,000-odd years, we are now able to manipulate individual genes in order to express specific traits. Genetic engineering has produced Golden Rice, designed to accumulate vitamin A in the edible portion of the grain, a boon for cultures where rice is the staple crop and a varied diet is often a luxury. Insufficient quantities of vitamin A can cause blindness and even death in children.

Researchers are looking into growing oral vaccines for hepatitis B and HIV in tomatoes, potatoes and even tobacco. Embedding drugs in plants promises a less expensive method than traditional vaccine production, which would make large-scale vaccination of the populations of poorer countries possible. Genetic tinkering has produced plants such as Monsanto's Roundup Ready corn, canola, soybeans and cotton, and Bayer CropScience's Liberty Link corn, which are, respectively, resistant to the proprietary herbicides Roundup and Liberty. Today, nearly all soy and half of the corn grown in the U.S. is genetically modified, as is 75 percent of cotton.

Scientists are also beginning to explore these methods for use on animals, seeking to increase egg and milk production, change fat content and speed maturity. Genetically modified varieties of catfish and tilapia, designed to grow faster, are already for sale in some countries, while bulls are being cloned in order to improve the breeding stock of cattle. Pet fish implanted with genes that produce luminescent proteins have been available for purchase since 2003.

However, such tinkering has spawned a number of advocacy groups that fear unforeseen consequences. Many groups argue that direct genetic manipulation could produce harmful side effects that simple hybridization and crossbreeding would not, while others warn that herbicide residue might remain in the tissues of resistant plant varieties, or that engineered genes might cross into wild plant populations. Environmental advocacy groups won a small victory in March 2007, when a federal judge halted the planting of Monsanto's Roundup Ready alfalfa, on the grounds that the plant had not undergone complete environmental impact testing before its 2005 release. The debate rages on, on a global scale: Mexico barred biotech companies from planting genetically-modified corn within its borders in October 2006. That same month, Japan increased its testing of rice imported from the U.S., sniffing out unapproved genetically modified rice in the 1.1 million tons of short- and medium-grain rice in its warehouses.

Visit Vault at **www.vault.com** for insider company profiles, expert advice, career message boards, expert resume reviews, the Vault Job Board and more.

VAULT CAREER LIBRARY

53

The organic green giant

Consumers, motivated by concerns about the above, as well as factory farming, animal cruelty and the health of the environment, are increasingly demanding organic, ethically-treated, free-range, and antibiotic- and hormone-free food products. And apparently they are willing to pay the premium price: according to the Organic Trade Association, Americans spent $17 billion on organic products in 2006, an increase of 22 percent over 2005. That year, organics accounted for 2.5 percent of all retail foods sold.

Many businesses are taking advantage of this surge in organic interest. The supermarket chain Whole Foods, one of the more popular purveyors of organic produce, has the highest profit margin per square foot of any grocery store. At the other end of the spectrum, Wal-Mart began offering organic products in 2006. While such produce's widespread availability will certainly have tangible benefits for the environment and for customers, there are some drawbacks. Faced with price competition, retailers will inevitably demand lower prices from organic farmers, which could put them out of business. In addition, though organic produce can be sourced from foreign countries—China, for instance—regulations stipulating what "organic" means are certain to differ from country to country, or could even be absent altogether.

You just can't get good help these days ...

Despite the increasing reliance on machinery to do the grunt work of the agriculture industry, there are still some jobs that require that human touch. Unskilled migrant and immigrant laborers have provided this necessary muscle power for relatively low pay for decades, often filling positions that more prosperous Americans don't want. However, as the sanctity of the nation's borders has come to the fore in this era of homeland security, the agriculture industry has struggled to find and keep cheap labor. In December 2006, immigration raids at Swift & Company's meat processing plants (Swift is the third-largest meatpacker in the nation, behind Cargill and Tyson Foods) netted more than 1,200 illegal immigrants—the replacement of which, coupled with lost production, cost the company $45 million. A solution to the problem remains elusive; an immigration bill that would give illegal immigrants a chance to obtain legal status was defeated in the Senate in June 2007, making meatpackers and farmers worry about increased raids and dwindling applicants.

Picking up the bill

Every so often Uncle Sam takes a look at the current policies aimed at aiding the agriculture industry in the form of the highly contentious Farm Bill. In terms of controversy, the 2008 incarnation (also known as the Food, Conservation and Energy Act of 2008) lived up to expectations, only becoming law when Congress overturned a Presidential veto of the bill. In many ways, the Farm Bill provides a snapshot of how politics work in Washington, pitting special interest groups and lobbyists against legislators (and one another), as each attempts to get the best possible deal out of the legislation. And, although easily ignored, the decisions of what to include within the bill have serious ramifications not only in the U.S., but all around the world. This is only exacerbated by the fact that the provisions of the bill shape the ag-industry for years to come; the 2008 bill, for example, will be in effect until 2013 (and possibly longer, given the length of time it can take to pass such a gargantuan piece of legislation).

One of the most controversial issues at stake in the 2008 bill was that of farm subsidies. Given the bumper crop prices being reaped by farmers due to record food prices and an ever-increasing demand for biofuel crops, there was a substantial body of feeling that farm subsidies should be cut, both to ease the cost for the U.S. taxpayer, and to encourage free trade around the globe. When the bill was passed by Congress, however, the subsidies were included within it, and even increased in some cases. The reasons for that are several-fold, and include a desire to keep agricultural jobs within the U.S., as well as security concerns, and the influence of lobbyists.

One example of how government subsidies affect the U.S. is in the ubiquity of junk food, much of which has ingredient lists that are heavily based on wheat, soybeans, corn, and corn-derived sugars and fats. All of those crops are subsidized by the

Government, making them less expensive to grow, meaning that they'll pop up more often in the American diet than non-subsidized crops.

Another bone of contention in the battle over the farm bill had to do with the influx of imported food. According to The New York Times, the U.S. is importing $65 billion in food a year, or double the amount it imported ten years ago. Consumer groups want clear labeling on imported food, arguing that Joe American has a right to know if the beef on his plate was slaughtered on foreign soil. Opponents (namely, the meat lobby) say that the cost of such labeling would overburden the industry, and have successfully limited such labeling to seafood despite 2002 legislation requiring country-of-origin labeling on meat, produce and nuts. However, in light of recent scares regarding imported foods—including the massive pet food recall in March 2007 due to tainted wheat gluten from China, and the subsequent closing of 180 Chinese food plants in June after a nationwide inspection—those calling for enforced labeling of imported food found more sympathetic ears in Congress, and a provision was included in the bill to place the country of origin on all meats, produce and certain types of nut.

Other provisions in the bill, meanwhile, included extensions to the food stamps program, and a pilot food aid program that involves buying locally-sourced food overseas to donate to poor countries rather than shipping American crops. On the "green" side, the bill included extra funding for research in organic farming, and the establishment of incentives and grants to encourage farms to increase energy efficiency and put renewable energy systems in place.

That wasn't the only eco-friendly piece of legislation, though. The bill also contained a raft of measures—including grants, subsidies and loan guarantees—for driving the biofuel industry forward. A significant amount of money was set aside for research and production of advanced biofuels (i.e., non-corn-based biofuels).

While the bill caused controversy within the U.S., the drubbing it received abroad was perhaps even more significant. Criticized as being anti-free trade, the bill has met a significant amount of opposition from foreign leaders who complain that it takes global agricultural policy in the wrong direction. The problem? Subsidies (surprise!), which allow U.S. products a price advantage in the marketplace, disadvantaging poorer countries.

From farmhand to finance

An enormous range of man- and womanpower is required to keep the culture of agri- humming along. The agriculture industry is exceptionally diverse when you consider the number of different segments it encompasses. Operations include fish hatcheries, apple orchards, flower nurseries, slaughterhouses and more. Farm workers (who account for 90 percent of industry employees) require minimal training, but the Bureau of Labor Statistics (BLS) expects that more efficient machinery will reduce the number of such jobs in the future. However, small-scale farming, especially of the organic variety, is expected to grow. Managers, meanwhile, include farm and ranch owners, as well as those who operate ripening facilities or cold storage. Agricultural graders sort products, such as fruits and eggs, and inspectors evaluate the cleanliness of processing facilities. These professionals generally require both an agriculture degree and a background in the field.

The agriculture industry has plenty of opportunities for those who want to avoid getting their hands dirty, as well. Commodities merchants are needed to buy and sell grain, cocoa and other articles of commerce to ensure a consistent supply. Ecologists consult for the farming world as consumers and the government grew more concerned about the environmental impact of factory farming on the land and ecosystems. Agronomists (researchers in the many disciplines involving agriculture) start at the bachelor degree level, and many have doctorates to perform "pure" research. Logistics experts get the stuff from where it is to where it's going, while veterinarians keep the livestock healthy (until its time to kill it). Along with the usual jobs in HR, sales and IT, lawyers and MBAs are needed to keep good business practices and make sure everyone plays by the rules.

Although agriculture has been around since, oh, say, the dawn of modern man, the industry is constantly trolling for advanced technologies and the scientists who create them. Chemists come up with coloring and flavoring agents and new uses for agricultural byproducts. Agricultural scientists devise new food-processing methods, study soil and animal management and

Visit Vault at www.vault.com for insider company profiles, expert advice, career message boards, expert resume reviews, the Vault Job Board and more.

VAULT CAREER LIBRARY

55

frequently consult for the government or food processing companies. Bioengineers tweak genetic codes to create herbicide-resistant plants, Mexican jumping beans that can do the Lindy hop, or whatever other special function is required of an organism. Agricultural engineers design farm equipment for increased efficiency and reduced environmental impact. Depending on the career path they wish to pursue, these people generally have advanced degrees. The BLS reports that the agricultural scientist and engineer industries, specifically, are expected to grow by 14 percent between 2004 and 2014.

Vault Q&A: Darryl Barbee, Archer Daniels Midland

As a product manager in Archer Daniels Midland Company's (ADM) Specialty Food Ingredients division, Darryl Barbee is responsible for shepherding new products through the development process. From ADM's headquarters in Decatur, Ill., Barbee spoke with Vault about his position.

Vault: Tell me a little bit about your position at ADM.

Barbee: I primarily work on new business development, looking at the possibility of new products in my division to see what will be profitable for the company. I'll perform market research, as well as find the current market price domestically and internationally. I take a look at competition. Also, as it is important to keep open lines of communication with our customers, I will go out on sales calls to see what ADM products are working best for them or what could be changed.

Vault: Who are these customers?

Barbee: Our division's customers are typically major baking and beverage companies. ADM products go into food, animal feed, fuel and industrial products, so as a company we have customers in all of those markets.

Vault: As a product manager, what types of positions are your main customer contacts?

Barbee: I interact with research and development, as well as purchasing. I speak with R&D to find out what their likes and dislikes are about the products. With purchasing, I discuss the price of our products.

Vault: Is there a particular product set you work on?

Barbee: Yes. They're called acidulants, which covers citric acid and lactic acid. These are additives that go into food and industrial products.

Vault: Tell me a little bit about your background. Where did you earn your MBA?

Barbee: I received my MBA from Indiana Wesleyan in Indianapolis in May 2002.

Vault: Was it a full-time or part-time program?

Barbee: It was part-time. At the time, I was working for a different company as a financial analyst. Once I earned my MBA, I joined ADM as an assistant product manager for lecithin, a release agent you can find in cooking spray and chocolates, among other things.

Vault: How did you end up transitioning from your finance background into your current position? Were you looking for a change?

Barbee: Actually, when I was in graduate school, one of my professors asked me what I was currently doing. As I told him I was in finance, he told me I was in the wrong profession, and that I needed to get in sales. When I joined ADM, that was the direction that I wanted to pursue. As a product manager, I'm not only in sales, but also using my finance background, as I'm working a lot with numbers—P&L's, etc. It was a perfect fit.

Vault: So what is the project cycle like? How long does it take to launch a new product?

Barbee: It takes about 18 months to two years to get a new product out.

Vault: And how many would you release in a year?

Barbee: I'd say about one. Products can be tweaked many different times before they are released. I would say, if you get one product out a year, you're doing a good job. There are usually about eight to 10 products in the pipeline.

Vault: Does your involvement with a product end once the product is approved?

Barbee: No. From there a plant is built, and while the plant is being built, I interact with the plant to make sure everything is OK. I keep track of the timeline and make sure we're keeping up.

I'm also working with R&D. I'm passing along information I am gathering from the customers about the product. Our main goal is to use our resources to help meet the needs of today and tomorrow for our customers.

I get R&D, sales, marketing and regulatory affairs together. We all make sure we're on the same page. With marketing, I'll assist in developing a brand, logo and sales literature as needed. I'll also work with marketing to talk to the trade publications to let them know we're coming out with a new product.

Vault: What is the most recent product you launched?

Barbee: Calcium citrate. It's used in orange juice, and it's also used in tablets.

Vault: What sort of classes from business school do you find most helpful with what you're doing right now?

Barbee: I would probably say marketing and finance. Also, just being a leader in a group. My cost accounting skills definitely play a huge role in launching a new product. You're looking at estimating packaging costs, what type of packaging, how much do we need to start off with. You're doing this all without any preexisting data, so my MBA, maybe more than anything else, has given me the confidence to handle those challenges managing a new product as opposed to managing a product that's already on the market.

Vault: How do you find working for a large employer like ADM?

Barbee: ADM is a Fortune 50 company, so when I talk to people about working for ADM, they know I am working for a large, successful company. ADM tends to attract and hire the best people.

There are also benefits working at the headquarters of a large organization. There's a gym on site that's free to all employees, their spouses and dependents. At that wellness center, there is also a medical facility with an on-site doctor that employees can use.

Visit Vault at **www.vault.com** for insider company profiles, expert advice, career message boards, expert resume reviews, the Vault Job Board and more.

V∧ULT CAREER LIBRARY

57

Employer Directory

A. Duda & Sons, Inc
1200 Duda Terrace
Oviedo, FL 32765
Phone: (407) 365-2111
Fax: (407) 365-2010
www.duda.com

ADM Alliance Nutrition, Inc.
1000 North 30th Street
Quincy, IL 62301
Phone: (217) 222-7100
Fax: (217) 222-4069
www.admani.com

Ag Processing Inc
12700 West Dodge Road
Omaha, NE 68154
Phone: (402) 496-7809
Fax: (402) 498-2215
Toll free: (800) 247-1345
www.agp.com

Agri Beef Co.
1555 Shoreline Drive, 3rd Floor
Boise, ID 83702
Phone: (208) 338-2500
Fax: (208) 338-2605
Toll free: (800) 657-6305
www.agribeef.com

Alabama Farmers Cooperative, Inc.
121 Somerville Road SE
Decatur, AL 35601
Phone: (256) 353-6843
Fax: (256) 350-1770
www.alafarm.com

The Andersons, Inc.
480 West Dussel Drive
Maumee, OH 43537
Phone: (419) 893-5050
Fax: (419) 891-6670
www.andersonsinc.com

Archer Daniels Midland Company (ADM)
4666 Faries Parkway
P.O. Box 1470
Decatur, IL 62525
Phone: (217) 424-5200
Fax: (217) 424-6196
Toll free: (800) 637-5843
www.admworld.com

Associated British Foods plc
Weston Centre
10 Grosvenor Street
London, W1K 4QY
United Kingdom
Phone: +44-20-73-99-65-00
Fax: +44-20-73-99-65-80
www.abf.co.uk

Blue Diamond Growers
1802 C Street
Sacramento, CA 95814
Phone: (916) 442-0771
Fax: (916) 446-8461
www.bluediamond.com

Bunge Limited
2 Church Street
Hamilton, HM 11
Bermuda
Phone: (914) 684-2800
Fax: (914) 684-3497
www.bunge.com

Cargill
15407 McGinty Road West
Wayzata, MN 55391
Phone: (952) 742-7575
Fax: (952) 742-7393
Toll free: (800) 227-4455
www.cargill.com

Chiquita Brands, International, Inc.
250 East 5th Street
Cincinnati, OH 45202
Phone: (513) 784-8000
Fax: (513) 784-8030
www.chiquita.com

CHS Inc.
5500 Cenex Drive
Inver Grove Heights, MN 55077
Phone: (651) 355-6000
www.chsinc.com

ConAgra Foods, Inc.
1 ConAgra Drive
Omaha, NE 68102-5001
Phone: (402) 595-4000
Fax: (402) 595-4707
www.conagra.com

Corn Products International, Inc.
5 Westbrook Corporate Center
Westchester, IL 60154
Phone: (708) 551-2600
Fax: (708) 551-2570
Toll free: (800) 443-2746
www.cornproducts.com

D'Arrigo Bros. Company
383 West Market Street
Salinas, CA 93908
Phone: (831) 424-3955
Fax: (831) 424-3136
www.andyboy.com

Dunavant Enterprises, Inc.
3797 New Getwell Road
Memphis, TN 38118
Phone: (901) 369-1500
Fax: (901) 369-1608
www.dunavant.com

Golden Peanut Company, LLC
100 North Point Center East, Suite 400
Alpharetta, GA 30022
Phone: (770) 752-8205
Fax: (770) 752-8306
www.goldenpeanut.com

Griffin Industries, Inc.
4221 Alexandria Pike
Cold Spring, KY 41076
Phone: (859) 781-2010
Fax: (859) 572-2575
www.giffinind.com

Employer Directory, cont.

J.G. Boswell Company
101 West Walnut Street
Pasadena, CA 91103
Phone: (626) 583-3000
Fax: (626) 583-3090
www.jgbowelltomato.com

Iowa Turkey Growers Cooperative
207 West 2nd Street
West Liberty, IA 52776
Phone: (319) 627-2126
Fax: (319) 627-6334
Toll free: (888) 511-4500

Land O'Lakes Purina Feed LLC
1080 County Road
Shoreview, MN 55126
Phone: (651) 481-2222
www.lolfeed.com

MFA Incorporated
201 Ray Young Drive
Columbia, MO 65201
Phone: (573) 874-5111
Fax: (573) 876-5430
www.mfaincorporated.com

Monsanto Company
800 North Lindbergh Boulevard
St. Louis, MO 63167
Phone: (314) 694-1000
Fax: (314) 694-8394
www.monsanto.com

Murdock Holding Company
10900 Wilshire Boulevard, Suite 1600
Wayzata, MN 55391
Phone: (952) 742-7575
Fax: (952) 742-7393
Toll free: (800) 227-4455

Murphy-Brown LLC
2822 Highway 24 West
Warsaw, NC 28398
Phone: (910) 293-3434
Fax: (910) 289-6400
www.murphybrownllc.com

National Grape Cooperative Association, Inc.
2 South Portage Street
Westfield, NY 14787
Phone: (716) 326-5200
Fax: (716) 326-5494
www.nationalgrape.com

Orscheln Farm and Home LLC
101 West Coates Street
Moberly, MO 65270
Phone: (660) 263-4335
Fax: (660) 269-3500
www.orscheln.com

Perdue Farms Incorporated
31149 Old Ocean City Road
Salisbury, MD 21804
Phone: (410) 543-3000
Fax: (410) 543-3292
Toll free: (800) 473-7383
www.perdue.com

Pilgrim's Pride Corporation
4845 U.S. Highway 271 North
Pittsburg, TX 75686-0093
Phone: (903) 855-1000
Fax: (903) 856-7505
www.pilgrimspride.com

Pioneer Hi-Bred International, Inc.
7100 NW 62nd Avenue
Johnston, IA 50131
Phone: (515) 270-3200
Fax: (515) 334-4515
Toll free: (800) 247-6803
www.pioneer.com

Smithfield Foods, Inc.
200 Commerce Street
Smithfield, VA 23430
Phone: (757) 365-3000
Fax: (757) 365-3017
www.smithfieldfoods.com

Southern States Cooperative, Incorporated
6606 West Broad Street
Richmond, VA 23230
Phone: (804) 281-1000
Fax: (804) 281-1413
www.southernstates.com

Sun World International, LLC
16350 Driver Road
Bakersfield, CA 93308
Phone: (661) 392-5000
Fax: (661) 392-5092
www.sun-world.com

Syngenta Corporation
2200 Concord Pike
Wilmington, DE 19803
Phone: (302) 425-2000
Fax: (302) 425-2001
www.syngenta.com

Tyson Foods, Inc.
2210 West Oaklawn Drive
Springdale, AR 72762-6999
Phone: (479) 290-4000
Fax: (479) 290-4061
www.tysonfoodsinc.com

Western Farm Service, Inc.
3705 West Beechwood Avenue
Fresno, CA 93711
Phone: (559) 436-2800
Fax: (559) 436-2949
www.westernfarmservice.com

Wm. Bolthouse Farms, Inc.
7200 East Brundage Lane
Bakersfield, CA 93307
Phone: (661) 366-7270
Fax: (661) 366-9236
www.bolthouse.com

Wilbur-Ellis Company
345 California Street, 27th Floor
San Francisco, CA 94104
Phone: (415) 772-4000
Fax: (415) 772-4011
www.wilburellis.com

Visit Vault at **www.vault.com** for insider company profiles, expert advice, career message boards, expert resume reviews, the Vault Job Board and more.

VAULT CAREER LIBRARY 59

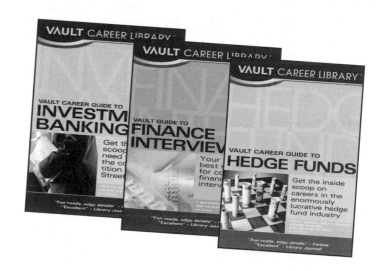

Brand Management/Consumer Goods

Consumer Goods

Ask for it by name

The consumer products industry produces and markets practically every item an individual can possibly purchase: from canned soup to shaving cream, chewing gum to washing machines—and everything in between.

To get a handle on the market, analysts often divide it into two categories, durable and nondurable goods. As the names imply, the former comprises items with (relative) staying power, like home furnishings, jewelry and electronics. The latter includes more ephemeral merchandise, with a life expectancy of fewer than three years, like soap, clothing, personal care items and cleaning supplies. Others, however, break the industry down into products that are staples and those that are discretionary— the difference between what consumers need and what they'd like to have. But however long they're intended to last, and whether consumers need them or not, these disparate products all have one thing in common: the overwhelming majority are sold under a brand name.

Brands exist ostensibly as a way for consumers to differentiate one manufacturer's goods from another—but of course, they mean so much more. A "brand" has two components. First, there's the association with the brand that the marketers and advertisers wish to cultivate in the minds of consumers, called the brand identity, where the brand promises (among other things) to make the consumer feel happier, more successful, more efficient or more popular. Then there's the idea of the brand that actually exists in the minds of consumers, called the brand image, which depends on how well it delivers on those promises. Effective brands communicate with consumers on an emotional level through advertising, and a buyer's feelings are also colored by previous experiences with the product. Of course, there can be considerable disconnect between the brand identity and the brand image, since a brand's image can be affected by all manner of scandal, rumor and negative press. There can also be a disconnect when the target audience fails to respond to the brand or finds it undesirable.

Internationalists

Regardless, branding these days drives an enormous amount of consumption. The numbers are staggering: spending on consumer products accounts for two-thirds of the volume of trade in the economy, and yearly spending on consumables hovers around $7 trillion in the U.S. alone. In addition, consumer products are making inroads into the furthest reaches of the globe: as American and European markets become increasingly saturated and competitive, manufacturers of consumer products are turning toward emerging markets in boom nations like those in the so-called BRIC (Brazil, Russia, India, China), Turkey and Eastern Europe.

These growing markets are like honey for consumer products manufacturers. Between 2003 and 2007, an index compiled by Morgan Stanley of the value of public companies in 25 developing nations increased nearly 250 percent. One reason for this phenomenal growth is tied to the World Bank's estimate that, by 2030, what it defines as the middle class will triple to include 1.2 billion people—and the overwhelming majority will live in the developing world.

Reaching customers in these dynamic economies is not simply a matter of shipping products to stores and advertising that they're ready to be taken home. There are a number of factors that companies must consider before taking on an emerging economy. Doing so is a risky endeavor, and is not a route to guaranteed gains. Emerging economies are unstable and prone to sudden financial crises, as in Russia in the late 1990s and Argentina in 2002. To further complicate matters, emerging economies often play by different rules than developed ones. Governments in these countries can be prone to cronyism and corruption, impeding the profitability and functions of businesses. Developing countries' infrastructure may be poorly

Visit Vault at **www.vault.com** for insider company profiles, expert advice, career message boards, expert resume reviews, the Vault Job Board and more.

VAULT CAREER LIBRARY

61

maintained or absent entirely: utilities necessary for the smooth operation of business—such as electricity, clean water and reliable modes of transport—may be sporadically or entirely absent, leading to manufacturing difficulties and fragile supply chains. While China's economic liberalization may have spurred a surprisingly high growth rate, it's still a communist country, operating under the dubious premise that bureaucracy can harness the market.

In addition, regulation of consumer products in developing markets may be notably absent, as in early 2007 when food products from China contaminated with melamine killed housepets in the U.S. In addition, cute toys coated in lead paint, counterfeit toothpaste full of lethal chemicals and defective tires that allegedly caused fatal accidents led to multiple recalls of Chinese-made imports and brought heavy media and legislative scrutiny to the issue.

The economic climate in a particular country is another hurdle that consumer products companies must sometimes overcome. While the elite in developing nations enjoy spending power and a standard of living roughly on par with that of Western countries, the majority of the population—95 percent, by some estimates—live on about $2,000 per year or less. Still, they are just like consumers everywhere: they desire products that make their lives easier and more pleasant, and are willing to shell out (within their means) for little luxuries. So, to tap this huge, profitable and underserved market, consumer products companies sell products like toothpaste, laundry detergent, shampoo, deodorant and moisturizer in small packets for a few pennies apiece. While the profit on such items might be mere fractions of a cent, they sell in large enough volumes to make serving this market a very profitable endeavor.

Of course, as branding guru Martin Lindstrom once noted, "A global brand-building strategy is, in reality, a local plan for every market." And when the markets are as disparate as Guangzhou and Cincinnati, what customers want will differ greatly. For instance, Crest toothpaste comes in flavors like tea and salt in China, flavors a Midwesterner would find mildly bewildering, to say the least. Lower-income consumers in China prefer to wash their clothes by hand, rather than pay for the excess water and electricity a washing machine consumes, and so they need washing detergent formulated specially for the task. In India, Whirlpool sells microwaves that can shallow-fry and sauté—cooking methods for a country that hasn't yet embraced convenience foods to the extent that the U.S. has.

Plan of ad-tack

That said, despite the developing world's growing importance in the consumer products industry, product sales in Western countries still account for the majority of these companies' income. But diverting new customers from Europe and the U.S. away from other products is increasingly difficult, as the people of developed nations are inundated with advertising. It's estimated that Americans, for example, see between 600 and 3,000 ads per day, and that most ignore them completely or view them as a nuisance, as users of ad-blocking software and fast-forwarding TiVo owners will attest. While traditional marketing techniques—catchy jingles, clever patter, happy housewives, etc.—have worked in years past, consumers are becoming increasingly immune to their effects.

In order to overcome consumers' jaded attitudes, marketers try to find new and clever ways to attract eyeballs to Product X, making the consumer products industry a cutthroat world. One recent trend has found companies running Internet contests in which audiences create their own ads for the product, with mixed results. Chevrolet gave Internet denizens stock footage of the Tahoe to craft into ads in 2006, and amateur muckracking documentarians promptly returned commentary on the cars' gas mileage and effect on the environment. A contest sponsored by Malibu Rum sparked particpants' ire when it altered the rules of its contest. Unilever's Dove and Pepsi's Frito Lay had better luck with entries submitted to run in coveted slots during the 2007 Super Bowl and the Oscars, respectively. And Heinz chose a winner in April 2008 from over 2,000 entries responding to call on its web site for homemade ads for its world-famous ketchup.

Companies now also customarily enter the public's space—MySpace, that is. Scores of companies have set up campaigns on social networking sites to draw the attention of bright young things with plenty of disposable income. Procter & Gamble began using social networking site Facebook to promote tooth whitening strips in 2006, while Unilever promoted its Axe brand of men's body spray on MySpace. Several other firms, including American Apparel, adidas and Dell, have set up presences in the virtual world Second Life, hoping to communicate with consumers wherever they go.

Trading up

It's a time-honored adage that the rich are getting richer and the poor are getting poorer. In the U.S., incomes at the high end have been growing dramatically, and the number of millionaires has doubled in the past 10 years. As a result, more consumers are demanding products with an aura of luxury about them. Brands cultivate such an image in a number of ways. Louis Vuitton, whose logo-splashed bags are more common than litter on some New York City streets, manages to maintain its high profile by sponsoring America's Cup races, and only sells its wares through a small group of stores.

Several other high-end brands—Gucci, Rolex, Nokia's Vertu—clamp down on the number of stores that sell their wares so that only the select few can buy them. Polo maintains its strong whiff of upper-crust appeal, even while expanding some lines into decidedly midmarket—even (gasp) discount—retail channels JCPenney and Kohl's by allowing the lower-priced brands to feed off the halo of their higher-end cousins. However, readily available objects can still be considered luxury items: Whirlpool's sleekly designed Duet washer (priced at about $1,000 more than your run-of-the-mill white box) was the best-selling front-loading washer in 2006.

As the midmarket becomes increasingly saturated with luxury products, some brands have moved into pricking consciences in order to make consumers shell out. In 2006, Apple, Armani, Gap and Converse all embarked on a co-branding initiative with Product (Red), a humanitarian campaign co-founded by the musician Bono. The deal with Product (Red) is that a portion of profits from certain items (T-shirts, MP3 players, sneakers) are sent to a charity that then funds the distribution of AIDS medication in Africa. Needless to say, the campaign sparked some backlash, especially in regards to its $100 million marketing budget. One site, Buylesscrap.org, launched in 2007, pointed out that charities would be better off if people donated money directly to them instead of shopping, and that Product (Red) hardly makes it clear exactly how much money is going towards charity and how much towards its strong marketing push.

It's a natural

Philanthropy isn't the only way that brands are grabbing consumers' attention. The overwhelming interest in all things green, organic and natural is currently a major force driving consumptive activity, and even Wal-Mart's gotten on the green wagon. The green energy division of GE was its fastest-growing segment in 2006, and in 2006, Levi's brought out jeans made from organic cotton—a smooth move, considering sales of organic cotton clothing will top $2.5 billion in 2008. The Hain Celestial Group and Dean Foods, segment leaders when it comes to organic, natural and/or soy-based products, have both been around for several decades and are now reaping the benefits of earlier investments. (Even companies that appeal to the sweet tooth have leaned towards the "nutritional" if not the "natural"; Nestlé acquired the medical nutrition business of drug company Novartis in July 2007, around the same time Coca-Cola came out with a vitamin-enhanced Diet Coke and bought the parent of Vitaminwater, Glaceau.) The significance of the trend hasn't been lost on the top consumer products companies; most consumers don't realize that Cascadian Farms (frozen fruits and vegetables) and Kashi (cereals) are actually cogs in the larger machinery of General Mills and Kellogg's, respectively.

However, as consumer interest in products designated as "natural" and "organic" increases, there's some fudge factor about what these terms actually mean. In 2007, a number of poultry processors, including Sanderson Farms, objected to the use of the word "natural" on chicken products that had been treated with such substances as salt water, chicken broth and carrageenan, a thickener derived from seaweed that is added to prevent the chicken from drying out when cooked. The processors petitioned the U.S. Agriculture Department to update its definition of "natural," which at present excludes only the use of artificial colors, flavors and ingredients.

Visit Vault at **www.vault.com** for insider company profiles, expert advice, career message boards, expert resume reviews, the Vault Job Board and more.

VAULT CAREER LIBRARY

63

This occurred only a few months after natural cosmetics company Burt's Bees introduced an initiative calling for manufacturers of natural cosmetics to voluntarily ban certain ingredients from items sold as "natural," like sodium laureth sulfate and p-thalates. (Its initiative, called The Greater Good, promotes a list of natural ingredients, such as "black currant oil" and buttermilk, which is praised for being "richer in fats and emollients than whole cow's milk.") The topic came up again in 2008: Dr. Bronner's Magic Soaps (officially named All One God Faith) accused 13 companies of false advertising by claiming their personal care products are organic; it subsequently filed a lawsuit in California on May 1, 2008 against the likes of consumer products groups Hain Celestial, Kiss My Face, Stella McCartney America, Estée Lauder and Whole Foods. Dr. Bronner's claims that certain components are made by treating them with petrochemicals, and others are suspected carcinogens.

The main problem is that there are a number of entities that certify products as organic, but no one definitive authority. In contrast to the food industry, there is no governmental body that governs lipsticks and face creams. However, the end of May 2008 did bring one authoritative statement: The California Attorney General filed suit against four companies (including Hain subsidiary Avalon Naturals) in an attempt to force them to append warning statements on their products about possible carcinogens.

As goes the economic climate, so goes consumer products

What may someday be referred to as "The Great Economic Turmoil of 2008" has affected a number of industries, perhaps none more so than consumer products. Escalating energy costs have raised shipping expenses, and petroleum-related products—integral to the process for making diapers, plastics, cleaners and packaging—have also driven costs. The price of basic ingredients, from peanuts to fruit, has climbed as well. Del Monte, Newell Rubbermaid, Kimberly Clark and Smucker's were just a few of the army of companies raising prices during the summer of 2008. Kellogg's sneakily kept cereal prices where they were while it made its boxes smaller.

Research showed that consumers, to save on gas, began to actively curtail their driving, which translated to fewer shopping trips, fewer products rung up and similarly poor results in the retail sector. They also cut out impulse buys, and bigger-ticket purchases such as food and other basic needs took up a larger slice of the take-home-pay pie. In the spring of 2008, the beauty market (which includes biggies L'Oreal and Estée Lauder), usually immune to the effects of financial stress, showed the largest one-quarter sales decline since 1997.

Brand Management

What is a marketer? The allure of brand management

Marketing encompasses a wide variety of meanings and activities. Some marketing positions are very close to sales, while others set overarching marketing strategy. What marketing positions have in common is the sense of ownership over the product or service, as well as the drive to understand customer needs and desires and translate those into some kind of marketing communication, advertising campaign or sales effort. The manager of product or service marketing is called the brand manager—he or she is the ruler of that marketing universe.

Careers within the marketing/branding arena are high profile. The business world is now realizing that strong brands and solid marketing programs drive shareholder value, and that companies can no longer make fundamental strategy decisions without truly understanding how to market a product. Today's business challenges—the quest for company growth, industry consolidation and deregulation, economic webs, and the emergency of new channels and technologies—make marketers even more valuable.

The titles of brand manager, product manager and, to a lesser extent, marketing manager are often used to describe the same function—some companies use one title, others use another. Marketing managers tend to be used in industries other than consumer packaged goods; product managers are often used in tech industries. "Brand management" implies more complete supervision of a product. The typical brand management framework gives a brand "group" or "team"—generally comprised of several assistant brand or assistant marketing managers and one supervising brand manager—responsibility for all matters relevant to their product or products. Whether this responsibility is, in fact, complete depends somewhat on the size of the company relative to the number of brands it has, the location of the brand group and most importantly on the company's attitude toward marketing.

How important is the individual brand manager?

Consider the company to determine the level of brand manager responsibility. The first factor is the size of the company relative to its number of brands. For a company with hundreds of different brands—Nabisco, for example—brand managers, or even assistant brand managers, may have a great deal of power over a specific brand. At companies with a few core products, brand managers will focus on narrower aspects of a brand. As one recently hired assistant brand manager at Coca-Cola comments: "They're not going to take an MBA and say, 'Okay, you're in charge of Sprite.'" Brand managers at such companies will instead be focused on marketing to a particular demographic or geographic group, or perhaps handling one aspect of the product's consumption (plastic bottles, cases of aluminum cans and so forth).

International brand managers have historically held more sway than managers in the company's home market, but keep in mind that the daily tasks of international brand managers often lean more toward questions of operations, rather than questions of strategy or marketing. ("How much should we produce?" or "How is our distribution network affecting sales?" rather than "What do we want our brand identity to be?") International brand management is sometimes split into two positions. Global brand managers are more strategic, concentrating on issues such as protecting brand equity and developing product offerings that can be rolled out into subsidiaries. Local brand managers are more tactical. Local managers focus on executing global plans that are delivered to them, and tweak them for local consumers. Also know that with the increasing trend toward globalization and the truly global presence of certain brands, companies have sought to impose more centralization and tighter controls on the marketing of those brands from country to country. In the past, individual country managers have had more discretion and leeway to make decisions about a brand's packaging, advertising, etc. Now, companies have established tighter guidelines on what can be done with regard to a brand around the world, with the goal of protecting and enhancing the value of the brand, and ensuring a consistent product and message worldwide.

Finally, consumer goods companies place varying levels of importance on their brand or marketing departments. Some, such as the Ford Motor Company, are driven as much by financial analyses of production costs or operations considerations as by marketing. The level of emphasis on finance or operations matters at a firm will influence not only the independence and authority of marketing managers, but also potential marketing career paths. At some companies, marketing is the training ground for general management. At General Mills, marketing is considered so important that employees in other functions who show promise are plucked from their positions and put into the department.

Visit Vault at **www.vault.com** for insider company profiles, expert advice, career message boards, expert resume reviews, the Vault Job Board and more.

VAULT CAREER LIBRARY

65

Careers in Marketing

Taking charge of a brand involves tackling many diverse job functions—and different subspecialties. Decide where you'd like your main concentration to lie.

Brand management

In a typical brand management organizational structure, positions are developed around responsibility for a particular product rather than a specific functional expertise (e.g., you're an assistant brand manager for Cheerios). This structure enables you to be the "master of all trades," acquiring an expertise in areas such as manufacturing, sales, research and development, and communications. In brand management, the marketing function is responsible for key general management decisions, such as long-term business strategy, pricing, product development direction and, in some cases, profit and loss responsibility. Brand management offers a terrific way to learn intensively about a particular product category (you could be a recognized expert on tampons!) and to manage the responsibility of running a business and influencing its performance.

The core of brand work is brand strategy. Brand managers must decide how to increase market share, which markets and demographic groups to target and what types of advertising and special promotions to use. And at the very heart of brand strategy is identifying a product's "brand identity." Brand groups then figure out how to exploit brand strategy or, in some cases, how to change it. PepsiCo's Mountain Dew has built its popularity among youth as a high-caffeine beverage into a "brand identity" of cutting-edge bravado that has boosted market share, while the Banana Republic chain underwent a transformation from an outdoor adventure store that sold actual Army-Navy surplus to an upscale, chic clothing store. In both cases, the brands have benefited from a shift in brand identity, and consequently, a shift in their market. Brand identity is normally created and confirmed through traditional print, radio and TV advertising. Advertising is usually produced by outside agencies, although brand insiders determine the emphasis and target of the advertising.

Some liken a brand manager to a hub at the center of a hub and spoke system, with the spokes going out to departments like finance, sales, manufacturing, R&D, etc. It is the brand manager's job to influence the performance of those groups—over whom he or she has no direct authority—in order to optimize the performance of his or her brand or product line.

Direct marketing

Ever wonder who is responsible for making those coupons you receive in the mail? Or the Saab videotape you've received every two years since you bought your car in 1993? You can thank direct marketers. Direct marketers are masters in one-to-one marketing. They assemble databases of individual consumers who fit within their target market, go after them with a personal approach and manage the production process from strategy inception to out-the-door distribution.

Direct marketers have two main objectives: to stay in touch with their current consumer base and to try to generate more business by finding individuals who fit a target set of criteria but are not currently using their particular product. For instance, if you've ever checked out of the supermarket and got a coupon for Advil after buying a bottle of Tylenol, chances are a direct marketer is trying to convince you to switch brands by offering you a monetary incentive.

It's important to note that direct marketing isn't just done through snail mail. It operates in multiple media, such as the Web, telemarketing and in-store promotions. Direct marketers have a powerful new tool in their arsenal—the Internet. Marketers are able to track the online habits and behavior of customers. They can then serve up customized banner advertisements that are much more likely to be relevant to them. Many consumers have agreed to receive promotional offers on certain subjects—marketers can then send them targeted e-mail messages that allow for much easier access to purchase or action (clicking on a link, for example) than a conventional mail direct marketing programs.

Affiliate/property marketing

If you're working with a major brand company like Nike, Disney, Pepsi or L'Oreal, chances are you'll do a lot of cross-promotion, or "affiliate marketing." For instance, Nike has marketing relationships with the NBA, NFL and a variety of individual athletes and athletic teams. Disney has a strong relationship with McDonald's; cute toys from the entertainment company's latest flick are often packaged with McDonald's Happy Meals upon the release of each new movie. L'Oreal works with celebrities, like Heather Locklear, and sponsors events, such as the annual Academy Awards.

Marketers must manage the relationship between any two entities. If Disney wants to promote the cartoon *du jour* with McDonald's, or Pepsi wants to make sure that all Six Flags theme parks have a Pepsi ride, then marketers need to ensure both parties get what they need out of the deal and stay true to their own brand images.

Price marketing/sales forecasting

Pricing is largely driven by market pressure. Most people, for example, won't pay more than $2 for a hamburger in a fast-food restaurant. On the other hand, brand managers always have some pricing leeway that can greatly affect market share and profitability. An increase of a nickel in the price of a product sold by the millions can make huge differences in revenue—assuming the price rise doesn't cause equivalent millions less of the products to be sold. Brand managers need to figure out the optimal pricing strategy for their product, though it's not always a case of making the most money. Sometimes it makes more sense to win market share while taking lower profits. How do brand managers justify their prices? Through extensive research. Paper towels, for example, may be much more price-sensitive than a luxury item like engagement rings or smoked salmon.

Brand and marketing managers don't always have free reign over pricing. At some companies, such as those that sell largely through mail order, or those with complex pricing systems, pricing and promotional offers may be limited to what the operational sales system can handle. Explains one marketing manager at a long-distance phone company (an industry with notoriously tangled pricing plans): "It's very easy to offer something to the customer. It's very difficult to implement that in the computer system."

Another large part of the general management duties of brand managers is forecasting product sales. This means not only keeping track of sales trends pertaining to one's product, but also anticipating responses to marketing campaigns and product launches or changes. The forecasts are used to determine production levels. Once a year, brand groups draw up budgets for their production, advertising and promotion costs, try to convince the finance folks that they absolutely need that amount, get less than they ask for, and then rework their budgets to fit the given budget. As one international brand manager at one of the world's biggest consumer goods companies puts it: "You don't determine the production and then get that budget; you get the budget, and then determine the production."

High-tech marketing

Not everyone markets applesauce for a living. Many people choose to enter the world of high-tech marketing because they want to work with products and technologies that reshape and improve the world around us. These marketers feel that they would rather change the way a person interacts with the world in a sophisticated way, rather than spend time understanding what hair color teenagers find most appealing. High-tech marketers spend much of their time understanding research and development issues, and working on new product launches.

Technology companies like Intel, Dell and Microsoft have recognized the power of branding and are utilizing traditional marketing tactics more and more. Amazon's extensive marketing campaign in 1998 helped brand that company in the mind of consumers still new to e-commerce as the company to purchase books (and other products) online. Intel became perhaps the first semiconductor company readily identifiable to the public through its heavily branded "bunny people." Marketing in

Visit Vault at **www.vault.com** for insider company profiles, expert advice, career message boards, expert resume reviews, the Vault Job Board and more.

VAULT CAREER LIBRARY   67

the high-tech world will continue to grow in importance over the next decade, as technology companies become more consumer-oriented (see Microsoft's X-Box). Marketing a service or software product versus a more tangible product is a bit different. It may be more challenging to understand how consumers relate to the product. Inventory and distribution issues may be tracked differently.

Market research

If you are an analytical person who likes numbers and analysis, and enjoys tracking consumer behavior, then market research may be the field for you. A product is much more effective when a company understands the consumer it is targeting. That's where market researchers come in. They employ a variety of different qualitative and quantitative research techniques to understand consumers. Surveys, tracking systems, focus groups, satisfaction monitors, psychographic and demographic models, and trial/repurchase estimations are all methods researchers use to understand how consumers relate to their products. Researchers who find that consumers associate lemon scents with cleanliness, for example, may suggest that cleansers could drive up sales by adding a lemon aroma.

Marketing consulting

Although most well-known consulting firms are known for their expertise in general strategy, many consulting firms now hire industry or functional experts that focus on marketing issues. These firms need people with expertise in the areas of branding, market research, continuous relationship marketing, pricing strategy and business-to-business marketing—they tend to hire people with previous marketing experience and value consultants who have been successful marketing managers and have lived through the full range of business issues from the inside. McKinsey and Monitor are two general strategy firms that have begun to hire marketing specialists. Other boutique marketing consulting firms, such as Kurt Salmon, focus on certain product categories like beverages, health care and retail. All major ad agencies are also attempting to reinvent themselves as marketing partners focused on marketing strategy beyond simple advertising.

A Day in the Life: Assistant Brand Manager

You can often spot the assistant brand managers because they are the ones running around like a chicken with its head cut off. Assistant brand managers must learn how to balance your time and prioritize. Here's a look at how their time might be spent:

Responsibilities	Percentage of time per day
Meetings	30 percent
Analysis/data tracking	30 percent
Writing memos	30 percent
Answering management queries	30 percent
Interfacing with other departments	30 percent
Actually marketing	Optional

Although this is a humorous take on the day of an ABM (talk about giving 150 percent), there is some truth to it. Days and weeks will go by where you feel like you've just been pushing paper and trying to stay afloat. It is very easy to get comfortable maintaining the businesses rather than creating new opportunities. Although the role of an ABM is mostly one of maintenance, if you want to be a "star," you must shape your brand, not just maintain it.

A more realistic look at a day in the life of a brand manager

8:30 a.m. Get into work. Listen to voicemails. Check e-mails. Print out calendar of today's events. Skim the markets section of *The Wall Street Journal* to find out what's happening "on the street." Go to the cafeteria and grab breakfast. (Of course, you're only eating products that your company produces or has some relationship with!)

9 a.m. Meet with market research department to discuss specifics of your latest round of quantitative research. You are trying to understand why people are not repurchasing your product, but you don't feel that the data presented actually answers your questions. You decide that you'll need to design another round of research—but where's the money going to come from?

10 a.m. Budget meeting to determine how you will be spending second quarter funds. Given the decision to spend more money on research, you might need to cancel an instant redeemable coupon or a local promotion in a poorly performing market.

10:30 a.m. You head to the long-awaited product development meeting. Your team has recently discussed reformulating your product to take advantage of new technology. This new technology may raise your product's performance levels, but it will cost more to manufacture and will take some advertising effort (and more money) to explain the changes to the consumer. The group must decide whether these changes are strategically and financially justified. As always, very few people agree. You decide to summarize all the costs and benefits to the project and present the issues to your brand manager at the status meeting you have scheduled for the end of the day.

12 p.m. A fancy lunch with a *People* magazine salesperson. For months the magazine has tried to convince you that your product should be advertised in *People*. During lunch, the represenative explains to you how the publication can effectively reach 18 percent of your target audience and how it can provide you with the extended reach you need to communicate with potential new users. You leave lunch with a fancy *People* backpack and a headache. Where can you find the money to add *People* to your media plan? Let's ask the media department (Note: While lunch with ad reps happens occasionally, the days of most brand managers are packed, without the time to spend schmoozing with ad reps. More often, brand managers, who are very focused on their jobs, grab lunch at a corporate cafeteria and take it back to their desks.)

1:30 p.m. Media planning meeting. Because sales of your product have come in slightly under budget, you have been forced to give up 10 percent of your media budget. You now must meet with the media department to determine how to cut media funds without sacrificing your goals (to reach 20 percent of your target group, and to have a continuous presence on TV). Maybe you can cut out two weeks of TV advertising in July when not many people are home anyway. But isn't that your product's peak purchase cycle? Decisions, decisions.

2:30 p.m. Time to review changes to the latest advertising campaign. Your ad agency presented a new concept about three weeks ago that needed work. You and your brand manager made comments to the storyboard (a drawing that explains a commercial) and now you are anxious to see what the agency has produced. You review the changes with the agency via conference call and promise to present the new work to your brand manager at your status meeting later in the day.

3:15 p.m. Keep the ad agency on the phone and bring in the in-house promotions department. This ad campaign will be introduced into a promotional campaign in the top-20 performing markets in the country. You want to make sure that before you get the promotions people working on a concept, they agree with the agency on the strategy going forward. The following 45 minutes is a creative brainstorming session that offers wonderful possibilities. You promise to type all ideas up and distribute them to the group later in the week.

4 p.m. Strategy development with sales manager. Your category manager is insisting that all brands work to gain a better presence in supermarkets. You meet with the regional sales manager to understand what types of strategies might work to get better shelf space and more consistent in-store promotions. Once you hear his ideas, you start to price options and see if this is possible within your (reduced) current budget.

Visit Vault at **www.vault.com** for insider company profiles, expert advice, career message boards, expert resume reviews, the Vault Job Board and more.

VAULT CAREER LIBRARY 69

5 p.m. Status meeting with brand manager. You present your proposal for increased research expending as well as the implications of the new product development issue. You also review the latest advertising changes and the changes to the media plan. You aggressively present your data and your opinion, and discuss these with your boss. The two of you decide on the next steps.

6 p.m. End of the day. You spend an hour checking the 23 e-mail/voicemail messages you received during the day but failed to return. You go through your "inbox" to read any documents relevant to your product. You start to attack all of the work you have to do and promise that tomorrow you'll block out some time to make some progress.

Employer Directory

Procter & Gamble

1 P&G Plaza

Cincinnati, OH 45202

Phone: (888) 486-7691

E-mail: careers.im@pg.com

www.pg.com/careers

Three billion times a day, P&G brands touch the lives of people around the world. Our company has one of the strongest portfolios of trusted, quality, including Pampers®, Tide®, Ariel®, Always®, Whisper®, Pantene®, Mach3®, Bounty®, Dawn®, Pringles®, Folgers®, Charmin®, Downy®, Lenor®, Iams®, Crest®, Oral-B®, Actonel®, Duracell®, Olay®, Head & Shoulders®, Wella, Gillette® and Braun. The P&G community consists of almost 140,000 employees working in almost 80 countries worldwide.

P&G embraces the principles of personal integrity, respect for the individual and doing what's right for the long term. We recognize our consumers, brands and employees as the pillars of our business.

Business schools Procter & Gamble recruits from

Various schools throughout the United States.

Visit Vault at **www.vault.com** for insider company profiles, expert advice, career message boards, expert resume reviews, the Vault Job Board and more.

VAULT CAREER LIBRARY

71

Employer Directory, cont.

3M Company
3M Center
St. Paul, MN 55144
Phone: (651) 733-1110
Fax: (651) 733-9973
www.3m.com

adidas AG
Adi-Dassler-Strasse 1-2
91074 Herzogenaurach
Germany
Phone: +49-9132-84-0
Fax: +49-9132-84-2241
www.adidas-group.com

Anheuser-Busch Companies, Inc.
1 Busch Place
St. Louis, MO 63118
Phone: (314) 577-2000
Fax: (314) 577-2900
www.anheuser-busch.com

Avon Products, Inc.
1345 Avenue of the Americas
New York, NY 10105-0196
Phone: (212) 282-5000
Fax: (212) 282-6049
www.avoncompany.com

Bose Corporation
The Mountain
Framingham, MA 01701
Phone: (508) 879-7330
Fax: (508) 766-7543
www.bose.com

Cadbury plc
Cadbury House, Uxbridge Business Park
Sanderson Road
Uxbridge UB8 1DH
United Kingdom
Phone: +44-18-95-61-50-00
Fax: +44-18-95-61-50-01
www.cadbury.com

Campbell Soup Company
1 Campbell Place
Camden, NJ 08103-1799
Phone: (856) 342-4800
Fax: (856) 342-3878
www.campbellsoup.com

The Clorox Company
1221 Broadway
Oakland, CA 94612-1888
Phone: (510) 271-7000
Fax: (510) 832-1463
www.thecloroxcompany.com

The Coca-Cola Company
1 Coca-Cola Plaza
Atlanta, GA 30313
Phone: (404) 676-2121
Fax: (404) 676-6792
www.thecoca-colacompany.com

Coach Incorporated
516 West 34th Street
New York, NY 10001-1394
Phone: (212) 594-1850
Fax: (212) 594-1682
www.coach.com

Colgate-Palmolive Company
300 Park Avenue
New York, NY 10022
Phone: (212) 310-2000
Fax: (212) 310-3284
www.colgate.com

Columbia Sportswear Company
14375 NW Science Park Drive
Portland, OR 97229-5418
Phone: (503) 985-4000
Fax: (503) 985-5800
www.columbia.com

ConAgra Foods Incorporated
1 ConAgra Drive
Omaha, NE 68102-5001
Phone: (402) 595-4000
Fax: (402) 595-4707
www.conagra.com

Del Monte Foods Company
1 Market at the Landmark
San Francisco, CA 94105
Phone: (415) 247-3000
Fax: (415) 347-3565
www.delmonte.com

Eastman Kodak Company
343 State Street
Rochester, NY 14650
Phone: (585) 724-4000
Fax: (585) 724-0663
www.kodak.com

The Estée Lauder Companies, Inc.
767 Fifth Avenue
New York, NY 10153
Phone: (212) 572-4200
Fax: (212) 572-3941
www.elcompanies.com

Fortune Brands, Inc.
520 Lake Cook Road
Deerfield, IL 60015
Phone: (847) 484-4400
Fax: (847) 478-0073
www.fortunebrands.com

General Electric Company
3135 Easton Turnpike
Fairfield, CT 06828
Phone: (203) 373-2211
Fax: (203) 373-3131
www.ge.com

General Mills Incorporated
1 General Mills Boulevard
Minneapolis, MN 55426
Phone: (763) 764-7600
Fax: (763) 764-7384
www.generalmills.com

H. J. Heinz Company
600 Grant Street
Pittsburgh, PA 15219
Phone: (412) 456-5700
Fax: (412) 456-6015
www.heinz.com

Employer Directory, cont.

Hasbro, Inc.
1027 Newport Avenue
Pawtucket, RI 02862-1059
Phone: (401) 431-8697
Fax: (401) 727-5544
www.hasbro.com

Henkel KGaA
Henkelstrasse 67
D-40191 Düsseldorf
Germany
Phone: +49-21-17-97-0
Fax: +49-21-17-98-24-84
www.henkel.com

The Hershey Company
100 Crystal A Drive
Hershey, PA 17033-0810
Phone: (717) 534-4200
Fax: (717) 534-7873
www.thehersheycompany.com

The J.M. Smucker Company
1 Strawberry Lane
Orrville, OH 44667
Phone: (330) 682-3000
Fax: (330) 684-3026
www.smuckers.com

Jockey International, Inc.
2300 60th Street
Kenosha, WI 53141
Phone: (262) 658-8111
Fax: (262) 658-1812
www.jockey.com

Johnson & Johnson
1 Johnson & Johnson Plaza
New Brunswick, NJ 08933
Phone: (732) 524-0400
Fax: (732) 214-0332
www.jnj.com

Kellogg Company
1 Kellogg Square
Battle Creek, MI 49016
Phone: (269) 961-2000
Fax: (269) 961-2871
www.kelloggcompany.com

Kimberly-Clark Corporation
351 Phelps Drive
Irving, TX 75038
Phone: (972) 281-1200
Fax: (972) 281-1435
www.kimberly-clark.com

Kraft Foods, Inc.
3 Lakes Drive
Northfield, IL 60093
Phone: (847) 646-2000
Fax: (847) 646-6005
www.kraft.com

L'Oréal
41, rue Martre Centre Eugene Schueller
Clichy, 92117
France
Phone: +33-47-56-82-65
Fax: +33-47-56-86-42
www.loreal.com

Levi Strauss & Co.
1155 Battery Street
San Francisco, CA 94111
Phone: (415) 501-6000
Fax: (415) 501-7112
www.levistrauss.com

Liz Claiborne, Inc.
1441 Broadway
New York, NY 10018
Phone: (212) 354-4900
Fax: (212) 626-1800
www.lizclaiborneinc.com

LVMH Moët Hennessy Louis Vuitton SA
22 Avenue Montaigne
75008 Paris
France
Phone: +33-44-13-22-22
Fax: +33-44-13-21-19
www.lvmh.com

MARS, Incorporated
6885 Elm Street
McLean, VA 22101
Phone: (703) 821-4900
Fax: (703) 448-9678
www.website.com

Mary Kay Inc.
16251 Dallas Parkway
Dallas, TX 75001
Phone: (972) 687-6300
Fax: (972) 687-1642
www.marykay.com

Mattel, Inc.
333 Continental Boulevard
El Segundo, CA 90245-5012
Phone: (310) 252-2000
Fax: (310) 252-2179
www.mattel.com

McCormick & Company, Inc.
18 Loveton Circle
Sparks, MD 21152
Phone: (410) 771-7301
Fax: (410) 527-8214
www.mccormick.com

MillerCoors LLC
1225 17th Street
Denver, CO 80202
Phone: (303) 279-6565
Fax: (303) 277-5415
www.millerbrewing.com

Molson Coors Brewing Company
311 10th Street
Golden, CO 80401-0030
Phone: (303) 279-6565
Fax: (303) 277-5415
www.molsoncoors.com

Nestlé SA
Avenue Nestle 55
Vevey, 1800
Switzerland
Phone: +41-924-2111
Fax: +41-924-4800
www.nestle.com

Visit Vault at **www.vault.com** for insider company profiles, expert advice, career message boards, expert resume reviews, the Vault Job Board and more.

V∧ULT CAREER LIBRARY   73

Employer Directory, cont.

New Balance Athletic Shoe, Inc.
Brighton Landing
20 Guest Street
Boston, MA 02135-2088
Phone: (617) 783-4000
Fax: (617) 787-9355
www.newbalance.com

Newell Rubbermaid, Inc.
10B Glenlake Parkway, Suite 300
Atlanta, GA 30328
Phone: (770) 407-3800
Fax: (770) 407-3986
www.newellrubbermaid.com

NIKE, Inc.
1 Bowerman Drive
Beaverton, OR 97005
Phone: (503) 671-6453
Fax: (503) 671-6300
www.nike.com

Nintendo Co., Ltd
11-1 Kamitoba Hokotate-cho Minami-ku
Kyoto-shi, KYT 601-8116
Japan
Phone: +81-35-820-22-51
Fax: +81-75-601-85-01

Nintendo of America Incorporated
4820 150th Avenue NE
Redmond, WA 98052
Phone: (425) 882-2040
Fax: (425) 882-3585
www.nintendo.com

PepsiCo, Inc.
700 Anderson Hill Road
Purchase, NY 10577
Phone: (914) 253-2000
Fax: (914) 253-2070
www.pepsico.com

Polo Ralph Lauren Corporation
650 Madison Avenue
New York, NY 10022
Phone: (212) 318-7000
Fax: (212) 318-7690
www.ralphlauren.com

Quiksilver, Inc.
15202 Graham Street
Huntington Beach, CA 92649
Phone: (714) 889-2200
Fax: (714) 889-3700
www.quiksilver.com

Revlon Inc.
237 Park Avenue
New York, NY 10017
Phone: (212) 527-4000
www.revlon.com

Royal Philips Electronics
Breitner Center, Amstelplein 2
1096 BC Amsterdam
Netherlands
Phone: +31-20-597-77177
Fax: +31-20-597-70710
www.philips.com

S.C. Johnson & Son, Inc.
1525 Howe Street
Racine, WI 53403-5011
Phone: (262) 260-2000
Fax: (262) 260-6004
www.scjohnson.com

Sara Lee Corporation
3500 Lacey Road
Downers Grove, IL 60515
Phone: (630) 598-6000
Fax: (630) 598-8482
www.saralee.com

Skechers USA, Inc.
228 Manhattan Beach Boulevard
Manhattan Beach, CA 90266
Phone: (310) 318-3100
Fax: (310) 318-5019
www.skechers.com

Sony Corporation
1-7-1 Konan
Minato-Ku, TKY 108-0075
Japan
Phone: +1-813-5448211
Fax: +1-813-5448224
www.sony.net

The Timberland Company
200 Domain Drive
Stratham, NH 03885
Phone: (603) 772-9500
Fax: (603) 926-9239
www.timberland.com

Tyson Foods, Inc.
2210 West Oaklawn Drive
P.O. Box 2020
Springdale, AR 72762-6999
Phone: (479) 290-4000
Fax: (479) 290-4061
www.tyson.com

Unilever PLC
Unilever House
PO Box 68
Blackfriars
London, ENG EC4Y 0DY
United Kingdom
Phone: +44-20-78-22-52-52
Fax: +44-20-78-22-69-07
www.unilever.com

Whirlpool Corporation
2000 M63
Benton Harbor, MI 49022
Phone: (269) 923-5000
Fax: (269) 923-5154
www.whirlpoolcorp.com

Wm. Wrigley Jr. Company
410 North Michigan Avenue
Chicago, IL 60611
Phone: (312) 644-2121
Fax: (312) 644-0015
www.wrigley.com

Energy/Oil and Gas

What is the Energy Sector?

Besides mc², what is energy?

The energy sector produces, converts and distributes fuels for heat, light and propulsion. Oil, natural gas and coal are burned to make heat and electricity. Wind, flowing water and sunlight are converted into electricity. Oil is refined to propel cars, planes and industrial machines. And to achieve these things, the companies who are producing, transporting, converting and distributing these energy sources are supported by a variety of service firms, investors and equipment providers.

There is a great divide between the oil and gas industries and the network of companies that produce electrical power, even though each side accounts for about half of the business jobs across both the sector. "Oil and gas" refers to the exploration for, and extraction and processing of oil and natural gas. In contrast, the electric power business revolves around converting fuel to electricity in power plants and distributing that electricity to consumers. The economics of the two fields, and the regulations that govern them, are quite distinct. Generally, people make their energy careers in one camp or the other, without too much crossover.

Just how big is the industry that comprises all those diverse activities? Companies in the energy sector take in over $1 trillion in revenue annually, out of the $20 trillion earned by all U.S. businesses. Energy-related businesses employ about three million people—or 2 percent of the U.S. workforce—far more than banking, high tech or telecommunications. Energy companies as a whole employ a high percentage of production workers (the people who drive local utility repair trucks, laborers on oil rigs and gas station attendants), compared to other industries. Of the millions of energy jobs in the U.S., about 90 percent of them are blue-collar jobs or technical positions. Even so, there are many energy-related business jobs out there: business analysts, finance associates, marketing managers, economic modelers and operations consultants, to name a few roles.

Energy sector positions capture about 4 percent of new MBA graduates, an amount roughly proportional to the industry's size. In contrast, the finance and accounting capture 22 percent of graduates, and consulting absorbs another 14 percent. Even the significantly smaller high-tech industry takes on three times the number of new MBAs as does the energy sector. What this means for you as a job seeker is that the energy sector is not as dominated by people with graduate business degrees as some other popular arenas. There is plenty of opportunity for smart, well-trained college graduates to rise through the ranks without going back to school.

Which Job Function?

In order to pursue a job in the energy sector, your first decision is what type of position you want—in other words, what functional role you want to play. Your function has a lot more impact on the nature of your job than does the type of company in which you work.

You can have a wide variety of business jobs in the energy sector:

- Asset development
- Corporate finance
- Quantitative analytics, risk management
- Trading, energy marketing
- Investment analysis
- Consulting

Visit Vault at www.vault.com for insider company profiles, expert advice, career message boards, expert resume reviews, the Vault Job Board and more.

VAULT CAREER LIBRARY   75

- Business development
- Banking
- Strategy and planning
- Economics and policy analysis

Different companies can have widely varying names by which they refer to these roles. For example, "marketing" in one company involves advertising and product promotion, whereas "marketing" in another can mean commodities trading. Similarly, "business development" can be more akin to sales in one company, or synonymous with strategic planning in another.

What Type of Company?

Job functions and company types intersect in numerous ways—for example, you can do corporate finance in a large oil company or with a small fuel cell manufacturer, or choose between asset development and trading within a given utility. Below, we have summarized the characteristics of each of the major energy sector employer types.

Oil companies

Oil companies engage in exploration and production of oil ("upstream" activities), oil transportation and refining ("midstream"), and petroleum product wholesale and retail distribution ("downstream"). The largest companies, known as the "majors," are vertically integrated, with business operations along the entire spectrum from exploration to gas stations. Smaller oil companies, known as "independents," are often exclusively involved in exploration and production. Upstream is considered the glamorous place to be, where all the big decisions are made. Upstream jobs also involve heavy international work, with many employees sent off to new postings around the world every three years or so. Some companies focus exclusively on midstream and downstream activities. They operate refineries to distill crude oil into its many commercially useful petroleum derivatives, like gasoline, jet fuel, solvents and asphalt. Refineries are, in theory, built to last 40 years, but some have been around for as long as 80 years. That means that new refineries are rarely built, and the refinery business is mostly about managing the razor-thin margins between purchased crude oil inputs and revenue from refined product outputs.

The majors are known for excellent rotational training programs, and a fair number of people take advantage of those programs and then jump over to independents for good salaries. Oil companies pay well in general, but jobs are not necessarily as stable as one might think. When oil prices drop, company operating profits are dramatically impacted, and layoffs are fairly common. American oil jobs are overwhelmingly concentrated in Houston. International hotspots include London, Calgary and the Middle East.

Aside from these are the sectors and businesses that feed off of oil. Oil services companies provide a range of outsourced operational support; for instance, they may rent out oil rigs, conduct seismic testing or transport equipment. Working for one of these probably means working in Texas or abroad, and can feel very much like working for an oil company, given the similarity in issues and activities. Equipment manufacturers make turbines, boilers, compressors, pollution control devices, well drilling and pipeline construction equipment, software control systems, and some provide engineering services and construction/installation of their equipment. Pipeline operators own and manage tens of thousands of miles of petroleum (and natural gas) pipelines. Many also operate oil intake terminals, engage in commodities trading and energy marketing, (and own natural gas storage facilities) or petroleum refineries as well. Pipeline companies are not household names; nonetheless, the largest ones take in several billion in annual revenue, comparable to the scale of a medium-sized oil company. The fortunes of these companies follow the price of oil: when oil is expensive, oil companies drill a lot and make a lot of money, so business volume and revenue increase for their contractors.

Oil services companies

Oil services companies provide a very wide range of outsourced operational support to oil companies, such as owning and renting out oil rigs, conducting seismic testing and transporting equipment. The fortunes of these companies follow the price of oil: when oil is expensive, oil companies drill a lot and make a lot of money, so business volume and revenue increase for their oil services contractors. Working for an oil services company probably means working in Texas or internationally, and can feel very much like working for an oil company, given the similarity in issues and activities.

Pipeline operators

Pipeline operators own and manage tens of thousands of miles of petroleum products and natural gas pipelines. Many of them also operate oil intake terminals, engage in commodities trading and energy marketing, and own natural gas storage facilities or petroleum refineries, as well. Unlike the major oil companies, pipeline operation companies are not household names—nonetheless, the largest ones take in several billion dollars in annual revenue, comparable to the scale of a medium-sized oil company.

Utilities

Utilities are, by definition, located all over the country—everyone has to get their electricity and gas from somewhere, of course. However, as a result of massive consolidation among utility holding companies, the corporate offices for your local utility may not necessarily be that local. There are presently about 50 investor-owned utilities in the country, but industry insiders predict that in a few years mergers may leave us with as few as 10. The "graying" of the utility industry is a well-documented trend; 60 percent of current utility employees are expected to retire by 2015, meaning there's lots of opportunity today for young job seekers.

"Utility" is actually a loose term that we use to succinctly refer to gas utilities and all types of power generation companies: investor-owned utilities, government-owned utilities, municipal power companies, rural electric co-ops and independent power producers (IPPs) or nonutility generators (NUGs). Utilities differ greatly in terms of their lines of business: some have sold off most of their generation assets and are primarily distribution companies with power lines as their primary assets. Others may own large numbers of regulated power plants, and may also own nonutility generators or individual independent power plants. As the electricity market fell apart starting in 2001, most IPPs sold off their assets piecemeal to large utility holding companies or financial institutions.

Transmission grid operators

Transmission grid operators, known as independent system operators (ISO) or regional transmission operators (RTO), provide a power generation dispatch function to a regional electricity market. They don't own the transmission lines, but coordinate how much power is generated when and where, such that supply and demand are equal at every moment. This is an extremely complex process, and necessitates the analytical skills of electrical engineers and other generally quantitative and analytical operations staff.

Equipment manufacturers

Equipment manufacturers make turbines, boilers, compressors, pollution control devices, well drilling and pipeline construction equipment, software control systems, pumps and industrial batteries. Many of them also provide engineering services and construction/installation of their equipment. The major gas turbine manufacturers, for example, also offer engineering, procurement and construction of entire power plants. Oil-related equipment makers are often characterized as

Visit Vault at **www.vault.com** for insider company profiles, expert advice, career message boards, expert resume reviews, the Vault Job Board and more.

VAULT CAREER LIBRARY   77

"oil services" firms. The equipment manufacturers in the energy industry are not particularly concentrated in one geographic area, though of course many of the oil business-oriented ones have major offices in Texas.

Investment funds

Investment funds are a diverse bunch: mutual funds, private equity funds and hedge funds. As a whole, the investment fund world is fairly concentrated in Boston, New York and San Francisco, but there are small funds dotted all over the country, as well.

Mutual funds hire stock analysts primarily out of MBA programs to track, value and recommend stocks in a particular sector (e.g., energy, natural resources, consumer goods) to the fund managers. However, there are a lot of other finance-related positions inside these massive firms for which graduating undergrads are sought.

The number of hedge funds in the U.S. has been growing at a phenomenal rate in the past few years, but they are still notoriously difficult places to get jobs. Hedge funds often hire people out of investment banking analyst programs. They tend not to hire people out of the mutual fund world, given that their valuation approach is so different, their investing horizon is so much shorter, and their orientation many times is towards short-selling, as well as buying stocks. While some hedge funds may focus exclusively on energy, most are generalist and opportunistic with respect to their target sectors.

Private equity funds invest money in private (i.e., not publicly traded) companies, often also obtaining operating influence through a seat on the portfolio company's board of directors. As a result, an analyst's work at a private equity fund is vastly different from that at a mutual fund or hedge fund. You are not following the stock market or incorporating market perception issues into your valuations and recommendations; instead, you are taking a hard look at specific operating issues, identifying concrete areas where the portfolio company can lower costs or enhance revenue. A few private equity firms specialize in energy investing, and many more do occasional deals in the energy space as part of a broader technology or manufacturing focus. Private equity firms hire just a few people straight out of college or MBA programs, and many others from the ranks of investment banking alumni.

Banks

Banks are primarily involved in lending money to companies, but they also have their own trading operations, private wealth management and investment analysis groups. Commercial and investment banks arrange for loans to energy companies, as well as syndicate loans for them (i.e., find other people to lend the money). Investment banks manage IPOs, and mergers and acquisitions (M&A) activities, as well. The banking world is overwhelmingly centered in New York (and London), with some smaller branches in Chicago and San Francisco.

Consulting firms

Consulting firms offer rich opportunities for those interested in the energy industry. Consulting on business issues (rather than information technology or technical, scientific issues) is done at three types of firms: management consultancies, risk consulting groups and economic consulting shops. Consulting firms are often interested in hiring people with good functional skills rather than requiring specific industry expertise and provide a broad exposure to energy sector business issues, as well as good training. Business consulting firm offices are located in most major cities, but much of the energy sector staff may be located in Houston, Washington, D.C. and New York.

Nonprofit groups

Nonprofit groups are tax-exempt corporations (pursuant to IRS code 501(c)3) engaged in issue advocacy or public interest research. Advocacy groups may focus on developing grassroots support for public policy changes, publicizing public interest issues or problems through direct actions, or working to influence politicians to enact or change legislation. Most of the energy-related advocacy groups focus on environmental topics, though some also cover corporate financial responsibility and investor protection issues. Think tanks are public policy research institutes, staffed mainly by PhDs who generate research and opinion papers to inform the public, policy-makers and media on current issues. Interestingly, the think tank is primarily a U.S. phenomenon, although the concept is slowly catching on in other countries. Some think tanks are independent and nonpartisan, whereas some take on an explicit advocacy role. Nonprofits are funded by individual donations and grants from foundations, and accordingly a substantial portion of their staffs are dedicated to fundraising. Most energy nonprofits are based in Washington, D.C., where they have access to the federal political process, but many of them have small regional offices or grassroots workers spread out across the country.

Government agencies

Government agencies at the federal and state levels regulate the energy markets and define public energy and environmental policy. Federal agencies are mostly located in Washington, D.C., and each state has staff in the state capital. Jobs can include policy analysis, research project management or management of subcontractors. The energy agencies tend to hire people with environmental or engineering backgrounds, and are lately following a policy of hiring people with general business and management education and experience.

Energy services firms

Energy services firms help companies (in any sector) reduce their energy costs. Working for an energy services firm is similar in many respects to consulting—except that you go much further down the path of implementation. Typically, an energy services firm first conducts an energy audit to understand where a company spends money on energy: electricity, heat and industrial processes. Then, the firm actually implements energy-saving measures "inside the fence" of the client company. This can involve investments and activities such as putting lightbulbs on motion sensors, upgrading the HVAC (heating, ventilation, air conditioning) system, negotiating better rates with the utility suppliers or developing a cogeneration power plant adjacent to the factory. Often, the energy services firm receives payment for these services in the form of a share in the net energy cost savings to the client. These firms are located across the country, with a few of the largest clustered in Boston.

Visit Vault at **www.vault.com** for insider company profiles, expert advice, career message boards, expert resume reviews, the Vault Job Board and more.

VAULT CAREER LIBRARY   79

Job Function	Possible Employer Types
Asset development	Utility; oil company; pipeline operator; energy services firm
Corporate finance	Utility; pipeline operator; oil company; equipment manufacturer
Quantitative analytics; risk management	Utility; oil company; transmission grid operator; pipeline operator; investment fund; bank
Trading; energy marketing	Utility; oil company; pipeline operator; investment fund; bank
Investment analysis	Investment fund; bank
Consulting	Consulting firm; oil services company
Business development	Equipment manufacturer; utility; oil services company; pipeline operator; energy services firm
Banking	Bank
Strategy and planning	Utility; oil company; pipeline operator; oil services company; equipment manufacturer
Economic and policy analysis	Government agency; nonprofit group; consulting firm

Who Gets Hired?

As in other technology-intensive sectors, the energy sector is populated by a disproportionate number of people with technical degrees (e.g., BS, MS or PhD in engineering, hard sciences and math). Whether it's true or not, traditional energy company employers often feel that success in a job correlates to having a certain degree. This pickiness about your undergraduate major or master's degree field gets even stronger during economic downturns, when companies act more conservatively and have more bargaining power in terms of new hires.

In many energy jobs, the prevalence of people with technical pedigrees is somewhat a function of self-selection; individuals interested enough in the energy sector to make it their career were usually also interested enough in related topics to focus on them academically. On top of that, the prevalence of technical people is also self-reinforcing; in other words, engineers like to hire other engineers. There is also arguably an element of reality underpinning the preference for people with certain academic backgrounds—engineers communicate best with other engineers, and have proven in school that they can learn the ins and outs of a complex subject area.

This tendency is most characteristic of hiring preferences among oil companies, oil services firms, refineries, pipelines, grid operators, equipment manufacturers, energy services companies and utilities. These firms want to hire people who have their heads around how their technologies work—people who can master the jargon quickly, and who can fit into their culture. Even for their MBA hires, these companies often look for technical undergraduate degrees or pre-MBA work in energy or another technical field.

However, there are certainly many people with liberal arts backgrounds doing great work at these types of companies. A nontechnical degree does not in any way shut you out of any energy sector career path; it simply makes you slightly more unusual in the eyes of some interviewers. If you can craft a compelling story about why you are passionate about and deeply understand the energy world, your degree becomes far less relevant. In addition, if you are applying for a finance, economics or accounting job with a degree in those fields, you are also less subject to scrutiny about your knowledge of geology, electrical engineering or chemistry. Once you have a couple years of experience in the industry, that serves as a degree equivalent and you will have established your credibility.

Many of the service jobs in energy are interested in simply hiring smart people who demonstrate an ability to learn a new industry quickly. Energy consulting, banking and investing jobs often screen for nothing different than their counterparts in other industries. Similarly, the newer, alternative energy companies are often heavily filled with people who studied liberal arts, economics and government in college. These companies are progressive in terms of their business strategies, and usually this comes across in their approach to hiring as well. In addition, nonprofits typically first look for passion and commitment to advocacy work before they look for technical background.

Where you're coming from

Apart from academic background, traditional energy employers are also keenly interested in people who have a strong connection to the geographic region in which the company is located. These companies like to hire for the long term, so will often grill out-of-state candidates about why they would want to move to, for example, Houston or Atlanta. This can mean that, for a Houston oil company position, an MBA from Rice is a more attractive candidate than one from Wharton.

In fact, the energy sector offers particularly rich opportunities for students from second-tier undergraduate and graduate schools. Energy companies know that their industry is not typically considered as hot and glamorous as some other industries, and they can therefore often be skeptical about recruiting from name-brand undergraduate and graduate schools. The bottom line is that energy, as an industry, is simply less hung up on name-brand schools than some other industries, e.g., consulting, law and banking.

Moreover, during the past few years of our sluggish economy, many traditional energy companies tightened their recruiting budgets and reduced focus on first-tier schools—at the same time as service companies like consulting and banking firms reacted to a slow economy by canceling recruiting at second-tier schools and concentrating on only a limited set of top schools. Of course, those in the know are well aware that the energy sector is one of the most intellectually challenging, influential arenas in which to work! If you want to work in the sector, you can certainly seek out the energy employers, regardless of whether they visit your campus or target people from your alma mater.

In general, the best time to jump into the energy sector is right out of undergraduate or graduate (MA/MS, MBA or PhD) school. Like most employers, energy companies expect less in the way of industry experience from people who have just graduated, so it's a good time to get your foot in the door of a new field. Lateral hires of people a few years out of college or post-MBA are relatively rare, unless you have some specific industry background or functional experience a company needs. For example, a pipeline company might realistically hire someone with a couple years of general banking experience into a corporate finance role, but would be very unlikely to hire someone with a couple of years of, say, real estate experience into that same role—so if you had just graduated and never spent those couple of years in real estate, you'd have a better shot at the job.

This reluctance to hire laterally from other industries is far less common in the services sector (consulting, banking, investing, nonprofits). These employers are more interested in functional knowledge and pure brainpower, rather than a track record in one particular industry or another (though they have their own intransigence about hiring people laterally from other functional areas, i.e., it's awfully hard to get into consulting or banking if you don't do so your first year out of school). As a result, these jobs are an excellent way to get into the energy sector, and offer lots of options down the road—in other words, for example, it's relatively easy to go from an energy consulting role into a corporate job at other energy firms.

One caveat for those who move from one firm to another to position themselves for a future job: traditional energy employers like stability. If you have a lot of different jobs on your resume, you should make sure to have a good story to explain the necessity of your job-hopping, and why you are long-term play for the company (whether you truly are or not). This is true when interviewing with any firm, but large, traditional energy firms are certainly more sensitive to the issue.

Visit Vault at www.vault.com for insider company profiles, expert advice, career message boards, expert resume reviews, the Vault Job Board and more.

VAULT CAREER LIBRARY   81

Employer Directory

The AES Corporation
4300 Wilson Boulevard, 11th Floor
Arlington, VA 22203
Phone: (703) 522-1315
Fax: (703) 528-4510
www.aes.com

ALLETE, Inc.
30 West Superior Street
Duluth, MN 55802
Phone: (218) 279-5000
Fax: (218) 720-2502
www.allete.com

Alliant Energy Corporation
4902 North Biltmore Lane
Madison, WI 53718
Phone: (608) 458-3311
Fax: (608) 458-4824
www.alliantenergy.com

American Electric Power Company, Inc.
1 Riverside Plaza
Columbus, OH 43215-2372
Phone: (614) 716-1000
Fax: (614) 716-1823
www.aep.com

Anadarko Petroleum Corporation
1201 Lake Robbins Drive
The Woodlands, TX 77380-1046
Phone: (832) 636-1000
Fax: (832) 636-8220
www.anadarko.com

Baker Hughes Incorporated
2929 Allen Parkway, Suite 2100
Houston, TX 77019-2118
Phone: (713) 439-8600
Fax: (713) 439-8699
www.bakerhughes.com

BJ Services Company
4601 Westway Park Boulevard
Houston, TX 77027
Phone: (713) 513-3300
Fax: (713) 513-3456
www.bjservices.com

BP p.l.c.
1 St James's Square
London SW1Y 4PD
United Kingdom
Phone: +44-20-7496-4000
Fax: +44-20-7496-4630
www.bp.com

Cameron International Corporation
1333 West Loop, Suite 1700
Houston, TX 77027
Phone: (713) 513-3300
Fax: (713) 513-3456
www.c-a-m.com

Chevron Corp.
6001 Bollinger Canyon Road
San Ramon, CA 94583
Phone: (925) 842-1000
Fax: (925) 842-3530
www.chevrontexaco.com

ConocoPhillips Company
600 North Dairy Ashford Road
Houston, TX 77079
Phone: (281) 293-1000
Fax: (281) 293-1440
www.conocophillips.com

Consolidated Edison, Inc.
4 Irving Place
New York, NY 10003
Phone: (212) 460-4600
Fax: (212) 982-7816
www.conedison.com

Duke Energy Corporation
526 South Church Street
Charlotte, NC 28202
Phone: (704) 594-6200
Fax: (704) 382-3814
www.duke-energy.com

Eaton Corporation
Eaton Center
1111 Superior Avenue
Cleveland, OH 44114-2584
Phone: (216) 523-5000
Fax: (216) 523-4787
www.eaton.com

Edison International
2244 Walnut Grove Avenue
Rosemead, CA 91770
Phone: (626) 302-1212
Fax: (626) 302-2517
www.edison.com

Entergy Corporation
689 Loyola Avenue
New Orleans, LA 70113
Phone: (504) 576-4000
Fax: (504) 576-4428
www.entergy.com

Exelon Corporation
10 South Dearborn Street, 37th Floor
Chicago, IL 60680-5379
Phone: (312) 394-7398
Fax: (312) 394-7945
www.exeloncorp.com

Exterran Holdings, Inc.
4444 Brittmoore Road
Houston, TX 77041
Phone: (713) 335-7000
Fax: (281) 854-3051
www.exterran.com

Exxon Mobil Corporation
5959 Las Colinas Boulevard
Irving, TX 75039-2298
Phone: (972) 444-1000
Fax: (972) 444-1350
www.exxonmobil.com

FirstEnergy Corp.
76 South Main Street
Akron, OH 44308
Phone: (800) 646-0400
Fax: (330) 84-3866
www.firstenergycorp.com

Employer Directory, cont.

Florida Power & Light Company
700 Universe Boulevard
Juno Beach, FL 33408
Phone: (561) 694-4000
Fax: (561) 694-4620
www.fpl.com

FMC Technologies, Inc.
1803 Gears Road
Houston, TX 77067
Phone: (281) 591-4000
Fax: (281) 591-4102
www.fmctechnologies.com

GE Energy
4200 Wildwood Parkway
Atlanta, GA 30339
Phone: (678) 844-6000
Fax: (678) 844-6690
www.gepower.com

Halliburton
5 Houston Center
1401 McKinney, Suite 2400
Houston, TX 77020
Phone: (713) 759-2600
Fax: (713) 759-2635
www.halliburton.com

Hess Corporation
1185 Avenue of the Americas
New York, NY 10036
Phone: (212) 997-8500
Fax: (212) 536-8593
www.hess.com

Koch Industries, Inc.
4111 East 37th Street North
Wichita, KS 67220
Phone: (316) 828-5500
Fax: (316) 828-5739
www.kochind.com

Marathon Oil Corporation
5555 San Felipe Road
Houston, TX 77056
Phone: (713) 629-6600
Fax: (713) 296-2952
www.marathon.com

MDU Resources Group, Inc.
1200 West Century Avenue
Bismarck, ND 58506
Phone: (701) 530-1000
Fax: (701) 530-1698
www.mdu.com

Nabors Drilling USA, LP
515 West Greens Road, Suite 1000
Houston, TX 77067
Phone: (713) 232-7500
Fax: (713) 232-7027
www.nabors.com

National Oilwell Varco, Inc.
7909 Parkwood Circle Drive
Houston, TX 77036
Phone: (713) 346-7500
Fax: (713) 435-2195
Toll free: (888) 262-8645
www.nov.com

Occidental Petroleum Corporation
10889 Wilshire Boulevard
Los Angeles, CA 90024
Phone: (310) 208-8800
Fax: (310) 443-6690
www.oxy.com

Pacific Gas and Electric Company
77 Beale Street
San Francisco, CA 94177
Phone: (415) 973 7000
Fax: (415) 267 7268
www.pge.com

PPL Corporation
2 North 9th Street
Allentown, PA 18101
Phone: (610) 774-5151
Fax: (610) 774-4198
www.pplweb.com

Progress Energy, Inc.
410 South Wilmington Street
Raleigh, NC 27601
Phone: (919) 546-6111
Fax: (919) 546-2920
www.progress-energy.com

Puerto Rico Electric Power Authority
Avenida Ponce de León 17½
Santurce, PR 00909
Phone: (787) 289-3434
Fax: (787) 289-4120
www.prepa.com

Schlumberger Limited
5599 San Felipe, 17th Floor
Houston, TX 77056
Phone: (713) 513-2000
www.slb.com

Sempra Energy
101 Ash Street
San Diego, CA 92101
Phone: (619) 696-2000
Fax: (619) 696-2374
Toll free: (877) 736-7721
www.sempra.com

Shell Oil Company
1 Shell Plaza
910 Louisana Street
Houston, TX 77002
Phone: (713) 241-6161
Fax: (713) 241-4044
www.shellus.com

Smith International, Inc.
16740 East Hardy Road
Houston, TX 77032
Phone: (281) 443-3370
Fax: (281) 233-5199
Toll free: (800) 877-6484
www.smith.com

Visit Vault at **www.vault.com** for insider company profiles, expert advice, career message boards, expert resume reviews, the Vault Job Board and more.

VAULT CAREER LIBRARY   83

Employer Directory, cont.

Southern Company
30 Ivan Allen Jr. Boulevard NW
Atlanta, GA 30308
Phone: (404) 506-5000
Fax: (404) 506-0455
www.southernco.com

Sunoco, Inc.
1735 Market Street, Suite LL
Philadelphia, PA 19103-7583
Phone: (215) 977-3000
Fax: (215) 977-3409
Toll free: (800) 786-6261
www.sunocoinc.com

Transocean Inc.
4 Greenway Plaza
Houston, TX 77046
Phone: (713) 232-7500
Fax: (713) 232-7027
www.deepwater.com

Valero Energy Corporation
1 Valero Way
San Antonio, TX 78249
Phone: (210) 345-2000
Fax: (210) 345-2646
Toll free: (800) 531-7911
www.valero.com

Weatherford International, Ltd.
515 Post Oak Boulevard
Houston, TX 77027
Phone: (713) 693-4000
Fax: (713) 693-4323
Toll free: (800) 257-3826
www.weatherford.com

The Williams Companies Inc.
1 Williams Center
Tulsa, OK 74172
Phone: (918) 573 2000
Fax: (918) 573 6714
www.williams.com

Xcel Energy Inc.
414 Nicollet Mall
Minneapolis, MN 55401
Phone: (612) 330-5500
Fax: (800) 895-2895
Toll free: (800) 328-8226
www.xcelenergy.com

Fashion

Fashion and the MBA

Like the entertainment industry, the fashion industry considers education to be less important than experience. So, if you want to go into the industry but don't have the previous experience, get a part-time job in sales or merchandising for an introduction to the industry. Unfortunately, most companies won't care much about your MBA unless it's a large corporation, such as Gap, Levi Strauss, Eddie Bauer, Limited or Nike. These companies tend to hire for finance, supply chain issues or CRM. Typically, you need a consulting, finance or marketing background to get a post-MBA job in the industry. Very few apparel companies have established programs to specifically hire MBAs. A few companies that do hire MBAs for the more creative positions include Cartier, LVMH, Macy's and the Gap.

Hillary Shor recruits for the strategy and business development and consulting and assurance services groups of Gap, Inc. These groups are relatively small (about 20 to 30 people per group). Almost all candidates have an MBA, although many are not hired directly as MBA graduates. Shor says, "We actually look at what a candidate did prior to business school. The strategy and consulting groups look for candidates with consulting or industry experience (such as consumer products, goods or retail). Some of our candidates come from consulting firms such as A.T. Kearney and McKinsey."

The strategy and business development group at Gap identifies, develops and drives longer-term strategies and initiatives that will result in profitable growth (usually with a focus on new opportunities). "Strategy involves brand management, research, as well as planning," says Shor. Consulting and assurance services involves financial/operational analysis, process analysis and design and project management. Basically, this group acts as an internal consulting group for Gap. Team members may work with outside consultants and vendors.

Getting Hired

Build your resume correctly and you can get the interviews you need. In apparel, most of the job functions are very specific, such as design, merchandising, marketing, production and so on. Because many of the companies are small, there aren't very many traditional MBA "management" positions. Many of the people who work at these companies may have gone to trade schools or been in the industry for a long time. For example, the president of Gucci used to work as vice president at Richard Tyler. He was young when he left Richard Tyler for Gucci, but he had started working there when he was 18.

The Gap, Limited and Eddie Bauer all have internal consulting groups that traditionally hire MBAs. If you are interviewing for an internal consulting position, more than likely it will resemble a traditional consulting interview. You may be given a case study as part of the interview. (See the *Vault Guide to the Case Interview* for more information on this type of business interview.) Other jobs at fashion companies for MBA graduates may include planning, finance or strategy.

Pay and Perks

MBA jobs in the fashion industry may not pay well in comparison with other MBA graduate options. Entry-level salaries may hover around the $50,000 mark, though a regional manager or director of sales can make more than $100,000, plus a wardrobe allowance and stock options. In general, there are two options—you work to get the experience or to learn enough to start your own business. If you are thinking of the latter, gain experience that will help you manage your own business. For example, if you want to open your own jewelry store, get a job merchandising or selling jewelry. The best way to learn all sides of the business is to experience it yourself. The pay in the fashion industry is more negotiable than other industries. Most companies will not release this information and, because these jobs are not necessarily geared toward MBAs, the salaries are not standard.

Visit Vault at **www.vault.com** for insider company profiles, expert advice, career message boards, expert resume reviews, the Vault Job Board and more.

VAULT CAREER LIBRARY   85

Vault Profile: Judy Chang, Fashion MBA

Judy Chang graduated from the Anderson School at UCLA with a MBA in 2002. Her previous education included a BS and master's in industrial and operations engineering from the University of Michigan. After college, she worked as a program manager for DaimlerChrysler to coordinate the launch of a particular program in the automotive plants. Chang says, "I would work on program launches for each car model year and style (for specific windshield specifications). I came to Anderson knowing that I wanted to do something totally different." She also says, "If you really want to change careers, getting an MBA is essential. Without my MBA, I don't think I would have been able to switch careers successfully. Fashion companies would have looked at my resume and questioned my interest."

At the Anderson School, her emphasis was marketing, and it was the first time she began to seriously consider a fashion career. She had worked at Armani Exchange during college and enjoyed it—but didn't think that fashion would be a practical career choice. At Anderson, she joined the Fashion and Retail Association and began to do her research so that she could merge her interests and career goals. On campus, Macy's and Neutrogena came for interviews. Through the database, she found alumni and contacted them to speak about their experiences. Chang landed a summer internship in planning at Macy's West. She worked there for three months in the summer and is now there fulltime.

At Macy's West, Chang did two projects over the summer. (The department store Macy's is split into two regions and run completely separately. Macy's East is headquartered in NYC, while Macy's West is based in San Francisco.) To her surprise, Chang's operations experience was extremely relevant during the internship. Her first project was about handbag assortments. Her goal was to figure the optimum assortment level. She analyzed the number of styles bought for each cluster of stores, available table space for the handbags and discounted handbag sales versus regular stock. She used Macy's sales data as well as active visits to the Macy's floor to make her recommendations. Her second project was to standardize colors across a group of buyers. Each buyer used an individual color coding system. Macy's had no way of tracking sales by color or across categories. For example, although each buyer bought "red," each red item could be a completely different shade. Chang created a color tracking system that allowed the planners to analyze the sales by color and buyer. Macy's could now see which color sold during any a one-week period.

During her internship, Chang was excited to go to work every day (especially compared to her previous position). She found everyone to be supportive and very friendly. Macy's was a very different experience for her. Chang says, "At Macy's, it seemed like the workforce was 90 percent women and only 10 percent men. At DaimlerChrysler, I used to work with 90 percent men and 10 percent women. If there is something you really think will make you happy, you should do it—even in this difficult economy."

Employer Directory

Abercrombie & Fitch Co.
6301 Fitch Path
New Albany, OH 43054
Phone: (614) 283-6500
Fax: (614) 283-6710
www.abercrombie.com

Alstyle Apparel, LLC
1501 East Cerritos Avenue
Anaheim, CA 92805
Phone: (714) 765-0400
Fax: (714) 765-0450
Toll free: (800) 225-1364
www.alstyle.com

Ann Taylor Stores Corporation
7 Times Square, 15th Floor
New York, NY 10036
Phone: (212) 541-3300
Fax: (212) 541-3379
www.anntaylor.com

Carter's, Inc.
The Proscenium
1170 Peachtree Street NE, Suite 900
Atlanta, GA 30309
Phone: (404) 745-2700
Fax: (404) 892-0968
www.carters.com

Chanel S.A.
135, Avenue Charles de Gaulle
92521 Neuilly-sur-Seine Cedex
France
Phone: +33-1-46-43-40-00
www.chanel.com

Coach, Inc.
516 West 34th Street
New York, NY 10001
Phone: (212) 594-1850
Fax: (212) 594-1682
www.coach.com

Crocs, Inc.
6328 Monarch Park Place
Niwot, CO 80503
Phone: (303) 848-7000
Fax: (303) 468-4266
www.crocs.com

Delta Apparel, Inc.
2750 Premiere Parkway, Suite 100
Duluth, GA 30097
Phone: (678) 775-6900
Fax: (678) 775-6992
Toll free: (800) 285-4456
www.deltaapparelinc.com

Dolce & Gabbana SPA
Via Santa Cecilia, 7
20122 Milan
Italy
Phone: +39-02-77-42-71
www.dolcegabbana.it

Donna Karan International Inc.
550 Seventh Avenue
New York, NY 10018
Phone: (212) 789-1500
Fax: (212) 921-3526
www.donnakaran.com

Eddie Bauer, Inc.
15010 NE 36th Street
Redmond, WA 98052
Phone: (425) 755-6100
Fax: (425) 755-7696
www.eddiebauer.com

Fruit of the Loom, Inc.
1 Fruit of the Loom Drive
Bowling Green, KY 42103
Phone: (270) 781-6400
Fax: (270) 781-6588
www.fruit.com

Gap Inc.
2 Folsom Street
San Francisco, CA 94105
Phone: (650) 952-4400
Fax: (415) 427-2553
www.gapinc.com

Guess?, Inc.
1444 South Alameda Street
Los Angeles, CA 90021
Phone: (213) 765-3100
Phone: (213) 744-7838
www.guess.com

Hanesbrands Inc.
1000 East Hanes Mill Road
Winston-Salem, NC 27105
Phone: (336) 424-6000
Fax: (336) 424-7631
www.hanesbrands.com

J. Crew Group Inc.
770 Broadway
New York, NY 10003
Phone: (212) 209-2500
Fax: (212) 209-2666
www.jcrew.com

Jockey International, Inc.
2300 60th Street
Kenosha, WI 53141
Phone: (262) 658-8111
Fax: (262) 658-1812
Toll free: (800) 562-5391
www.jockey.com

Jordache Enterprises, Inc.
1400 Broadway, 15th Floor
New York, NY 10018
Phone: (212) 944-1330
Fax: (212) 239-0063
www.jordachecorporate.com

Jones Apparel Group, Inc.
1411 Broadway
New York, NY 10018
Phone: (212) 642-3860
Fax: (215) 785-1795
www.jonesapparel.com

Tommy Hilfiger
25 West 39th Street, 14th Floor
New York, NY 10018
www.tommy.com

Kellwood Company
600 Kellwood Parkwway
Chesterfield, MO 63017
Phone: (314) 576-3100
Fax: (314) 576-3460
www.kellwood.com

Visit Vault at **www.vault.com** for insider company profiles, expert advice,
career message boards, expert resume reviews, the Vault Job Board and more.

V∧ULT CAREER LIBRARY

87

Employer Directory, cont.

Kenneth Cole Productions, Inc.
603 West 50th Street
New York, NY 10019
Phone: (212) 265-1500
Fax: (212) 830-7422
www.kennethcole.com

L'Oreal USA
575 5th Avenue
New York, NY 10017
Phone: (212) 818-1500
Fax: (212) 984-4999
www.lorealusa.com

Levi Strauss & Co.
1155 Battery Street
San Francisco, CA 94111
Phone: (415) 501-6000
Fax: (415) 501-7112
www.levistrauss.com

Limited Brands
3 Limited Parkway
Columbus, OH 43216
Phone: (614) 415-7000
Fax: (614) 415-7440
www.limited.com

Liz Claiborne, Inc.
1441 Broadway
New York, NY 10018
Phone: (212) 354-4900
Fax: (212) 626-3416
www.lizclaiborneinc.com

Louis Vuitton North America, Inc.
19 East 57th Street
New York, NY 10222
Phone: (212) 318-7000
Fax: (212) 888-5780
Toll free: (800) 377-7656

Macy's, Inc.
7 West Seventh Street
Cincinnati, OH 45202
Phone: (513) 579-7000
Fax: (513) 579-7555
www.federated-fds.com

Nike, Inc.
1 Bowerman Drive
Beaverton, OR 97005-6453
Phone: (503) 671-6453
Fax: (503) 671-6300
Toll free: (800) 344-6543
www.nikebiz.com

Nine West Group Inc.
1129 Westchester Avenue
White Plains, NY 10604
Phone: (914) 640-6400
Fax: (914) 640-1676
Toll free: (800) 999-1877
www.ninewest.com

Nordstrom, Inc.
1617 Sixth Avenue
Seattle, WA 98101-1742
Phone: (206) 628-2111
Fax: (206) 628-1795
www.nordstrom.com

Oxford Industries, Inc
222 Piedmont Avenue NE
Atlanta, GA 30308
Phone: (404) 659-2424
Fax: (404) 653-1545
www.oxfordinc.com

Polo Ralph Lauren Corporation
650 Madison Avenue
New York, NY 10222
Phone: (212) 318-7000
Fax: (212) 888-5780
Toll free: (800) 377-7656
www.ralphlauren.com

OshKosh b'Gosh, Inc.
112 Otter Avenue
Oshkosh, WI 54901
Phone: (920) 231-8800
Fax: (920) 231-8621
www.oshkoshbgosh.com

Polo Ralph Lauren Corporation
650 Madison Avenue
New York, NY 10022
Phone: (212) 318-7000
Fax: (212) 888-5780
www.polo.com

Reebok International Ltd.
1895 J.W. Foster Boulevard
Canton, MA 02021
Phone: (781) 401-5000
Fax: (781) 401-7402
www.reebok.com

Renfro Corporation
661 Linville Road
Mt. Airy, NC 27030
Phone: (336) 719-8000
Fax: (336) 719-8215
Toll free: (800) 334-9091
www.renfro.com

Samsonite Corporation
575 West Street, Suite 110
Mansfield, MA 02048
Phone: (508) 851-1400
Fax: (508) 851-8715
www.samsonite.com

The Timberland Company
200 Domain Drive
Stratham, NH 03885
Phone: (603)772-9500
Fax: (603) 773-1640
www.timberland.com

Employer Directory, cont.

V.F. Corporation
105 Corporate Center Boulevard
Greensboro, NC 27408
Phone: (336) 424-6000
Fax: (336) 424-7631
www.vfc.com

The Warnaco Group, Inc.
501 7th Avenue
New York, NY 10018
Phone: (212) 563-2000
Fax: (212) 971-2250
Toll free: (800) 759-4219
www.warnerco.com

Visit Vault at **www.vault.com** for insider company profiles, expert advice,
career message boards, expert resume reviews, the Vault Job Board and more.

VAULT CAREER LIBRARY

89

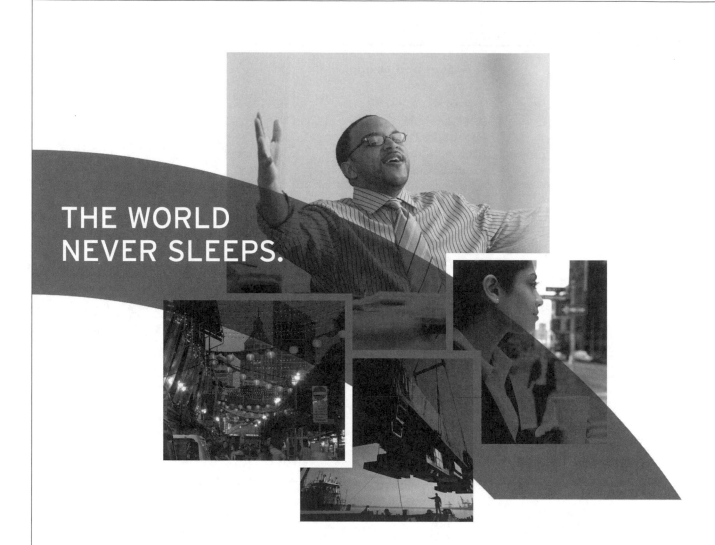

THE WORLD NEVER SLEEPS.

Dreams. | **Realities.**

In Harvard Square, Jackson has just cracked an equation. Meanwhile, in Austin, Texas, Rita – the woman who will soon give Jackson an analyst position – is on her way to give a presentation on microfinance. And in Singapore, a team of Global Capital Markets Associates are projecting the impact of the growth of the global middle class.

Working in more than 100 countries means being open-minded in every way: how we do business, how we find solutions, and how we choose our colleagues. To us, inclusion isn't a rule to follow; it's a way of life. Because we're all different, and we're proud to be. That's why at Citi, the world never sleeps. **oncampus.citi.com**

Citi never sleeps™

citi®

Financial Services and Insurance

State of the Industry

Like a bazaar that offers something to satisfy every customer's potential needs, the financial services industry presents a little bit of everything to prospective clientele. But while the trade is a vast one, its subdivisions are specialized to meet individuals' fiscal needs. Many of these specialized financial categories are covered in this guide.

The firms we chose to profile as the top financial services firms primarily operate in one of the following categories: credit cards, insurance, mortgages, auto financing, ratings, financial data services or diversified financials. (Noticeably missing categories include accounting, investment banking, commercial banking and investment management—all of which are covered in other Vault guides.)

Although the evolution of the financial services business has been a long and storied one, its development and expansion continues well into this century. What follows is a brief overview of the financial services fields covered in this guide.

Credit Card Services

Looming large

Issuing credit cards is one of the most common ways in which financial services firms provide credit to individuals. Via the credit card, firms provide individuals with the funds required to purchase goods and services, and in return, individuals repay the full balance at a later date, or make payments on an installment basis. Via the debit card, people avoid debt by withdrawing the purchase amount from their bank accounts and transferring it to the seller. Though you're most likely familiar with how credit and debit cards work, you might not be familiar with just how large the industry is. According to Reuters, as of 2007, there were more than 640 million credit cards in circulation in the U.S. And according to CreditCards.com, Visa had a 46 percent U.S. market share based on credit card receivables outstanding in 2007, followed by MasterCard with 36 percent, American Express with 12 percent and Discover with 6 percent. On a global scale, Visa accounted for 65 percent of the market, MasterCard had a 30 percent share, followed by American Express and Japan-based JCB card (both of which had unknown shares).

A bumpy ride

In the first quarter of 2008, Visa and MasterCard spent $860,000 and $720,000 apiece in order to attempt to combat proposed federal regulations, which would shield consumers from high interest rates and let merchants who take credit cards negotiate their transaction fees. The proposed legislation, called the "Credit Card Fair Fee Act of 2008," as spearheaded by the Federal Reserve, the Office of Thrift and Supervision, and the National Credit Union Administration.

Potential legislation against Visa and MasterCard was only the tip of the iceberg of credit card companies' difficulties in 2008. MasterCard posted a $746 million loss for the second quarter of the year, due in no small part to the $1.8 billion the company ended up paying American Express in a settlement stemming from a 2004 lawsuit contending that MasterCard—along with competitor Visa—had barred some financial companies from distributing cards through American Express. In the third quarter of 2008, MasterCard will make its first $150 million payment to American Express—a practice that will continue for 12 quarters. Meanwhile, Visa, in its settlement, is paying American Express a total of $2.25 billion.

Consumer credit purgatory

Credit card companies were hardly the only ones to feel the pinch of the credit crunch. Consumers worldwide felt the breakdown of the subprime market in many ways, and those in the U.S. took the brunt of the fallout. In late 2007, International Monetary Fund Director Rodrigo Rato predicted the U.S. would be the hardest hit throughout 2008. Sadly, his

Visit Vault at www.vault.com for insider company profiles, expert advice, career message boards, expert resume reviews, the Vault Job Board and more.

VAULT CAREER LIBRARY 91

predictions seemed to be fulfilled quickly—by June 2008, *The Guardian* reported on the trend of more and more middle-class citizens being forced to live in their cars due to the foreclosures brought on by the subprime crisis. And that wasn't the end of the market backlash. In July 2008, the Senior Loan Officer Opinion Survey on Bank Lending Practice reported that 65 percent of U.S. banks admitted to stiffening their overall lending practices over the course of the year as a result of the credit crisis, a 30 percent jump versus its April 2008 report.

Heavy metal

The credit card traces its roots back to 1914 when Western Union began doling out metal cards, called "metal money," which gave preferred customers interest-free, deferred-payment privileges. Ten years later, General Petroleum Corporation issued the first metal money for gasoline and automotive services, and by the late 1930s, department stores, communication companies, travel and delivery companies had all began to introduce such cards. Then, companies issued the cards, processed the transactions and collected the debts from the customer. The popularity of these cards grew until the beginning of World War II, when "Regulation W" restricted the use of cards, and as a result, stalled their growth.

After the war, though, cards were back on track. Modes of travel were more advanced and more accessible, and more people were beginning to buy expensive modern conveniences such as kitchen appliances and washing machines. As a result, the credit card boomed in popularity, as consumers could pay for these things on credit that otherwise they couldn't afford to buy with cash.

Charge-it

In 1951, New York's Franklin National Bank created a credit system called Charge-It, which was very similar to the modern credit card. Charge-It allowed consumers to make purchases at local retail establishments, with the retailer obtaining authorization from the bank and then closing the sale. At a later date, the bank would reimburse the retailer and then collect the debt from the consumer. Acting upon the success of Franklin's Charge-It, other banks soon began introducing similar cards. Banks found that cardholders liked the convenience and credit line that cards offered, and retailers discovered that credit card customers usually spent more than if they had to pay with cash. Additionally, retailers found that handling bank-issued cards was less costly than maintaining their credit card programs.

The association and the Master

Bank of America masterminded credit card innovations in the 1960s with the introduction of the bank card association. In 1965, Bank of America began issuing licensing agreements that allowed other banks to issue BankAmericards. To compete with the BankAmericard, four banks from California formed the Western States Bankcard Association and introduced the MasterCharge. By 1969, most credit cards had been converted to either the MasterCharge (which changed its name to MasterCard in 1979) or the BankAmericard (which was renamed Visa in 1977).

Cutting the cost of transaction processing and decreasing credit card fraud were the next innovations introduced to the industry. Electronic authorizations, beginning in the early 1970s, allowed merchants to approve transactions 24 hours a day. By the end of the decade, magnetic strips on the back of credit cards allowed retailers to swipe the customer's credit card through a dial-up terminal, which accessed the issuing bank cardholder's information. This process gave authorizations and processed settlement agreements in a matter of minutes. In the 1980s, the ATM (Automatic Teller Machine) began to surface, giving cardholders 24-hour access to cash.

The debut of the debit, the climb of the cobrand

The 1990s saw the debit card rise in popularity. The debit card grew from accounting for 274 million transactions in 1990 to 8.15 billion transactions in 2002. (According to the Packaged Facts report "Debit Cards in the U.S.," there were 28 million debit card transactions in the U.S. in 2007, worth a total of $1.4 trillion.) The 1990s also witnessed the surge of cobranded and affinity cards, which match up a credit card company with a retailer to offer discounts for using the card (think Citibank's AAdvantage cards and American Express' Mileage Rewards program). Although cobranded cards took a dip in the late 1990s—according to some industry experts, this was because issuers had exhausted the most lucrative partners—they returned in full force during the early part of the new millennium. In 2003 alone, MBNA—called "The King of the Plastic Frontier" by *BusinessWeek*—struck some 400 new deals with various companies such as Merrill Lynch, Royal Caribbean and Air Canada. Additionally, it renewed deals with another 1,400 organizations, including the National Football League and the University of Michigan. In 2004, MBNA signed agreements with numerous other companies and organizations such as A.G. Edwards & Sons, the Massachusetts Institute of Technology, Arsenal Football Club (U.K.), Charles Schwab and Starwood Hotels and Resorts. (In 2005, MBNA was acquired by Bank of America.)

And then there were four

In September 2003, a federal court upheld a lower court ruling that cost credit card powerhouses Visa and MasterCard a combined $3 billion. The court found Visa and MasterCard rules preventing the companies' member banks from also issuing American Express and Morgan Stanley's Discover cards to be illegal and harmful to competition. MasterCard was forced to pay $2 billion in damages and Visa paid $1 billion.

In October 2004, the U.S. Supreme Court decided not to hear Visa and MasterCard's appeal in the government's antitrust suit against them, effectively ending the two companies' rules that had prevented banks from issuing cards on rival networks. As a result, Amex and Discover became free to partner with the thousands of banks that issue Visa and MasterCard. This allows Amex and Discover to gain ground on the two credit powerhouses that, together, control at least 80 percent of the U.S. credit card purchase volume (as of July 2007), according to the National Retail Federation.

Re-Discovering the possibilities

In the midst of Morgan Stanley's great personnel exodus of March 2005, the firm announced plans to spin off its Discover credit card unit. Former Morgan Stanley CEO Philip Purcell reasoned that Discover "will be more properly valued as a stand-alone entity" than as a piece of Morgan Stanley. Soon after the announcement, analysts began estimating the Street value of the huge credit card unit. The range fell between $9 billion and $16 billion. Analysts also disagreed over whether or not the spin-off would maximize shareholder value.

However, new CEO John Mack's first big after taking over the reins in mid-2005 was to reverse course on the Discover business, which predecessor Purcell had talked of selling off. "Discover is not only a strong business, but also an attractive asset for Morgan Stanley," Mack said in a statement. "It is a unique, successful franchise with growth opportunities that gives Morgan Stanley a consistent stream of stable, high-quality earnings and substantial cash flow, diversifies the company's earnings and broadens our scale and capital base."

But despite the kind words, there was ultimately a change of heart for Morgan Stanley. Although Discover delivered record before-tax earnings of $16 billion in 2006, Morgan Stanley announced the same year that it planned to spin off Discover, which some analysts said would allow both businesses to grow more quickly. The deal was finally completed in June 2007, and though financial terms weren't disclosed, analysts estimated Discover's worth to be $13 billion at the time.

As an autonomous firm, Discover is now led by CEO David W. Nelms, and as of August 2008, its stock was trading at $15.52 a share. Net income for the second quarter 2008 was $234.15 million, up from $209.24 million in the second quarter 2007. Being its own entity has hardly exempted Discover from dealing with a few roadblocks. In August 2008, a lawsuit from Discover asserting a conspiracy between MasterCard and Visa was deemed limited in reach by a judge who also rejected allegations from Discover that MasterCard was excluding Discover from distributing debit cards.

Visit Vault at **www.vault.com** for insider company profiles, expert advice, career message boards, expert resume reviews, the Vault Job Board and more.

VAULT CAREER LIBRARY   93

The big buy

In June 2005, BofA announced its acquisition of credit card behemoth MBNA in a $35 billion deal, following closely on the heels of its $49 billion purchase of FleetBoston Financial in 2003. The MBNA purchase made Bank of America one of the largest card issuers in the U.S., with $143 billion in managed outstanding balances and 40 million active accounts. Bank of America added more than 20 million new customer accounts as well as affinity relationships with more than 5,000 partner organizations and financial institutions. It achieved overall expense efficiencies of $850 million after-tax, fully realized in 2007, and a restructuring charge of $1.25 billion after-tax. Cost reductions came from a range of sources, including layoffs. (In unrelated cuts, the bank announced plans to slash 7,500 jobs in its mortgage, home-equity and insurance groups in summer 2008).

In November 2006, BofA announced that it had agreed to acquire US Trust, the wealth management subsidiary of Charles Schwab Corporation. The $3.3 billion acquisition, completed in July 2007, helped BofA strengthen its capabilities in serving high-net-worth clients and increase its assets under management.

The big IPOs

At the end of August 2005, MasterCard, which became a private share corporation in 2002, announced plans to become a publicly-traded company. On May 25, 2006, MasterCard finally went public, and began trading on the New York Stock Exchange (NYSE) under the ticker 'MA.' "Listing on the NYSE marks a major milestone for MasterCard and reinforces our commitment to continued growth and building value for our customers and stockholders," Robert Selander, the company's president and chief executive officer, told the Associated Press. The market had expected the issue to open in the $40 to $43 range, but MasterCard was at $39 after a series of setbacks delayed the process. But by most accounts, the IPO has been a huge success. As of August 2008, the stock had zoomed to over $234 per share, thanks in part to solid growth rates. During the second quarter 2008, 951 million MasterCard cards were issued, up 11 percent. MasterCard's worldwide purchase volume went up 12.8 percent to $655 billion, while transactions processed went up 13.6 percent to 5.2 billion.

MasterCard wasn't the only piece of plastic that's dazzled IPO investors. On March 19, 2008, Visa set a record for stateside IPOs when it raised $17.9 billion in its initial public offering. (The deal got even bigger when Visa's underwriters decided to exercise their option to buy 40.6 million more shares at $44 each for about $1.8 billion.) The firm's shares were initially valued at $44 per share—higher than the expected $37 to $42 range—and increased 35 percent to $59.50 almost immediately upon going public. At the end of the first day of trading, Visa's shares (which trade on the NYSE under the symbol 'V') closed at $56.50, a 28.4 percent increase from its opening price. As of September 2008, Visa's stock was still going strong, trading for around $74 a share.

The road, however, has been rocky as MasterCard and Visa have recently weathered some storms. In November 2007, MasterCard and Visa announced that they would be paying American Express $1.8 billion and $2.25 billion, respectively, in a settlement stemming from a 2004 lawsuit contending that the companies had barred some financial companies from distributing cards through American Express.

No contact credit

"Contactless" cards and finger-swiping systems are the latest advances in the world of plastic purchasing. According to CreditCards.com, by mid-2007, banks had issued about 27 million debit and credit cards that could be scanned via a radar-like beam, rather than having to be run through a machine. The popularity of contactless credit and debit cards—which can be used at numerous retailers such as McDonald's, 7-Eleven and CVS—is only expected to skyrocket. According to market research firm Packaged Facts, there will be approximately 109 million cards in circulation by 2011. Other than not having to run the cards through a machine, another benefit is that no signature is required for purchases less than $25.

Another no-contact credit payment system is now in place: the pay-by-finger system, in which individuals' fingers are scanned and linked to their payment information. All you have to do is press your finger (its print) against a device, enter some personal information, such as your phone number on a keypad and your payment is made; fingerprints are linked up with credit or debit cards. The system is already in place at hundreds of U.S. supermarkets such as Albertsons and Piggly Wiggly.

A worrying trend

There's been a number of reports detailing the disturbing trend of cash-strapped homeowners declining to pay their mortgages as the U.S. economy has continued to tank. Maybe because of this trend—or in spite of it—American Express and Visa began a rewards program that allows customers to pay their monthly mortgage or rent with a credit card. Although the companies said that customers have the potential to earn exponentially more bonus points than they had before, some analysts pointed out that the main concern with such a program is that credit card owners who are already in debt will only continue to fall deeper into credit issues. And those debt issues already run deep with Americans to begin with. A Sallie Mae/Gallup poll released in August 2008 revealed that parents of college students who borrowed on credit cards put an average of more than $5,800 on their cards while students put about $2,500 on their plastic. Besides big-ticket items like education, other accouterments of wealth are also frequently put on Americans' credit cards without a second thought—swimming pools and car payments are no longer a rarity to charge.

But is it preferable to put college payments on a credit card rather than luxury items that would otherwise be out of reach? It may be, according to some credit card companies. CompuScore, which markets Visa cards, came under fire from the Federal Trade Commission in August 2008 for profiling cardholders' transactions, reducing the credit limits of customers who used their cards at marriage counselors, tire shops, billiard halls and pawn shops. The FTC hasn't called the company's actions illegal, but it did allege that the company wasn't upfront about its actions. Either way, it may pay for consumers to watch where they use their cards.

Insurance

Risky business

The insurance industry combines to form a multi-trillion-dollar market dealing in risk. In exchange for a premium, insurers promise to compensate, monetarily or otherwise, individuals and businesses for future losses, thus taking on the risk of personal injury, death, damage to property, unexpected financial disaster and just about any other misfortune that could occur.

The industry is often divided into categories such as life/health and property/casualty. Life insurance dominates the mix, making up about 60 percent of all premiums. The bigger categories can be subdivided into smaller groups; property insurance, for instance, may cover homeowner's, renter's, auto and boat policies, while health insurance is made up of subsets including disability and long-term care.

But these days, you can find insurance for just about anything, including weddings and bar mitzvahs, policies for the chance of weather ruining a vacation and policies for pets (a market that grew 342 percent from 1998 to 2002, had sales of $160 million in 2005 and exploded to $195 million by 2007, according to the industry publication Small Business Trends). Even insurance companies themselves can be insured against extraordinary losses—by companies specializing in reinsurance.

Although insurance isn't the sexiest business around, celebrity policies always get a lot of press. While rumors that Jennifer Lopez had insured her famous asset for $1 billion proved to be unfounded, other such policies do indeed exist. In fact, the phrase "million dollar legs" comes from Betty Grable's policy for that amount (a similar policy is held by TV's Mary Hart); other notable contemporary policies include Bruce Springsteen's voice, reportedly covered at around $6 million.

The world's top five

Though the U.S. is well ahead of the rest of the world in terms of insurance coverage, insurance is a truly global business. The industry is the biggest in the world, raking in more than $4 trillion in revenue annually, according SocialFunds, an

Visit Vault at www.vault.com for insider company profiles, expert advice, career message boards, expert resume reviews, the Vault Job Board and more.

VAULT CAREER LIBRARY   95

investment news site. Ranked by sales, the top five insurance companies are Germany's Allianz, the Netherlands' ING, New York-based American International Group (AIG), France's AXA and Japan's Nippon Life Insurance Company. Other leading U.S. insurers include State Farm, MetLife, Allstate, Prudential, Aetna and Travelers.

Consolidation is the name of the game—Hoovers reports that the top 10 property/casualty insurers account for nearly half of all premiums written. Perhaps the most notable example of the mergers and acquisitions mania in the industry was the $82 billion merger in 1998 between Citicorp and the Travelers Group, which created Citigroup (now known as Citi). Some insurance companies have also begun to reconfigure themselves from mutual insurers, or those owned by policyholders (e.g., State Farm), to stock insurers, or those held by shareholders (e.g., Allstate). This process, known as "demutualization," promises to raise even more capital for insurance companies to indulge in more acquisitions.

The last 25 years have seen a shift in the industry away from life insurance toward annuity products, focusing on managing investment risk rather than the (inevitable) risk of mortality. With increasing deregulation in the U.S. and Japan, these insurers are moving ever closer to competition with financial services firms. Indeed, the business of the insurance industry doesn't end with insurance. The world's top insurance companies have broadened their array of financial services to include investment management, annuities, securities, mutual funds, health care management, employee benefits and administration, real estate brokerage and even consumer banking. The move towards financial services followed the 1999 repeal of the Glass-Steagall Act, which barred insurance companies, banks and brokerages from entering each other's industries, and the Gramm Leach-Bliley Act of 1999, which further defined permissible acts for financial holding companies. Now insurance companies are free to partner with commercial banks, securities firms and other financial entities.

At the speed of the Internet

Like many other industries, the insurance market has been transformed in recent years by the Internet. Traditionally, insurance products have been distributed by independent agents (business people paid on commission) or by exclusive agents (paid employees). But insurers who sell over the Web reap the benefits of lower sales costs and customer service expenses, along with a more expedient way of getting information to consumers, which is transforming traditional methods by cutting costs and increasing the amount of information available to consumers. Celent Communications estimates that the online insurance market takes in over $200 billion in sales each year. Of course, an automated approach to doing business means fewer sales people are needed—Celent reported that insurance giant Cigna, for instance, eliminated 2,000 jobs in 2002 because of increased efficiencies.

With more IT comes a greater need for IT security—Celent estimates that U.S. insurers spend about 2.5 to 3 percent of premium on security. Aside from the threat of viruses, hackers and the like, regulations have made security a top priority—the Health Information Portability and Accountability Act (HIPAA), for instance, which went into effect in 2003, sets strict standards for the privacy and security of the patient information transferred between health insurers and providers.

Recovering from September 11th

The September 11 terrorist attacks sent shockwaves through the industry. Not only did they constitute perhaps the largest insured loss in U.S. history—with estimates ranging between $40 billion and $50 billion in claims for loss of life and property, injuries and workers' compensation—but they also caused insurers and re-insurers to take a hard look at how they would handle the risks associated with possible future terrorist acts. The Terrorism Risk Insurance Act, signed into law by President Bush in November 2002, aimed to deal with the nearly incalculable risk posed by this threat. Among other things, the law defines a terrorism-related event as one with a minimum of $5 million in damages. It provides for the sharing of risk between private insurers and the federal government over a three-year period, with each participating company responsible for paying a deductible before federal assistance is available. If losses are incurred above the insurer's deductible, the government is obliged to pay 90 percent. While the measure met with a considerable amount of grumbling from all parties involved, for the most part the industry acknowledged that the plan at least allows for the potential risk to insurers from terrorism-related disasters to be quantified.

Property insurance stalemate?

In parts of the U.S. such as California and Louisiana, which have dealt with rampant wildfires and Hurricane Katrina in recent years, another trend has arisen. More and more, property insurers are requiring homeowners to take precautions to protect their houses or confront the possibility of being dropped—a trend that has continued into 2008 with precautions from companies encouraging homeowners to guard against floods and winter freezing.

Some insurance companies in California are requiring homeowners to replace their roofs with fire-resistant ones, and other companies in hurricane-prone coastal areas are requiring policyholders to install storm-resistant shutters. Still, since the requirements are following three years of record profits for the property insurance industry, the Associated Press reported in June 2007 that many homeowners are up at arms about the potential cost. But the insurance industry isn't backing down on their requirements, and some companies have even decided to pull out of certain states altogether. For example, Farmers Insurance said in August 2008 that it would pull out of the North Carolina homeowners' market by the end of the year.

Despite the deluge of flood-related insurance claims in the Midwest in 2008, many companies are surprisingly weathering the financial storm. In July 2008, rating agency Standard & Poor's (S&P) said that the Midwest floods were unlikely to impact the ratings of many insurance companies. S&P added that the Midwest flooding was likely to have fairly little impact on insurance companies in general, although financial consequences are expected to vary across Midwest states that have experienced particularly vigorous flooding.

Unhealthy health care

Medical malpractice remained a hot topic through 2008. Health insurers generally get a bad rap from the public, and the media and politicians give plenty of air time to horror stories about managed care companies slighting critically ill patients, and insurers refusing to cover necessary treatments or technologies. Is this reputation deserved? Depends on who you ask, but the industry has its own battles in health care—for example, it sees medical malpractice claims, which have skyrocketed in recent years, as a true crisis. Indeed, according to the Insurance Information Institute, some insurers have quit writing malpractice policies entirely rather than shoulder the risk (the median malpractice award in 2001, the latest year for which this figure is available, was $1 million). And it looks like costs keep increasing—a report by reinsurance company Aon said that malpractice awards tend to go up by 6 percent each year. Insurance company Farmers, which racked up more than $100 million in malpractice-related losses in 2003, finally got out of malpractice overage in September of the same year. But by August 2008, there was more brewing on the medical malpractice front. New York Governor David Paterson signed a bill that gives a little financial relief to doctors with high premiums. The bill also deferred the possibility of a surcharge for doctors. Those backing the bill said that doctors were likely to have to pay a 30 percent hike in insurance rates without the passage of the proposal.

Lots of jobs

In the U.S., the insurance industry employs around 2.36 million people, according to industry trendwatcher Plunkett Research. Of these jobs, 62 percent are with insurance carriers, while 38 percent are with insurance agencies, brokerages and providers of other insurance-related services, as reported by the U.S. Bureau of Labor Statistics in its most recent survey. Most insurance agents specialize in life and health insurance, or property and casualty insurance. But a growing number of "multi-line" agents sell all types of insurance. An increasing number of agents also work for banking institutions, non-depository institutions, or security and commodity brokers.

Visit Vault at **www.vault.com** for insider company profiles, expert advice, career message boards, expert resume reviews, the Vault Job Board and more.

VAULT CAREER LIBRARY

97

Ratings

Making the grade

Credit rating is another sector of the financial services industry that serves a highly specific purpose. Founded by John Knowles Fitch as the Fitch Publishing Company in 1913, Fitch was one of the early leaders in providing financial statistics. The Fitch rating system of "AAA" to "D," introduced in 1924, has become the standard for the financial community. Fitch, one of the four major credit-rating agencies (the others are Moody's Investors Service, Standard & Poor's and DBRS), is the leader in providing ratings on debt issued by companies, covering entities in more than 80 countries.

Moody's, founded in 1900, is one of the most prominent and widely utilized sources for credit ratings, research and risk analysis on debt instruments and securities. In addition, Moody's provides corporate and government credit assessment and training services, credit training services and credit software to financial institutions, with 9,000 accounts at 2,400 institutions worldwide. The firm's ratings and analyses track 100 sovereign nations, 11,000 company insurers, 25,000 public finance issuers and 70,000 structured finance obligations. Moody's ratings business consists of four groups: structured finance, corporate finance, financial institutions and sovereign risk and public finance. The firm's primary clients include corporate and government issuers as well as institutional investors, banks, creditors and commercial banks.

Standard & Poor's operates through six main divisions: credit ratings, data services, equity research, funds, indices and risk solutions. Nearly $1.5 trillion in investor assets was directly tied to S&P indices as of June 2008, more than all other indices combined. The firm has the world's largest network of credit ratings analysts, and its equity research division is the world's largest producer of independent equity research. More than 1,000 institutions—including 19 of the top 20 securities firms, 13 of the top 20 banks, and 11 of the top 20 life insurance companies—license its research for their investors and advisors.

DBRS, an international ratings agency, is headquartered in Toronto and gives ratings to borrowing entities. The company is split into corporate, financial institutions, public finance and structured finance divisions. The firm prides itself on being "the leading rating agency in Canada" as well as being the first rating agency to have a full-service web site for customers.

Suspect practices

Rating agencies have recently come under severe scrutiny for their ratings of mortgage-backed securities—specifically, whether or not these ratings helped contribute to the subprime mortgage crisis. In late 2007, the Securities and Exchange Commission (SEC) began an inquiry into whether appropriate procedures were followed for ratings companies like Moody's and S&P. The SEC has alleged that some ratings agencies gave unnaturally high rankings to mortgage-backed securities and some debt products.

The problems for the rating agencies didn't end with the SEC. In July 2008, Connecticut Attorney General Richard Blumenthal filed a lawsuit against Fitch, Moody's and S&P, alleging that the firms gave municipal bonds falsely low ratings and, consequently, caused customers to pay for unneeded bond insurance as well as elevated interest rates. Additionally, Blumenthal said the agencies ran afoul of the Connecticut Unfair Trade Practices Act by neglecting to mention "material facts that caused bond insurers in Connecticut to purchase bonds at higher interest rates."

Employer Directory

Citi

388 Greenwich Street
New York, NY 10013
Phone: (212) 559-1000
www.oncampus.citi.com

Your ambitions are more than plans for the future. They're your hopes and dreams. They're a part of who you are and who you aspire to be. When you join Citi you'll cultivate those aspirations with market-leading training and exposure to the most complex and groundbreaking transactions around the world. You'll join a company with an impressive, far-reaching heritage. Among our proud alumni are finance ministers, Nobel Prize winners, and even New York's mayor. While ambitions have taken them in different directions, their business foundation began with Citi.

Whatever your dreams Citi can make them a reality.

Visit Vault at **www.vault.com** for insider company profiles, expert advice, career message boards, expert resume reviews, the Vault Job Board and more.

VAULT CAREER LIBRARY   99

Employer Directory, cont.

Aflac (American Family Life Assurance Company)
1932 Wynnton Road
Columbus, GA 31999
Phone: (706) 323-3431
Fax: (706) 324-6330
www.aflac.com

Alliance Data (Alliance Data Systems Corporation)
17655 Waterview Parkway
Dallas, TX 75252
Phone: (972) 348-5100
Fax: (972) 348-5335
www.alliancedata.com

The Allstate Corporation
2775 Sanders Road
Northbrook, IL 60062-6127
Phone: (847) 402-5000
Fax: (847) 326-7519
Toll free: (847) 402-5000
www.allstate.com

American Express
World Financial Center
200 Vesey Street
New York, NY 10285
Phone: (212) 640-2000
www.americanexpress.com

American Family Insurance Group
6000 American Parkway
Madison, WI 53783-0001
Phone: (608) 249-2111
www.amfam.com

AmeriCredit
801 Cherry Street, Suite 3900
Fort Worth, TX 76102
Phone: (817) 302-7000
Toll free: (800) 284-2271
www.americredit.com

Aon Corporation
Aon Center
200 East Randolph Street
Chicago, IL 60601
Phone: (312) 381-1000
Fax: (312) 381-6032
www.aon.com

Arthur J. Gallagher & Co.
The Gallagher Centre
2 Pierce Place
Itasca, IL 60143-3141
Phone: (630) 773-3800
Fax: (630) 285-4000
www.ajg.com

Assurant
1 Chase Manhattan Plaza
New York, NY 10005
Phone: (212) 859-7000
Fax: (212) 859-5893
www.assurant.com

Berkshire Hathaway Inc.
1440 Kiewit Plaza
Omaha, NE 68131
Phone: (402) 346-1400
Fax: (402) 346-3375
www.berkshirehathaway.com

Capital One Financial
1680 Capital One Drive
McLean, VA 22012
Phone: (703) 720-1000
www.capitalone.com

CB Richard Ellis Group, Inc.
100 North Sepulveda Boulevard
Suite 1050
El Segundo, CA 90245
Phone: (310) 606-4700
Fax: (949) 809-4357
www.cbre.com

The Chubb Corporation
15 Mountain View Road
Warren, NJ 07059
Phone: (908) 903-2000
Fax: (908) 903-2027
www.chubb.com

Citigroup
399 Park Avenue
New York, NY 10043
Phone: (212) 559-1000
Fax: (212) 793-3946
www.citigroup.com

Countrywide Financial Corp.
4500 Park Granada
Calabasas, CA 91302-1613
Phone: (818) 225-3000
Fax: (818) 225-4051
www.countrywide.com

Daimler Financial Services
Eichhornstraße 3
10875 Berlin
Germany
Phone: +49-30-2554-0
Fax: +49-30-2554-2525

36455 Corporate Drive
Farmington Hills, MI 48331
Phone: (248) 991-6700
Fax: (248) 957-2997
www.daimler-financialservices.com

Discover Financial Services
2500 Lake Cook Road
Riverwoods, IL 60015
Phone: (224) 405-0900
Fax: (224) 405-4993
www.discoverfinancial.com

DST Systems
333 West 11th Street
Kansas City, MO 64105
Phone: (816) 435-1000
Fax: (816) 435-8618
www.dstsystems.com

Employer Directory, cont.

The Dun & Bradstreet Corporation
103 JFK Parkway
Short Hills, NJ 07078
Phone: (973) 921-5500
Fax: (973) 921-6056
www.dnb.com

Equifax
1550 Peachtree Street NW
Atlanta, GA 30309
Phone: (404) 885-8000
Fax: (404) 885-8055
www.equifax.com

Fidelity National Financial
601 Riverside Avenue
Jacksonville, FL 32204
Phone: (888) 934-3354
www.fnf.com

First American Corp.
1 First American Way
Santa Ana, CA 92707
Phone: (800) 852-3643
Fax: (714) 250-3000
www.firstam.com

First Data Corporation
6200 South Quebec Street
Greenwood Village, CO 80111
Phone: (303) 967-8000
Fax: (303) 967-6701
www.firstdata.com

Fiserv
255 Fiserv Drive
Brookfield, WI 53045
Phone: (262) 879-5000
Fax: (262) 879-5013
www.fiserv.com

Fitch Ratings
1 State Street Plaza
New York, NY 10004
Phone: (212) 908-0500
Fax: (212) 480-4435
www.fitchratings.com

Genworth Financial Inc.
6620 West Broad Street
Richmond, VA 23230
Phone: (804) 281-6000
Fax: (804) 662-2414
www.genworth.com

GMAC Financial Services
200 Renaissance Center
Detroit, MI 48265
Phone: (313) 556-5000
Fax: (313) 556-5108
www.gmacfs.com

Guardian (The Guardian Life Insurance Company of America)
7 Hanover Square
New York, NY 10004-2616
Phone: (212) 598-8000
Fax: (212) 919-2170
www.guardianlife.com

Hartford Financial Services
Hartford Plaza
690 Asylum Avenue
Hartford, CT 06115-1900
Phone: (860) 547-5000
Fax: (860) 547-2680
www.thehartford.com

Leucadia National Corporation
315 Park Avenue South
New York, NY 10010-3607
Phone: (212) 460-1900
Fax: (212) 598-4869
www.leucadia.com

Liberty Mutual
175 Berkeley Street
Boston, MA 02117
Phone: (617) 357-9500
Fax: (617) 350-7648
www.libertymutualgroup.com

Lincoln Financial Group
1500 Market Street, Suite 3900
Philadelphia, PA 19102
Phone: (215) 448-1400
Fax: (215) 448-3962
www.lfg.com

Loews Corporation
667 Madison Avenue
New York, NY 10021-8087
Phone: (212) 521-2000
Fax: (212) 521-2525
www.loews.com

Marsh & McLennan Companies, Inc.
1166 Avenue of the Americas
New York, NY 10036-2774
Phone: (212) 345-5000
Fax: (212) 345-4838
www.marshmac.com

MassMutual
1295 State Street
Springfield, MA 01111-0001
Phone: (413) 744-1000
Fax: (413) 744-6005
www.massmutual.com

MasterCard Worldwide
2000 Purchase Street
Purchase, NY 10577
Phone: (914) 249-2000
Fax: (914) 249-4206
www.mastercard.com

Moody's Investors Services
99 Church Street
New York, NY 10007
Phone: (212) 553-0300
Fax: (212) 553-4820
www.moodys.com

Nationwide
1 Nationwide Plaza
Columbus, OH 43215-2220
Phone: (614) 249-7111
Fax: (614) 854-5036
www.nationwide.com

New York Life Insurance Company
51 Madison Avenue
New York, NY 10010
Phone: (212) 576-7000
Fax: (212) 576-8145
www.newyorklife.com

Visit Vault at **www.vault.com** for insider company profiles, expert advice, career message boards, expert resume reviews, the Vault Job Board and more.

VAULT CAREER LIBRARY 101

Employer Directory, cont.

Pacific Life Insurance Company
700 Newport Center Drive
Newport Beach, CA 92660
Phone: (949) 219-3011
www.pacificlife.com

The Progressive Corporation
6300 Wilson Mills Road
Mayfield Village, OH 44143
Phone: (800) 766-4737
www.progressive.com

Prudential Financial, Inc.
751 Broad Street
Newark, NJ 07102-3777
Phone: (973) 802-6000
Fax: (973) 802-4479
www.prudential.com

Sallie Mae
12061 Bluemont Way
Reston, VA 20190
Phone: (703) 810-3000
Fax: (703) 984-5042
www.salliemae.com

Scottrade
12800 Corporate Hill Drive
St. Louis, MO 63131-1834
Phone: (314) 965-1555
Fax: (314) 543-6222
www.scottrade.com

Standard & Poor's
55 Water Street
New York, NY 10041
Phone: (212) 438-2000
Fax: (212) 438-7375
www.standardandpoors.com

State Farm
1 State Farm Plaza
Bloomington, IL 61710
Phone: (309) 766-2311
Fax: (309) 766-3621
www.statefarm.com

SunGard Data Systems
680 East Swedesford Road
Wayne, PA 19087-1586
Phone: (800) 825-2518
www.sungard.com

Thornburg Mortgage
150 Washington Avenue, Suite 302
Santa Fe, NM 87501
Phone: (505) 989-1900
Fax: (505) 989-8156
www.thornburgmortgage.com

Toyota Financial Services
19001 South Western Avenue
Torrance, CA 90509
Phone: (310) 468-1310
Fax: (310) 468-7829
www.toyotafinancial.com

The Travelers Companies, Inc.
385 Washington Street
St. Paul, MN 55102
www.travelers.com

Unum
1 Fountain Square
Chattanooga, TN 37402
Phone: (423) 294-1011
Fax: (423) 294-3962
www.unum.com

USAA
9800 Fredericksburg Road
San Antonio, TX 78288
Phone: (210) 498-2211
Fax: (210) 498-9940
www.usaa.com

Visa USA
900 Metro Center Boulevard
Foster City, CA 94404
Phone: (650) 432-3200
Fax: (650) 432-3631
www.usa.visa.com

Government and Politics

Washington, D.C. has largely been an untapped source of career opportunities for business school students and MBAs. However, several recent trends indicate that MBAs may start looking to Washington for positions not available elsewhere. These trends include a heightened interest in employment with nonprofits and a burgeoning effort by some federal agencies to recruit MBAs. Additionally, there are MBA employers that exist only in Washington, such as the World Bank.

Despite increased interest in hiring MBAs by many of these employers, in general, these organizations have limited and spotty recruiting efforts on business school campuses. The onus remains on interested students to research appropriate opportunities and network with individuals with similar interests. The section below contains a guide to several of the employment options for MBAs in Washington along with advice on how to identify opportunities and successfully apply for positions.

Federal Government

Washington, D.C. is slowly, but increasingly, becoming more aware of the benefits of the MBA as well as the need to bring in qualified managers with more than just government experience. When George W. Bush was sworn in as the 43rd President of the United States, he was commonly referred to as the "MBA President," since, as a graduate of the Harvard Business School, he is the first chief executive of the United States to hold the degree. Several of his appointments to fill key administration posts were also MBAs, including Elaine Chao, the Secretary of Labor, a Harvard Business School alumna; Don Evans, the Secretary of Commerce, who received an MBA from the University of Texas; and the current Secretary of the Treasury, Hank Paulson, also a Harvard Business School alumnus. Many other of his top appointments were culled from the world of business, including Paul O'Neil, his first Secretary of the Treasury and former CEO of Alcoa, as well as his first replacement, John Snow, who was the head of CSX Corp.

The change at the top has not yet translated into widespread opportunities for MBAs, but the government has grown more receptive to MBAs as it begins to appreciate the skills and capabilities they bring to bear. For example, there have been recent efforts to recruit on MBA campuses. In the 2003 recruiting season, the U.S. Department of the Treasury visited select campuses seeking to fill internships and full-time positions. At times, the CIA has promoted opportunities with MBA programs and advertised for MBAs as part of its financial analysis teams on popular job posting sites, such as HotJobs.com and *The Washington Post*.

In addition, federal departments have been creating rotational programs for recent MBA grads. The Securities and Exchange Commission (SEC) has a two-year Business Associate Program that teaches participants about the securities industry and the role the SEC plays in the economy. In 2002, Secretary Chao of the U.S. Department of Labor launched an initiative specifically to recruit MBAs to the department. With a large proportion of senior department personnel scheduled to retire in the coming years, Secretary Chao moved aggressively to create a new pipeline of talent and specifically identified hiring MBAs as the future of the department.

Finding a position with the federal government

As would be expected with the federal government, bureaucracy rules the hiring process. However, as with any organization, there are paths around the human resources quagmire. MBAs interested in finding an appropriate position with the federal government should apply the tools emphasized by any career counseling office: identify your interests, find out the general requirements for position, network, and utilize internships.

Since the federal government is required to post nearly all vacancies, one potential resource to use in identifying appropriate opportunities is its career listing web site, www.usacareers.com. However, a word of warning: while the site provides a useful starting point and a valuable research tool, using it exclusively for a job search with the federal government would sell your efforts short. Instead, for MBAs it can be best used as means to examine the types of positions available and the general

Visit Vault at **www.vault.com** for insider company profiles, expert advice, career message boards, expert resume reviews, the Vault Job Board and more.

VAULT CAREER LIBRARY **103**

salary ranges. Still, even the position descriptions can be overly bureaucratic, and therefore the site should only be considered a starting point in the research process.

According to several MBAs employed by the federal government in Washington, the best way to identify opportunities is by networking with those already working in the federal government and with those in the nonprofits and other entities that regularly partner or interact with the federal agencies. Two good ways to make such contacts are through MBA alumni networks and student- or school-sponsored conferences focusing on the public sector and nonprofit management.

Applying for positions can also be highly bureaucratic, and again, interested applicants are well advised to use their networks to begin the application process. While all applicants must eventually go through the human resources department to determine whether they are qualified and if so, their pay level, it is far more fruitful to begin the application process with the office one wishes to join than with the human resources department. This is where networking can pay off, since ultimately hiring decisions are made within a specific office for high-level candidates. In fact, many government managers already have an applicant in mind before a position is posted.

One MBA graduate who returned to the federal government after graduation says that while finding government position can take effort, the MBA is definitely seen as a benefit. "There are a lot of hiring managers who will be receptive to talking with MBAs simply because they hold the credential," he says. "MBAs with a specific interest should seek out managers in the federal government, send them their resumes, and then try to follow up."

The insider also confirmed that there is a growing awareness of the value of an MBA, but that the government hasn't been fast enough to quickly establish the right recruiting policies to bring more business students into the federal workforce. "The fact of the matter is that the government just doesn't pay what the private sector does," he says. "But, for those with a strong interest in government work, there are many ways in and many rewarding career paths."

Areas of Interest to MBAs

Since most MBAs aren't interested in becoming lifetime bureaucrats, they usually consider specific opportunities in order to gain the experience they need to advance in their chosen professions. The following are areas of the federal government that provide career enhancing opportunities.

Community and economic development

Community and economic development is an area that has captured the interest of MBAs. Since community and economic development is often the result of cooperation among public sector, private sector and nonprofit entities, a position with the federal government can be an effective way to build experience, gain contacts within the development community and gain an understanding of the government's role in community and economic development and the resources it makes available.

There are several agencies within the federal government that have community and economic development functions. These include the U.S. Department of Treasury, the U.S. Department of Commerce and the Small Business Administration. Since roles within each agency will vary with the specific mission of the department, interested candidates should try to learn about each department's operations and opportunities through networking with organizations such as Net Impact, alumni, and by contacting hiring managers directly to discuss opportunities.

Management

There are many opportunities within the federal government for MBAs to gain management experience. However, these opportunities must be ferreted out, and will depend on what the MBA hopes to gain by joining the federal government. For example, an MBA with an interest in the federal budget process could attempt to locate an analyst position with the Office of

Management and Budget. Another potential source of management positions will be the Department of Homeland Security. Since the Homeland Security Department is free of some of the federal employment regulations imposed on virtually every other federal entity, there may be more opportunities for MBAs to utilize their management abilities to a greater degree than elsewhere in the federal bureaucracy. MBAs need to think creatively about how their skills relate to government management.

One avenue for MBAs into the federal government is through the Presidential Management Internship (PMI) program, which is open to all students pursuing master's or doctoral degrees. To be considered for the program, students must submit an application and be nominated by the dean, chairperson or program director of their academic program. Once accepted, PMIs must find an appropriate position within the federal government. The program lasts two years, with PMIs beginning at the GS-9 level (approximately $35,500 to $46,100). After one year, they are eligible for promotion to the GS-11 level ($42,900 to $55,800). At the end of the program, PMI program participants may be converted to a permanent position with the federal government and are eligible for the GS-12 grade level ($51,500 to $66,900). For detailed information on the program, see its web site at www.pmi.opm.gov.

Additionally, the Department of Labor has begun to actively recruit MBAs for general management positions with strong results. For 2002, its first year in operation, the department's MBA recruitment program reported receiving more than 250 applications for 30 openings. While MBAs start at the GS-9 level, the department is offering other incentives, including recruitment bonuses and loan forgiveness programs.

Upon acceptance into the program, MBAs will be allowed to rotate through several different assignments before being placed in a permanent position. The permanent assignments are based on the needs of the department and the long-term interests of each participant.

A senior official working on the program glows about its initial results: "We didn't know what to expect when we fist put the program into place, but we have been very pleased with the results. In fact, several other offices within the federal government have approached us about putting up similar recruitment programs for themselves."

Application information is available on the department's web site at www.dol.gov.

International development

The federal government also provides options for MBA students interested in international development, a field that has traditionally and still remains dominated by economists.

Since there are no formal recruitment programs in place for MBAs for international development positions with the federal government, interested students will have to network with both on-campus and outside organizations to uncover opportunities.

The U.S. Department of Treasury's Office of International Affairs often recruits MBAs for financial analysis positions covering such issues as debt policy or international trade. It is particularly interested in MBAs with strong experience in the banking and financial service sector, as well as international experience. The office's recruitment efforts include posting position openings with MBA career offices and general advertising.

Visit Vault at www.vault.com for insider company profiles, expert advice, career message boards, expert resume reviews, the Vault Job Board and more.

VAULT CAREER LIBRARY   105

Employer Directory

Central Intelligence Agency
1423 Chain Bridge Road
McLean VA 22101
Phone: (703) 482-1100
Fax: (703) 482-1739
www.cia.gov

Democratic National Committee
430 South Capitol Street SE
Washington, DC 20003
Phone: (202) 863-8000
www.democrats.org

Federal Bureau of Investigation
J. Edgar Hoover Building
935 Pennsylvania Avenue, NW
Washington, DC 20535
Phone: (202) 324-3000
www.fbi.gov

Federal Reserve System
20th Street and Constitution Avenue NW
Washington, DC 20551
Phone: (202) 452-3000
www.federalreserve.gov

Federal Trade Commission
600 Pennsylvania Avenue NW
Washington, DC 20580
Phone: (202) 326-2222
www.ftc.gov

Financial Management Professional Training Program (NAVY)
520 Turner Street, Suite B
Pensacola, FL 32508-5245
Phone: (850) 452-3785
Fax: (850) 452-3821
www.navyfmtp.com

National Security Agency
9800 Savage Road
Fort Meade, MD 20755
Phone: (301) 688-6524
Fax: (301) 688-6198
www.nsa.gov

Office of the Chief Financial Officer
Budget, Planning and Performance Division
810 7th Street NW
Washington, DC 20531
Phone: (202) 307-0623
Fax: (202) 616-5962
www.ojp.usdoj.gov/obms

Republican National Committee
310 1st Street SE
Washington, DC 20003
Phone: (202) 863-8500
Fax: (202) 863-8820
www.rnc.org

Securities and Exchange Commission
100 F Street NE
Washington, DC 20549
Phone: (202) 942-8088
www.sec.gov

Small Business Administration
409 3rd Street SW
Washington, DC 20024
Phone: (800) 827-5722
www.sba.gov

Social Security Agency
6401 Security Boulevard
Baltimore, MD 21235
Phone: (800) 772-1213
www.ssa.gov

U.S. Department of Commerce
1401 Constitution Avenue NW
Washington, DC 20230
Phone: (202) 482-2000
Fax: (202) 219-8979
www.commerce.gov

U.S. Department of Defense
The Pentagon
Washington, DC 20301
Phone: (703) 428-0711
www.defenselink.mil

U.S. Department of Energy
1000 Independence Avenue SW
Washington, DC 20585
Phone: (202) 586-5575
Fax: (202) 586-4403
www.energy.gov

U.S. Department of Health and Human Services
200 Independence Avenue SW
Washington, DC 20201
Phone: (202) 619-0257
www.hhs.gov

U.S. Department of Justice
950 Pennsylvania Avenue NW
Washington, DC 20530
Phone: (202) 514-2000
Fax: (202) 307-6777
www.usdoj.gov

U.S. Department of Labor
200 Constitution Avenue NW
Washington, DC 20210
Phone: (202) 693-6000
Fax: (202) 693-6111
www.dol.gov

U.S. Department of State
2201 C Street NW
Washington, DC 20520
Phone: (202) 647-4000
Fax: (202) 647-1558
www.state.gov

U.S. Department of the Treasury
1500 Pennsylvania Avenue NW
Washington, DC 20220
Phone: (202) 622-2000
Fax: (202) 622-6415
www.ustreas.gov

Health Care

Industry Overview

An industry in flux

You can't live with it and you can't live without it—this pretty much sums up the attitude many Americans have toward today's health care industry. The sector is a veritable Rube Goldberg machine of providers of patient care, manufacturers, middlemen and insurance companies. It's no secret that the sector is a volatile one despite making up around 16 percent of the nation's gross domestic product (GDP). U.S. health care spending totaled $2.3 trillion in 2007, more than what people spent on housing or food. Despite the awesome quantities of money involved in the industry, industry players have a tough time figuring out how to turn a profit in such a way that benefits both providers and patients—not to mention shareholders. Economists predict health care spending will make up 20 percent of the country's GDP in 2016, a percentage considered unsustainable by many analysts. It is estimated that the public sector will pay for nearly half of all health spending in the U.S. by that year—not a healthy number.

Big trouble

Another unhealthy number is the growing number of people who will need medical attention in the coming decades due to the increasing prevalence of bariatric and geriatric patients. In 2007, census data revealed that Americans were the fattest people on the planet. One quarter of adults are classified as clinically obese. Carrying a few extra pounds won't be listed as a cause of death, but it also doesn't just mean that one's trousers are a tad snug: overweight and obese people are increasingly at risk for disorders like heart disease, stroke, osteoarthritis, type II diabetes, certain types of cancer and a number of other long-term (and expensive) conditions. Economists are continually trying to figure the economic impact of overweight and obese Americans. In 2006, researchers estimated that obesity cost insurers around $80 billion per annum, and the number is rising. However, the term "overweight" is difficult to define consistently; additionally, there are a number of subtle effects, like depressed wages from weight discrimination and missed productivity due to disability, that can have profound economic consequences. More worryingly, the incidence of obesity in children has tripled since the 1970s, according to data from the Centers for Disease Control and Prevention; studies have shown that children who were overweight had an 80 percent chance of growing up to be obese adults.

Having a senior moment

Speaking of adults, according to the American Association of Retired Persons (AARP), by the year 2050, seniors will outnumber children for the first time ever. With approximately one million people turning age 60 each month worldwide, the phenomenon known as "global aging" promises to have a profound effect on the demand for and delivery of health care services. This shift is sparking interest in all issues affecting senior health, from preventive care to programs promoting home care and assisted living as alternatives to merely shunting the elderly to oft-dreaded nursing home care.

The United States' aging population is also putting pressure on the nation's reimbursement system for seniors and low-income patients. The Medicaid program is funded by the federal government but administered by the states, serving low-income individuals who do not have access to health care through their employers, while the Medicare program serves people over the age of 65. Because of this, the federal government looms large in health care. In fact, ranked by sales, the government's own Centers for Medicare & Medicaid Services (CMS) is the No. 1 provider in the insurance industry, covering around one in four people, and distributing $554 billion in benefits in 2006—more than a fifth of the spending of the federal government. Expenditures from the program are expected to rise to 11 percent of GDP through 2008.

Visit Vault at www.vault.com for insider company profiles, expert advice, career message boards, expert resume reviews, the Vault Job Board and more.

VAULT CAREER LIBRARY 107

As the 77 million members of the baby boomer generation reach age 65 and sign up for Medicare, the government will foot an even larger share of the health care bill. In 2007, Ben Bernanke, chairman of the Federal Reserve, warned in a Senate hearing that the spiraling costs of Social Security and government-funded health care could precipitate a budgetary crisis if not swiftly addressed. He predicted that the programs, burdened by the baby boomers, could increase publicly held government debt from 37 percent of the GDP in 2007 to 100 percent of GDP in 2030, and that it would increase astronomically thereafter, requiring large increases in taxes and deep cuts in government spending.

Let's go to Part D

The solution to this problem, of course, is to expand the benefits offered by Medicare. In 2006, Part D, a prescription drug benefit plan, was rolled out. (Medicare parts A, B and C govern hospital stays, doctor's visits and plans offered through other insurers, respectively.) The Bush administration has made several attempts to tweak the program, with mixed results. The revised Medicare drug plan, known as Medicare Part D, which came into effect in 2006, provided seniors with a flurry of plan options provided by various private insurance companies. But the Byzantine regulations for the program left many seniors confused and worried they were not getting the coverage they needed. Befuddled seniors notwithstanding, insurance companies have posted record profits from administering Part D.

In 2007, new regulations refigured the rates at which Medicare compensates hospitals and physicians for various procedures. Compensation for surgeries, such as hip and knee replacements and various cardiac procedures, will be cut by as much as a third. In response, the American Medical Association (AMA) announced that if compensation for Medicare patients is reduced, physicians will be forced to restrict the number of such cases they can handle. This legislation represents the opening salvo in a series of laws that will try to rein in Medicare spending by 34 percent over the next decade. Further economic fallout may include hospitals seeking higher reimbursement from insurance companies, which will then raise premiums, further increasing the cost of health care.

Flying without a net

Then there is the problem of the remaining 86 percent of the population, who aren't eligible for Medicare or Medicaid and either must buy private insurance on their own, get it through an employer or just go without and hope for the best. An alarming number of Americans, including many children, are uninsured—15.8 percent of the population at last count, or some 48 million people.

What's more, this number, along with the number of those who must purchase insurance on their own, will grow. As generally healthy people opt not to pay for health insurance—the cost of which increased at twice the rate of inflation in 2006—the pools of people buying insurance increasingly consists of people with expensive, chronic conditions or those who think they will imminently need expensive medical care—an actuarial nightmare that's driving up premiums. At such high costs, employers are increasingly unwilling or unable to pay to insure their employees, further enlarging the ranks of the uninsured.

Uninsured individuals increase pressure on the price of health care in other ways, as well. They are less likely to get regular checkups and treat minor medical problems before they become major issues, causing many to end up seeking treatment in the emergency room. Since many of the uninsured don't have the financial reserves to buy health insurance in the first place, a hospital stay can be devastating, and many default on their debts or are forced into bankruptcy by medical bills. In order to defray the costs of essentially providing free medical care, hospitals must charge higher prices. Reports also indicate that health care is more expensive overall for the uninsured. For example, hospitals bill uninsured clients a higher rate for the same procedures provided to those with health coverage, since big insurance companies are able to negotiate discounts with providers.

The solution to America's health care woes is not as simple as forcing everyone to purchase insurance, however. The fragmented nature of the industry, with so many different players jockeying for their slice of profits, has played a role in increasing the amount that patients must pay for care, since administrative costs only drive up the price of services.

The situation isn't so rosy for consumers fortunate enough to have coverage, either. As the cost of providing health care coverage continues to rise, many employers are finding they can no longer afford this benefit, and are passing more of the costs on to employees in the form of higher premiums, deductibles and stingier reimbursement plans.

Instead of pointing fingers or complaining about the situation, some people are doing something about high health care costs. Seattle's Virginia Mason Medical ran into trouble when the insurance companies that referred patients there pointed out that, despite the stellar quality of the care it delivered, it cost significantly more than other hospitals in the area. Virginia Mason went on a cost-cutting campaign, eliminating pricey medical equipment and specialists. Oddly, the hospital kept losing money, due to the skewed way insurers reimburse procedures. High-tech options, like MRI scans, net big checks from insurers, while simple, equally effective procedures, which cost far less, may cause hospitals to lose money.

In short, insurers are paying caregivers based on how much they do to a patient, as opposed to how effective—or even necessary—the treatments are. The doctors at Virginia Mason and the insurance companies reworked the payment scheme for the hospital so that patients were treated more efficiently. Instead of seeing scads of specialists for back pain, getting an MRI, and finally going to physical therapy, patients are now sent directly to physical therapy, which costs much less, and immediately starts to alleviate the patient's pain.

The quest for reform

The health care crisis had been a hot topic throughout the Presidential primaries, but the issue is taking a back seat to broader economic woes. Still, the health care system is a problem that the newly-elected President, whether it be Obama or McCain, will have to revisit regardless. Legislators have been notably reluctant to deal with the issue ever since Hillary Clinton's attempt to create a universal coverage plan was shot down early in her husband's tenure as president. In 2007, however, California Governor Arnold Schwarzenegger outlined a plan to insure the 36 million residents of his state. Individuals would be required to purchase insurance, either privately or through their employers, and health insurance companies would be obliged to cover them. Employers not offering insurance would pay 4 percent of payroll into a state fund for coverage; government assistance in purchasing this insurance would be given to people below a certain income level. To defray future costs, the state will sponsor initiatives against obesity and diabetes, and will levy a fee of 4 percent of gross revenue on hospitals and 2 percent on doctors to pay for it all. Needless to say, many groups oppose the plan: business owners say that mandated coverage is a sneaky form of tax and will stunt economic growth in the state; a nurses' group says it panders to insurance companies; conservatives cry socialism and liberals claim Schwarzenegger stole their idea. With so few groups happy with the plan, it just might work.

The need for heath care reform was also addressed by President Bush in his State of the Union address in January 2007. He proposed a tax break for people who have to purchase their own insurance, in order to make it more affordable, while taxing employer-provided plans as income. The plan is expected to make coverage affordable for a few million people at best. Critics have rushed to point out the flaws in the proposal. It does not take into account that smaller groups of people, or worse yet, groups of elderly or sick people, are a greater actuarial risk than larger groups, and premiums increase to reflect that. They also point out that this tax scheme would have the effect of driving people towards less expensive plans (which offer skimpier coverage, naturally) in order to reduce spending on unnecessary procedures. Furthermore, it dangerously destabilizes the system under which workers receive health insurance through their employers, the only part of the nation's health insurance plan that could be remotely described as functional. The President also proposed federal funding for states that are creating ways to cover their uninsured populations.

Visit Vault at **www.vault.com** for insider company profiles, expert advice, career message boards, expert resume reviews, the Vault Job Board and more.

VAULT CAREER LIBRARY

109

CDHC—the new wave of care?

Another plan for health care that has generated a buzz in the Bush administration is the idea of "consumer-driven health care," or CDHC. The idea is elegant in theory: If consumers can control their own health care spending, providers and insurers will be forced to compete for business, thus (hopefully) increasing quality of care while driving down costs. At the crux of CDHC are health savings accounts (HSAs), or tax-free accounts offered along with low-cost, high-deductible insurance plans. Either employee or employer (or both) stow away a certain amount of money in the HSA each year, which consumers can spend on virtually any health treatment or medication they want; whatever is unused remains in the account for any future health-related expenses.

Proponents of CHDC point out that the cost of plastic surgery and other elective procedures not covered by insurance has effectively kept pace with inflation, since consumers can shop around and find the best care for the best price. Since 1998, the average price of a tummy tuck has risen 19 percent, only slightly higher than inflation, and far below the 49 percent rise in per capita spending on health care for the same period. Opponents of the plan suggest that employers will use CDHC as a cover to reduce employee compensation. What CDHC plans do not take into account is that the bulk of the cost of health care spending is not from overconsumption of medical care by people who can afford it, but rather from treating people with chronic conditions, which can easily require in excess of thousands of dollars per year to manage. CDHC also fails to take into account that competitive pricing only works when one is in a position to make rational, informed decisions about which doctors to visit; in the event of a medical emergency, a severely wounded, unconscious or similarly incapacitated person is in no position to comparison shop.

Liability looms

Another type of reform that gets plenty of congressional buzz is medical malpractice liability, which the powerful AMA has made its top priority. The association has taken to identifying states that are in a "medical liability crisis" owing to exploding insurance premiums and the aftereffects of those costs—namely, that some providers are limiting or halting certain services because of liability risks. As of July 2006, there were 22 states on the AMA's list. One such state, Massachusetts, is a case in point: According to Massachusetts Medical Society research, 50 percent of the state's neurosurgeons, 41 percent of orthopedic surgeons and 36 percent of general surgeons had been forced to limit their scopes of practice due to insurmountable medical liability costs.

The Bush administration said an end to "junk lawsuits" was one of its primary goals for the president's second term, calling for "medical liability reform that will reduce health care costs and make sure patients have the doctors and care they need." In the early months following his January 2005 inauguration, Congress passed Bush-backed legislation to restrain class-action lawsuits and overhaul bankruptcy laws. However, Bush's influence has not fared as well for the "med-mal" bill, which was passed through the House but not the Senate. Bush's proposal would have limited the amount a health provider could be required to pay a patient for "pain and suffering" to $250,000 beyond actual cost of medical services; the proposal also provided for payout of judgments over time instead of in a lump sum.

It's a seemingly unending loop: multimillion-dollar judgments against providers, brought by a solid industry of trial lawyers devoted to representing mistreated patients, make headlines regularly. These judgments then cause liability insurers to panic, with many refusing to cover health care providers at all. As such, the insurers who have stayed in the medical liability market charge a premium providers increasingly can't afford to pay.

For lawmakers, the issue is a tough one: how do you set a cap on the amount a plaintiff can receive for the preventable death of a loved one? Patient advocates frame the issue as a David-versus-Goliath scenario, charging that the monolithic medical community wants to limit consumers' rights to sue providers for poor care. Meanwhile, as the industry waits for the federal government to come up with a solution, states have begun to tackle the issue themselves by setting their own limits on the amount of money a malpractice judgment can reap for the plaintiff. Voters in the state of Texas, which was listed on the

AMA's liability list, recently approved a constitutional amendment capping awards for non-economic damages at $250,000. (Similar measures are in place in West Virginia and Ohio.) Though these states' actions are a far cry from the national reform physicians and insurers desire, it is at least a start in a definitive direction.

Hot hospitals

In 2006, $607 billion was spent on care in hospitals. Growing demand for hospital services, along with higher rates from private insurers, have led to an increase in capital expended in this area. Among the approximately 5,700 registered hospitals in the U.S., a few tower over the rest. Each year, *U.S. News & World Report* publishes a ranking of the nation's top hospitals, surveying doctors around the country about hospitals' reputations in 16 medical specialties, as well as other factors like staffing, morbidity rates and technology. In 2008, the magazine's list named Baltimore's Johns Hopkins Hospital No. 1 overall—a position the institution has held for 18 years running. The Mayo Clinic came in second, followed by the Ronald Reagan UCLA Medical Center and the Cleveland Clinic.

MBAs in Health Care

What is health care management?

Health care management, also known as health care administration, encompasses a wide range of jobs in a variety of organizations. Health care managers are involved in the delivery of health care and the development of public policy regarding financing of and access to care. It is a field that has evolved over the last 50 years and continues to evolve as the health care delivery system changes. Health care managers work for organizations and individuals, from physician groups to hospitals, insurance companies and government agencies. Their roles are diverse, as well, ranging from line supervisors to directors and middle managers, to executives.

As the health care field has grown through advances in medicine, new technology and new types of health care facilities, so has the number of disciplines that health care managers oversee. In addition to expanding clinical areas requiring managers, such as imaging centers, ambulatory surgery centers, home care, occupational health, assisted living and adult day care, to name a few, disciplines in need of professional management have developed. These include specialists in the realm of financial management, reimbursement, revenue cycle management, planning, fundraising and development, performance improvement, medical management and business development.

The health care field is one of the most rapidly growing in the United States today. An aging population, longer life expectancy and new technology, treatments and medication are major contributors to this growth. As such, the need for health care professionals, including managers at all levels, will increase. The roles and responsibilities of health care managers may change as the health care system continues to do so. But the primary objective of management will remain constant: creating a work environment within an organization that promotes the accomplishment of goals and objectives.

Who are health care managers and what do they do?

Health care managers come from a large number of professions. In addition to the majority of managers who graduate from programs in health care administration, public administration or business administration, there are many different kinds of health care managers. These include clinical managers, financial managers, information systems managers, and public relations and marketing managers. Individuals with undergraduate or graduate degrees in management generally enter the field after the completion of their training with the goal of obtaining a middle management or upper-level management position in a health care organization. Managers in professions, such as finance, often have worked in another field, have

Visit Vault at **www.vault.com** for insider company profiles, expert advice, career message boards, expert resume reviews, the Vault Job Board and more.

VAULT CAREER LIBRARY   111

developed their skills and can readily transfer these skills to the health care environment. Clinical managers, including nurses and physicians, may work as clinicians for a period of time before entering management.

The organizations in which health care managers work include those that provide direct patient care and those that support the provision of care and services. Along what is referred to as the continuum of care, organizations provide different levels of direct care.

The highest level of care is provided in acute care hospitals. Hospitals are large complex organizations with hundreds or even thousands of employees and dozens or hundreds of supervisory and management personnel. Hospitals may be freestanding or part of a health system. They are classified according to ownership and control, number of beds, by the levels and types of services they provide and whether they have physician training programs, research programs and academic affiliations.

The next level of care on the continuum is called long-term acute care (LTAC). These are hospitals either freestanding or units within an acute care hospital that provide care to patients with chronic conditions. This is a relatively new level of care that is in a growth mode as units and facilities open throughout the country.

Sub acute care is provided in hospital and nursing homes. Hospital units are often referred to as transitional care units in which patients receive intense rehabilitation. Nursing homes operate sub acute or short-term units in which patients discharged from the hospital receive rehabilitation and other clinical services. Nursing homes or skilled nursing facilities provide care to the elderly and disabled and others requiring long-term care. Nursing homes may be freestanding, part of a regional or national company or hospital based.

Assisted living facilities provide a lower level of care than nursing homes. These facilities are generally for elderly residents who are unable to live on their own who require supervision and assistance with activities of daily living. Adult day care programs may be a medical model or social model. These programs provide socialization and medical services in the case of the medical model to elderly individuals who live in the community.

Other levels include home health care and ambulatory care. These services are provided by a variety of organizations and individuals including hospitals, physicians, nurses, therapists and technologists.

Organizations that support the provision of care may be classified into the following categories:

- Managed care organizations and insurance companies
- Management services organizations
- Consulting firms
- Public health and community health organizations
- Health care information services organizations
- Health related companies
- Research organizations, associations and educational institutions
- Regulatory and government agencies

Each of these entities plays a role in the delivery, financing and regulation of health care services. Managers in these organizations may have worked for a direct care provider previously or in another field.

Levels of health care management

As in any organization, there are different levels of management in health care. Entry-level management positions are generally referred to as line supervisors. These people supervise the day-to-day activities of a group of employees. Examples of this type of position are a chemistry lab supervisor in a hospital, a nursing supervisor in a nursing home, a food services supervisor in an assisted living facility and a case management supervisor in a managed care company. Many of these individuals are trained in a clinical or technical field, such as X-ray technology, ultrasound or nursing, and have come up through the ranks.

Manager

The next management level is department manager, or department head. These individuals are responsible for an entire department in a hospital, nursing home or other health care organization. An environmental services manager in a nursing home, a health information management (also known as medical records) department head in a hospital, and a project manager in a consulting firm are all at this management level. Many of these individuals have formal management training (a bachelor's or master's degree or other training program) and/or certification in their specific discipline other than management.

Director

The level above department manager is often called director, although some organizations refer to their managers as directors. Director usually implies the management of a broad function in the company, such as director of public relations or director of staff development, who is responsible for their specific area in multiple departments and often for the entire organization. Managers in these roles may have clinical experience (e.g., certified oncology manager or registered record administrator).

In health care systems with corporate structures, like Community Health Systems and Hospital Corporation of America (two national hospital chains), the title of director is often used for individuals with corporate or systemwide responsibility for a function such as the director of materials management who is in charge of this function for all of the hospitals and other facilities in the system. Another example of a corporate director is the director of managed care at a smaller hospital system in the New York area, Atlantic Health.

Physicians

Physicians assume management roles, as well. These include the head of a clinical department in a hospital (e.g., medicine, surgery, obstetrics), the head of a clinical section in a large hospital (e.g., cardiology, urology) and various positions in hospitals that are administrative in nature, including medical director, chief medical officer, director of performance improvement, director of clinical effectiveness and medical director of a managed care organization. Many of these physician-executives obtain management degrees and attend management training courses prior to or after achieving these positions.

Executive-level

There are several designations for executive-level management in health care organizations. One title sequence uses administrator to signify the highest management level. In this scheme, there are associate administrators and assistant administrators. In hospitals and nursing homes that use these titles, the administrator is the highest ranking executive responsible for the entire organization. Associate administrators and assistant administrators report to this individual and are responsible for multiple departments and/or large functional areas. A common variation of this structure is president and chief executive officer, executive and senior vice presidents and vice presidents. For the most part, the roles and responsibilities of these individuals correspond to the first set of titles. Another set of titles designates executive director as the top person, and associate and assistant executive director for the top managers reporting to this individual. Those who hold these positions may have worked their way up through the management ranks and almost always have graduate degrees in health care management, business administration or a similar discipline.

Corporate management

In health systems, multihospital organizations or hospitals operating other facilities, such as nursing homes and ambulatory care centers, there is also a corporate management level. These executives have system responsibilities for the operations and

Visit Vault at **www.vault.com** for insider company profiles, expert advice, career message boards, expert resume reviews, the Vault Job Board and more.

VAULT CAREER LIBRARY   113

specific functions (e.g., financial management) for the entire organization and usually have the title corporate director or vice president. There is also a corporate president or chief executive officer and a corporate chief financial officer. These companies may be regional, national or international and either for-profit or nonprofit. They may be comprised of one type of health care facility, such as a nursing home, or many types, such as hospitals, physician practices and insurance companies. Manor Care, a for-profit chain, for example, operates long-term care facilities throughout the country. Kaiser Permanente is comprised of physician practices, affiliated hospitals and provides various insurance plans.

In an academic setting, deans and university vice presidents often have overall responsibilities for the hospitals and other health care facilities in the organization. The health care executives at the hospital or other health care facilities report to these individuals.

Functional areas

New roles and positions continue to evolve. Administrators and managers for organizational effectiveness, and managers of clinical effectiveness are two examples.

And there is good reason to believe that as the health care system continues to evolve, new roles for managers will be created. These positions may be in areas of outcomes management, health education, information systems and ambulatory services. As access to health and health care increases via the Internet, people have more information on which to base their health care decisions. This will lead to increased accountability in terms of quality of care and health outcomes. Health information systems managers will be needed to develop ways to compile, store and share the data that is used in diagnosing and treating illness. The promotion of healthy lifestyles has become a high priority and will continue to be driven by health education. The need to control escalating health care costs will continue to result in less health care provided in expensive inpatient settings and more in ambulatory care settings. Alternatives to institutional long-term care will also have an impact. New models for the provision of care to the growing elderly population are being developed and tested. One such demonstration project is PACE (programs of all-inclusive care for the elderly). These programs provide comprehensive primary care, acute care and long-term care services to individuals as an alternative to nursing home admission. An interdisciplinary team develops care plans for program enrollees, and Medicare and Medicaid reimburse services provided on a capitation (pre-determined monthly payment per enrollee) basis.

Government policy and regulation will play a major role in shaping new management positions in a number of ways. Limiting Medicare reimbursement for specific procedures (e.g., surgeries) and treatments, and reporting requirements for infection rates and hospital acquired infections will further stimulate the growth of ambulatory care. Government reporting requirements for infections rates and hospital acquired infections will result in an increase in the number of quality improvement professionals and managers. All of these factors contribute to field that is expected to expand and diversify for years to come.

Employer Directory

Aetna Inc.
151 Farmington Avenue
Hartford, CT 06156
Phone: (860) 273-0123
Fax: (860) 273-3971
Toll free: (800) 872-3862
www.aetna.com

AMERIGROUP Corporation
4425 Corporation Lane
Virginia Beach, VA 23462
Phone: (757) 490-6900
Fax: (757) 222-2330
www.amerigrp.com

Applied Biosystems Inc.
850 Lincoln Centre Drive
Foster City, CA 99404
Norwalk, CT 06856-5435
Phone: (650) 638-5800
Fax: (650) 638-5884
Toll free: (800) 327-3002
www.appliedbiosystems.com

Beckman Coulter, Inc.
4300 North Harbor Boulevard
Fullerton, CA 92834-3100
Phone: (714) 871-4848
Fax: (714) 773-8283
Toll free: (800) 233-4685
www.beckman.com

Beverly Enterprises, Inc.
1000 Beverly Way
Fort Smith, AR 72919-0001
Phone: (479) 201-2000
www.berverlycares.com

Blue Cross and Blue Shield Association
225 North Michigan Avenue
Chicago, IL 60601-7680
Phone: (312) 297-6000
Fax: (312) 297-6609
www.bcbs.com

Boston Scientific Corporation
1 Boston Scientific Place
Natick, MA 01760-1537
Phone: (508) 650-8000
Fax: (508) 650-8910
www.bostonscientific.com

Caremark Pharmacy Services
211 Commerce Street, Suite 800
Nashville, TN 37201
Phone: (615) 743-6600
Fax: (205) 733-9780
www.caremark.com

CIGNA Corporation
2 Liberty Place
1601 Chestnut Street
Philadelphia, PA 19192
Phone: (215) 761-1000
Fax: (215) 761-5515
www.cigna.com

Community Health Systems, Inc.
4000 Meridian Boulevard
Franklin, TN 37067
Phone: (615) 465-7000
www.chs.net

Coventry Health Care, Inc.
6705 Rockledge Drive, Suite 900
Bethesda, MD 20817
Phone: (301) 581-0600
Fax: (301) 493-0731
www.cvty.com

DaVita Inc.
601 Hawaii Street
El Segundo, CA 90245
Phone: (310) 536-2400
Fax: (310) 536-2675
Toll free: (800) 310-4872
www.davita.com

Express Scripts, Inc.
1 Express Way
St. Louis, MO 63121
Phone: (314) 996-0900
www.express-scripts.com

Fresenius Medical Care AG & Co. KGaA
Else-Kröner-Straße 1
61346 Bad Homburg
Germany
Phone: +49-6172-609-0
Fax: +49-6172-608-2488
www.fmc-ag.com

HCA Inc.
1 Park Plaza
Nashville, TN 37203
Phone: (615) 344-9551
Fax: (615) 344-2266
www.hcahealthcare.com

Health Management Associates, Inc.
5811 Pelican Bay Boulevard, Suite 500
Naples, FL 34108-2710
Phone: (239) 598-3131
Fax: (239) 598-2705
www.hma-corp.com

Health Net, Inc.
21650 Oxnard Street
Woodland Hills, CA 91367
Phone: (818) 676-6000
Fax: (818) 676-8591
Toll free: (800) 291-6911
www.healthnet.com

HealthSouth Corporation
1 HealthSouth Parkway
Birmingham, AL 35243
Phone: (205) 967-7116
Fax: (205) 969-3543
Toll free: (888) 476-8849
www.healthsouth.com

Henry Schein, Inc.
135 Duryea Road
Melville, NY 11747
Phone: (631) 843-5500
Fax: (631) 843-5658
www.henryschein.com

Visit Vault at **www.vault.com** for insider company profiles, expert advice, career message boards, expert resume reviews, the Vault Job Board and more.

VAULT CAREER LIBRARY   115

Employer Directory, cont.

Hillenbrand, Inc.
1 Batesville Boulevard
Batesvill, IN 47006-7798
Phone: (812) 934-7500
Fax: (812) 934-7613
www.hillenbrandinc.com

Hill-Rom Holdings
1069 State Route 46 East
Batesville, IN 47006-9167
Phone: (812) 934-7777
Fax: (812) 934-8329
ir.hill-rom.com

Humana Inc.
The Humana Building
500 West Main Street
Louisville, KY 40202
Phone: (502) 580-1000
Fax: (502) 580-3677
Toll free: (800) 448-6262
www.humana.com

Johns Hopkins Health System
600 North Wolfe Street
Baltimore, MD 21287
Phone: (410) 955-5000
Fax: (410) 955-0890
www.hopkinshospital.org

Kaiser Permanente
1 Kaiser Plaza
Oakland, CA 94612
Phone: (510) 271-5800
Fax: (510) 267-7524
www.kaiserpermanente.org

Kindred Healthcare, Inc.
680 South 4th Street
Louisville, KY 40202-2412
Phone: (502) 596-7300
Fax: (502) 596-4170
Toll free: (800) 545-0749
www.kindredhealthcare.com

Laboratory Corporation of America Holdings
358 South Main Street
Burlington, NC 27215
Phone: (336) 229-1127
Fax: (336) 436-1205
www.labcorp.com

Magellan Health Services, Inc.
55 Nod Road
Avon, CT 06001
Phone: (860) 507-1900
Fax: (860) 507-1990
Toll free: (800) 410-8312
www.magellanhealth.com

Mariner Health Care, Inc.
1 Ravinia Drive, Suite 1250
Atlanta, GA 30346
Phone: (678) 443-7000
Fax: (770) 393-8054
www.marinerhealth.com

Mayo Foundation for Medical Education and Research
200 1st Street SW
Rochester, MN 55905
Phone: (507) 284-2511
Fax: (507) 284-0161
www.mayo.edu

Medco Health Solutions, Inc.
100 Parsons Pond Drive
Franklin Lakes, NJ 07417-2603
Phone: (201) 269-3400
Fax: (201) 269-1109
www.medco.com

Medical Mutual of Ohio
2060 East 9th Street
Cleveland, OH 44115-1355
Phone: (216) 687-7000
Fax: (216) 687-6044
Toll free: (800) 700-2583
www.mmoh.com

Medtronic, Inc.
710 Medtronic Parkway
Minneapolis, MN 55432-5604
Phone: (763) 514-4000
Fax: (763) 514-4879
Toll free: (800) 328-2518
www.medtronic.com

Quest Diagnostics Incorporated
3 Giralda Farms
Madison, NJ 07940
Phone: (201) 393-5000
Fax: (201) 729-8920
Toll free: (800) 222-0446
www.questdiagnostics.com

Sierra Health Services, Inc.
2724 North Tenaya Way
Las Vegas, NV 89128
Phone: (702) 242-7000
Fax: (702) 242-9711
www.sierrahealth.com

St. Jude Medical, Inc.
1 Lillehei Plaza
St. Paul, MN 55117-9983
Phone: (651) 483-2000
Toll free: (800) 328-9634
www.sjm.com

Stryker Corporation
2825 Airview Boulevard
Kalamazoo, MI 49002-1802
Phone: (269) 385-2600
Fax: (269) 385-1062
www.stryker.com

Sun Healthcare Group, Inc.
18831 Von Karman, Suite 400
Irvine, CA 92612
Phone: (949) 255-7100
Fax: (949) 255-7054
Toll free: (800) 729-6600
www.sunh.com

Employer Directory, cont.

Tenet Healthcare Corporation
13737 Noel Road
Dallas, TX 75240
Phone: (469) 893-2200
Fax: (469) 893-8600
www.tenethealth.com

UnitedHealth Group Incorporated
UnitedHealth Group Center
9900 Bren Road East
Minnetonka, MN 55343
Phone: (952) 936-1300
Fax: (952) 936-1819
Toll free: (800) 328-5979
www.unitedhealthgroup.com

Universal Health Services
Universal Corporate Center
367 South Gulph Road
King of Prussia, PA 19406-0958
Phone: (610) 768-3300
Fax: (610) 768-3336
www.uhsinc.com

WellPoint, Inc.
120 Monument Circle
Indianapolis, IN 46204
Phone: (317) 488-6000
Fax: (317) 488-6028
www.wellpoint.com

Visit Vault at **www.vault.com** for insider company profiles, expert advice,
career message boards, expert resume reviews, the Vault Job Board and more.

VAULT CAREER LIBRARY   117

Hedge Funds

What is a Hedge Fund?

Hedge funds are considered an "alternative investment" vehicle. The term "alternative investment" is the general term under which unregulated funds operate; this includes private equity and real estate funds. The total "alternative" category (including private equity and real estate) is not covered within the scope of this section but it is useful to know that often people refer to hedge funds as alternative investments. Mainstream funds are investment funds that everyday investors can purchase, mutual funds are the prime example of a mainstream fund.

Over the past decade, hedge funds have grown tremendously in terms of assets under management and also garnered a lot of media attention. Although, despite their growth and popularity, hedge funds still remain a mystery to many people who do not understand exactly what they are and how they work. So what exactly is a hedge fund?

A Concise Definition of "Hedge Fund"

A "private unregistered investment pool" encompassing all types of investment funds, companies and private partnerships that can use a variety of investment techniques such as borrowing money through leverage, selling short, derivatives for directional investing and options.

During the early years of the hedge fund industry (1950s to 1970s), the term "hedge fund" was used to describe the "hedging" strategy used by managers at the time. "Hedging" refers to the hedge fund manager making additional trades in an attempt to counterbalance any risk involved with the existing positions in the portfolio. Hedging can be accomplished in many different ways but the most basic technique is to purchase a long position and a secondary short position in a similar security. This is used to offset price fluctuations and is an effective way of neutralizing the effects of market conditions.

Today, the term "hedge fund" tells an investor nothing about the underlying investment activities, similar to the term "mutual fund." So how do you figure out what the hedge fund manager does? You are able to figure out a little more about the underlying investment activities by understanding the trading/investment strategies that the hedge fund manager states he trades. The "investment strategy" is the investment approach or the techniques used by the hedge fund manager to have positive returns on the investments. If a manager says he trades long/short equity then you know he is buying undervalued equities and selling overvalued equities. Although this description is the long/short equity strategy at its most basic, it is important to understand the strategies that the manager says he employs.

Distinguishing Characteristics

So now that you have reviewed some of the basic terminology in the industry, we will explain the key points in depth. The main distinguishing characteristics of hedge funds are the following:

- Hedge funds can "hedge" their portfolio.
- Hedge funds use derivatives.
- Hedge funds can short sell.
- Hedge funds have the ability to use leverage.

Visit Vault at www.vault.com for insider company profiles, expert advice, career message boards, expert resume reviews, the Vault Job Board and more.

VAULT CAREER LIBRARY   119

These characteristics make hedge funds different from most other investment funds, especially mutual funds. To get a good understanding of how a hedge fund manager operates, it is very important to understand these concepts. The four concepts are now defined in detail.

Hedging

Hedging can be accomplished in many different ways, although the most basic technique is to purchase a long position and a secondary short position in a similar security (see Gap example). This is used to offset price fluctuations and is an effective way of neutralizing the effects of market conditions.

Hedging Example

Courtney is a hedge fund manager who invested in the Gap stores. Here we will see how he hedges his risk. Courtney is "long" (he's bought) 100 shares of Gap stores but he now believes the retail industry may be vulnerable to a down turn in the market. He wants to hedge this risk and does this by going "short" (selling) Abercrombie & Fitch, which is in the same retail industry.

Q. What would happen if the retail industry did poorly?
A. The share prices of both Gap and Abercrombie & Fitch might decline.

Q. How would this affect any money Courtney makes?
A. Since Courtney is long on Gap (he owns it) he would lose money on this trade. Since Courtney is also short (he has already sold it) Abercrombie & Fitch, he would make money on that trade. Therefore he can offset some of his losses from Gap with gains from Abercrombie & Fitch. He reduces his risk of Gap by hedging with Abercrombie & Fitch.

Q. When you say Courtney gains from the Abercrombie & Fitch trade, what does this mean?
A. When Courtney goes short A&F, it means he has sold it before he owns it. So say he sells 100 A&F shares short for $50 each. He receives $5,000 cash for doing so. This transaction is conducted through his broker and he now owes 100 A&F shares to his broker, to be paid back at some time the future. As time goes by, the retail industry does poorly and the share price of A&F falls to $40.

Q. If the stock price of A&F falls to $40, what does this mean for Courtney's profits?
A. Since Courtney owes 100 A&F shares to his broker, he can now go out and buy the 100 shares for $40 each, costing him a total of $4,000. Therefore, Courtney has made $1,000 profit. (He receives $5,000 from the original short sale and then pays $4,000 to buy A&F, so his profit is $1,000)

Derivatives

Derivatives that are used by hedge funds can take on many forms, and the more complex derivatives (interest rate swaps, foreign currency swaps, contract for differences, total return swaps, etc.) are not covered in this book. Discussed now are the most basic forms of derivatives: "put" and "call" options on stocks.

Option Definitions

Put option
A "put" option gives the holder the right to sell the underlying stock at a specified price (strike price) on or before a given date (exercise date).

Call option
A "call" option gives the holder the right to buy the underlying stock at specified price (strike price) on or before a given date (exercise date).

Option writer
The seller of these options is referred to as the "writer"—many hedge funds will often write options in accordance with their strategies. This is the person who originates an option contract by promising to perform a certain obligation in return for the price or premium of the option. Any investor can sell options (write options) provided they have answered an options questionnaire provided to them by their broker. This would determine the knowledge of the investor and whether they understand the risks associated with writing options.

Short selling (going "short")

Short selling involves the selling of a security that the seller does not own. Short sellers believe that the stock price will fall and that they will be able to repurchase the stock at a lower price in the future. Thus, they will profit from selling the stock at a higher price, then buy it in the future at a lower price. (The opposite of going "short" is going "long," when investors buy stocks they believe will rise.)

Short Selling Example

Jimmy believes that McDonald's is overvalued and that he can profit by selling short "MCD." Jimmy sells short 100 shares at $50 which means he has sold stock that he does not yet own, this is a stock loan. In the future he has to buy the stock to repay the stock loan he entered into when shorting the stock. But, McDonald's price continues to rise to $75, this means that in order to buy the stock (this is called "covering" his stock loan), Jimmy pays $75 per share, which results in him losing $2,500 (100*$25)

Before Jimmy enters into the short sale, he must ensure that he is able to borrow the stock (get a stock loan), usually through its prime broker. Jimmy will call the stock loan department of the prime broker to see if the prime broker has the stock available to lend to him. If the stock loan department has the stock to lend, then Jimmy can short sell the stock (borrowing it from the prime broker). If the stock is not available for borrow, Jimmy cannot sell short the security.

Visit Vault at **www.vault.com** for insider company profiles, expert advice, career message boards, expert resume reviews, the Vault Job Board and more.

VAULT CAREER LIBRARY   121

The Chicago Board Options Exchange (CBOE)

The CBOE created an orderly market with well-defined contracts on 16 stocks when it began trading call option contracts in 1973. The exchange began trading put options in 1977. The CBOE now trades options on over 1,200 stocks and many different stock indices. Many other exchanges throughout the world also trade option contracts. To learn more, visit the exchange's web site at www.cboe.com.

Leverage

Leverage measures the amount of assets being borrowed for each investment dollar. Leverage (borrowing additional funds) is utilized by hedge fund managers when they believe that the cost of the borrowed funds will be minimal compared to the returns of a particular position. It can be a key component to hedge fund management since it gives the hedge fund managers the ability to have higher returns (and potentially lose more) with borrowed funds.

Typical hedge fund leverage depends on the type of financial instruments that the hedge fund trades. Fixed income has lower risk levels so it is not uncommon to have four or five times the value of the fund borrowed. Equities have a higher risk profile and therefore typical leverage is one and a half to two times the value of the fund. However, hedge funds are usually comprised of long and short positions, so a large market rise or fall has little impact if their profitable positions were equally balanced by their losing positions.

The simplest examples in everyday life of leverage are house mortgages and car loans. The bank manager uses the house or the car as collateral for the loan from the bank. The bank manager can then sell the house or the car if you default on your loan. Similarly, the hedge fund manager uses the financial instruments in his account as collateral for the funds they have borrowed from their bank (prime broker). The primary sources of leverage are financial institutions and banks. If the hedge fund manager cannot pay the loan back, the financial institution can then sell the collateral (the financial instruments in the account) to pay back the loan.

Leverage Calculation Example

If the hedge fund has $1 million of invested money and is borrowing another $2 million, to bring the total dollars invested to $3 million, then the leverage used is 200 percent. The amount of leverage typically used by the fund is shown as a percentage of the fund.

Organizational Structure of a Typical Hedge Fund

So who exactly are hedge fund managers and what do they do? A hedge fund manager is normally the founder and the key person in charge of overseeing the whole operation of the hedge fund. This means that he/she is responsible for overseeing the portfolio, often making trading decisions, hiring personnel, monitoring the risk of the portfolio and ensuring that the accounting and operations departments are in order. The hedge fund manager is often referred to as the principal or president and can often also be called the portfolio manager.

Hedge funds vary in size from assets under management from as little as $1 million to over $10 billion. Unlike a typical investment bank, the roles of the employees at hedge funds are not the same for each hedge fund. Someone entering an investment bank as a trader will likely have a similar role to someone else entering another investment bank as a trader. Traders at hedge funds are likely to have different responsibilities, which are usually determined by the size of the fund. At a smaller fund the trader is much more likely to be involved with the operations of the trade, whereas a larger hedge fund would have a separate operations person to handle this element. A smaller hedge fund may have three or four employees, whereas a larger hedge fund may employ over 300 people.

A typical hedge fund will have various departments: operations, accounting, trading, and risk and investor relations. These departments support the trading decisions and operations of the hedge fund. Since the size of hedge funds vary dramatically, the number of people in each department can range from one to over 20. As a hedge fund grows in size (manages more money), more personnel are added to support the increased trading volume.

It is very important to note that specific job titles are not important at hedge funds. This is because one role (job) can have many different titles depending on the hedge fund. For example, an operations analyst can also be called portfolio analyst, trading assistant or accountant depending on the size and environment of the fund.

In addition, due to the varying sizes of hedge funds, employees tend to have a more diverse range of responsibilities, which may overlap between several different departments. This unique nature of the hedge fund job requires superior teamwork skills and the ability to deal with a variety of people.

Visit Vault at **www.vault.com** for insider company profiles, expert advice, career message boards, expert resume reviews, the Vault Job Board and more.

VAULT CAREER LIBRARY   123

Director of Operations

Most individuals carrying this title either have several years of experience in the same capacity, a MBA or both. At this stage one generally has a staff of two to 10 people who are direct reports. The job functions are similar to the operations specialist although there is much more responsibility for the employees working under you as well as maintaining relationships between prime broker, banks and offshore administrators.

This position will generally pay between $100,000 and $250,000 depending on experience, background and size of hedge fund.

A Day in the Life: Director of Operations

7:30 a.m. Arrive at the office and log onto the computer, along will various back office and portfolio systems such as DTC.

8:15 a.m. Go over exception reports (available only to a manager) that show trades that have not settled and any margin calls for accounts and speak to the member of staff who works on it to get status on the item.

9 a.m. Have weekly team meeting and go over team workload and coverage for the week.

10 a.m. Get on a call with a manager in the prime broker because a large wire needs to be sent out for management fees and there needs to be extra attention give to it to make sure it goes through properly. The prime broker department at an investment bank offers products, technology and clearing services to a hedge fund.

11 a.m. Have a meeting with the head trader on the convertible trading desk who does not agree with the final position on a particular security. Go over each transaction and see if anything was incorrectly booked. Have one of the staff members print all transaction reports internally and ask the prime broker to find a solution to this problem as it may involve large losses for the desk.

1 p.m. Have lunch at the desk while browsing through some stories on Bloomberg.

2 p.m. Field calls and help the staff resolve any pending problems.

4 p.m. Re-review all reports from the morning and make sure all highlighted discrepancies are resolved otherwise jot them down as "open items."

5 p.m. Create a list of agenda items for the next day and look at the calendar of any meetings.

6 p.m. Leave work and meet the prime broker for dinner who is taking the operations team out.

7 p.m. Discuss rates with the prime broker over dinner and get to know them better.

10 p.m. Head home and try to get the motivation to go to the gym before crashing.

Risk Management

The risk department proactively monitors each hedge fund, identifying potential risks and then determining and understanding the importance of various types of risks. This department uses various propriety or vendor tools and methodologies for risk management and implements strategies to prevent any risk completely or to deal with them if they occur.

At a hedge fund, a risk management role can vary depending on the size of the fund. At a small fund, generally the principals or the trading group may monitor the risk and there are no specific risk personnel; while at a larger fund, there is a group who is solely responsible for monitoring risk. Many hedge funds are also known to outsource their risk controls through third party vendors specialized in providing this service to corporations, hedge funds, mutual funds, etc. Many investment banks also provide such added value service through their prime broker departments.

Fund of funds are known to have a very large risk teams because of two reasons. Firstly, due to the way fund of funds operate they are dealing with a large variety of securities product base; and secondly, the risk group plays a large role in alleviating concerns of existing and potential investors.

Risk associate

This associate level position will play a supporting role in the risk department. Many hedge funds don't have a separate risk department but this position would be available at an investment bank's prime broker department.

In a prime broker department, the risk associate will perform the same duties, except he will be monitoring risk for several hedge funds that are prime broker clients. This position generally requires a minimum of a bachelor's degree and a few years of relevant experience. A thorough understanding of a variety of trading products (i.e., options, fixed income, mortgage backed securities, swaptions), options risks (i.e., delta, gamma, vega, rho and theta) and strong analytical skills are strongly recommended. The daily job duties include but are not limited to maintaining value at risk (VAR) data, back-testing and stress-testing securities within a portfolio and reporting the analyzed data to senior risk management.

For example, Heather works with the trading group to monitor risk. The hedge fund where she works subscribes/utilizes a risk monitoring system designed by a large investment bank. Every morning she will perform analysis to the short portfolio measuring how minor changes in the stock market, such as the Dow Jones Industrial Average decreasing substantially in one day, could affect the value of the portfolio. Heather does not have to compute everything manually because the risk system has built in mathematical models to attribute for different scenarios, although Heather needs to understand what the output of results mean and be able to verbally communicate those clearly to the traders and portfolio mangers along with having spreadsheets and graphs as back up of her analysis.

Base salary depends on geographical location, previous experience, education skills and size of the corporation. The risk position could potentially have interaction with clients (investors) depending on the size of the fund. Some hedge funds have a designated investor relations employee whose sole responsibility is to field calls from investors. Although, in smaller funds investors may call the risk group directly to state and address any risk concerns. It is important that a hedge fund has a strong risk monitoring system because this reduces the likelihood of error and losses in the fund and will also help alleviates the investor's worries.

Risk jobs are found through job agencies or through connections. Generally, traders are also well aware of job openings in the risk groups and can be a good source of contact/network.

Visit Vault at www.vault.com for insider company profiles, expert advice, career message boards, expert resume reviews, the Vault Job Board and more.

VAULT CAREER LIBRARY 125

A Day in the Life: Risk Analyst at a Large Hedge Fund

7:30 a.m. Get into the office and check e-mail. Chat with colleagues about interesting stories in the *WSJ*.

8 a.m. Daily risk conference call with traders, portfolio manager and principals

9:30 a.m. Monitoring the portfolios on one screen while looking at the markets affecting the various securities on another screen. Quantify illiquid positions and valuations risk and compare margin requirements of all positions with the custodian/prime broker making sure you are in agreement.

10 a.m. Call the prime broker risk department and discuss risks involved in utilizing more leverage for a particular option arbitrage fund. Write up a report based on the call to present to the principals.

11 a.m. Compile statistics for the ongoing exception report for non-investment risk issues such as trade settlement, particular trader leaving the organization, etc.

12 p.m. Making sure that the portfolio is maintained within established risk parameters

1 p.m. Eat lunch at the desk while preparing for the 1:30 meeting with potential investors of the hedge fund who want to discuss business and corporate structure of the hedge fund and its links to the investment manger.

1:30 ro 2:30 p.m. Meeting with investors in a conference room. Emphasize the safety of assets to the investor because of proper risk monitoring.

2:30 p.m. Recap the meeting with principals, see how it went and make a list of items to follow up with the investor. It is very important that the risk manager gets rid of any potential investors concerns of sudden losses.

4 p.m. Work with the CFO to have him clarify a problem you noticed on last month's audit.

5 p.m. Field calls and answer e-mails on all risk and portfolio inquiries to internal and external people.

7 p.m. Look over notes from today and jot down any items that needs to be addressed tomorrow.

7:15 p.m. Review schedule for next day.

7:30 to 8 p.m. Head home and get to bed early for a good night's sleep.

Employer Directory

Andor Capital Management
1 American Lane, 3rd Floor
Greenwich, CT 06831
Phone: (203) 742-7200
www.andorcap.com/index.html

Angelo, Gordon & Co.
245 Park Avenue
New York, NY 10167
Phone: (212) 692-2000
Fax: (212) 867-9328
Toll free: (800) 805-0024
www.angelogordon.com

Arden Asset Management
375 Park Avenue, 32nd Floor
New York, NY 10152
Phone: (212) 751-5252
Fax: (212) 751-8546
www.ardenasset.com

Atticus Capital
152 West 57th Street
New York, NY 10019
Phone: (212) 373-0800

Avenue Capital
535 Madison Avenue
New York, NY 10022
Phone: (212) 878-3535
www.avenuecapital.com

Bank of America
100 North Tryon Street
Bank of America Corporate Center
Charlotte, NC 28255
Phone: (704) 386-5681
Fax: (704) 386-6699
www.bankofamerica.com

Blackstone Alternative Asset Management
345 Park Avenue, Floor 30
New York, NY 10154
Phone: (212) 583-5000

Brevan Howard Asset Management
590 Madison Ave, 9th Floor
New York, NY 10022-2524
Phone: (212) 418-8200
www.brevanhoward.com

Bridgewater Associates
1 Glendinning Place
Westport, CT 06880
Phone: (203) 226-3030
Fax: (203) 291-7300
www.bwater.com

Campbell & Co.
210 West Pennsylvania Avenue
Suite 770
Towson, MD 21204
Phone: (800) 698-7235
Fax: (410) 296-3311
www.campbell.com

Caxton Associates
500 Park Avenue
New York, NY 10022-1606
Phone: (212) 418-8300
www.caxton.com

Cerberus Capital Management
299 Park Avenue
New York, NY 10171
Phone: (212) 891-2100
Fax: (212) 891-1540
www.cerberuscapital.com

Citadel Investment Group
131 South Dearborn Street
Chicago, IL 60603
Phone: (312) 395-2100
Fax: (312) 977-0270
www.citadelgroup.com

CSFB Alternative Capital (Credit Suisse)
Credit Suisse
11 Madison Avenue
Phone: (212) 325-2000
www.csfb.com/investment_managemen
t/private_equity/index.shtml

D. E. Shaw & Co.
120 West 45th Street, 39th Floor
Tower 45
New York, NY 10036
Phone: (212) 478-0000
Fax: (212) 478-0100
www.deshaw.com

Davidson Kempner Capital Management
65 East 55th Street, 19th Floor
New York, NY 10022-3355
Phone: (212) 371-3000

DB Absolute Return Strategies
Phone: (212) 454-2118
ars.db.com/arsportal/index.jsp

EIM
750 Lexington Avenue
New York, NY 10022
Phone: (212) 371-9000
Fax: (212) 371-9111
www.eimgroup.com

ESL Investments
200 Greenwich Avenue
Greenwich, CT 06830
Phone: (203) 861-4600

Fortress Investment Group
1345 Avenue of the Americas
New York, NY 10105
Phone: (212) 798-6100
www.fortressinv.com

Goldman Sachs Asset Management
1 New York Plaza
New York, NY 10004
Phone: (800) 292-4726
goldmansachs.com

Grosvenor Capital Management
900 North Michigan Avenue
Suite 1100
Chicago, IL 60611

Visit Vault at **www.vault.com** for insider company profiles, expert advice, career message boards, expert resume reviews, the Vault Job Board and more.

VAULT CAREER LIBRARY   127

Employer Directory, cont.

Harris Alternatives
227 West Monroe Street, 60th Floor
Chicago, IL 60606-5055
Phone: (312) 762-6700
www.harrisalternatives.com

HBK Capital Management
300 Crescent Court
Dallas, TX 75201-1836
Phone: (214)758-6100
www.hbk.com

Ivy Asset Management
1 Jericho Plaza, Suite 304
Jericho, NY 11753
Phone: (516) 2286500
Fax: (516) 228-6515
www.ivyasset.com

J.P. Morgan Alternative Asset Management
245 Park Avenue
New York, NY 10167
Phone: (212) 483-2323
im.jpmorgan.com

Man Investments
123 North Wacker Drive, 28th Floor
Chicago, IL 60606-1749
Phone: (312) 881-6800
www.maninvestments.com

Mesirow Advanced Strategies
350 North Clark Street
Chicago, IL 60610
Phone: (312) 595-6000
Fax: (312) 595-4246
Toll free: (800) 453-0600
www.mesirowfinancial.com

Oaktree Capital Management, LLC
333 South Grand Avenue, 28th Floor
Los Angeles, CA 90071
Phone: (213) 830-6300
Fax: (213) 830-6393
www.oaktreecapital.com

Och-Ziff Capital Management
9 West 57th Street, 39th Floor
New York, NY 10019
Phone: (212) 790-0120
Ozcap.com

Pacific Alternative Asset Management Co.
19540 Jamboree Road, Suite 400
Irvine, CA 92612
Phone: (949) 261-4900
Fax: (949) 261-4901
www.paamco.com

Pequot Capital Management
500 Nyala Farm Road
Westport, CT 06880
Phone: (203) 429-2200
Fax: (203) 429-2400
www.pequotcap.com

Permal Group
900 3rd Avenue, 28th Floor
New York, NY 10022
Phone: (212) 418 6500
www.permal.com

Perry Capital
3113 Woodcreek Drive
Downers Grove, IL 60515-5412
Phone: (630) 719-7800
www.perrycap.com

Pirate Capital LLC
200 Connecticut Avenue, 4th Floor
Norwalk, CT 06854
Phone: (203) 854-1100
www.piratecapitalllc.com

Quellos Capital Management
601 Union Street, Suite 5600
Seattle, WA 98101-4059
Phone: (206) 613-6700
www.quellos.com

RBS Asset Management
71 South Wacker Drive, 28th Floor
Chicago, IL 60606-4637
Phone: (312) 777-3500
www.rbsam.com

Renaissance Technologies Corp.
800 3rd Avenue, 33rd Floor
New York, NY 10022
Phone: (212) 486-6780
Fax: (212) 758-7136
www.rentec.com

SAC Capital Advisors
72 Cummings Point Road
Stamford, CT 06902-7912
Phone: (203) 614-2000

Soros Fund Management
888 7th Avenue, 33rd Floor
New York, NY 10106
Phone: (212) 262-6300
Fax: (212) 245-5154

Superfund Group
489 5th Avenue
New York, NY 10017
Phone (212) 750-6300
Fax: (212) 750-2206
www.superfund.com

Tremont Capital Management
555 Theodore Fremd Avenue
Rye, NY 10580
Phone: (914) 925-1140
Fax: (914) 921-3499
www.tremont.com

Tudor Investment Corporation
1275 King Street
Greenwich, CT 06831
Phone: (203) 863-6700
Fax: (203) 863-8600
www.tudorfunds.com

UBS Global Asset Management
51 West 52nd Street, 22nd Floor
New York, NY 10019-6119
Phone: (212) 713-2000

High Tech

Technology is Everywhere

It's a tech, tech world

As industries go, the tech sector is a fairly new one, but is revolutionizing the way people conduct themselves socially and in business. Technology has been so rapidly integrated into the fabric of modern life that the semiconductor chip, a device that hardly existed 50 years ago, has become a commonplace part of modern life. The sector is fairly broad, and encompasses companies that manufacture hardware—the guts of the computer—like hard drives, chips, circuit boards and wiring, and software, the programs that run on said chips. Other companies offer their customers some combination of hardware and software—like Hewlett-Packard and Dell, who ship computers with operating systems and programs already installed.

Chips off the old block

Microchips are up there with the wheel and domesticated animals in terms of human inventions that have had a dramatic effect on history. The microchip as we know it—which consists of multiple circuits embedded in a semiconductive substrate—was invented by Jack Kilby, an employee of Texas Instruments, in 1958. The first semiconductors, which only had a handful of circuits, were initially used in highly-funded government projects, like the Apollo Moon mission and in the guidance systems for Minuteman missiles. As the production of chips became less expensive, they began their inexorable move into the realm of consumer goods during the late 1970s and early 1980s. Unlike those first microchips, which combined tens of circuits on a single chip, microchips produced today can have billions of circuits in an area that can fit on a fingertip.

While the first microchips were soldered together by hand in a lab, today's versions are assembled by building up multiple layers of silicon on a chip in clean rooms. Chip manufacturing involves hundreds of steps, which gradually build up the microscopic circuitry on the face of the chip. Chips are built on a substrate of pure silicon, called a wafer. A machine cuts wafers—which are about a millimeter thick—off of an enormous cylindrical crystal of pure silicon. After cutting, the surfaces of wafers are polished; any imperfections in the surface of the wafer will result in chips that do not function properly. As chip manufacturing technology improved, wafers increased in size from about four inches in the 1960s to 12 inches (30 cm) today; some memory chips are still made on smaller wafers. Anywhere from a few hundred to 1,000 can fit on a 30-centimeter wafer. After polishing, the wafer is transferred to a machine that coats the surface with an insulating layer of silicon dioxide a few atoms thick, which, in turn, is coated with a light-sensitive material called a photoresist. The wafer is then exposed to light filtered through a lithographic plate, which allows an acid etch bath to remove the photresist that was exposed to light, as well as some of the silicon underneath it. An atom-thick layer of metal, such as copper or aluminum, can be deposited on these exposed parts of the chip; when the photoresist is removed, only the metal remains to connect the various parts of the chip. Other electrical features can be added to the surface of the chip by implanting the silicon with a smattering of individual atoms, often of boron or arsenic, known as dopants. The boron or arsenic atoms are shot into the crystal structure of the silicon with a particle accelerator. Successive layers of insulating and conducting pathways are gradually built up by repeating these processes, often hundreds of consecutive times.

Since the electrical pathways of modern processor chips are measured in mere nanometers—billionths of an inch—nearly any errant piece of schmutz can short out a circuit. Therefore, chips must be manufactured in what are known as 'clean rooms,' where the ambient level of dust is significantly reduced by filtration. Workers in these environments also wear bunny suits, which protect the wafers from hair or skin cells that they might shed.

Visit Vault at **www.vault.com** for insider company profiles, expert advice, career message boards, expert resume reviews, the Vault Job Board and more.

VAULT CAREER LIBRARY   129

Bumpy road

The semiconductor industry is highly cyclical, prone to vertiginous highs and astonishing lows. This is partly due to the industry's high cost of entry; a fab or foundry, a plant where microchips are made, can take several years—not to mention $2 billion and change—to build. As the price of chips rises, more fabs are built; as they add their capacity to the marketplace, the price of chips falls. This has already happened several times over the course of the industry's history, notably in the 1980s, when Japanese manufacturers flooded the marketplace with inexpensive chips. The market reached a high in 1999—in time to fuel the tech boom—and again in 2004, in order to power the recovery from the tech bust.

In Soviet Russia, you power your devices

Tech isn't just chips, however—batteries present their own host of problems for designers of computer gadgets. In addition to adding to the size and weight of the product, they are often taxed by the demands of fueling features like bigger, brighter displays—for days at a time. Engineers are nearly at a loss to provide products that can stand up to the rigors of powering zippy processors, big displays and Internet connections between charges. As batteries are pushed to their limits, they can suddenly fail—or worse, explode.

One explosion-free plan for powering the next generation of cell phones would harvest power from the gadgets' human hosts. While this sounds like a premise for a horror movie, it's really quite clever. Carrying a cell phone while walking—having the device jiggling up and down in a purse or pocket—can generate a small charge, which can be stored in a capacitor for later use. Piezoelectric materials, which generate electricity when compressed, can be put beneath buttons to ease the battery's output during those epic games of Brick Breaker.

Giving the customers what they want

Speaking of those power-hungry gizmos, the overwhelming trend in the tech industry is to add more features to products. The scheme is a surefire crowd-pleaser: feature-laden gadgets attract customers and sell at a premium, and adding a chip that turns a cell phone into a music player doesn't contribute much to its manufacturing cost. This process, known as feature creep, has a downside, however. Consumers only spend about 20 minutes on average fussing around with a new product—and if they can't figure out all the bells and whistles in that period of time, they're likely to return it. While it may be easy and cheap to add more features, it's extremely difficult to design an elegant, easy-to-use interface for the device, instead of just adding more menus and buttons.

Data, data everywhere

People are also producing more data than ever. Luckily, the cost of data storage is also falling, currently at a rate of around 15 percent every three months. While the cost of data storage has dropped precipitously—from $10,000 per megabyte in 1956 to less than $1 per gigabyte in 2008, the amount of data that people and businesses want to store has increased dramatically. A great deal of this data, especially the portion created by companies—from credit card transactions to funny cat pictures sent to the office via e-mail—must be saved for several years according to regulations like Sarbanes-Oxley. This translates into strong growth for the data-storage products industry, but stand clear of falling margins, since price competition in this sector can be intense.

One laptop per lap

Developing economies are a hot market for tech companies—and not just those who want to manufacture goods there. The wealth of the citizens in these countries is increasing dramatically, pushing people into a growing middle class. Combine that factor with competitive Western markets saturated with products and jaded consumers—and the solutions are obvious. The companies bringing the gospel of the byte to the citizens of growing economies have diverse motives for doing so, from increasing computer literacy among the world's poorest people to seeking profits and gaining market share. Nicholas Negroponte, a former MIT professor, has a plan to bring a $100 laptop (actual cost: $130) to poor people in developing countries. The laptops, whose design is not yet finalized, can be used as an e-book (with a black-and-white screen that can be read in sunlight), laptop or game device—and can also be networked over a wireless connection, just like conventional machines. The laptops run on a version of Fedora Linux, to encourage children to develop their own software, and also to keep prices down. The governments of Egypt and Argentina are particularly interested in the devices, which are expected to ship in the latter half of 2007.

Microsoft is pursuing customers in the developing world, partly in search of profits, and to curb the growth of free operating systems, which can erode the market share of Windows and its Office suite. In 2007, Microsoft announced that it would begin selling PCs aimed at children in India, which has not adopted the laptops for children initiative. The plan is intended to supplement education in areas where public schools may lack such necessities as running water, electricity, teachers and books. Microsoft's computer, which will cost about $500, or $100 more than some of the less expensive models, will come equipped with a Windows operating system, Word, Encarta and programs tailored to help children cram for school exams. The device isn't designed to get poor children up to speed with the Internet, but will help the company gain market share in the growing Indian economy, where it has the potential to lose ground to less expensive machines running Linux—it hopes to grab one billion customers by 2015. Intel is also looking to sell low-cost computers in Asia in 2007. Aimed at middle-class customers, who make around $5,000 per year, the devices will cost about $300. Company officials say that despite the low prices, they are still making a profit.

An Apple a day

Microsoft is seeking new markets because its dominance at home is increasingly coming under threat. Apple—whose computers were once the purview of a small, rabid fringe of computer users—is now the mainstream. In the younger generation, it's hard to find someone who doesn't own some kind of iPod (and have it permanently welded to his ears). The iPhone has been a roaring success, as well—the company reported that it sold 1 million of them four months after the launch, and expects to make it an even 10 million by early 2009. However, the company is not just about spiffy consumer electronics—it's been gaining in the computer race as well. Although it still hangs behind industry behemoths Hewlett-Packard and Dell, its share of the pie has been growing—Apple holds over 20 percent of the U.S. personal computer market, up from single-digits just a few years ago. Industry pundits note that consumers enjoy Apple computers' modern-looking cases, pretty graphics and relative imperviousness to viruses.

The MBA in Tech

So you're in IT and you decided to get an MBA. Perhaps your degree even came with a technology specialty, which is an increasingly common option. Where will your degree get you?

Despite the lore of the 1970s-era computer "hackers" who revolutionized personal computing by working out of garages, many other people even then were studying for MBA degrees and were interested in technology. In the five-year period from 1976 to 1981, Harvard Business School produced Dan Bricklin (VisiCalc), Scott Cook (Intuit), Donna Dubinsky (Palm), Meg Whitman (eBay), and many others. Bricklin was an MIT-educated engineer, but has stated that he thought of many core ideas for the electronic spreadsheet while in business school.

Today, working in IT or working at a technology manufacturer offers many opportunities for MBAs to advance. Some of the popular fields are consulting, director-level positions, finance, law, marketing, project management, sales, training and the ultimate, which is C-level leadership.

Visit Vault at **www.vault.com** for insider company profiles, expert advice, career message boards, expert resume reviews, the Vault Job Board and more.

V/\ULT CAREER LIBRARY   131

Project management

As a project (or product) manager, you have a very specific set of goals to meet. They typically include detailed technology specifications to follow, deadlines to make and, of course, a budget to stick with. Maybe you'd be put in charge of an IT department's rollout of a new software product for internal users, or in charge of a certain operating system version of a certain piece of hardware. Either way, acquiring an MBA as a project/product manager can lead to doing the same job but with a bigger company, or to a position with a VP title. As in marketing, project/product managers need a very wide range of skills and knowledge, so having your MBA can only help. If you're a hardcore engineer or programmer, the MBA will help you break into project/product management.

Marketing

If the intensity of the IT lifestyle makes you feel burned out, and you have some creative DNA, then you may be a good fit for a position in technology marketing. The field involves dealing with advertising, partners, the press and anything related to corporate outreach. In technology marketing, more so than in other fields, you will be expected to know quite a bit about the technology in question. By getting that MBA you can also understand the technology's business strategic situation, and have a good chance at moving up into upper management.

Tech consulting

Many tech consultants are former successful technologists who desire to share what they've learned with others. With just IT experience, you can get an entry-level consulting job, which means interfacing with your client's own IT staff about their special needs. With a few years of experience and the addition of an MBA degree, you can open your own consulting firm, be invited to participate in panels at trade shows, or perhaps move from out of consulting and into the exciting world of venture capital. (To be a VC, you need to excel at understanding business and technology hand-in-hand, just as good consultants do.) You can also become an in-house consultant for a very large company, which may involve more deadlines and politics to play, but leaves you not having to worry about finding new customers.

Director jobs

If you work for a company that makes technology products, instead of working in the IT department of a company that simply utilizes technology, then possessing an MBA degree will often lead you into a "director" level job. For example, you might become the director of printers for a company that makes business technology, or the director of R&D for a military software contractor. As a director, your role is a notch below the division vice president and a notch above the various product managers. Product managers work on just one thing, but as director you're also working on a technology group's sales, marketing, manufacturing, etc.

Finance and law

Finance and law positions in an IT department or at a technology vendor have some aspects that are unique compared to working in other fields. You may have to deal with patent issues, foreign employee visas, international licensing laws, making sure the IT staff follows legal compliance rules for backing up data, and working with multiple layers of distributors, partners and resellers. By getting an MBA degree as well, you are in good position to become a company's operations director, or even to get a C-level position if you have extensive sales or technology experience as well.

Sales

In sales the job description is very clear: generate revenue for the company. By having an MBA you can manage entry-level staff, get the best and biggest clients, get into working with partners and resellers, or even enter the field of "competitive intelligence," which is a nice way of saying corporate espionage.

Training

As an IT trainer you have many career options. You can work in a classroom setting, manage advanced customer support, become involved with technical writing, educate the sales staff or work with your company's technology partners. With an MBA degree you can become a manager and get a title such as call center director or VP of user experience.

Upper management

Last, and the hardest job to get, is technology upper management. To become a CIO, CTO or even a CEO in the technology field, an MBA degree is almost a requirement, especially at large companies. There are a lucky few who become business leaders straight out of core technology jobs (and with a lot of natural talent)—the world's richest person, Bill Gates, never even finished his undergraduate degree. But for mere mortals, if you want to become an IT business leader, you can't go wrong with an MBA: it will help you close big sales, manage your company's logistics, strategize for growth and prepare you for the executive suite.

Tech Experience and the MBA

Of course, getting an MBA is not enough for a successful career in tech. "My gut reaction is, get the real-world experience," says Paul Buonaiuto, director of recruiting for Computer Associates International Inc., the Islandia, NY company specializing in business management software. The problem with classroom experience alone, he says, is that "Unless you're really out in the trenches, it's difficult to implement sometimes what you read in a book. Real-world experience I hold in more high regard." And even when a rookie MBA gets hired, there is usually the need for some amount of retraining, as "a lot of the [MBA] case studies are dot-com [or] an Enron or a latest-greatest merger," Buonaiuto explains.

To really stand out in the hiring process, the ideal job candidate should also have some kind of hands-on technology experience, Buonaiuto said. Candidates that well rounded come along "almost never," he says. When a pure MBA interviews in technology, "What's sorely lacked in those folks looking for a job is research skills. It becomes painfully evident in the interview" that they know about CA's stock performance but know nothing about its technology other than what's on the web site, he said.

Many future executive candidates start out as technical employees or lower-level managers. For them, many companies will pay for a portion of their MBA educations. There are a wide range of choices for where to get it—a traditional MBA program gives you the recognition that business is business and profits are profits, regardless of your industry, while a specialized technology MBA program (such as in e-commerce or systems management) will make you stand out but can be risky if your chosen specialty market has a downturn. Magazines like *Computerworld*, *BusinessWeek* and *U.S. News & World Report* sometimes publish features dedicated to ranking the graduate programs. The relative newness of specialized degrees is another common point of debate: it's been noted many times before that the leading rankings often wildly disagree.

Visit Vault at **www.vault.com** for insider company profiles, expert advice, career message boards, expert resume reviews, the Vault Job Board and more.

VAULT CAREER LIBRARY   133

Vault Q&A: Catherine Wang, Intuit

Prior to attending the Stanford Graduate School of Business, Catherine Wang had little experience in high tech. While at Stanford, however, she landed an internship at Silicon Valley stalwart Intuit and took a position as a marketing manager upon graduating in 2005. Wang took some time out from her busy schedule to talk to Vault about her experience as an MBA at a tech company.

Vault: Tell me a little about your experience prior to business school

Wang: I was in consulting at McKinsey for two years and then worked with Charles Schwab for two years before going to business school.

Vault: Did you know going into business school that you wanted to move into high-tech marketing?

Wang: I actually wanted to do marketing in general, so technology was less important. I chose Intuit less because Intuit is a software company, but more because of Intuit's approach to customers. Intuit is definitely not a technology company for the sake of being a technology company. It just happens that they use technology to solve their customer's needs. Frankly, I didn't interview with many tech companies, but was interested in Intuit's strong marketing organization.

I did my summer internship at Intuit. You can do either marketing or product development on the MBA side. The internship was very structured—lots of meetings with senior executives of the company, intern events, things like that.

Vault: Were there a lot of MBAs that joined Intuit at the same time you did?

Wang: There really isn't an MBA class my year; Intuit kind of hires MBAs as needed. That said, there's tons of MBAs at Intuit and there's tons of Stanford MBAs at Intuit.

There are many people who have very very similar backgrounds to you. We are a big company, but the culture at Intuit is very collaborative, it's very much about helping people out, getting to know people. You don't really have to be very proactive in networking, a lot of people reach out to get to know you. It's part of the company culture to make sure you have the mentors you need that you have the network that you need.

Vault: Tell me about your current position at Intuit.

Wang: I'm a marketing manager, working on our payroll service, which is a small business solution that enables small businesses to do payroll in house. It's a service within the Quickbooks product.

Vault: How is it delivered? Is it a CD or through the Web?

Wang: It's functionality that we turn on in Quickbooks. Think about your cable TV, and how there are different packages. If you pay more, you get HBO versus if you didn't pay for it. It's kind of like that—we turn it on for you. Quickbooks itself can be downloaded from the Web or you can buy it off the shelf and install it.

Vault: So what does it mean to be a marketing manager at Intuit?

Wang: So marketing manager is comparable to a brand management position. What I manage is one of our channels, the phone channel. I work a lot through our call centers, to make sure that they have the materials they need. Our main call centers are in Tucson and Reno, so I go to each of them about once a month. Right now, I'm in Tucson.

We have a group of 12 marketing folks within payroll. For example, there's someone focused on retail, so packaging is a more important part of her responsibilities than it is for me. We also have someone who focuses on the web channel who's responsible for the content displayed on the Web.

Vault: What is your impression of how marketing management at Intuit and other high-tech companies compares to brand management at traditional packaged goods companies?

Wang: My perception is that with many consumer packaged goods companies, there's more of a focus on marketing. I would say it's less so that way here, because technology plays an important role. It's more of a balance.

I think a big difference between Intuit and a lot of other tech companies, however, is that marketing is very important. I did interview at tech companies where the folks I was interviewing with would say, "Honestly, we have some products that have certain functionality because the engineers thought it was cool." Here, the focus is on the customer and so I don't think you have that tension between engineering and marketing.

Vault: In brand management at traditional packaged goods companies, brand managers interface with a wide variety of departments in an organization. Who are you working with mainly?

Wang: People from all levels, starting from sales managers to coaches who lead a team of about 15 agents. We're very customer focused, so I spend a lot of time listening on calls to agents, to see who what our customers are saying, or doing agent focus groups.

For example, we did six focus groups around what types of marketing messages we should emphasize. This starts with identifying what are the benefits that customers really value, that has implications that they really sell—so if customers are saying that a benefit is not important, the salespeople aren't going to focus on that.

Vault: What about getting customers in the door in the first place?

Wang: So I also deal with lead generation—getting calls into the call center. That involves working with our managers who manage Quickbooks.com or Payroll.com, as well as working with our direct marketing organization. Direct marketing is a centralized function at Intuit, so all marketing managers coordinate with that team.

Vault: What other responsibilities do you have?

Wang: Although we're largely structured by channels, we also spend some time on different issues that affect all channels. For me, beyond telesales, I work on pricing promotion across channels. These promotions must be coordinated with other channels.

Vault: Was there a particular reason that pricing promotion fell under your oversight? Does it have particular relevance to the telesales channel?

Wang: No, it was just how things were divided up.

Vault: So are you frequently interacting with the marketing managers overseeing other channels?

Wang: Yes, definitely—every day, if not more frequently. Things that we do in one channel affect other channels. If we do a promotion on the Web, we know not everyone is going to order through the Web, some will call. If we are trying to grow sales of one particular product, that affects all channels.

Vault: Are you often in contact with the engineers building the products?

Wang: Not so much. We interface more with the product marketing folks. Of the four Ps in marketing, the marketing side is really focused on the pricing, promotions and placement. The product piece is really the ownership of the product managers. The product managers are the ones who take customer requirements, find out what functionality is missing, and they work with engineers with the product themselves.

The product managers and engineers work on future functionality, the marketing group focuses on selling current functionality.

Visit Vault at **www.vault.com** for insider company profiles, expert advice, career message boards, expert resume reviews, the Vault Job Board and more.

V/\ULT CAREER LIBRARY   135

Employer Directory

3Com
350 Campus Drive
Marlborough, MA 01752-3064
Phone: (508) 323-5000
Fax: (508) 323-1111
Toll free: (800) 638-3266
www.3Com.com

Adobe Systems
345 Park Avenue
San Jose, CA 95110-2704
Phone: (408) 536-6000
Fax: (408) 537-6000
Toll free: (800) 833-6687
www.adobe.com

Advanced Micro Devices
1 AMD Place
P.O. Box 3453
Sunnyvale, CA 94088-3453
Phone: (408) 749-4000
Fax: (408) 749-4291
Toll free: (800) 538-8450
www.amd.com

Affiliated Computer Services Incorporated
2828 North Haskell
Dallas, TX 75204
Phone: (214) 841-6111
Fax: (214) 821-8315
www.acs-inc.com

Akamai Technologies, Inc.
8 Cambridge Center
Cambridge, MA 02142
Phone: (617) 444-3000
Fax: (617) 444-3001
www.akamai.com

Apple Incorporated
1 Infinite Loop
Cupertino, CA 95014
Phone: (408) 996-1010
Fax: (408) 974-2113
www.apple.com

Applied Materials
3050 Bowers Avenue
Santa Clara, CA 95054-3299
Phone: (408) 727-5555
Fax: (408) 748-9943
www.appliedmaterials.com

CA - Computer Associates
1 CA Plaza
Islandia, NY 11749
Phone: (631) 342-6000
Fax: (631) 342-6800
www.ca.com

Cisco Systems
170 West Tasman Drive, Building 10
San Jose, CA 95134
Phone: (408) 525-4000
Fax: (408) 526-4100
Toll free: (800) 553-6387
www.cisco.com

Dell Incorporated
1 Dell Way
Round Rock, TX 78682
Phone: (512) 338-4400
Fax: (512) 283-6161
www.dell.com

Freescale Semiconductor Incorporated
6501 William Cannon Drive West
Austin, TX 78735
Phone: (512) 895-2000
www.freescale.com

Fujitsu Limited
Shiodome City Center
1-5-2 Higashi-Shimbashi, Minato-ku
Tokyo 105-7123
Japan
Phone: +81-3-62-52-22-20
Fax: +81-3-62-52-27-83
www.fujitsu.com

Hewlett-Packard
3000 Hanover Street
Palo Alto, CA 94304
Phone: (650) 857-1501
Fax: (650) 857-5518
www.hp.com

Hitachi Limited
6-6, Marunouchi 1-chome, Chiyoda-ku
Tokyo 100-8280
Japan
Phone: +81-3-32-58-11-11
Fax: +81-3-32-58-23-75
www.hitachi.com

IBM
New Orchard Road
Armonk, NY 10504
Phone: (914) 499-1900
Fax: (914) 765-7382
Toll free: (800) 426-4968
www.ibm.com

Intel
2200 Mission College Boulevard
Santa Clara, CA 95054
Phone: (408) 765-8080
Fax: (408) 765-3804
www.intel.com

Intuit
2631 Marine Way
Mountain View, CA 94043
Phone: (650) 944-6000
Fax: (650) 944-3699
www.intuit.com

Lenovo Group Limited
1009 Think Place
Morrisville, NC 27560
Phone: (866) 458-4465
Fax: (877) 411-1329
www.lenovo.com

McAfee Incorporated
3965 Freedom Circle
Santa Clara, CA 95054
Phone: (408) 988-3832
Fax: (408) 970-9727
www.mcafee.com

Employer Directory, cont.

Microsoft Corporation
1 Microsoft Way
Redmond, WA 98052-6399
Phone: (425) 882-8080
Fax: (425) 936-7329
www.microsoft.com

National Semiconductor Corporation
2900 Semiconductor Drive
P.O. Box 58090
Santa Clara, CA 95052-8090
Phone: (408) 721-5000
Fax: (408) 739-9803
www.national.com

Network Appliance Incorporated
495 East Java Drive
Sunnyvale, CA 94089
Phone: (408) 822-6000
Fax: (408) 822-4501
www.netapp.com

Novell Incorporated
404 Wyman Street, Suite 500
Waltham, MA 02451
Phone: (781) 464-8000
Fax: (781) 464-8100
www.novell.com

NVIDIA Corporation
2701 San Tomas Expressway
Santa Clara, CA 95050
Phone: (408) 486-2000
Fax: (408) 486-2200
www.nvidia.com

Oracle Corporation
500 Oracle Parkway
Redwood City, CA 94065
Phone: (650) 506-7000
Fax: (650) 506-7200
www.oracle.com

QUALCOMM Incorporated
5775 Morehouse Drive
San Diego, CA 92121
Phone: (858) 587-1121
Fax: (858) 658-2100
www.qualcomm.com

Red Hat, Inc.
1801 Varsity Drive
Raleigh, NC 27606
Phone: (919) 754-3700
Fax: (919) 754-3701
www.redhat.com

Samsung
250, 2-ga, Taepyung-ro, Jung-gu
Seoul, 100-742
South Korea
Phone: +82-2-751-7114
Fax: +82-2-727-7892
www.samsung.com

SAP AG
Dietmar-Hopp-Allee 16
69190 Walldorf
Germany
Phone: +49-6227-74-7474
Fax: +49-6227-75-7575
www.sap.com

SAS Institute Incorporated
100 SAS Campus Drive
Cary, NC 27513-2414
Phone: (919) 677-8000
Fax: (919) 677-4444
www.sas.com

Seagate Technology LLC
920 Disc Drive
Scotts Valley, CA 95066
Phone: (831) 438-6550
Fax: (831) 429-6356
Toll free: (877) 271-3285
www.seagate.com

Sun Microsystems Incorporated
4150 Network Circle
Santa Clara, CA 95054
Phone: (650) 960-1300
Fax: (408) 276-3804
www.sun.com

Symantec Corporation
20330 Stevens Creek Boulevard
Cupertino, CA 95014-2132
Phone: (408) 517-8000
Fax: (408) 517-8186
www.symantec.com

Texas Instruments Incorporated
12500 TI Boulevard
Dallas, TX 75243-4136
Phone: (972) 995-2011
Fax: (972) 927-6377
www.ti.com

Toshiba America, Inc.
1251 Avenue of the Americas, Suite 4110
New York, NY 10020
Phone: (212) 596-0600
Fax: (212) 593-3875
www.toshiba.com

Unisys Corporation
Unisys Way
Blue Bell, PA 19424
Phone: (215) 986-4011
Fax: (215) 986-2312
www.unisys.com

Vmware
3401 Hillview Avenue
Palo Alto, CA 94304
Phone: (650) 475-5000
Fax: (650) 427-5001
www.vmware.com

Visit Vault at **www.vault.com** for insider company profiles, expert advice, career message boards, expert resume reviews, the Vault Job Board and more.

VAULT CAREER LIBRARY   137

Human Resources

Every organization has people, which means every organization needs human resources (HR) professionals. HR helps manage and develop the people in an organization. Sometimes called "personnel" or "talent management," HR is the function in charge of an organization's employees, which includes finding and hiring employees, helping them grow and learn in the organization, and managing the process when an employee leaves. Human resources takes care of people from the time they're interested in the organization to long after they leave.

The History of Human Resources

Now a thriving, growing profession, human resources wasn't always a key part of most organizations—if at all. Until the early 1900s, all human resources functions were typically handled by the workers themselves or their bosses (often called master craftsmen). As more workers were needed, master craftsmen would just go out and find them (talk about the birth of recruiting!).

When the 1900s brought inventions and changes in the workplace, like machines that automated production, human resources began to take shape. The addition of machines made factories run more quickly and smoothly, but also meant that the workers had to learn how to use them, and forced factory managers to introduce rules and procedures on the factory floor.

Frederick Taylor, a businessman and researcher, first introduced the concept of scientific management. Taylor's theory took workplace rules and procedures one step further, declaring that there was only one best way to do a job. He spent years collecting data on the tasks making up specific jobs and then researching the workers who performed each small task. Workers who performed well, following tasks to the letter, remained employed and were paid well. Those who didn't were among the first to hear "you're fired."

Taylor's research was the first to increase worker productivity, but his robotic approach didn't prove to be an effective management tool. Still, his work showed the importance of managing workers to increase a company's success. While Taylor's work focused more on company success than that of the worker, it propelled many companies to begin to personalize the workplace, anticipating the first appearance of HR. One of the earliest HR roles was that of a welfare secretary whose role was to look out for the welfare of the workers. An ancestor of what's now called a benefits manager, welfare secretaries created libraries and recreation areas in the workplace, as well as primitive medical and health programs.

But HR really took shape in the 1930s when a company called Western Electric asked a team of researchers to figure out how to increase workers' productivity at one of their plants in Chicago. The Hawthorne Studies, taking their name after the targeted plant, set out to determine whether changing the lighting in the plant could help the employees work faster. What they found instead was how important it was for plant managers to pay attention to the workers, reward them for a good job and make sure they were satisfied. The idea of happy workers being productive workers took hold and still remains true today. If a company wants to perform well, it has to create and manage a content workforce. HR plays a critical role in making sure that happens.

The Hawthorne Studies fueled the study of worker behavior in organizations, and what was called behavioral science. The growth of behavioral science as a field studied how jobs and the workplace affect workers and how workers affect the performance of a company.

The study of behavioral science reinforced the importance of welfare secretaries. The secretaries' jobs became more and more complex as governments introduced labor laws to keep up with the changing workplace. These laws, restricting the rights of both employers and employees, required the welfare secretaries to keep paper records of employees and their activities. One of the first human resources laws, the Fair Labor Standards Act (FLSA) created a minimum wage, set rules for child labor and required employers to treat employees fairly in regards to wage and hours worked.

Visit Vault at **www.vault.com** for insider company profiles, expert advice, career message boards, expert resume reviews, the Vault Job Board and more.

VAULT CAREER LIBRARY   139

In many industries, workers also began organizing into unions—groups of workers banding together to lobby for rights in the workplace. New laws around union activity also required companies and welfare secretaries to understand and comply with the laws.

Many companies began hiring multiple welfare secretaries—one responsible for hiring employees, another responsible for employee benefits and perhaps another to train employees on the factory floors. These specialty areas evolved into the specialty areas of the human resources profession today.

Human Resources Today

Today, human resources is essential to the success of business. The level of importance HR holds does differ from organization to organization, but businesses consistently rely on HR professionals to help them through high-growth times and periods of turmoil. Regardless of how successful (or not) an organization is, there is always a need for HR staff. The welfare secretary title may be long gone, but the idea of having human resources professionals focus on specific areas of managing and developing a company's workers has remained. Now, in most organizations, there are HR professionals who focus specifically on hiring, training, benefits, labor relations, health and safety and more.

While it's important to like working with people and wanting to help them to be successful in HR, that's definitely not the only skill or attribute you need to be a successful HR professional. HR is about creating systems, processes and environments where employees perform better and are satisfied, and there are many different career paths and opportunities in the profession. For example, HR professionals can take center stage as a recruiter or trainer. In these roles, you're interacting with people all day long, whether conducting interviews or running a training course. But HR professionals can also serve behind the scenes, administering payroll, tracking HR metrics (statistics about company workers) or running an organization's Human Resource Information System (HRIS), technical databases where all employee data is stored and managed.

While HR continues to grow as a function, in many companies it does not carry the importance or value of its colleagues in finance, sales or marketing. Know that as satisfying as an HR career can be, the profession still struggles to gain respect in many places.

What Do HR Professionals Do?

Typical HR responsibilities are focused in major areas such as recruiting and staffing, compensation and benefits, training and learning, labor and employee relations, and organization development. Most HR professionals have experience in one or more of these specialty areas. These areas all deal with helping employees in an organization perform more effectively and satisfactorily on the job.

Recruiting and staffing

You're either in or you're out. When an employee leaves and a job opens up or new jobs are created, HR is usually in charge of the process. Recruiting and staffing is one of the largest areas of HR. Recruiters start the process—working with specific departments to write job descriptions and understand what skills and abilities the new employee should have. Then they're off and running—responsible for finding candidates, determining who might be a good fit, conducting interviews and making job offers. While recruiters involve department employees in the process to interview and make the hiring decisions, it's the recruiters who are usually in charge of finding the talent, managing interview scheduling, negotiating offers and making sure departments have all the information they need to make the best hiring decisions possible.

While recruiters work to find and hire the talent, staffing experts determine who should go where. They strategize with different departments to anticipate hiring needs and help determine where a new employee might best fit in an organization.

Staffing professionals are heavily relied on in high-growth companies to make sure the company is prepared to hire enough new employees to grow the company, and that employees are in the right positions.

Recruiting and staffing professionals are also called upon to help an organization market to prospective employees. This can include creating and managing recruiting events, designing marketing pieces, such as company brochures and commercials, and staffing career fairs to educate prospective employees about open opportunities. Many organizations also have recruiting and staffing professionals dedicated to working with universities. These roles are focused on finding talent on undergraduate and graduate school campuses and can include a great deal of travel and campus presentations.

Compensation and benefits

Finding talent is important, but employees also have to be paid. HR, specifically compensation and benefits professionals, are in charge of making sure new employees are given an appropriate salary and benefits, and current employees continually receive their salary and benefits.

Compensation experts focus on the money. This includes processing regular payroll (making sure that the check is in the mail) and payroll changes, including raises and tax changes. Compensation experts also work closely with an organization's finance department to ensure salaries stay within each department's budget, as well as conducting and researching salary surveys to make sure they're paying the going rate.

Benefits professionals also have to make sure employees are taken care of—they specialize in helping employees with medical and other company benefits. This may include teaching new employees about their medical plan choices, implementing and managing the plans offered by the company, and managing the cost of benefits for the company.

Compensation and benefits professionals are also often tasked with communicating salary and benefits information to employees. This may include marketing and promoting new benefits offerings to a company or managing a company's open enrollment period—a brief period of time where employees can change medical plans and other benefit options.

One-on-one counseling may also be part of the job. If an employee leaves an organization, the benefits manager may counsel the employee on access to health insurance available after departure. Employees also often seek guidance on understanding their compensation packages, making changes to employment tax forms or managing a difficult medical insurance claim.

Training and learning

Part teacher, part manager, part leader—that's a training professional. Helping employees become oriented to a new job or company is just one of the many responsibilities of training and learning professionals. Sometimes called training, or learning and development, it's helping both new and tenured employees develop and grow as professionals both on and off the job.

Training and learning professionals are typically responsible for running programs designed to educate and develop employees. This can include programs for an entire employee population, such as new hire orientation or ethics training, but also includes more specialized programs for different groups of workers within a company, like online training courses, in-class instruction or on-the-job training.

Training managers, for example, are called upon to do everything from registering and tracking training courses, to developing new courses and evaluating the effectiveness of training programs after they happen. This may include designing surveys or determining if newly trained employees perform better than they did before the training. They also may be responsible for providing information to employees on training classes and programs outside the company.

In some organizations, training and learning professionals actually deliver the training courses. They might create a presentation skills course and then send trainers on the road to teach the new course to employees around the country. Since it's often cheaper to train current employees rather than hire new ones, training and learning is becoming increasingly

Visit Vault at **www.vault.com** for insider company profiles, expert advice, career message boards, expert resume reviews, the Vault Job Board and more.

V∧ULT CAREER LIBRARY   **141**

important in the business world. A company's strong commitment to training and development is also a boost to its workers' morale.

Labor and employee relations

Just like welfare secretaries responded to new laws in the early 1900s, labor and employee relations professionals ensure that anything dealing with employee contracts, rights, responsibilities and complaints is taken care of right quick.

Labor relations is a function typically found in companies whose employees are members of unions. Labor relations professionals are called upon to deal directly with unions, doing everything from interpreting current union contracts to negotiating new ones. They also analyze and monitor union activity and work with unions during organizing campaigns—the time when unions recruit new members.

Employee relations professionals need to be familiar and comfortable with the law; they are also responsible for equal employment opportunity and affirmative action programs. For government agencies or companies that do work for the government, this may include creating reports to demonstrate a company is complying with the law and making an effort to hire and retain employees from underrepresented ethnicities. Other key responsibilities may include counseling or conflict resolution within an organization, helping employees who are dealing with disagreements in the workplace or have issues preventing them from doing their jobs.

Labor and employee relations is not found in every human resources department. Organizations that don't have government contracts or unionized employees may rely on outside attorneys or consultants to deal with any legal issues or employee conflicts that arise.

Organization development (OD)

While developing employees is important, perhaps just as important is developing an organization. A relatively new field, organization development focuses on evaluating how a company is structured and how employees work together to see where improvements can be made. Also referred to as organization effectiveness, this might include helping to restructure the chain of command in a department to helping employees cope with a major change, such as the introduction of a new company-wide technical system.

OD professionals are experts in understanding behavior and psychology. They often act as internal consultants, helping their fellow employees understand how a new company program might affect the employees' behavior.

They often work closely with training professionals to address development needs for the company. OD professionals may develop companywide team-building activities or introduce new programs for leadership development.

OD specialists often manage the performance review process, making sure that employees are evaluated and moved within the organization based on how well they're working. OD specialists may also help companies develop succession plans (determining who is in line to be the next person in a leadership position, such as CEO or CFO) and mentoring programs, making sure less experienced employees can learn from their more experienced comrades. OD professionals may also be called upon to help an employee address individual issues through executive coaching, or a department address a leadership or performance challenge.

Less common OD work may include coaching or career development. Coaches, common at the executive level, help employees overcome poor teamwork or management skills. Many large firms are hiring external coaches, or creating coaching functions in order to help valuable employees deal with singular issues that may prevent them from being promoted.

Health and safety

Factory machines, hazardous chemicals and construction sites are all potentially dangerous situations for workers. This is where health and safety professionals come in. One of the oldest HR specialties, health and safety professionals are responsible for ensuring a safe working environment for all workers—this is more of an issue in industries with risky work settings, such as manufacturing, health care and construction. While all organizations must protect the safety of their employees while at work, it is more complicated in industries that have work sites beyond a typical office environment.

One of the major components of the role of a health and safety professional is to be proactive—assessing a work environment to anticipate where the dangers might be and correcting them before an injury occurs. This might include periodic tours of a work site, or research into the latest workplace safety options.

Health and safety professionals are also responsible for reacting to issues, concerns or problems related to the workplace environment. They might handle a complaint from a worker about a dangerous factory machine or an on-site injury. They work closely with compensation and benefits professionals to handle any injuries and determine how to prevent future injuries from occurring.

Working with an organization's legal team and employee law specialists is also part of the role. Health and safety professionals are responsible for following federal and state rules governing workplace safety, including, in some industries, submitting reports that demonstrate a company's compliance with the law.

Why HR?

While HR professionals have varying degrees of interaction with an organization's employees, all HR people can enjoy the satisfaction of knowing that the work they do has a direct impact on people every day. HR professionals like helping employees navigate through tough problems and get back to normal on the job. Whether it's helping an employee overcome a performance problem or fix an expensive and stressful medical claim, there is an inherent satisfaction in these types of tasks.

They also enjoy the ability to interact with different groups of people; HR professionals may be working with employees in many different parts of the company. Organization development specialists may act like internal consultants helping different departments in a company work better together. This means they might be working with a sales team one week and a product design team the next. So there is a ton of variety in their day-to-day tasks.

In his role at Bank of America, Phil Skeath likes the diversity of projects. "Each time I am on a new project," he says, "I find myself identifying general concepts I learned in my educational experience, adapting them and applying them to a specific issue in the bank."

They also like contributing to the business and bottom line. For example, one of the most common issues CFOs are facing in 2005 (according to *CFO Magazine*) is the rising cost of health care. HR and benefits professionals who analyze how to lower these costs can save a company millions of dollars. Talk about making an impact.

Why not?

For most HR professionals, the positives of working in HR (such as extending a job offer to a very excited job candidate) are enough to outweigh the drawbacks (in the opposite category, downsizing or laying off employees). Otherwise, they wouldn't be there in the first place. But no job is perfect. Even rock stars have to deal with annoying paparazzi and screaming fans. While it's highly unlikely you'll be chased by reporters working in HR, you may be chased by unhappy employees. One of the toughest things about working in HR is providing a service many employees take for granted. No one says, "thanks HR," every time they get a paycheck. But if something goes wrong, if employees don't get paid, if benefits disappear or new employees aren't trained properly, you may end up with a mailbox full of angry callers to contend with.

Visit Vault at **www.vault.com** for insider company profiles, expert advice, career message boards, expert resume reviews, the Vault Job Board and more.

VAULT CAREER LIBRARY   143

Like many professions, starting out in HR, you may also have your fair share of administrative work. Many HR careers begin with processing paperwork for new employees, or entering and maintaining resumes in an online database. This might seem like menial work, especially if you've just received a college degree, but don't walk away too quickly. These roles, while tedious, provide a great learning opportunity and a chance to prove you're ready for more responsibilities. HR also suffers from some common misconceptions, like being a touchy-feely profession or being female-dominated.

Ready to help your colleagues and organization perform better? Before you determine what type of HR role you might best be cast in, it's important to understand that HR as a function isn't the same in every organization.

Human Resource Management

Human resource management (HRM) is the set of traditional HR activities that manage or support the people in the organization, and every working organization has to have at least one person responsible for HRM. The major areas of HRM include:

- Recruiting and staffing
- Compensation and benefits
- Labor and employee relations
- Health and safety

In HRM roles, professionals need to keep the HR motor humming and wheels turning. Imagine if you stopped receiving your paycheck or if your company stopped recruiting altogether. HRM functions are key to keeping organizations running smoothly, and HRM professionals are responsible for preventing any interruption in services that employees expect.

HRM professionals are also responsible to the organization as a whole. Running all of these processes can cost a lot of money, and it is up to HRM professionals to make decisions that help save the company money and make sure employees are well served. In each of the major areas of HRM, professionals are continually evaluating processes and implementing new programs and systems to serve the organization better. Examples include:

- **Recruiting and staffing:** Recruiting management systems (RMS) or applicant tracking systems (ATS) are the latest trend in electronically managing the influx of resumes during busy recruiting times. These systems save organizations money by streamlining the recruiting process and requiring fewer staff members to manage employee records.

- **Labor and employee relations:** Legal training for managers on topics, such as sexual harassment and workplace law, is becoming more and more common, in order to proactively reduce lawsuits related to workplace behavior.

- **Health and safety:** While injuries at plants and hazardous sites are common, HR professionals are also recognizing the increase in office injuries; many health and safety professionals are introducing ergonomically correct office furniture. While these fancy chairs and glare-reducing computer screens may be expensive, such investments can prevent future injuries and their associated costs.

- **Compensation and benefits:** Benefits outsourcing is a popular way to reduce costs and responsibility for an organization. Some compensation and benefits professionals work with outside vendors to manage programs such as an employee stock purchase plan. Since these outside vendors already have the expertise and systems in place to manage these programs, it saves the company the expense of creating them from scratch.

Companies such as the Home Depot are well known for their HR practices, and are consistently looking for ways to ease and automate the function in order to serve customers, and ultimately the organization, better. The Home Depot has become more recently renowned for creatively recruiting veterans who have recently finished their military careers. Since advertising on online job boards can be expensive, finding new channels to recruit prospective employees is an important way to save valuable recruiting dollars.

As a human resources VP for a consulting firm professes, improving the way employees are served is an important part of the job. "In the last five years, over 75 percent of our HR transactions have been automated to better serve our customers. We created a company Intranet and put our benefits elections process online, as well as all of our employee policies and procedures. No more paper!"

HRM professionals are also often charged with reporting HR's return on investment (ROI) to the company through tracking HR metrics (statistics on how a company's employees are performing) and demonstrating the value HR brings to the company. Compensation and benefits professionals might track how much employees are spending on health care costs and seek ways to reduce them. On the other hand, an employee relations professional might track statistics on how many minorities are employed in an organization for an affirmative action report. Measuring such activity is important for HRM professionals to show their commitment to an organization's bottom line.

HR management professionals must continually be thinking about ways to better serve and save a company money at the same time.

Common Human Resource Management (HRM) Roles

Common HRM roles include:

- Compensation manager
- Senior recruiter
- Health and safety manager
- Employment lawyer

- Labor relations specialist
- Benefits specialist
- HR generalist

Human Resource Development

Human resource development (HRD) is the second part (albeit much smaller) of the HR world. If HRM professionals are keeping the wheels turning smoothly, HRD professionals are helping them turn faster and better. Human resource development refers to the activities in an organization that help develop and grow employees. Many organizations simply refer to HRD as training or learning and development but in reality, it's much more than that. HRD includes:

- Training and learning
- Organization development, which includes:
  - Succession planning (determining who is next in line for a CEO or other senior job)
  - Coaching (helping employees overcome on-the-job problems)
  - Performance management (those pesky performance reviews)

HRD is the area of HR that is growing most quickly as organizations recognize the need to go way beyond simply managing their workforce. While smaller organizations often have HR generalists assume the responsibility for training alongside other HR tasks, large companies, such as Medtronic, Bank of America and Texas Instruments, have entire functions devoted to subsets of HRD such as organization development.

"Organization development is a key part of human resources," says Phil Skeath, a performance improvement consultant at Bank of America. "We are business partners who support our line managers' needs, but we are also an integral part in driving the company's strategy."

Visit Vault at **www.vault.com** for insider company profiles, expert advice, career message boards, expert resume reviews, the Vault Job Board and more.

V/\ULT CAREER LIBRARY 145

HRD professionals may be responsible for a certain subset of the workforce (such as training the sales force), or may serve as internal consultants working on projects as they arise, such as helping to restructure a department or working on the succession plan for an entire division. Other HRD responsibilities include employee performance evaluations, training new employees and helping companies deal with change as the result of a new program, technology, merger or acquisition.

HRD careers are growing every year. Training and development is one area in which the Bureau of Labor Statistics (BLS) predicts growth in 2005 and beyond. This is due not only to how complex jobs are becoming, but also the aging of the workforce, and the many changes in technology requiring more and more training and development programs for workers. What does this mean for HR professionals? HRD might well be an increasingly popular career path.

Because HRD is not only growing, but is structured very differently from organization to organization, if you see HRD as a viable career path, it's important to research where it fits in specific companies. Organizations that only have a training and learning function may not see as much value in HRD as a company that has a specific organization development function.

Employer Directory

Accord Human Resources
Oklahoma Tower
210 Park Avenue, Suite 1200
Oklahoma City, OK 73102
Phone: (405) 232-9888
Fax: (405) 232-9899
Toll free: (800)725-4004
www.accordhr.com

Administaff
19001 Crescent Springs Drive
Kingwood, TX 77339
Phone: (281) 358-8986
Fax: (281) 348-3718
Toll free: (800) 237-3170
www.administaff.com

ADP Total Source Group
10200 Sunset Drive
Miami, FL 33173
Phone: (305) 630-1000
Fax: (305) 630-2006
www.adptotalsource.com

Adecco SA
Sägereistrasse 10
8152 Glattbrugg
Switzerland
Phone: +41-44-878-8888
Fax: +41-44-829-8888
www.adecco.com

Allegis Group, Inc.
7301 Parkway Drive
Hanover, MD 21076
Phone: (410) 579-4800
Fax: (410) 540-7556
Toll free: (877) 388-3823
www.allegisgroup.com

Aon Consulting Worldwide
Aon Center
200 East Randolph Street, 10th Floor
Chicago, IL 60601
Phone: (312) 381-4844
Fax: (312) 381-0240
www.aon.com

ATC Healthcare, Inc.
1983 Marcus Avenue
Lake Success, NY 11042
Phone: (516) 750-1600
Fax: (516) 750-1683
www.atchealthcare.com

Automatic Data Processing, Inc.
1 ADP Boulevard
Roseland, NJ 07068
Phone: (973) 974-5000
Fax: (973) 974-3334
Toll free: (800) 225-5237
www.adp.com

Barrett Business Services
8100 NE Parkway Drive, Suite 200
Vancouver, WA 98662
Phone: (360) 828-0700
Fax: (360) 828-0701
Toll free: (800) 494-5669
www.barrettbusiness.com

Buck Consultants
1 Pennsylvania Plaza
New York, NY 10119
Phone: (212) 330-1000
Fax: (212) 695-4184
www.buckconsultants.com

Ceridian Corporation
3311 East Old Shakopee Road
Minneapolis, MN 55425
Phone: (952) 853-8100
Fax: (952) 853-4430
www.ceridian.com

COMFORCE Corporation
415 Crossways Park Drive
Woodbury, NY 11797
Phone: (516) 437-3300
Fax: (516) 396-9528
Toll free: (877) 266-3672
www.comforce.com

Convergys
201 East 4th Street
Cincinnati, OH 45202
Phone: (513) 723-7000
Fax: (513) 421-8624
www.convergys.com

Cross Country Healthcare, Inc.
6551 Park of Commerce Boulevard NW
Boca Raton, FL 33487
Phone: (561) 998-2232
Fax: (800) 768-8128
www.crosscountryhealthcare.com

Employco Group, Ltd.
350 E. Ogden Avenue
Westmont, Il 60599
Phone: (630) 920-0126
Fax: (630) 920-0157
www.employco.com

Entegee, Inc.
70 Blanchard Road, Suite 102
Burlington, MA 01803
Phone: (781) 221-5800
Fax: (781) 221-4544
Toll free: (800) 368-3433
www.entegee.com

Express Employment Professionals
8516 Northwest Expressway
Oklahoma City, OK 73162
Phone: (405) 840-5000
Fax: (405) 717-5669
Toll free: (800) 222-4057
www.expresspros.com

Hay Group
The Wanamaker Building
100 Penn Square East
Philadelphia, PA 19107
Phone: (215) 861-2000
Fax: (215) 861-2111
www.haygroup.com

Visit Vault at **www.vault.com** for insider company profiles, expert advice,
career message boards, expert resume reviews, the Vault Job Board and more.

VAULT CAREER LIBRARY

147

Employer Directory, cont.

Hewitt Associates
100 Half Day Road
Lincolnshire, IL 60069
Phone: (847) 295-5000
Fax: (847) 295-7634
www.hewitt.com

Kforce Inc.
1001 East Palm Avenue
Tampa, FL 33605
Phone: (813) 552-5000
Fax: (813) 254-9640
Toll free: (800) 395-5575
www.kforce.com

Kelly Services, Inc.
999 West Big Beaver Road
Troy, MI 48084
Phone: (248) 362-4444
Fax: (248) 244-4360
www.kellyservices.com

Manpower Inc.
100 Manpower Place
Milwaukee, WI 53212
Phone: (414) 961-1000
Fax: (414) 906-7985
www.manpower.com

Maxim Healthcare Services, Inc.
7227 Lee Deforest Drive
Columbia, MD 21046
Phone: (410) 910-1500
Fax: (410) 910-1515
www.maximhealthcare.com

Meador Staffing Services, Inc.
722 A Fairmont Parkway
Pasadena, CX 77504
Phone: (713) 941-0616
Fax: (713) 941-3582
Toll free: (800) 332-3310
www.meador.com

Mercer LLC
1166 Avenue of the Americas
New York, NY 10036
Phone: (212) 345-7000
Fax: (212) 345-7414
www.mercerHR.com

Medical Staffing Network Holdings, Inc.
901 Yamato Road, Suite 110
Boca Raton, FL 33431
Phone: (561) 322-1300
Fax: (561) 322-1200
Toll free: (877) 676-8326
www.msnhealth.com

Modern Business Associates
9455 Koger Boulevard, Suite 200
St. Petersburg, FL 33702
Phone: (727) 563-1500
Fax: (727) 563-1501
Toll free: (888) 622-6460

MPS Group, Inc.
1 Independent Drive, Suite 2500
Jacksonville, FL 32202
Phone: (904) 360-2000
Fax: (904) 360-2350
www.mpsgroup.com

Nursefinders, Inc.
524 East Lamar Boulevard, Suite 550
Arlington, TX 76011
Phone: (817) 460-1181
Fax: (817) 462-9146
Toll free: (800) 445-0459
www.nursefinders.com

On Assignment, Inc.
26651 West Agoura Road
Calabasas, CA 91302
Phone: (818) 878-7900
Fax: (818) 878-7930
www.onassignment.com

Paychex, Inc.
911 Panorama Trail South
Rochester, NY 14625-2396
Phone: (585) 385-6666
Fax: (585) 383-3428
www.paychex.com

Paystaff Corporation
7361 Calhoun Place, Suite 510
Rockville, MD 20855
Phone: (301) 340-3800
Fax: (301) 340-3801
Toll free: (800) 776-0076
www.paystaff.com

PDS Technical Services, Inc.
1925 West John Carpenter Freeway
Suite 550
Irving, TX 75063
Phone: (214) 647-9600
Fax: (214) 647-9636
Toll free: (800) 270-4737
www.pdstech.com

Robert Half International Inc.
2884 Sand Hill Road
Menlo Park, CA 94025
Phone: (650) 234-6000
Fax: (650) 234-6999
www.rhi.com

Select Staffing
1511 North Westshore Boulevard
Suite 900
Tampa, FL 33607
Phone: (813) 830-7700
Fax: (813) 830-7029
www.selectstaffing.com

SOI Holdings, Inc.
5260 Parkway Plaza Boulevard
Suite 140
Charlotte, NC 28217
Phone: (704) 523-2191
Fax: (704) 523-2158
Toll free: (800) 572-2412
www.soi.net

Employer Directory, cont.

Spherion Corporation
2050 Spectrum Boulevard
Fort Lauderdale, FL 33309
Phone: (954) 308-7600
Fax: (954) 308-7666
www.spherion.com

Technisource, Inc.
2050 Spectrum Boulevard
Fort Lauderdale, FL 33309
Phone: (954) 308-7600
www.technisource.com

The TemPositions Group of Companies
420 Lexington Avenue, 21st Floor
New York, NY 10170
Phone: (212) 490-7400
Fax: (212) 867-1759
www.tempositions.com

Towers Perrin
263 Tresser Boulevard
Stamford, CT 06901
Phone: (203) 326-5400
www.towersperrin.com

Vedior North America LLC
60 Harvard Mill Square
Wakefield, MA 01880
Phone: (781) 213-1500
Fax: (781) 213-1520
www.vediorna.com

Volt Information Sciences, Inc.
560 Lexington Avenue
New York, NY 10022
Phone: (212) 704-2400
Fax: (212) 704-2417
www.volt.com

Watson Wyatt Worldwide
901 North Glebe Road
Arlington, VA 22203
Phone: (703) 258-8000
Fax: (703) 258-8585
www.watsonwyatt.com

Westaff, Inc.
298 North Wiget Lane
Walnut Creek, CA 94598
Phone: (925) 930-5300
Fax: (925) 934-5489
Toll free: (877) 937-8233
www.westaff.com

Visit Vault at www.vault.com for insider company profiles, expert advice, career message boards, expert resume reviews, the Vault Job Board and more.

VAULT CAREER LIBRARY   149

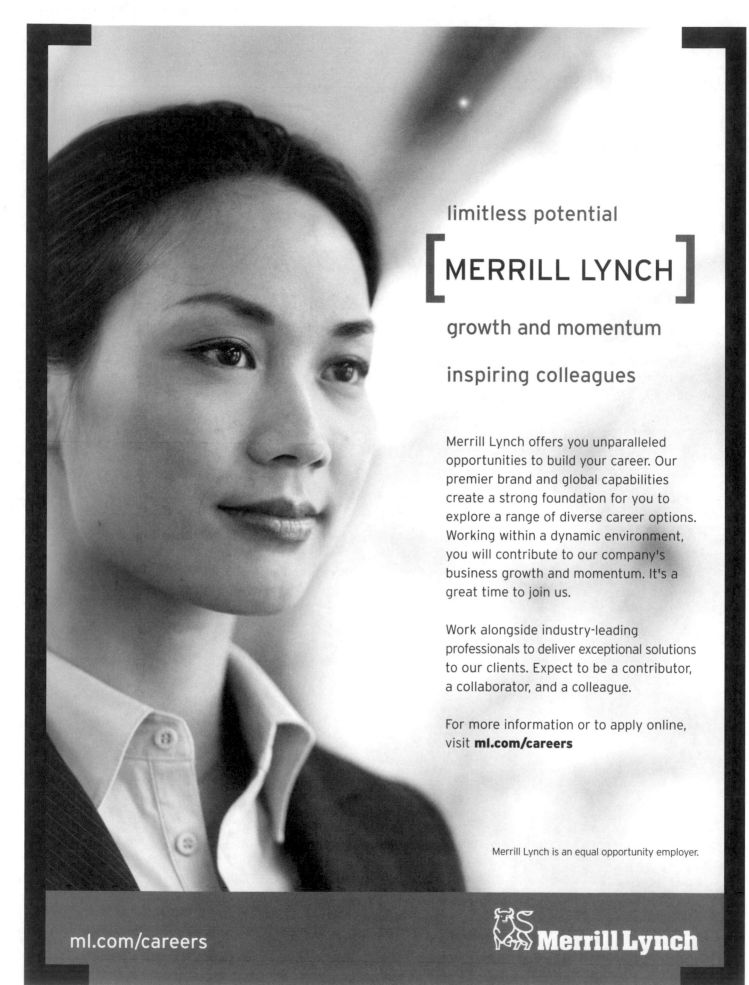

Investment Banking

What is investment banking? Is it investing? Is it banking? Really, it is neither. Investment banking, or i-banking, as it is often called, is the term used to describe the business of raising capital for companies and advising them on financing and merger alternatives. Capital essentially means money. Companies need cash in order to grow and expand their businesses; investment banks sell securities (debt and equity) to investors in order to raise this cash. These securities can come in the form of stocks, bonds or loans. Once issued, these securities trade in the global financial markets.

Generally, an investment bank comprises the following areas:

Corporate finance

The bread and butter of a traditional investment bank, corporate finance generally performs two different functions: (1) mergers and acquisitions advisory, and (2) underwriting. On the mergers and acquisitions (M&A) advising side of corporate finance, bankers assist in negotiating and structuring a merger between two companies. If, for example, a company wants to buy another firm, then an investment bank will help finalize the purchase price, structure the deal and generally ensure a smooth transaction. The underwriting function within corporate finance involves raising capital for a client. In the investment banking world, capital can be raised by selling either stocks or bonds to investors.

Sales

Sales is another core component of an investment bank. Salespeople take the form of: (1) the classic retail broker, (2) the institutional salesperson or (3) the private client service representative. Brokers develop relationships with individual investors and sell stocks and stock advice to the average Joe. Institutional salespeople develop business relationships with large institutional investors—those who manage large groups of assets, like pension funds or mutual funds. Private client service (PCS) representatives, often referred to as private wealth managers, lie somewhere between retail brokers and institutional salespeople, providing brokerage and money management services for extremely wealthy individuals. Salespeople make money through commissions on trades made through their firms.

Trading

Traders also provide a vital role for the investment bank. Traders facilitate the buying and selling of stock, bonds or other securities, either by carrying an inventory of securities for sale or by executing a given trade for a client. Traders deal with transactions, large and small, and provide liquidity (the ability to buy and sell securities) for the market—often called making a market. Traders make money by purchasing securities and selling them at a slightly higher price. This price differential is called the "bid-ask spread."

Research

Research analysts follow stocks and bonds and make recommendations on whether to buy, sell or hold those securities. Stock analysts (known as equity analysts) typically focus on one industry and will cover up to 20 companies' stocks at any given time. Some research analysts work on the fixed-income side and will cover a particular segment, such as high-yield bonds or U.S. Treasury bonds. Salespeople within the investment bank utilize research published by analysts to convince their clients to buy or sell securities through their firm. Corporate finance bankers rely on research analysts to be experts in the industry in which they are working. Reputable research analysts can generate substantial corporate finance business and substantial trading activity, and thus are an integral part of any investment bank.

Visit Vault at **www.vault.com** for insider company profiles, expert advice, career message boards, expert resume reviews, the Vault Job Board and more.

VAULT CAREER LIBRARY   151

THE WORLD NEVER SLEEPS.

Dreams. | **Realities.**

In Harvard Square, Jackson has just cracked an equation. Meanwhile, in Austin, Texas, Rita – the woman who will soon give Jackson an analyst position – is on her way to give a presentation on microfinance. And in Singapore, a team of Global Capital Markets Associates are projecting the impact of the growth of the global middle class.

Working in more than 100 countries means being open-minded in every way: how we do business, how we find solutions, and how we choose our colleagues. To us, inclusion isn't a rule to follow; it's a way of life. Because we're all different, and we're proud to be. That's why at Citi, the world never sleeps. **oncampus.citi.com**

Citi never sleeps™

Syndicate

The hub of the investment banking wheel, syndicate provides a vital link between salespeople and corporate finance. Syndicate exists to facilitate the placing of securities in a public offering, a knock-down-drag-out affair between and among buyers of offerings and the investment banks managing the process. In a corporate or municipal debt deal, syndicate also determines the allocation of bonds.

Corporate Finance

Stuffy bankers?

The stereotype of the corporate finance department is stuffy, arrogant (white and male) MBAs who frequent golf courses and talk on cell-phones nonstop. While this is increasingly less true, corporate finance remains the most white-shoe department in the typical investment bank. The atmosphere in corporate finance is, unlike that in sales and trading, often quiet and reserved. Junior bankers sit separated by cubicles, quietly crunching numbers.

Depending on the firm, corporate finance can also be a tough place to work, with unforgiving bankers and expectations through the roof. Although decreasing, stories of analyst abuse run rampant and some bankers come down hard on new analysts simply to scare and intimidate them. The lifestyle for corporate finance professionals can be a killer. In fact, many corporate finance workers find that they literally dedicate their lives to the job. Social life suffers, free time disappears and stress multiplies. It is not uncommon to find analysts and associates wearing rumpled pants and wrinkled shirts, exhibiting the wear and tear of all-nighters. Fortunately, these long hours pay remarkable dividends in the form of six-figure salaries and huge year-end bonuses.

Personality-wise, bankers tend to be highly intelligent, motivated, and not lacking in confidence. Money is very much a driving motivation for bankers, and many anticipate working for just a few years to earn as much as possible, before finding less demanding work. Analysts and associates tend also to be ambitious, intelligent and pedigreed. If you happen to be going into an analyst or associate position, make sure to check your ego at the door but don't be afraid to ask penetrating questions about deals and what is required of you.

The deal team

Investment bankers generally work in deal teams which, depending on the size of a deal, vary somewhat in makeup. In the paragraphs below, we will provide an overview of the roles and lifestyles of the positions in corporate finance, from analyst to managing director. (Often, a person in corporate finance is generally called an I-banker.) Because the titles and roles really do not differ significantly between underwriting to M&A, we have included both in this explanation. In fact, at most smaller firms, underwriting and transaction advisory are not separated, and bankers typically pitch whatever business they can scout out within their industry sector.

The Players

Analysts are the grunts of the corporate finance world. They often toil endlessly with little thanks, little pay (when figured on an hourly basis), and barely enough free time to sleep four hours a night. Typically hired directly out of top undergraduate universities, this crop of bright, highly motivated kids does the financial modeling and basic entry-level duties associated with any corporate finance deal.

Modeling every night until 2 a.m. and not having much of a social life proves to be unbearable for many an analyst. Furthermore, when not at the office, analysts can be found feverishly typing on their BlackBerries. Not surprisingly, after two years, many analysts leave the industry. Unfortunately, many bankers recognize the transient nature of analysts and work

Visit Vault at **www.vault.com** for insider company profiles, expert advice,
career message boards, expert resume reviews, the Vault Job Board and more.

VAULT CAREER LIBRARY 153

them hard to get the most out of them they can. The unfortunate analyst who screws up or talks back too much may never get quality work, spending his days bored until 11 p.m. waiting for work to come, stressing even more than the busy analyst. These are the analysts who do not get called to work on live transatctions and do menial work or just put together pitchbooks all of the time. The very best analysts often get identified early by top performing MDs and VPs, thus finding themselves staffed on many live transactions.

When it comes to analyst pay, much depends on whether the analyst is in New York or not. In NYC, salary often begins for first-year analysts at $55,000 to $70,000 per year, with an annual bonus of approximately $60,000 to $85,000. While this seems to be quite a lot for a 22-year-old with just an undergrad degree, it's not a great deal if you consider per-hour compensation. Bonuses at this level are also force-ranked, thus identifying and compensating top talent. At most firms, analysts also get dinner every night for free if they work late, and have little time to spend their income, often meaning fat checking and savings accounts and ample fodder to fund business school or law school down the road. At regional firms, pay typically is 20 percent less than that of their New York counterparts. Worth noting, though, is the fact that at regional firms (1) hours are often less, and (2) the cost of living is much lower. Be wary, however, of the small regional firm or branch office of a Wall Street firm that pays at the low end of the scale and still shackles analysts to their cubicles.

Regardless of location, while the salary generally does not improve much for second-year analysts, the bonus will dramatically increase for those second-years who demonstrate high performance. At this level, bonuses depend mostly on an analyst's contribution, attitude and work ethic, as opposed to the volume of business generated by the bankers with whom he or she works.

Associates

Much like analysts, associates hit the grindstone hard. Working 80- to 100-hour weeks, usually fresh out of top-tier MBA programs, associates stress over pitchbooks and models all night, become experts with financial modeling on Excel, and sometimes shake their heads wondering what the point is. Unlike analysts, however, associates more quickly become involved with clients and, most importantly, are not at the bottom of the totem pole. Associates quickly learn to play quarterback and hand-off menial modeling work and research projects to analysts. However, treatment from vice presidents and managing directors doesn't necessarily improve for associates versus analysts, as bankers sometimes care more about the work getting done, and not about the guy or gal working away all night to complete it.

Usually hailing directly from top business schools (sometimes law schools or other grad schools), associates often possess only a summer's worth of experience in corporate finance, so they must start almost from the beginning. Associates who worked as analysts before grad school have a little more experience under their belts. The overall level of business awareness and knowledge a bright MBA has, however, makes a tremendous difference, and associates quickly earn the luxury of more complicated work, client contact and bigger bonuses.

Associates are at least much better paid than analysts. A $95,000 to $100,000 salary generally starts them off, and usually bonuses hit $35,000 to $55,000 or more in the first six months. (At most firms, associates start in August and get their first prorated bonus in January.) Newly minted MBAs cash in on signing bonuses and forgivable loans as well, especially on Wall Street. These can amount to another $35,000 to $55,000, depending on the firm, providing total first-year compensation over $200,000 for top firms. Associates beyond their first year begin to rake it in, earning $250,000 to $500,000 and up per year, depending on the firm's profitability and other factors.

Vice presidents

Upon attaining the position of vice president (at most firms, after four or five years as associates), those in corporate finance enter the realm of real bankers. The lifestyle becomes more manageable once the associate moves up to VP. On the plus side, weekends sometimes free up, all-nighters drop off, and the general level of responsibility increases—VPs are the ones telling associates and analysts to stay late on Friday nights. In the office, VPs manage the financial modeling/pitchbook production process in the Corporate Finance office. On the negative side, the wear and tear of traveling that accompanies VP-level banker responsibilities can be difficult. As a VP, one begins to handle client relationships, and thus spends much more time on the road than analysts or associates. As a VP, you can look forward to being on the road at least two to four days per week, usually visiting current and potential clients. Don't forget about closing dinners (to celebrate completed deals), industry conferences (to drum up potential business and build a solid network within their industry), and, of course, roadshows. VPs are perfect candidates to baby-sit company management on roadshows.

Directors/managing directors

Directors and managing directors (MDs) are the major players in corporate finance. Typically, MDs set their own hours, deal with clients at the highest level, and disappear whenever a drafting session takes place, leaving this grueling work to others. (We will examine these drafting sessions in depth later.) MDs mostly develop and cultivate relationships with various companies in order to generate corporate finance business for the firm. At this point in a banker's career, the job completes the transition from managing a process to managing a relationship. MDs typically focus on one industry, develop relationships among management teams of companies in the industry, and visit these companies pitching ideas on a regular basis. These visits are aptly called sales calls.

A Day in the Life: Associate, Corporate Finance

We've asked insiders at leading investment banks to offer us insight into a day in the life of their position. Here's a look at a day of an associate I-banker at Goldman Sachs.

8:15 a.m. Arrive at 85 Broad Street. (Show Goldman ID card to get past the surly elevator guards.)

8:25 a.m. Arrive on 17th Floor. Use "blue card" to get past floor lobby. ("Don't ever forget your blue card. Goldman has tight security and you won't be able to get around the building all day.")

8:45 a.m. Pick up work from word processing department, review it, make changes.

9 a.m. Check voicemail, return phone calls.

9:30 a.m. Eat breakfast; read *The Wall Street Journal*. ("But don't let a supervisor see you with your paper sprawled across your desk.")

10 a.m. Prepare pitchbooks, discuss analysis with members of deal team.

12 p.m. Conference call with members of IPO team, including lawyers and client.

1 p.m. Eat lunch at desk. ("The Wall Street McDonald's delivers, but it's the most expensive McDonald's in New York City; Goldman's cafeteria is cheaper, but you have to endure the shop talk.")

2 p.m. Work on restructuring case studies; make several document requests from Goldman library.

3 p.m. Start to prepare analysis; order additional data from DRG (data resources group).

5 p.m. Check in with vice presidents and heads of deal teams on status of work.

6 p.m. Go to gym for an abbreviated workout.

6:45 p.m. Dinner. ("Dinner is free in the IBD cafeteria, but avoid it. Wall Street has pretty limited food options, so for a quick meal it's the Indian place across the street that's open 24 hours.")

8 p.m. Meet with VP again. ("You'll probably get more work thrown at you before he leaves.")

Visit Vault at **www.vault.com** for insider company profiles, expert advice, career message boards, expert resume reviews, the Vault Job Board and more.

VAULT CAREER LIBRARY   155

9:45 p.m. Try to make FedEx cutoff. Drop off pitchbook to document processing department on the 20th Floor. ("You have to call ahead and warn them if you have a last-minute job or you're screwed.")

10 p.m. Order in food again. ("It's unlikely that there will be any room left in your meal allowance—but we usually order in a group and add extra names to bypass the limit.")

11 p.m. Leave for home. ("Call for a car service. Enjoy your nightly 'meal on wheels' on the way home.")

Mergers & Acquisitions

Mergers & Acquisitions (M&A) transactions can be roughly divided into either mergers or acquisitions. These terms are often used interchangeably in the press, and the actual legal difference between the two involves arcana of accounting procedures, but we can still draw a rough difference between the two.

Acquisition: When a larger company takes over another (smaller firm) and clearly becomes the new owner, the purchase is typically called an acquisition on Wall Street. Typically, the target company ceases to exist post-transaction (from a legal corporation point of view) and the acquiring corporation swallows the business. The stock of the acquiring company continues to be traded.

Merger: A merger occurs when two companies, often roughly of the same size, combine to create a new company. Such a situation is often called a "merger of equals." Both companies' stocks are tendered (or given up), and new company stock is issued in its place. For example, both Chrysler and Daimler-Benz ceased to exist when their firms merged, and a new combined company, DaimlerChrysler was created.

M&A advisory services

For an I-bank, M&A advising is highly profitable, and there are many possibilities for types of transactions. Perhaps a small private company's owner/manager wishes to sell out for cash and retire. Or perhaps a big public firm aims to buy a competitor through a stock swap. Whatever the case, M&A advisors come directly from the corporate finance departments of investment banks. Unlike public offerings, merger transactions do not directly involve salespeople, traders or research analysts, although research analysts in particular can play an important role in "blessing" the merger. In particular, M&A advisory falls onto the laps of M&A specialists and fits into one of either two buckets: seller representation or buyer representation (also called target representation and acquirer representation).

Representing the target

An I-bank that represents a potential seller has a much greater likelihood of completing a transaction (and therefore being paid) than an I-bank that represents a potential acquirer. Also known as sell-side work, this type of advisory assignment is generated by a company that approaches an investment bank (also an investment bank may also make the initial approach and "pitch" the idea of the company being sold or merged) and asks the bank to find a buyer of either the entire company or a division. Often, sell-side representation comes when a company asks an investment bank to help it sell a division, plant or subsidiary operation.

Generally speaking, the work involved in finding a buyer includes writing a Selling Memorandum and then contacting potential strategic or financial buyers of the client. If the client hopes to sell a semiconductor plant, for instance, the I-bankers will contact firms in that industry, as well as buyout firms that focus on purchasing technology or high-tech manufacturing operations. In the case of many LBO transactions, a sell-side firm might even hold an "auction" in which it will accept bids for the company, in order to get the seller the best price possible for its property.

Representing the acquirer

In advising sellers, the I-bank's work is complete once another party purchases the business up for sale, i.e., once another party buys your client's company or division or assets. Buy-side work is an entirely different animal. The advisory work itself is straightforward: the investment bank contacts the firm their client wishes to purchase, attempts to structure a palatable offer for all parties, and makes the deal a reality. (Again, the initial contact may be from the acquiring company. Or the investment bank may "pitch" the idea of an acquisition of Company X to the acquiring company.) However, most of these proposals do not work out; few firms or owners are readily willing to sell their business. And because the I-banks primarily collect fees based on completed transactions, their work often goes unpaid. However, this doesn't stop investment banks from dreaming up new proposals.

Consequently, when advising clients looking to buy a business, an I-bank's work often drags on for months. Often a firm will pay a nonrefundable retainer fee to hire a bank and say, "Find us a target company to buy." These acquisition searches can last for months and produce nothing except associate and analyst fatigue as they repeatedly build merger models and pull all-nighters. Deals that do get done, though, are a boon for the I-bank representing the buyer because of their enormous profitability. Typical fees depend on the size of the deal, but generally fall in the one-two percent range. For a $100 million deal, an investment bank takes home $1 to $2 million. Not bad for a few months' work.

The Year in Review

Crisis marks the end of an era

During summer 2007, the phrase "credit crisis" took center stage. The nation watched helplessly as the subprime housing market imploded, affecting nearly every sector imaginable. Among the first to feel the crunch were the U.S. banking giants, some of which had seemed infallible. The crisis set off instability in financial markets both international and stateside, resulting in skittish investors. The crisis continued into 2008, and within the first quarter, more write-downs (reductions in book values of assets due to their being overvalued compared to their market values) at financial institutions only made investors wary, setting off drops in market liquidity. By March 2008, conditions were explosive, setting off the demise of global investment bank Bear Stearns. A few months later, the crisis took down another investment bank, as the U.S. government took control of the leading but ailing home mortgage companies, Fannie Mae and Freddie Mac. U.S. Treasury Secretary Henry Paulson indicated that allowing either of the giants to fail would "cause great turmoil" for domestic and international financial markets. To this end, his predictions seemed accurate; stocks rallied after the takeover announcement was made.

But the market gains were short-lived, and not long after, the credit crisis claimed its second investment bank, as Lehman Brothers filed for Chapter 11 bankruptcy in September 2008 after the federal government refused to support a takeover of the bank as it did for Bear. However, a few days after the filing, British giant Barclays stepped in, agreeing to purchase Lehman's U.S. investment banking operations, saving 10,000 jobs in the process. This was followed by Japan's Nomura agreeing to buy Lehman's Asian operations, which included about 3,000 employees.

On the same day that Lehman filed Chapter 11, Merrill Lynch—attempting to avoid a bankruptcy filing—agreed to be bought by Bank of America for $44 billion. The combination of BofA and Merrill Lynch—which was worth about $100 million not too long before the deal was announced—will create the country's largest brokerage house and consumer banking franchise. Merrill's 17,000 brokers and BofA's wealth managers will combine to form a powerful unit that will be known as Merrill Lynch Wealth Management.

And this was just the beginning of the changes on Wall Street. Two days after Lehman's bankruptcy filing and Merrill's acquisition of BofA, the crisis hit another boiling point, as the U.S. government seized control of American International Group, the monstrous insurance giant commonly known as AIG. The deal was a monumental one, putting a private insurance firm into the hands of the government and thus placing U.S. taxpayer dollars on the hook. The deal sent $85 billion to AIG in the form of a federal loan and handed the U.S. government an approximate 80 percent stake in the insurance company. The deal also sent banking stocks

Visit Vault at www.vault.com for insider company profiles, expert advice, career message boards, expert resume reviews, the Vault Job Board and more.

VAULT CAREER LIBRARY   157

plummeting, as investors feared that more banks than were thought had huge liquidity issues. Included in those financial firms were the last two large independent investment banks still standing: perennial league table leader Goldman Sachs and perennial runner-up Morgan Stanley. Both firms' shares took nosedives when the AIG rescue was announced, with Morgan Stanley's shares falling about 24 percent and Goldman's slipping 19 percent (at one point, Morgan's shares were down an astounding 44 percent and Goldman's were in the hole by as much as 26 percent). Although both firm's shares rebounded a day later, they would soon make moves that would significantly change the face of investment banking as we know it.

On the heels of its seizing control of Fannie Mae, Freddie Mac and AIG, the Feds stepped in again to try to help curtail the financial crisis plaguing bank's and other financial institution, temporarily banning short selling and backing $50 billion in money market funds as well entering talks to buy up distressed mortgages, putting the U.S. government on the hook for up to $1 trillion. This was indeed good news for banks in distress, and the U.S. stock market reacted with making a huge leap. But this also underscored just how bad the situation was for everyone, including the top dogs on Wall Street. And on September 21, 2008, Goldman Sachs and Morgan Stanley decided to take matters into their own hands. In the midst of Congress endeavoring to pass a $700 billion rescue package for big Wall Street players, Goldman and Morgan both requested to become bank holding companies. The requests were granted by the Federal Reserve, giving them the backing of bank deposits instead of relying on high-risk forms of financing.

By becoming bank holding companies—which gives the two venerable Wall Street firms a similar status as commercial banking behemoths Citi, BofA and JPMorgan Chase—Goldman and Morgan Stanley will now be closely regulated by several federal supervising organizations, and not only overseen by the SEC. The holding company status also means Goldman and Morgan will have to lower the amount they can borrow versus their capital, resulting in financially safer institutions with limited upside potential with respect to profits.

On the same day it became a bank holding company, Morgan Stanley also entered into an agreement with Mitsubishi UFJ Financial Group, which will buy 10 to 20 percent of Morgan Stanley's common stock. The Japanese bank has been making a big move in the U.S. recently. In August 2008, it acquired the remaining one-third of San Francisco-based UnionBanCal that it did not already own.

The fall of Bear

Though the effects of the credit crisis were felt throughout the industry, Bear Stearns—the investment house with the highest exposure to overvalued mortgage-backed securities—was harder hit than most. In October 2007, the bank announced that it would let go more than 310 staffers and combine its separate mortgage businesses into one. Its two home loan-related hedge funds—the High Grade Structured Credit Strategies Fund and its similarly named Enhanced Leverage counterpart—had imploded in July, turning $1.6 billion of investors' funds to dust (this was seen by some as the beginning of the credit crisis). Bear Stearns was forced to write off $200 million with the stroke of a pen—and fired the executive responsible for the asset management department, co-president Warren Spector.

Despite the lingering cloud and a disastrous third quarter (in which its revenue in fixed income declined 88 percent), Bear Stearns management asserted in October that it was cautiously optimistic, asserting that "most of our businesses are beginning to rebound." This cautious optimism proved unfounded, and in December 2007, the firm revealed its quarterly results, including a staggering $854 million loss—the first quarterly loss in Bear Stearns' history. Most of the losses came from write-downs, which the firm reported were $700 million greater than expected. Despite the quarterly results, Bear CEO James Cayne claimed his confidence in the company was "rock solid." In response to the disappointing results, Cayne and other Bear executives noted that they were foregoing their holiday bonuses—"as it should be," according to Cayne himself. In January 2008, when Bear's future took a turn for the worse, Cayne resigned.

In March 2008, facing collapse, Bear received a temporary reprieve when JPMorgan Chase & Co. and the New York Federal Reserve moved in to provide the firm with emergency funding. Bear, whose shares immediately fell 53 percent on the news, admitted that its financial situation had "significantly deteriorated" after it fell prey to a cash shortage brought on by the credit crisis. But within a matter of days, the situation turned even more dire. Fearing Bear's cash shortage, the firm's clients withdrew approximately $17 billion over two days, leaving the 85-year-old Bear with no choice (other than claiming bankruptcy) but to sell. And on Monday, March 16th, that sale became official when JPMorgan Chase announced it would buy Bear for $2 a share—just $236 million, or approximately 97 percent less than Bear's value in the previous week. (After much grumbling from Bear shareholders, the deal was cut at a higher value: $10 a share.) To help finance the deal, the Federal Reserve agreed to provide J.P. Morgan with about a $30 billion credit line, "believed to be the largest Fed advance on record to a single company," according to *The Wall Street Journal.*

Aftershocks of the buyout were felt all around the world. In Japan, stocks immediately sunk to the lowest they'd been in two years. Analysts in the U.K. predicted a depression on the scale of that which occured in the 1930s. Swiss-based UBS announced it would likely cut another 8,000 jobs. And in the U.S., financial stocks plummeted during the first few hours of trading on March 17th.

JPMorgan Chase, meanwhile, stepped forward to answer questions about what would become of Bear Stearns' employees. The bank stated that about 50 percent of job offers extended by Bear Stearns would be rescinded. Summer interns had it a little better—the firm assured summer interns that they "will be offered 10 weeks of pay if they work for a certain nonprofit organization and will get an early chance to apply for fall positions." Graduates denied full-time jobs were allowed to keep their signing and relocation bonuses, and given access to career services. The cuts came mostly in areas where there was overlap, such as M&A, equity underwriting and corporate finance. Offers in investment management and other areas such as commodities, merchant banking and prime brokerage (Bear's jewel) were unaffected.

Plenty of pink slips

For others in the banking trenches, the situation didn't look much rosier. Credit Suisse was one of the first big finance firms to downsize in response to the credit crisis, slashing about 150 jobs in September 2007. By the beginning of 2008, Credit Suisse confirmed that market conditions had caused the company to cut about 500 investment banking positions—a total of about 20 percent of the group. Goldman Sachs, which had estimated job cuts to be around 10 percent earlier in the year, said in June 2008 that 25 percent of its investment banking employees (about 1,500) at the vice president level had been cut. Morgan Stanley didn't fare much better, announcing in February 2008 that it would cut 1,000 jobs in its operations, technology and asset management units, in addition to shutting down its U.K. home loan business and decreasing the size of its U.S. counterpart. And in reaction to a $6 billion write-down in the first quarter of 2008 and its third quarterly loss in a row, Merrill Lynch announced in April 2008 that it would cut 3,000 positions (adding to the 1,100 the firm slashed in the first quarter of 2008).

Deutsche Bank, meanwhile, announced in April 2008 that it was cutting nearly 1,000 investment banking jobs in mortgage banking and other areas. Though the number was not in the realm of some its banking brethren, it still spelled trouble for Deutsche, which reported its first quarterly loss in five years—a €131 million net loss for the first quarter of 2008, contrasted with a €2.12 billion profit in the first quarter of 2007. UBS felt the pinch of the credit crunch, too, announcing in May 2008 that it would be cutting approximately 5,500 jobs, in addition to the 1,500 positions it eliminated in 2007. No doubt the news had just a little bit to do with UBS's first quarter loss of $10.9 billions.

Citi fared the worst of all the big banks, announcing at the beginning of 2008 that it was cutting 4,200 jobs, bringing its ultimate total number of layoffs close to 20,000 to 24,000. A few months later, it slashed another 2,000 positions. (Citi, perhaps in a damage control move, announced that it was simply culling the "bottom 5 percent of performers" each year.)

Though no bank was able to remain truly impervious to the credit crunch, some firms had it worse than others. In March 2008, Lehman Brothers announced that it was laying off about 5 percent of its total workforce of 28,600 employees. The cuts, which affected all of its business units, were hardly the first wave of cutbacks for Lehman—in 2007, the company slashed about 4,000 jobs, mostly in its mortgage operations arm. In the second quarter of 2008, some analysts were predicting that Lehman would be the next firm to fall—in a July 2008 poll on the financial site Motley Fool, more than 40,000 respondents chose Lehman Brothers as the next firm to have a "Bear Stearns-style implosion." (As of mid-July, Lehman's stock price was hovering around $20 per share, well below its 52-week high of $70, but higher than its 52-week low of $12 per share, which the stock traded at in early July.)

Visit Vault at **www.vault.com** for insider company profiles, expert advice, career message boards, expert resume reviews, the Vault Job Board and more.

VΛULT CAREER LIBRARY   **159**

Cuts at all levels

All in all, estimated layoffs for the banking industry since its mortgage-related downfall were a staggering 79,000 jobs, the Bureau of Labor Statistics reported in January 2008. And those at the top were hardly exempt from the axe. In addition to the resignation of Bear Stearns' Cayne, there were quite a few shake-ups at the top of banking pyramids.

In July 2007, UBS's CEO Peter Wuffli was cut from the firm, and replaced by deputy CEO Marcel Rohner. Wuffli's removal was largely attributed to the collapse of a hedge fund the firm managed. In November 2007, Merrill Lynch took drastic action after posting a $8.4 billion write-down and a $2.3 billion loss for the third quarter of 2007 (its largest quarterly loss ever), forcing CEO Stan O'Neal to step down. In his place Merrill substituted New York Stock Exchange Chief John Thain, after BlackRock CEO Larry Fink declined the position, insisting on full transparency of Merrill's exposure to the subprime market.

In December 2007, Citi had a full-time search on its hands after CEO Charles Prince resigned in November. The firm settled on Vikram S. Pandit to take over the reins. Pandit had only spent six months at the firm, but still managed to beat out such candidates as Robert B. Willumstad, Citi's former president, and Michael A. Neal, the head of GE Capital's commercial finance division. Wachovia also made a major change, asking CEO Ken Thompson to retire in June 2008. The request followed Wachovia's significant losses (including $707 million in the first quarter of 2008) due to failure to successfully integrate A.G. Edwards and buying mortgage lender Golden West not long before the subprime mess. A month later, Wachovia found Thompson's replacement, naming Robert K. Steel—former undersecretary of the U.S. Treasury—as its new chief executive and president.

Tough times for the top women of Wall Street

In April 2008, Morgan Stanley co-president Zoe Cruz—heir-apparent to Morgan's CEO throne and the 16th most powerful woman in the world, according to *Forbes* magazine—was summarily dismissed by CEO John Mack. Some argue that Cruz took the fall for Mack, who lobbied for her firing as a preemptive move to save his own job.

Lehman Brothers' Erin Callan—considered the most powerful woman on Wall Street after Cruz—suffered a similar fate in June 2008, when she was demoted from her position as chief financial officer, a spot she only held for a few short months. In July 2008, Callan left Lehman to head up Credit Suisse's global hedge fund unit. Callan's departure came as little surprise for Lehman Brothers, which had suffered a net loss of $2.8 billion in the second quarter of 2008. (Throughout her term as financial officer at Lehman, Callan argued for more transparency in financial reporting.) Callan's move to the Swiss giant's hedge fund arm was a coming home of sorts—she worked for Lehman's hedge fund unit at the start of her 13-year career with the firm.

The ballad of Fannie and Freddie

Although the departure of CEOs and other top executives certainly made good drama, virtually nothing made the credit crisis more pronounced than the consumer fear surrounding the uncertainty of the future of mortgage giants Freddie Mac and Fannie Mae. The mortgage agencies' stocks both lost half their value in July 2008—an event that some analysts said was worse for the financial markets than the collapse of Bear Stearns. (Fannie has lost about $7.2 billion since mid-2007 and Freddie has lost about $4.6 billion.) Following the stock nosedives, the U.S. Treasury finagled a few favors from Congress on behalf of the two agencies: a temporary increase in a credit line for Fannie and Freddie, along with temporary authority to purchase equity in one or both of the mortgage companies.

After much negotiation regarding the fate of Fannie and Freddie, House and Senate heads reached a tentative agreement within a few weeks. The Congressional Budget Office reported that a temporary plan to bail out Fannie and Freddie could cost the government $25 billion, including a $4 billion provision that would let local governments purchase and restore previously foreclosed houses.

You can run, but you can't hide

In early 2008, the FBI announced that it had begun a criminal investigation into 14 companies, as part of a larger inquiry into what had gone wrong with the mortgage industry. Goldman Sachs, Morgan Stanley and famously-defunct Bear Stearns received requests for information about subprime mortgage-linked securities. The FBI investigation, which is being carried out in cooperation with the Securities and Exchange Commission, has also targeted mortgage lenders and loan brokers.

By June 2008, effects of the investigation finally began to trickle down. Former Bear Stearns hedge fund managers Ralph Cioffi and Matthew Tannin were taken into custody—the first two arrests in conjunction with the probe. Cioffi and Tannin each face nine counts of conspiracy, securities fraud and wire fraud for purportedly deceiving investors about the stability of Bear's hedge funds. More arrests—at additional firms—are expected to follow as the query into the $396.6 billion fraud deepens.

The tables don't lie

Despite the rocky second half of 2007, investment banking league tables looked much as they did in 2006. In total global debt, equity and equity-related underwriting volume, Citi ranked No. 1 for the second consecutive year, according to Thomson Reuters. Citi, which worked on 1,740 deals worth a total of $617.6 billion, had its hands in two of the world's largest deals of the year: Blackstone's $4.75 billion IPO, underwritten by Citi, Morgan Stanley and 15 other banks; and MF Global Ltd.'s $2.92 billion IPO, underwritten by Citi, J.P. Morgan, Lehman Brothers, Merrill Lynch and UBS Investment Bank.

In worldwide announced M&A deal volume, perennial powerhouse Goldman Sachs again ranked No. 1, with Morgan Stanley in second place and Citi in third. Goldman also again took the top spot in the U.S., with Morgan in second and Lehman Brothers in third. As far as the largest worldwide transactions, BHP Billiton's acquisition of Rio Tinto down under in Australia for $192.7 billion came in at No. 1, followed by ABN-AMRO Holding's $99.4 billion sale and the $61.4 billion spinoff of Kraft Foods. By industry sector, financial services was the busiest when it came to merging, acquiring and divesting in 2007, with about 5,000 announced deals worth a total of $700 billion. In the U.S., overall M&A deal volume for the year hit a record $1.57 trillion, a 5.5 percent increase versus 2006.

The Fortune-ate ones

The 2008 Fortune 500 list included in its top 40 a number of big banking players, including Citi (No. 8), Bank of America (No. 9), JPMorgan Chase (No. 12), Goldman Sachs (No. 20), Morgan Stanley (No. 21), Merrill Lynch (No. 30), Lehman Brothers (No. 37) and Wachovia (No. 38). Goldman Sachs also ranked No. 2 on *Fortune*'s Best Companies to Work For list.

Small goes big time

Since the credit crunch began, it's been a big time for smaller boutique banks such as Moelis & Co., which advised on a number of big-ticket deals, including Yahoo!'s $44.6 billion unsolicited proposal from Microsoft, Allied Waste's pending $12.7 billion sale to Republic Services and Anheuser-Busch's $61.2 billion sale to InBev.

There has also recently been a good deal of jockeying for status between big name banking players. For years, J.P. Morgan Chase was the third-biggest bank in the U.S., trailing just behind Citi (Bank of America being No 1.). This rankled J.P. Morgan CEO Jamie Dimon, who spent many years at Citi under Sanford Weill. But Weill turned on Dimon in the late 1990s, ousting him and installing former CEO Charles Prince in his place. Dimon went on to a career at Bank One, which he then merged with JPMorgan Chase. In January 2008, Dimon had reason to cheer (despite the fact that his firm had taken a $1.3 billion subprime write-down and posted lower-than-expected earnings for 2007): for the first time, JPMorgan Chase's market value surpassed that of Citigroup's—$136 billion to $129.8 billion, to be exact. Although Citi still holds more assets, Dimon won bragging rights, declaring his firm the second-largest bank in America by market value.

Visit Vault at **www.vault.com** for insider company profiles, expert advice, career message boards, expert resume reviews, the Vault Job Board and more.

VAULT CAREER LIBRARY 161

Final completion

The long-awaited ABN AMRO transaction was finally completed in October 2007 after many months of anticipation and talks with Barclays, which ultimately bowed out of the deal. In April 2007, ABN AMRO received a letter from a consortium made up of Banco Santander, the Royal Bank of Scotland and Fortis—an invitation to start exploratory merger talks. The three-bank consortium ultimately offered about $90 billion for ABN AMRO—$10 billion more than Barclays was offering. In October 2007, Barclays withdrew its bid for ABN AMRO and received break-up fees of €200 million from ABN AMRO. ABN AMRO was then officially purchased by the consortium.

Other high-profile (but less pricey) banking buys include Jefferies' June 2007 purchase of the Putnam Lovell investment banking business from Canada's National Bank Financial Group, and Oppenheimer Holdings' January 2008 acquisition of most of CIBC World Markets' U.S. investment banking business.

Down and out on Wall Street

Following the onslaught of the credit crisis, job security for those working in the industry became shaky at best. And a 2008 report by the National Association of College & Employers concerning the job outlook for several industries confirmed the gloomy career picture: For jobs in the financial sector—including banking and other fields—hiring was down overall by 7 percent.

Compensation will also be down in 2008. At a news conference in Albany in July 2008, New York Governor David Paterson said that Wall Street banks could end up slashing bonuses by approximately 20 percent in 2008. Paterson also scoffed at economists who believe the U.S. will not experience a recession: "This has finally confirmed to me that flying saucers have landed and that people from outer space are in our midst, influencing policy."

Whether alien life forms are trying to infiltrate legislative bodies or not, it's highly probable that, given the hits that most banks have already taken, bankers will close 2008 with significantly lighter wallets.

More failures ahead?

Analysts have predicted more bank failures in the industry's immediate future. *The New York Times* reported in July 2008 that federal regulators are steadying themselves for more bank closures, and analysts predict that some 150 of 7,500 small and mid-sized banks may fail over the next year to year-and-a-half.

Meanwhile, in 2007, the Federal Deposit Insurance Corporation flagged 76 "problem" banks, up from 50 at the end of 2006. Still, the FDIC has also assured customers that the state of the industry has been much worse—there were more than 1,000 banks on the same list toward the end of the last banking crisis, in 1992.

The final chapter in Lehman's history: 11

After being unsuccessful in its efforts to find a corporate buyer, Lehman announced on September 15, 2008, that it would file for Chapter 11 bankruptcy, a form of bankruptcy under which the firm would have its assets protected. The bankruptcy filing did not apply to Lehman Brother Asset Management or Neuberger Berman, LLC, whose portfolio management, research and operating functions will remain intact.

Over the course of the weekend leading up to the bankruptcy decision, potential buyers Bank of America and Barclays Plc both pulled out of talks to acquire Lehman (in parts or as a whole). As far as the possibility of a government loan goes, it looks like the U.S. Treasury may be using Lehman as an example. Treasury Secretary Henry Paulson said in a briefing regarding the firm's demise that he "never once considered it appropriate to put taxpayer money on the line" to save Lehman Brothers. On September 15th, the firm's stock was down to a mere 21 cents a share—quite a tumble from the high of $67 a share it had traded at within the past 12 months.

One day after it filed bankruptcy, Lehman Brothers found a financial savior in the form of Barclays, which agreed to purchase parts of the struggling firm for $2 billion. The transaction will include Lehman's equity, fixed income and M&A advisory units. In addition to avoiding bankruptcy, the Barclays takeover prevented about 10,000 Lehman investment banking jobs from being cut (for the time being, at least).

Merrill's surprise selloff

After witnessing the demise of Lehman Brothers and deciding to take matters into its own hands, Merrill Lynch agreed to be acquired by Bank of America in an all-stock transaction for $29 a share (about $44 billion in total) in September 15, 2008. Some Street insiders speculated that the Federal Reserve might have played a part in helping to arrange the sale as a way to attempt damage control. The deal, which is expected to close in early 2009, has received approval from directors of Merrill Lynch and Bank of America. Shareholder and regulatory approvals are also needed before the transaction is finalized.

Meanwhile, Bank of America CEO Ken Lewis appeared confident regarding the bank's acquisition of Merrill. In a statement, Lewis said that BofA "could have rolled the dice and possibly got it at a cheaper price," but added that "the long-term benefits" and "a strategic opportunity" were attractive for the bank. Once Merrill is officially incorporated with Bank of America, Merrill will become the biggest brokerage house in the U.S., employing more than 20,000 financial advisers. The combined entity will also be the largest consumer banking company. At the end of the day on which the transaction was announced, Merrill sold for $17 a share (compared with the $29 a share it was purchased for). Merrill can only back out of the agreement if its shareholders vote against the transaction, but if Bank of America's shareholders oppose the deal, Bank of America or Merrill can terminate the agreement.

An end of an era

On September 21, 2008, while Morgan Stanley and Goldman Sachs—the last two large independent investment banks still standing—were granted requests to become bank holding companies, giving them the backing of bank deposits instead of relying on high-risk forms of financing (as of August 31, 2008, Morgan Stanley had $36 billion in retail deposits and Goldman had $20 billion). Morgan Stanley and Goldman will now be similar in status and will soon directly compete with the likes of Bank of America, Citi and JPMorgan Chase. The moves changed the face of Wall Street, ending the reign of the large independent brokerage house. Many analysts and industry observers expect both Goldman and Morgan Stanley to acquire commercial banking firms to beef up deposits, so in the near future, the banking landscape will likely look a lot different than it does now.

Visit Vault at **www.vault.com** for insider company profiles, expert advice, career message boards, expert resume reviews, the Vault Job Board and more.

VAULT CAREER LIBRARY 163

Employer Directory

Citi

388 Greenwich Street

New York, NY 10013

(212) 559-1000

www.oncampus.citi.com

Your ambitions are more than plans for the future. They're your hopes and dreams. They're a part of who you are and who you aspire to be. When you join Citi you'll cultivate those aspirations with market-leading training and exposure to the most complex and groundbreaking transactions around the world. You'll join a company with an impressive, far-reaching heritage. Among our proud alumni are finance ministers, Nobel Prize winners, and even New York's mayor. While ambitions have taken them in different directions, their business foundation began with Citi.

Whatever your dreams Citi can make them a reality.

Credit Suisse

11 Madison Avenue

New York, NY 10010

www.credit-suisse.com/standout

Active in over 50 countries and employing more than 45,000 people, Credit Suisse provides investment banking, private banking and asset management services to companies, institutional clients and high-net-worth individuals. In 2006, we announced record profits and launched an integrated banking platform. Now there are exceptional opportunities for further growth in new product areas and emerging markets; there are equally exceptional opportunities for people who can help deliver that growth.

We typically recruit MBAs to specialize in investment banking, fixed Income, equities, alternative investments, private banking and asset management. More information is available at www.credit-suisse.com/careers

Business Schools Credit Suisse Recruits From: University of Chicago GSB, Columbia University GSB, Cornell University Johnson School of Management, Harvard Business School, New York University Stern School of Business, University of Michigan Business School, Wharton Graduate School (University of Pennsylvania), as well as many other top business programs.

Employer Directory, cont.

Goldman, Sachs and Co.

85 Broad Street
New York, NY 10004
MBA Recruiting Contact: (212) 902-1000
www.gs.com/careers

Goldman Sachs is a leading global investment banking, securities and investment management firm that provides a wide range of services worldwide to a substantial and diversified client base that includes corporations, financial institutions, governments and high-net-worth individuals. Founded in 1869, it is one of the oldest and largest investment banking firms. The firm is headquartered in New York and maintains offices in London, Frankfurt, Tokyo, Hong Kong and other major financial centers around the world. Please visit our careers site for information about applying online and our recruiting process.

Schools Goldman recruits from

The following is a list of our primary cross-divisional target schools. The firm also hires from a number of additional schools on a divisional basis, and welcomes online applications from all business schools.

University of Chicago, Columbia University, Cornell University (Johnson), Dartmouth College (Tuck), Duke University (Fuqua), Harvard University, Indiana University (Kelley), University of Michigan (Ross), MIT (Sloan), Northwestern University (Kellogg), NYU (Stern), Stanford University, University of Texas (Rice), UCLA (Anderson), University of North Carolina (Kenan-Flagler), University of Pennsylvania (Wharton), University of Virginia (Darden), Vanderbilt University (Owen), Yale University.

Visit Vault at **www.vault.com** for insider company profiles, expert advice, career message boards, expert resume reviews, the Vault Job Board and more.

VAULT CAREER LIBRARY   165

Employer Directory, cont.

Allen & Company
711 Fifth Avenue, 9th Floor
New York, NY 10022
Phone: (212) 832-8000
Fax: (212) 832-8023
Firm does not have a web site.

Bank of America
100 North Tryon Street
Charlotte, NC 28255
Phone: (704) 388-2547
Fax: (704) 386-6699
www.bankofamerica.com

Bank of New York Mellon
1 Wall Street
New York, NY 10286
Phone: (212) 495-1784
Fax: (212) 809-9528
www.bnymellon.com

Barclays Capital
5 The North Colonnade
Canary Wharf
London, E14 4BB
United Kingdom
Phone: +44-20-7623-2323

200 Park Avenue
New York, NY 10166
Phone: (212) 412-4000
Fax: (212) 412-7300
www.barcap.com

The Blackstone Group
345 Park Avenue
New York, NY 10154
Phone: (212) 583-5000
Fax: (212) 583-5712
www.blackstone.com

BNP Paribas
16, boulevard des Italiens
Paris 75009
France
Phone: +33-1-4014-4546
Fax: +33-1-40-14-69-73

787 Seventh Avenue
New York, NY 10019
Phone: (212) 841-2000
Fax: (212) 841-2146
www.bnpparibas.com

Brown Brothers Harriman
140 Broadway
New York, NY 10005-1101
Phone: (212) 483-1818
Fax: (212) 493-8545
www.bbh.com

CIBC World Markets
MG Corporate Finance
300 Madison Avenue
New York, NY 10017
Phone: (212) 856-4000
www.cibcwm.com

Citi Consumer Banking
399 Park Avenue
New York, NY 10043
Phone: (800) 285-3000
Fax: (212) 793-3946
www.citi.com

Citi Institutional Clients Group
388 Greenwich Street
New York, NY 10013
www.citigroup.com

Citi Markets & Banking
388 Greenwich Street
New York, NY 10013
Phone: (212) 816-6000
www.citigroupcib.com

Citigroup Inc. (Citi)
399 Park Avenue
New York, NY 10043
Phone: (800) 285-3000
Fax: (212) 793-3946
www.citi.com

Cowen and Company LLC
1221 Avenue of the Americas
New York, NY 10020
Phone: (646) 562-1000
Fax: (646) 562-1741
www.cowen.com

Deloitte & Touche Corporate Finance LLC
600 Renaissance Center, Suite 900
Detroit, MI 48243-1704
Phone: (313) 396-3000
Fax: (313) 396-3618
www.investmentbanking.deloitte.com

Deutsche Bank
60 Wall Street
New York, NY 10003
Phone: (212) 250-2500
www.db.com

Dresdner Kleinwort
30 Gresham Street
P.O. Box 52715
London, EC2V 2XY
United Kingdom
Phone: +44-20-76-23-80-00

1301 Avenue of the Americas
New York, NY 10019
Phone: (212) 969-2700
www.dresdnerkleinwort.com

Evercore Partners
55 East 52nd Street, 43rd Floor
New York, NY 10055
Phone: (212) 857-3100
Fax: (212) 857-3101
www.evercore.com

Employer Directory, cont.

FBR Capital Markets
1001 19th Street North
Arlington, VA 22209
Phone: (703) 312-9500
Fax: (703) 312-9501
www.fbrcapitalmarkets

Gleacher Partners
660 Madison Avenue, 19th Floor
New York, NY 10021
Phone: (212) 418-4200
Fax: (212) 752-2711
www.gleacher.com

Greenhill & Co.
300 Park Avenue
New York, NY 10022
Phone: (212) 389-1500
www.greenhill.com

Houlihan Lokey
1930 Century Park West
Los Angeles, CA 90067
Phone: (310) 553-8871
Fax: (310) 553-2173
www.hl.com

HSBC North America Holdings Inc.
26525 North Riverwoods Boulevard
Mettawa, IL 60045
Phone: (224) 554-2000
Fax: (224) 552-4400
www.hsbcnorthamerica.com

Jefferies & Company
520 Madison Avenue, 12th Floor
New York, NY 10022
Phone: (212) 284-2300
www.jefferies.com

JMP Securities
600 Montgomery Street, Suite 1100
San Francisco, CA 94111
Phone: (415) 835-8900
Fax: (415) 835-8910
www.jmpsecurities.com

J.P. Morgan Chase Commercial Bank
270 Park Avenue
New York, NY 10017
Phone: (212) 270-6000
Fax: (212) 270-2613
www.jpmorganchase.com

J.P. Morgan Investment Bank
270 Park Avenue
New York, NY 10017
Phone: (212) 270-6000
Fax: (212) 270-2613
www.jpmorgan.com

Keefe Bruyette & Woods, Inc.
The Equitable Building
787 Seventh Avenue, 4th Floor
New York, NY 10019
Phone: (212) 887-7777
Fax: (212) 541-6668
www.kbw.com

KPMG Corporate Finance
120 Broadway, 23rd Floor
New York, NY 10271
Phone: (888) 957-5764
www.kpmgcorporatefinance.com

Lazard
30 Rockefeller Plaza
New York, NY 10020
Phone: (212) 632-6000
www.lazard.com

Macquarie Group
125 West 55th Street
New York, NY 10019
Phone: (212) 231-1000
www.macquarie.com/us

Moelis & Company
245 Park Avenue, 32nd Floor
New York, NY 10167
Phone: (212) 880-7300
Fax: (212) 880-4260
www.moelis.com

Morgan Keegan
Morgan Keegan Tower
50 Front Street, 17th Floor
Memphis, TN 38103
Phone: (901) 524-4100
Fax: (901) 579-4406
www.morgankeegan.com

Morgan Stanley
1585 Broadway
New York, NY 10036
Phone: (212) 761-4000
Fax: (212) 762-0575
www.morganstanley.com

Nomura Holdings, Inc.
1-9-1, Nihonbashi, Chuo-ku
Tokyo 103-8645
Japan
Phone: +81-3-52-55-10-00
Fax: +81-3-32-78-04-20

2 World Financial Center, Building B
New York, NY 10281-1198
Phone: (212) 667-9300
Fax: (212) 667-1058
www.nomura.com

Oppenheimer & Co.
125 Broad Street
New York, NY 10004
Phone: (212) 668-8000
www.opco.com

Perella Weinberg Partners
767 Fifth Avenue
New York, NY 10153
Phone: (212) 287-3200
Fax: (212) 287-3201
www.pwpartners.com

Piper Jaffray & Co.
800 Nicollet Mall, Suite 800
Minneapolis, MN 55402
Phone: (612) 303-6000
Fax: (612) 303-8199
www.piperjaffray.com

Visit Vault at www.vault.com for insider company profiles, expert advice,
career message boards, expert resume reviews, the Vault Job Board and more.

VAULT CAREER LIBRARY   167

Employer Directory, cont.

Raymond James Financial
880 Carillon Parkway
St. Petersburg, FL 33716
Phone: (727) 567-1000
Fax: (727) 567-5529
www.rjf.com

RBC Capital Markets
Royal Bank Plaza
200 Bay Street
Toronto, ON M5J 2W7
Canada
Phone: (416) 842-2000

1 Liberty Plaza
165 Broadway
New York, NY 10006-1404
Phone: (212) 428-700
www.rbccm.com

Robert W. Baird & Company
777 East Wisconsin Avenue
Milwaukee, WI 53202
Phone: (414) 765-3500
Fax: (414) 765-3633
www.rwbaird.com

Rothschild
Rothschild North America
1251 Avenue of Americas, 51st Floor
New York, NY 10020
Phone: (212) 403-3500
Fax: (212) 403-3501
www.us.rothschild.com

Royal Bank of Scotland
36 St Andrew Square
Edinburgh, EH2 2YB
Scotland
Phone: +44-13-15-56-85-55
www.rbs.com

Thomas Weisel Partners
1 Montgomery Street
San Francisco, CA 94104
Phone: (415) 364-2500
Fax: (415) 364-2695
www.tweisel.com

U.S. Bancorp
800 Nicollet Mall
Minneapolis, MN 55402
Phone: (800) 872-2657
www.usbank.com

UBS Investment Bank
299 Park Avenue
New York, NY 10171
Phone: (212) 821-3000
www.ibb.ubs.com

Wachovia Corporation
301 South College Street, Suite 4000
1 Wachovia Center
Charlotte, NC 28288-0013
Phone: (704) 374-6161
Fax: (704) 383-0996
www.wachovia.com

Wells Fargo
420 Montgomery Street
San Francisco, CA 94163
Phone: (866) 249-3302
www.wellsfargo.com

William Blair & Company LLC
222 West Adams Street
Chicago, IL 60606
Phone: (312) 236-1600
Fax: (312) 368-9418
www.williamblair.com

Investment Management

Do you enjoy following the financial markets—whether it be reading *The Wall Street Journal*, watching CNBC, or checking stock prices on the Internet? Do you consider yourself to be creative and analytical, opinionated and objective? If that is the case, you may find a career in investment management an appealing option.

Imagine an industry that rewards individuals for working independently, thinking on their feet and taking calculated risks. Additionally, how many industries can you think of that broadly impact households all over the world? Very few. That is one of the many exciting aspects of the asset management industry—with household increasing and the demise of Social Security as a tool for long-term savings, more people than ever before are planning for their future financial needs. As a result, the industry is growing and more visible than ever.

Investment Management vs. Asset Management

A quick note about the terms **investment management** and **asset management**: these terms are often used interchangeably. They refer to the same practice—the professional management of assets through investment. Investment management is used a bit more often when referring to the activity or career (i.e., "I'm an investment manager" or "That firm is gaining a lot of business in investment management"), whereas "asset management" is used more with reference to the industry itself (i.e., "The asset management industry").

More stability

Because of the stability of cash flows generated by the industry, investment management provides a relatively stable career when compared to some other financial services positions (most notably, investment banking). Investment management firms are generally paid a set fee as a percentage of assets under management. (The fee structure varies, and sometimes is both an asset-based fee plus a performance fee, especially for institutional investors.) Still, even when investment management fees involve a performance incentive, the business is much less cyclical than cousins like investment banking. Banking fees depend on transactions. When banking activities, such as IPOs and M&A transactions, dry up, so do fees for investment banks, which translates into layoffs of bankers. This occurred in 2000-2001, with the tech bubble burst, and most recently in late 2007 and 2008, with the subprime mortgage debacle. In contrast, assets are quite simply always being invested.

History

To better understand why asset management has become such a critical component of the broader financial services industry, we must first become acquainted with its formation and history.

The beginnings of a separate industry

While the informal process of managing money has been around since the beginning of the 20th century, the industry did not begin to mature until the early 1970s. Prior to that time, investment management was completely relationship-based. Assignments to manage assets grew out of relationships that banks and insurance companies already had with institutions—primarily companies or municipal organizations with employee pension funds—that had funds to invest. (A pension fund is set up as an employee benefit. Employers commit to a certain level of payment to retired employees each year and must manage their funds to meet these obligations. Organizations with large pools of assets to invest are called institutional investors.)

Visit Vault at **www.vault.com** for insider company profiles, expert advice, career message boards, expert resume reviews, the Vault Job Board and more.

VAULT CAREER LIBRARY   169

These asset managers were chosen in an unstructured way—assignments grew organically out of pre-existing relationships, rather than through a formal request for proposal and bidding process. The actual practice of investment management was also unstructured. At the time, asset managers might simply pick 50 stocks they thought were good investments—there was not nearly as much analysis on managing risk or organizing a fund around a specific category or style. (Examples of different investment categories include small cap stocks and large cap stocks.) Finally, the assets that were managed at the time were primarily pension funds. Mutual funds had yet to become broadly popular.

ERISA, 401(k) plans and specialist firms

The two catalysts for change in the industry were: (1) the broad realization that demographic trends would cause the U.S. government's retirement system (Social Security) to be under-funded, which made individuals more concerned with their retirement savings; and (2) the creation of ERISA (the Employment Retirement Income Security Act) in 1974, which gave employees incentives to save for retirement privately through 401(k) plans. (401(k) plans allow employees to save pre-tax earnings for their retirement.) These elements prompted an increased focus on long-term savings by individual investors and the formation of what can be described as a private pension fund market.

These fundamental changes created the opportunity for professional groups of money mangers to form "specialist" firms to manage individual and institutional assets. Throughout the 1970s and early 1980s, these small firms specialized in one or two investment styles (for example, core equities or fixed income investing).

During this period, the investment industry became fragmented and competitive. This competition added extra dimensions to the asset management industry. Investment skills, of course, remained critical. However, relationship building and the professional presentation of money management teams also began to become significant.

The rise of the mutual fund

In the early to mid 1980s, driven by the ERISA laws, the mutual fund came into vogue. While mutual funds had been around for decades, they were only generally used by almost exclusively financially sophisticated investors who paid a lot of attention to their investments. However, investor sophistication increased with the advent of modern portfolio theory (the set of tools developed to quantitatively analyze the management of a portfolio. Asset management firms began heavily marketing mutual funds as a safe and smart investment tool, pitching to individual investors the virtues of diversification and other benefits of investing in mutual funds. With more and more employers shifting retirement savings responsibilities from pension funds to the employees themselves, the 401(k) market grew rapidly. Consequently, consumer demand for new mutual fund products exploded (mutual funds are the preferred choice in most 401(k) portfolios). Many specialists responded by expanding their product offerings and focusing more on the marketing of their new services and capabilities.

Modern Portfolio Theory

Modern Portfolio Theory (MPT) was born in 1952 when University of Chicago economics student Harry Markowitz published his doctoral thesis, "Portfolio Selection," in the *Journal of Finance*. Markowitz, who won the Nobel Prize in economics in 1990 for his research and its far-reaching effects, provided the framework for what is now known as MPT. The theory quantifies the benefits of diversification, looking at how investors create portfolios in order to optimize market risk against expected returns. Markowitz, assuming all investors are risk averse, proposed that investors, when choosing a security to add to their portfolio, should not base their decision on the amount of risk that an individual security has, but rather on how that security contributes to the overall risk of the portfolio. To do this, Markowitz considered how securities move in relation to one another under similar circumstances. This is called "correlation," which measures how much two securities fluctuate in price relative to each other. Taking all this into account, investors can create "efficient portfolios," ones with the highest expected returns for a given level of risk.

Consolidation and globalization

The dominant themes of the industry in the 1990s were consolidation and globalization. As many former "specialists" rapidly expanded, brand recognition and advanced distribution channels (through brokers or other sales vehicles) became key success factors for asset management companies. Massive global commercial and investment banks entered the industry, taking business away from many specialist firms. Also, mutual fund rating agencies such as Lipper (founded in 1973, now a part of Reuters) and Morningstar (founded in Chicago in 1984) increased investor awareness of portfolio performance. These rating agencies publish reports on fund performance and rate funds on scales such as Morningstar's five-star rating system.

These factors led to a shakeout period of consolidation. Over the last 20 years, there have been well over 150 mergers in the industry, creating well-established and formidable players such as BlackRock and JP Morgan Asset Management. The top-10 mutual fund firms now control roughly 50 percent of total assets, while the top-20 mutual funds control roughly 65 percent of total assets.

Traditional vs. alternative asset managers

The dominant theme over the past five to 10 years has been the proliferation of alternative asset managers. It is necessary to make the distinction between traditional asset managers and alternative asset managers. Traditional asset managers (such as mutual funds) are highly regulated entities that are governed by strict laws and regulations. The Securities and Exchange Commission (SEC) is the principal governing body and regulates these funds under the Investment Company Act of 1940. The rules governing traditional asset managers are primarily instilled to protect the investors and limit the amount of unnecessary risk-taking. Traditional asset managers have defined investment mandates, which determine what types of securities and strategies they can pursue in a given portfolio.

Alternative asset managers include assets classes such as hedge funds, private equity and venture capital. Their investment strategies and regulation differ from traditional asset managers as they are lightly regulated investment vehicles that do not always have defined investment strategies or risk tolerances. These asset classes are often designed to be uncorrelated with the broad stock and bond markets and seek to provide positive returns in a variety of economic situations. Since alternative investments are very risky, investors need to be deemed "accredited" (which is determined by net worth) in order to invest in these products.

The Industry Today

A robust economy has led to ever-increasing wealth creation, which in turn led to even greater demand for money management services today. Some analysts estimate the total global investable asset universe to be worth around $60 trillion, having grown by roughly 10 percent annually over the past decade. According to Merrill Lynch, there are 9.5 million people across the world with greater than $1 million in financial assets, up from 8.2 million in 2004. Mutual fund demand has continued to increase; as of 2006, there were 9,000 different funds in the market (up from just 3,000 in 1990). In fact, nearly 50 million households invest in mutual funds, with a total worth of $24 trillion as of June 2007 ($1 trillion as recently as 1990).

As the industry has matured, total assets under management (AUM) in the United States have grown to $60 trillion. Consolidation and globalization have created a diverse list of leading industry players that range from well-capitalized divisions of investment banks, global insurance companies and multinational commercial banks to independent behemoths, such as Fidelity and Capital Group.

Working in the industry, unlike other areas of financial services like investment banking, does not require that you live in a particular region of the country.

Visit Vault at **www.vault.com** for insider company profiles, expert advice, career message boards, expert resume reviews, the Vault Job Board and more.

VAULT CAREER LIBRARY   **171**

The Three Segments

As you know, the investment management is usually considered the "buy-side" of the finance industry. (The buy-side refers to the asset managers who represent individual and institutional investors. The sell-side refers to the functions of an investment bank. Specifically, this includes investment bankers, traders and research analysts.) In general, investment management companies are less structured than most other types of finance firms, especially those on the sell-side. As a result, investment management positions have less defined job descriptions than positions at other types of finance firms.

For example, investment banking typically has a three-year analyst program for college grads, a three-year associate program for MBA grads (or directly promoted analysts), and then promotions to vice president and managing director. Investment management careers have a much less rigid hierarchy and there is usually no formal training program. Job descriptions for similar job titles in the investment management industry differ from firm to firm (for example, a new undergrad hire is considered an associate, not an analyst).

This presents the opportunity for very intelligent and successful individuals to be promoted at a very young age. In general, buy-side firms have a three-segment professional staff consisting of:

- Portfolio managers who invest money on behalf of clients
- Research analysts who provide portfolio managers with potential investment recommendations and in some cases invest money in their respective sectors
- Account and product managers who manage client relationships and distribute the investment products to individual and institutional investors

Asset management firms are organized into three segments: portfolio management, investment research and account/product management (marketing/sales). Below is a diagram that explains this structure.

As you can see from the diagram, both portfolio management and account/product management serve the client (whether they be individuals, institutions or high-net-worth investors). Alternatively, investment research falls under portfolio management, indicating its support of the investment process. While this represents a traditional hierarchy, asset managers can have varying structures. In many cases, the research analyst can also report directly to the client if he/she has money management responsibilities. An example of this would be Fidelity's "Select" funds in which the industry analysts manage money directly in their industries of expertise.

Portfolio Management

The portfolio management segment of the firm makes the ultimate investment decision; it's the department that "pulls the trigger." There are three jobs that typically fall under this component of the firm: portfolio managers, portfolio analysts (or associate portfolio managers) and portfolio manager assistants. Recent college graduates often fill portfolio assistant positions, while individuals with many years of investment experience hold associate and senior portfolio manager assignments. MBAs are not hired as portfolio managers right out of business school, unless they have a ton of experience. Typically, MBAs who wish to pursue a career in portfolio management join investment management firms in their investment research divisions. After several years in research, MBAs will then have a choice: either stay in research or leverage their research experience to move into an associate portfolio manager position or broaden their experience by covering additional sectors.

Senior portfolio manager

Portfolio managers are responsible for establishing an investment strategy, selecting appropriate investments and allocating each investment properly. All day long, portfolio managers are presented with investment ideas from internal buy-side analysts and sell-side analysts from investment banks. It is their job to sift through the relevant information and use their judgment to buy and sell securities. Throughout each day, they read reports, talk to company managers, and monitor industry and economic trends looking for the right company and time to invest the portfolio's capital.

The selection of investments must adhere to the style of the portfolio. For instance, a large-capitalization growth manager might be screening for only companies that have a market-capitalization in excess of $10 billion and earnings growth characteristics that exceed its industry average. Therefore, the portfolio manager would not even consider a $500 million utility stock, with a 6 percent dividend yield.

Once investment opportunities are recognized, portfolio managers must decide what percentage of their portfolio to allocate to the respective security. This decision is based on the mandate of the portfolio—active or passive—and the risk expectation of the overall portfolio. For example, riskier portfolios invest in a small number of securities and take large "bets." The popular Janus Twenty fund invests in only 20 liquid large-capitalization companies. These are often referred to as "concentrated" funds. Alternatively, diversified portfolios may invest in over 100 securities to spread the risk of any one holding.

Portfolio managers also spend time meeting with their clients to review investment strategy and performance results. While account and product management professionals lead this process, portfolio managers are often an integral part of client discussions. In the mutual fund world, portfolio managers do not spend time talking to individual customers, but they are often called on to present at sales conferences and at product road shows. However, institutional and high-net-worth portfolio managers have fewer clients, and they only meet with them one to two times a year.

Portfolio managers are the most seasoned investment professionals in the firm. Typically, people with at least seven to 10 years of investment experience occupy these positions, and most have either an MBA and/or a CFA designation.

Visit Vault at **www.vault.com** for insider company profiles, expert advice, career message boards, expert resume reviews, the Vault Job Board and more.

V∧ULT CAREER LIBRARY   173

Associate portfolio manager

The associate portfolio manager position requires an MBA, CFA or considerable investment experience. Typically, the job is filled by successful research analysts who have at least three to five years of post-MBA experience. Larger firms may also recruit MBAs to fit this role straight out of business school. The job itself is very similar to that of the senior portfolio manager with one main exception: associates interact less with clients than senior managers do. Associate portfolio managers usually are assigned smaller, less sophisticated portfolios to manage or serve as lieutenants on large, complicated portfolios.

The role of the associate portfolio manager differs depending on which segment of the market is being served—mutual fund, institutional or high-net-worth. For instance, associate portfolio managers at many mutual fund firms will either act as the lead investor on a sector fund or as second-in-command on a large diversified fund. Depending on the firm, an associate could also act as a lead on a sector fund and a second-in-command on a diversified fund at the same time. Alternatively, on the institutional side, associate portfolio managers typically apprentice with seasoned portfolio managers on the largest and most complicated portfolios. After they have succeeded in that role, the firm will assign them smaller institutional accounts to manage on their own.

While there is no defined career track, successful associate portfolio managers could be promoted to senior portfolio managers within three to five years depending on the associate's track record.

A Day in the Life: Portfolio Manager, Major Mutual Fund Firm

6:30 a.m. Take train into office. Read *The Wall Street Journal* and several trade magazines. An article in an aviation magazine mentions a small aerospace firm that designs generic aftermarket parts. It sounds like an interesting company. I send the portfolio analyst a quick e-mail to gather additional information.

7 a.m. Arrive at work. I have 100 e-mails sitting in my inbox. I quickly sift through the e-mails, paying particular attention to companies that have released quarterly earnings. Three companies whose stocks I own in the portfolio have reported earnings.

7:30 a.m. The portfolio analyst comes into my office with preliminary research on the aerospace company. He has printed out several sell-side reports and a financial model. He tells me the company is growing the top line at 20 percent and generating positive free cash flow. I ask him if it will generate increasing returns on invested capital, which he tells me he expects it to. The company seems very interesting and meets our portfolio's initial screening process, so I ask the portfolio analyst to continue researching and build out a detailed financial model.

8 a.m. Review my calendar with my analyst. She notifies me that CEOs from four companies will be visiting the offices today. I ask to be signed up for two of the meetings.

8:30 a.m. Attend the morning investment meeting. A new senior analyst covering pharmaceuticals has joined the firm and is initiating coverage on the industry. He puts hold ratings on two stocks in my portfolio. I ask several questions during his presentation. He agrees to follow up with me later in the day.

9 a.m. Dial-in to earnings conference call. I'll try to listen to as much of it as possible but realize I will probably be interrupted.

9:30 a.m. My co-portfolio manager walks into my office. While we each manage 50 percent of the portfolio independently, we constantly inform each other of our ideas and trades. We discuss the week's upcoming economic releases and how our portfolio is structured to react to certain data points.

10:30 a.m. I attend a meeting with a CEO on his company's road show. A "road show" occurs when a company files an initial public offering (IPO) and seeks to sell the equity to institutional investors. While I find the company and presentation to be interesting, I am going to pass on investing in the IPO.

11:30 a.m. Return to my office. I have five new voicemails and 20 new e-mails. One message is from the product manager of the fund I manage. He is getting several inquiries from account managers over the quarterly performance of my portfolio. We set up a time to meet later in the day.

12 p.m. Eat lunch while attending an industry update. The technology analyst is providing an annual update and outlook to our firm's portfolio managers. Our firm provides lunch while the analyst formally presents his research and projections.

1 p.m. Monitor portfolio. Check to see if any stocks have particularly large gains or losses. There are currently no abnormal returns.

1:30 p.m. Attend another meeting with the CEO of a restaurant company. CEOs and CFOs often go on the road several times a year to meet with institutional investors. I have owned this particular stock at several points throughout the last five years and know the CEO quite well. The meeting is quite casual and we discuss the outlook for his business amidst a potential pending recession.

2:30 p.m. Contact trader. Make several trades in order to meet new fund flows.

3 p.m. Meet with the pharmaceuticals industry analyst to gain further understanding behind his investment theses on the two stocks I hold in my portfolio.

4 p.m. Meet with the product manager for my fund. While our performance has been decent in the last quarter, it fared much better than some of its closest competitors. The product manager wants a detailed understanding of the "moving parts." He conveys this information to several account managers whose clients have large positions in the fund.

5 p.m. Touch base with the portfolio analyst and see if he has gotten any further work done on the aerospace company from this morning. He has set up a conference call with a sell-side analyst the next day to discuss the company.

5:30 p.m. Leave for home.

Investment Research

The investment research segment is responsible for generating recommendations to portfolio managers on companies and industries that they follow. Similar to the portfolio management segment, there are several positions in the research hierarchy: senior research analyst, research associate-analyst (or junior analyst), and research associate.

On the sell-side, senior analysts typically have three to five years of post-MBA research experience or six to 10 years of post-college experience (if an MBA was not pursued). On the buy-side, new MBA graduates typically occupy the senior analyst position. The research associate-analyst is typically a sell-side position for recent MBA graduates. These positions are usually occupied for several years or until the candidate is deemed capable of covering his own sector. Both buy-side and sell-side firms employ recent college graduates as research associates. It is typically a two- or three-year program that can lead to a more senior position or result in the associate returning to business school.

Senior research analyst

Senior research analysts are investment experts in their given industry focus. An equity analyst covers stocks; a fixed income analyst covers bonds.

Visit Vault at **www.vault.com** for insider company profiles, expert advice, career message boards, expert resume reviews, the Vault Job Board and more.

VAULT CAREER LIBRARY   175

Their role is to predict the investment potential of the companies in their sector. For instance, take an equity analyst covering computer hardware companies, including Apple Computer. The analyst would be responsible for predicting Apple's future earnings and cash flow, and comparing the fair value of Apple to the expectations of the stock market. To do this, the analyst would build a financial model that included all of the potential variables to derive Apple's earnings and appropriate value (e.g., sales growth, business costs, as well as research and development).

A fixed income analyst focusing on Telecom, for example, might be looking at a new high-yield corporate bond issued by Qwest. The main thing the analyst will be looking for is Qwest's ability to pay off that loan—the amount of the bond. The analyst will look at historical cash flows, project future cash flows and look at other debt obligations that might be more senior to the new bond. This will tell the analyst the likelihood that Qwest will be able to pay off the bond.

Analysts spend a considerable amount of time attending industry conferences, meeting with company management and analyzing industry supply and demand trends to derive business forecasts. Sell-side analysts follow around 15 to 25 companies and must be an expert on each while buy-side analysts typically follow even more companies.

An important part of a senior research analyst's job is to convey their recommendations to the portfolio management teams. Therefore, senior analysts spend considerable time presenting to portfolio managers and issuing investment reports. Because of this, senior research analysts must be articulate and persuasive in their convictions in order to earn respect within the firm.

Senior research analysts typically have served as investment research associates for three to five years, post MBA or CFA, before assuming their position. If successful in their role, many senior analysts move into portfolio management roles later in their careers.

Investment research associate-analyst

This is the role for most MBAs or those with equivalent experience. It is typically a sell-side position but some larger buy-side firms employ the position as well. Essentially, associate-analysts have the same responsibilities as senior research analysts with one exception: associate-analysts are given smaller industries to follow. Typically for the buy-side, the industry assigned to an associate-analyst is a component of a broader sector that is already being analyzed by a senior analyst. For instance, an associate-analyst might be assigned HMOs and work closely with the senior analyst in charge of insurance companies. As stated above, the more likely scenario is for the MBA to enter the buy-side as the senior analyst. On the sell-side, the associate-analyst will typically work under the senior analyst for several years before branching off on his own to cover a sub-sector.

The associate-analyst creates investment recommendations in the same manner as a senior analyst. In general, they spend several weeks familiarizing themselves with their industry by reading industry papers, journals and textbooks, and attending industry conferences. A large percentage of a research analyst's time is spent monitoring industry and company trends to predict financial results for the company. Therefore, associate-analysts are constantly speaking with management, customers and suppliers to gauge the current status of the company they are analyzing. Armed with financial models and fundamental company analysis, they develop investment recommendations that they distribute to the senior analyst or firm's portfolio managers (on the buy-side).

One of the greatest challenges for a new associate-analyst is the steepness of the learning curve. Senior analysts and portfolio managers do not have the patience or the luxury to allow an analyst to be uninformed or consistently incorrect. New associate-analysts work extremely hard building trust with their superiors.

Obviously, financial acumen and quantitative skills are a must for an associate-analyst, but communication skills are also critical. Associate-analysts need to be able to clearly and persuasively communicate their investment recommendations. They must also be able to respond to detailed inquiries from portfolio managers that challenge their ideas—which requires a strong tact and a great deal of patience. Furthermore, associate-analysts need to be energetic, diligent and intellectually curious.

A Day in the Life: Senior Analyst, Hedge Fund

5:45 a.m. Wake up and check BlackBerry for any news.

6 a.m. Check foreign markets on CNBC from home before I leave for work. (Foreign stock markets and the futures market are a good proxy of how the U.S. markets will open.)

6:30 a.m. Arrive at work. Monitor foreign positions and comb through e-mail, checking for any upgrades or downgrades from sell-side analysts.

7 a.m. Attend morning meeting with the other five members of our portfolio team. We discuss two positions. Company XYZ has doubled in three months and now represents a significant concentration of the portfolio. We decide to trim our position. The other stock has underperformed significantly. Our investment thesis remains intact and we decide to schedule a call with Company XYZ's CFO for later in the day.

8 a.m. Receive phone call from a sell-side analyst that downgraded a stock I have a large position in. He explains his reasoning for the downgrade. I expect the stock to drop significantly and may use the opportunity to purchase more stock.

8:30 a.m. Read the sell-side analyst's downgrade report. Revisit my financial model and assumptions. I disagree with certain key conclusions and check the pre-market trading activity. It appears the stock is down 12 percent.

9 a.m. Notify the portfolio manager that I want to purchase more of the stock. He approves the decision.

9:30 a.m. The market opens and the stock is down 15 percent. I contact our trader and let him know I want to purchase an additional 100,000 shares.

9:35 a.m. The trader calls me and confirms he was able to find 100,000 shares and made the purchase.

9:45 a.m. Meet with a colleague on the options desk for coffee. As an analyst covering three industries, I brief him on my industry outlooks. He is trying to devise an options strategy to capitalize on the volatility of one of my industries. I assist by notifying him of upcoming catalysts that will increase volatility in the industry.

11 a.m. Meet with the portfolio manager to further discuss Company XYZ and why the stock is underperforming. He asks extremely detailed questions on the company's inventory levels. I answer most of the questions but need to get back to him on others.

11:30 a.m. Call up several distributors of the company to discuss inventory levels. Determine that inventory remains at all-time low levels. Write the portfolio manager a quick e-mail.

1 p.m. Eat lunch with a sales representative from J.P. Morgan. The purpose of the lunch is to introduce me to a new sell-side analyst the firm has hired and to hear his investment ideas.

2 p.m. Prepare for the conference call with Company XYZ's CFO. Write down five topics I plan on discussing with him.

2:30 p.m. Conference call with CFO of company XYZ.

3:30 p.m. Discuss the call with the portfolio manager. We agree to hold onto the position.

4 p.m. Go through e-mail and return phone calls.

6 p.m. Prepare for earnings releases of three companies for the next day.

7 p.m. Go home.

Visit Vault at **www.vault.com** for insider company profiles, expert advice, career message boards, expert resume reviews, the Vault Job Board and more.

VAULT CAREER LIBRARY   **177**

Employer Directory

AllianceBernstein
1345 Avenue of the Americas
New York, NY 10105
Phone: (212) 969-1000
Fax: (212) 969-2229
www.alliancebernstein.com

Allianz Group
Königinstrasse 28
D-80802 Munich
Germany
Phone: +49-89-3800-0
Fax: +49-89-3800-3425
www.allianz.com

American Century Investments
4500 Main Street, Suite 1500
Kansas City, MO 64111
Phone: (816) 340-4200
Fax: (816) 340-7962
Toll free: (800) 345-2021
www.americancentury.com

Ameriprise Financial
55 Ameriprise Financial Center
Minneapolis, MN 55474
Phone: (612) 671-3131
Fax: (612) 671-5112
Toll free: (800) 386-2042
www.ameriprise.com

Bank of America
Bank of America Corporate Center
100 North Tryon Street, 18th Floor
Charlotte, NC 28255
Phone: (704) 386-5681
Fax: (704) 386-6699
www.bankofamerica.com

Barclays Global Investors
45 Fremont Street
San Francisco, CA 94105
Phone: (415) 597-2000
Fax: (415) 597-2171
www.barclaysglobal.com

BlackRock
40 East 52nd Street
New York, NY 10022
Phone: (212) 810-5300
Fax: (212) 754-3123
www.blackrock.com

The Blackstone Group
345 Park Avenue
New York, NY 10154
Phone: (212) 583-5000
Fax: (212) 583-5712
www.blackstone.com

CalPERS
Lincoln Plaza, 400 P Street
Sacramento, CA 95814
Phone: (916) 795-3829
Fax: (916) 795-4001
www.calpers.ca.gov

Capital Group Companies
333 South Hope Street, 53rd Floor
Los Angeles, CA 90071
Phone: (213) 486-9200
Fax: (213) 486-9217
www.capgroup.com

Charles Schwab
120 Kearny Street
San Francisco, CA 94104
Phone: (415) 636-7000
Fax: (415) 636-8538
www.schwab.com

Credit Suisse Asset Management
11 Madison Avenue
New York, NY 10010
Phone: (212) 325-2000
Fax: (212) 538-3395
www.credit-suisse.com/am/en

D.E. Shaw & Co., L.P.
120 West 45th Street
39th Floor, Tower 45
New York, NY 10036
Phone: (212) 478-0000
Fax: (212) 478-0100
www.deshaw.com

DC Energy
8065 Leeburg Pike, 5th Floor
Vienna, VA 22182
Phone: (703) 506-3901
Fax: (703) 506-3905
www.dc-energy.com

Deutsche Bank
345 Park Avenue
New York, NY 10017
Phone: (212) 454-3600

Theodor-Heuss-Allee 70
Frankfurt am Main, 60262
Germany
Phone: +49-69-910-00
Fax: +49-69-910-34225
www.db.com

Dreyfus Corporation
200 Park Avenue
New York, NY 10166
Phone: (212) 922-6000
Fax: (212) 922-7533
www.dreyfus.com

Fidelity Investments
82 Devonshire Street
Boston, MA 02109
Phone: (617) 563-7000
Fax: (617) 476-6150
www.fidelity.com

E*TRADE FINANCIAL
135 East 57th Street
New York, NY 10022
Phone: (646) 521-4300
Fax: (888) 276-9771
www.etrade.com

Edward Jones
12555 Manchester Road
Des Peres, MO 63131
Phone: (314) 515-2000
Fax: (314) 515-2820
www.edwardjones.com

Employer Directory, cont.

Federated Investors
Federated Investors Tower
1001 Liberty Avenue
Pittsburgh, PA 15222-3779
Phone: (412) 288-1900
Fax: (412) 288-6823
www.federatedinvestors.com

Franklin Resources, Inc.
(Franklin Templeton Investments)
1 Franklin Parkway
Building 970, 1st Floor
San Mateo, CA 94403
Phone: (650) 312-2000
Fax: (650) 312-3655
www.franklintempleton.com

GAMCO Investors, Inc.
1 Corporate Center
Rye, NY 10580-1422
Phone: (914) 921-5100
Fax: (914) 921-3710
www.gabelli.com

Goldman Sachs
85 Broad Street
New York, NY 10004
Phone: (212) 902-1000
Fax: (212) 902-3000
www.gs.com

HSBC North America Holdings
26525 North Riverwoods Boulevard
Mettawa, IL 60045
Phone: (224) 554-2000
Fax: (224) 552-4400
www.hbscusa.com

ING Investment Management
10 State House Square
Hartford, CAT 06103-3607
Phone: (860) 275-3720
www.inginvestment.com

INVESCO
1 Midtown Plaza
1360 Peachtree Street NE
Atlanta, GA 30309
Phone: (404) 892-0896
www.invesco.com

Janus Capital Group
151 Detroit Street
Denver, CO 80206
Phone: (303) 333-3863
Fax: (816) 218-2452
www.janus.com

JPMorgan Investment Management
245 Park Avenue
New York, NY 10067
Phone: (212) 270-6000
Fax: (212) 270-2613
im.jpmorgan.com

Lazard Asset Management
30 Rockefeller Plaza, 58th Floor
New York, NY 10112-6300
Phone: (800) 821-6474
www.lazardnet.com

Legg Mason
100 Light Street
Baltimore, MD 21202-1099
Phone: (410) 539-0000
Fax: (410) 528-3999
www.leggmason.com

Mellon Financial Corporation
1 Mellon Center
500 Grant Street
Pittsburgh, PA 15258-0001
Phone: (412) 234-5000
Fax: (412) 234-9495
www.mellon.com

MFS Investment Management
500 Boylston Street
Boston, MA 02116
Phone: (617) 954-5000
www.mfs.com

Morgan Keegan—Wealth Management Division
Morgan Keegan Tower
50 North Front Street, 17th Floor
Memphis, TN 38103
Phone: (901) 524-4100
Fax: (901) 579-4406
www.morgankeegan.com

Morgan Stanley Investment Management
1221 Avenue of the Americas
New York, NY 10020
Phone: (212) 762-7100
www.morganstanley.com/im

Northern Trust Corporation
50 South LaSalle Street
Chicago, IL 60603
Phone: (312) 630-6000
Fax: (312) 444-7843
www.ntrs.com

Nuveen Investments
333 West Wacker Drive
Chicago, IL 60606
Phone: (312) 917-7700
Fax: (312) 917-8049
www.nuveen.com

Pacific Investment Management Co. (PIMCO)
840 Newport Center Drive, Suite 300
Newport Beach, CA 92660
Phone: (949) 720-6000
Fax: (949) 720-1376
www.pimco.com

Pequot Capital Management
500 Nyala Farm Road
Westport, CT 06880
Phone: (203) 429-2200
Fax: (203) 429-2400
www.pequotcap.com

Putnam Investments
1 Post Office Square
Boston, MA 02109
Phone: (617) 292-1000
Fax: (617) 482-1581
Toll free: (800) 225-1581
www.putnam.com

Visit Vault at **www.vault.com** for insider company profiles, expert advice,
career message boards, expert resume reviews, the Vault Job Board and more.

VAULT CAREER LIBRARY   179

Employer Directory, cont.

Raymond James Financial
880 Carillon Parkway
St. Petersburg, FL 33716
Phone: (727) 567-1000
Fax: (727) 567-8915
Toll free: (800) 248-8863
www.rjf.com

Schroders plc
31 Gresham Street
London, EC2V 7QA
United Kingdom
Phone: +44-20-76-58-60-00
Fax: +44-20-76-58-69-65
www.schroders.com

State Street Corporation
1 Lincoln Street
Boston, MA 02111
Phone: (617) 786-3000
Fax: (617) 654-3386
www.statestreet.com

T. Rowe Price
100 East Pratt Street
Baltimore, MD 21202
Phone: (410) 345-2000
Fax: (410) 752-3477
www.troweprice.com

TD Ameritrade
4211 South 102nd Street
Omaha, NE 68127
Phone: (402) 331-7856
Fax: (402) 597-7789
www.amtd.com

TIAA-CREF
730 3rd Avenue
New York, NY 10017
Phone: (212) 490-9000
Fax: (212) 916-4840
Toll free: (800) 842-2252
www.tiaa-cref.org

UBS Financial Services
1285 Avenue of the Americas
New York, NY 10019
Phone: (212) 713-2000
Fax: (212) 713-9818
financialservicesinc.ubs.com

The Vanguard Group
100 Vanguard Boulevard
Malvern, PA 19355
Phone: (610) 648-6000
Fax: (610) 669-6605
Toll free: (800) 662-7447
www.vanguard.com

Wellington Management Co., LLP
75 State Street
Boston, MA 02109
Phone: (617) 951-5000
Fax: (617) 951-5250
www.wellington.com

Leveraged Finance

What is Leveraged Finance?

The financial markets can be divided into two major sections: debt and equity. Under this overarching organization structure, think of leveraged finance as the intersection of investment banking, commercial banking, hedge funds, private equity, and sales and trading on the debt side of the financial markets.

Generally speaking, leveraged finance is a platform in all major investment and commercial banks. It is a function that taps into two major financial markets (the high-yield bond market and the leveraged loan market), is accessed by nearly all private equity shops and hedge funds on a regular basis, and has been one of the booming profit centers of Wall Street for the past two decades. For analysts and associates, it has become a prime training ground for the most elite private equity shops and hedge funds. Subsequently, for careers on Wall Street, leveraged finance is one of the most sought-after fields.

Why leveraged finance?

Along with its role as a potential springboard to careers in private equity and hedge funds, leveraged finance is also unique from a career perspective because it provides a vantage point into most of the other areas of investment banking, as well as sales and trading. For analysts and associates, working in leveraged finance allows one to see what else is out there career-wise in the financial markets, without ever having to leave the field.

Another advantage of working in leveraged finance is that in general, it is an area of investment banking that is focused on closing transactions. In a corporate finance role within a coverage team in an investment bank (a team that covers a specific industry and pitches deals to companies in that industry), one analyst might close one or two deals a year in an investment bank. By contrast, in leveraged finance, it's feasible to close five to 10 transactions a year. Leveraged finance affords analysts and associates a continually busy pace and good deal and client exposure along the way.

Major deals

One of the great advantages to working in leveraged finance is that you will typically work on notable transactions. As an analyst or associate in a major leveraged finance firm, you may even see at least one of your deals make the cover of *The Wall Street Journal*. Notable brands like RJR Nabisco, Burger King, United Airlines, Domino's Pizza and Sony MGM have all accessed the leveraged finance markets. From multibillion-dollar leveraged buyouts to major corporate restructurings, there are plenty of headline transactions across the field.

Leveraged Finance vs. Corporate Finance/Investment Banking

Are the leveraged finance and investment banking the same animal? Sort of. As leveraged finance was originally a commercial banking function, most of the premier leveraged finance shops can be found within the investment banks of the largest finance institutions, such as JPMorgan Chase, Bank of America and Citigroup. Because of the sheer amount of leveraged finance deal volume at these institutions, there will typically be entire floors and groups dedicated to "originating deals" (proposing deals to existing or new clients), following the capital markets, trading in and out of loan/bond positions, selling these products to investors, and monitoring the firm's exposure to loans and bonds of issuers. Naturally, at pure investment banks such as Goldman Sachs that do not originate as many of these types of debt transactions, there will typically be smaller groups dedicated to following the markets, in more of a debt capital markets generalist role. However, in both types of institutions, the leveraged finance platform is typically part of a debt capital markets group—it just depends on the volume of deals to determine how specific and/or large the groups will be.

Visit Vault at **www.vault.com** for insider company profiles, expert advice, career message boards, expert resume reviews, the Vault Job Board and more.

VAULT CAREER LIBRARY   181

A common misperception is that traditional investment banking only involves providing solutions and advice to companies (such as mergers and acquisitions advice). In this regard, leveraged finance is different from investment banking, since a leveraged finance bank is not only offering advice for a financial problem, but also a product as a solution. However, most people these days broaden their definition of investment banking to include both offering advice to companies, as well as executing a financial transaction, such as an initial public offering (IPO). In this sense, leveraged finance is identical—just as an investment bank covers a company in an industry coverage group and works with its equity capital markets team to structure an IPO, so does it provide the same service for leveraged finance transactions. In the case of a leveraged finance transaction, the investment bank also covers the company and works with people from its debt capital markets team to structure a syndicated loan and/or high-yield bond.

Unlike investment banking, however, there exist a number of other financial institutions, such as General Electric or CIT Group, that arrange these similar financing packages for companies, but do so without a coverage group or an industry platform (which an investment bank would have). These financial institutions still have relationships with companies, but they don't typically provide M&A or IPO advice like an investment bank. The loan market is a private market, and as such is not limited in terms of what type of firm can provide lending solutions. If you're a treasurer of a multibillion dollar company and you need a large loan for an acquisition, you'll go to the firm with the best interest rate, regardless of whether it's an investment bank or not. In this regard, leveraged finance is more similar to commercial lending (e.g., lending to a company so that they can buy copiers, printers, etc.) than it is similar to investment banking.

Different experiences: working in the coverage group of an investment bank vs. leveraged finance

Working in a coverage group or M&A at an investment bank differs greatly from working in a debt capital markets (DCM) or equity capital markets (ECM). There is more execution of deals in a DCM or ECM role. Whereas someone in this role may not be as familiar with every facet of an industry like their counterpart in a coverage group, they will generally have more breadth of financial market knowledge.

This breadth vs. depth trade-off is directly related to the amount of transaction experience offered in leveraged finance. For example, the day-to-day grind might be a little more hectic in a leveraged finance role, as a deal team could potentially be closing two multibillion-dollar transactions on the same day—something that would be quite unlikely in a coverage role. However, this transaction-oriented environment involves substantially less idea generation and pitching of ideas to clients than one would find in an investment banking industry coverage group. That is not to say that someone in leveraged finance will not do any pitching—quite the contrary. While the industry coverage group might come up with and pitch the idea of a syndicated loan or high-yield bond to finance an M&A deal, they will surely bring along the appropriate people from the leveraged finance platform to comment on the markets, comparable transactions and provide other relevant advice.

If you are beginning your career in finance, it is important to think about your long-term career goals when considering a role in investment banking coverage versus leveraged finance. If your goal is to work in a specific industry—let's say running a health care company—you would probably be better served in a health care coverage group at an investment bank. However, if you are interested in working at a hedge fund or private equity shop, working in leveraged finance will give you the opportunity to interact with many of these firms, as you close numerous deals of theirs. Furthermore, you will be trained in certain debt metrics (what's typically called "credit" training), which are useful in understanding the industry and are not typically emphasized in the coverage side of the bank. This is not to say that moving from a coverage group to a private equity shop or hedge fund can't happen—it certainly does, and even the top-tier PE shops and hedge funds seek people with very specific industry knowledge. However, it's definitely the case that your exposure (most likely in late-night financial modeling revisions) to the private equity shops will be higher in leveraged finance groups when compared to your exposure working in an industry coverage group. In an industry where relationships are everything, this exposure will definitely matter.

Types of leveraged finance deals

There are a wide variety of deals executed within leveraged finance. Most common are syndicated loans and high-yield bonds for working capital or general corporate purposes (day-to-day financing needs). However, in leveraged finance you'll also find leveraged buyouts, when private equity shops and financial sponsors use borrowed money to purchase companies. There are also corporate restructurings and DIP (Debtor-in-Possession) facilities, where companies are entering/exiting bankruptcy and are trying to avoid Chapter 7 bankruptcy (liquidation). In this case, the companies will work with both the financial institutions' leveraged finance groups and the federal bankruptcy court to get financing packages in order to stay in business. Leveraged finance also covers dividend transactions, where loans/bonds are used to pay out the owners of a business, recapitalizations, where a company's financial structure is changed, IPO/spin-off financings, where the proceeds of a loan/bond are in tandem with an IPO or a spin-off of a business unit, and even general debt refinancings, where an existing loan/bond is taken out with a new loan/bond.

Opportunities in Leveraged Finance

There are so many different areas within leveraged finance and so many related to the field that there is place for almost everyone. For example, there is deal origination, for the person who enjoys managing numerous processes such as putting together presentations, financial modeling and pitching. There is also capital markets work (for both syndicated loans and high-yield bonds) for the person who enjoys understanding the flow of the markets and conducting research about the market's trends. For the person who enjoys the asset management aspect of managing a firm's exposure to the syndicated loan/high-yield bond markets, there are positions in internal credit/portfolio management work. Finally, there is a sales and trading function for both syndicated loans and high-yield bonds.

However, very generally speaking, leveraged finance refers to the deal origination function—when a team goes out to pitch a client, wins the mandate, structures the loan/bond, markets it to investors, sells it, and then closes and funds the transaction. This role as an analyst or associate caters to the individual who enjoys managing numerous deals throughout this process, who is a jack-of-all-trades from financial modeling to talking to investment firms, and who thrives in the pace of a seemingly never-ending day. Furthermore, when considering if leveraged finance is/is not the field for you, it is important to realize that some firms are organized in a typical investment banking "cubicle/office" atmosphere, whereas some are organized like trading floors. Some people feed off the energy from a football field-sized area crammed with people chatting all day long, while others would prefer the quieter nature of a cube or an office, where personal phone calls are not heard by their neighbors and neighbor's neighbors. This type of setup can make a substantial difference in the day-to-day enjoyment of someone's role in leveraged finance.

The culture of leveraged finance depends almost entirely on the culture of the firm in general. At a pure investment bank such as Goldman Sachs, you might find the culture to be almost entirely opposite from that of the commercial lending arm of a larger financial institution, such as General Electric Commercial Finance. Whereas one might be very rigid and hierarchical, the other might be golf shirt and khakis on Fridays, where an analyst can chat it up with any managing director at any time.

Structuring/organization

Within structuring/origination, there are four major roles: managing director, vice president, associate and analyst. As the hierarchy is structured, there are generally more analysts than associates, more associates than VPs, and more VPs than MDs. At most firms, the ratio tends to be one MD for every one to two VPs, two to three associates, and three to four analysts.

Visit Vault at **www.vault.com** for insider company profiles, expert advice, career message boards, expert resume reviews, the Vault Job Board and more.

VAULT CAREER LIBRARY   183

Managing director

Sitting at the top of the leveraged finance food chain, the MD generally spends most of his/her time speaking with treasurers and CFOs of companies, in order to assess their financial status and need for debt facilities. The MD is usually the key relationship manager for the bank because of continuous dialogue with the client. As senior members of the deal team, MDs have something of a sales role, and interact with a limited number of clients with whom they have worked throughout the years. The top MDs are group heads, who may have contracts outlining their compensation structure.

Managing directors will spend quite a bit of time pitching ideas to clients, as their salary is typically determined based on the fees they earn from their deal flow. In this sense, it is not uncommon for the best-of-the-best MDs to command multiple-millions of dollars in compensation in good years (think $3 million or more in bonuses). Naturally, it pays to be an MD in a leveraged finance group that executes a high volume of exceptionally profitable LBOs, DIP facilities, and recapitalizations. However, more often than not, the salary of an MD is enough to support his/her basic lifestyle and the bulk of pay comes in the form of a bonus paid with stock options that must vest over a certain period of years. These "golden handcuffs" are usually incentive enough for senior MDs to stay at their current firms for long periods of time, which generally ensures consistency at the most senior ranks.

As for lifestyle, managing directors typically work "market" hours—from 8 a.m. to 7 p.m. However, when working on more complex transactions, they will often work later, reviewing financial presentations and editing offering memorandums. Rarely is a weekend worked from the office, but it is not uncommon for an MD to review materials and make calls from their homes on the weekend or on the train ride home from work. MDs also tend to have access to corporate expense accounts, in order to entertain clients over lunch, dinner, a ball game or on the golf course.

Vice president

The vice president on a deal team is the right hand man of the MD. Once a mandate has been won, the VP generally takes over and manages the process going forward. From the negotiating and signing of legal documents to the final signoff of the information memorandum, the VP's role is to ensure that everything in the deal goes smoothly. Throughout the deal lifecycle, a VP will often act as the relationship manager, delivering the periodic client update call and subsequently laying the future foundation for his promotion to MD.

Although, like MDs, VPs interact frequently with clients, VPs tend to be salaried and not commission-based they way MDs typically are. The very best VPs are paid extremely well, commanding salaries in the multiple hundreds of thousands of dollars, like their other corporate finance investment banking counterparts. In great years, it is not uncommon for a top performing VP in a very active team to clear $1 million. However, in bad economic times, or working in groups that do not originate many transactions, these VPs tend to make closer to $250,000.

The high performing VPs are generally on the fast track to promotion, spending three to four years in the role before becoming a managing director. At some firms a vice president will be referred to as a "principal" or "director"—the main distinction of this role from that of a managing director is a lower salary. VP titles are also quite often awarded to those who spend a good amount of time interacting with clients.

Associate

Either fresh out of a top-tier MBA program or recently promoted from third-year analyst, the associate role is highly soughtafter. For those top-performing analysts fortunate enough to land the analyst-to-associate ("A-to-A") promotion, this position has a lot of upsides. Able to hit the ground running more quickly than their just-out-of-B-school counterparts, these associates stand a much higher chance to be ranked near the top of their class. The downside is that an A-to-A might have trouble separating herself from the day-to-day financial modeling that came with the analyst lifestyle and subsequently, might run the risk of becoming a micromanager. The deal lifecycle is so process-oriented that this can easily become the downfall of an associate.

Associates generally have a very similar lifestyle to that of an analyst. Eager to be promoted to VP, they arrive in the office early. They typically leave late, reviewing work with their analysts to get projects completed. It is not uncommon for even the most senior associates to work 80+ hour workweeks, including nearly every weekend. As is the case with the deal cycle in leveraged finance, there are typically quite a few projects needing to be completed at any given time. This lifestyle lends itself to the never-ending workday.

However, associates are paid accordingly with other corporate finance investment banking associates, which tends to reward them handsomely for their work ethic. With base salaries as high as $95,000, signing bonuses in the $25,000 to 45,000 range, and full-year bonuses well in excess of $150,000, the first-year associate gets paid well for his efforts. The more experienced associates can expect to be compensated very well in the good economic years. This can translate into bonuses near $300,000, with salaries clearing $150,000 to 200,000. However, in slower years, this bonus amount can easily be cut in half. Whereas analysts are generally very excited to make their base salary in their bonus in a good year, senior associates are hoping to double their salary amount.

Generally staffed by a VP in their team, analysts and associates are usually placed on a variety of deals, which means that they should not all be "live" or closing at the same time. Inevitably, this is never actually the case. This deal variety helps to ensure that these junior resources will be able to work with different issuers, deal teams and financial products. At first, most junior resources are staffed alongside other seasoned ones.

Capital markets/loan sales and distribution

Managing director/vice president

In a capital markets function, the managing director and vice president often have very similar job responsibilities; one's title reflects not job responsibilities but years of experience in the field. As loan sales and distribution is typically grouped with these capital markets professionals (if not one and the same at most firms), these positions are compensated similarly. Managing directors and vice presidents spend most of their time advising deal teams and clients on market conditions, as well as delivering these deals to investors.

With years of relevant experience, these professionals generally hail from origination and structuring teams or another section of the investment bank's corporate finance practice, and are typically compensated on a scale comparable to their managing director and vice president peers in origination and corporate finance. Although their function is not specifically "on the line" (they are not directly responsible for generating revenues for a firm), and this means that their pay scale might not be quite the same as those successful at originating many deals, it is generally very close. However, because the pay for a capital markets MD does not depend as much on fee generation as it does for an origination MD, this can lead to more consistent earnings for the capital markets MD/VP year after year.

In this sense, the capital markets and loan sales teams are like head coaches of professional sports teams: whereas the players (the deal team) are out winning the games, the coach is directing the team during games, drawing up new plays (adjusting the terms of the deal in market), conducting research on other competition (market comparables), talking to fans (investors), and interacting with the team's owners (the client). While marquee players bring in extraordinary financial contracts, the very best coaches are generally not too far behind.

As the firm's eyes and ears of the financial markets, the capital markets and loan sales positions tend to work more "market" hours. In at 7 a.m. and out by 7 p.m. is somewhat typical for these senior professionals. However, even the senior capital markets professionals will commonly find themselves working with origination teams and issuers to structure large deals well into the evenings. Loan sales professionals often work late too, but in a different capacity and outside of the office. Often, they are attending dinners/sporting events with investors and/or clients. Regardless, the lifestyles of senior professionals in both capacities tends to be quite hectic: following the markets, talking to clients, answering questions from investors and

Visit Vault at **www.vault.com** for insider company profiles, expert advice, career message boards, expert resume reviews, the Vault Job Board and more.

VAULT CAREER LIBRARY   **185**

spending the day attached to a BlackBerry. Weekends for these teams are typically freer than origination teams', but there is always occasional work that needs to be done.

Associate/analyst

As part of the corporate finance program, the associate and analyst role within these teams is much like their peers in other groups. On a junior level, in capital markets these tend to be positions that are more geared towards research, while in loan sales these roles are more focused on investment-grade deals and coverage of smaller clients. Because they are paid on the same scale as an origination associate/analyst, it appears on first glance that the capital markets analyst or associate role would offer a better lifestyle than in origination. However, because of the pace of the job, that's not necessarily true.

While an origination analyst or associate completes a number of different tasks over the span of a week (such as writing an info memo, adding pages to a credit deck, or completing slides in a pitch), the capital markets associate/analyst usually completes tasks on a daily or hourly basis. The nature of the job is like a sprint, not a marathon, often involving numerous fire drills. For example, deal teams might ask for league tables and credential slides, investors might want to know the spread differential between a particular syndicated loan and a high-yield bond, a senior MD of the bank might want a deck of slides outlining market conditions, and a client might want a set of recent second lien LBO deals. These are all likely requests in the first half of a day for a capital markets associate or analyst.

Therefore, it is not uncommon for an associate/analyst in these groups to spend the entire day at his desk, working through a large list of requests. On the upside (if you can call it that), the day will most likely end before midnight (and usually closer to 9 or 10 p.m.) and resume again promptly at 8 a.m. Although the capital markets have closed and the MD and VPs might have gone home, there are always materials needing preparation for early morning meetings and late-night, last-minute requests from deal teams. This is quite different from origination, where the day of an analyst might not end until 4 a.m., but the next day will not usually start until 10 a.m., as there is less market sensitivity in origination/structuring.

Weekend work for capital markets associates and analysts is usually a regular occurrence. While unlike the weekends of their origination counterparts, weekends for capital markets analysts and associates are usually not spent entirely in the office, the variety of the requests is less predictable than in origination. In origination, there are usually projected deadlines for projects. In capital markets, those deadlines are usually ASAP. As for sales, working on a weekend would be quite out of the ordinary. A quick phone call or BlackBerry message to a client might occur, but not the creation of market update slides or league tables, which usually happens in capital markets.

Credit/risk/corporate banking/ratings advisory

These functions are essential to the leveraged finance platform but are not generally aligned with revenue generation. As such, they are typically compensated on a lower pay scale, and the lifestyle in these groups is better.

Managing director/vice president

Similar to other senior resources, the lifestyles of the managing director and vice president roles within these teams is less intense than their coverage counterparts. With the exception of corporate banking, these roles are not usually the primary client contacts for the firm. Also, since they are not usually aligned with revenue generation, they are compensated on a different scale. Whereas an all-star managing director in origination might get the credit for bringing in $25 million of fees for a deal and will be paid in-line with this fee generation (or lack thereof in a bad year), someone in a non-revenue generation role will have more stable earnings. This means that the top-tier ratings advisory managing director will most likely not earn as much as the top-tier origination managing director. However, when it comes to compensation for group/department heads, all bets are off.

In terms of hours, the senior resources in these functions can expect to work even more predictable hours than those senior professionals in origination. Like their counterparts, weekends are usually free and you will not usually find them in the office at 9 p.m. However, as with any other major leveraged finance function, if a large or complex deal is coming to the market, everyone on a deal team usually works well past their "normal" hours.

Associate/analyst

Much like the origination/structuring and capital markets junior resources, these individuals are part of the corporate finance program at the investment banks. However, the ebb-and-flow of workload in these positions tends to be more similar to origination than to capital markets. Their day-to-day will fluctuate based on their group and or deal-flow, but will generally be long hours, marked with long-term projects and firm deadlines, such as the creation of a ratings agency presentation. Also, the pay will generally coincide with the entire corporate finance program. As for weekend work, junior resources in all of these groups can definitely expect it. Usually working intensely on one or two deals, as opposed to three to five in origination, their weekend lifestyle is slightly more predictable.

Commercial banks and commercial finance companies

Organizationally, commercial banks and commercial finance companies tend to set up their leveraged finance platforms in relation to their deal flow. Whereas some of the larger players like GE have dedicated origination teams to cover large cap and small cap issuers, smaller middle-market players might combine all of their origination, capital markets and sales roles. Typically though, the large players are set up in a manner similar to the investment banks, although they will combine the complementary functions such as sales/capital markets and underwriting/credit/risk. At these firms, the titles/hierarchy are similar to that of investment banks, as is the way that pay for each function depends on how closely tied that group is to revenue generation. However, at the commercial banks, pay and lifestyle are often very different than that at an investment bank.

A Day in the Life: Leveraged Finance Structuring/Origination Associate

7 a.m. It's a little bit early for you to be up, but you want to get a head start on the day. Since it's a Friday and your analyst has been cranking late on an info memo for a new deal, you definitely want to get into the office and review it ASAP. Also, your MD has called a 9 a.m. meeting for this deal and you want to be prepared. So, you grab the BlackBerry and head to the office.

8:15 a.m. Even as a third-year associate, you still are not used to the early morning hours, which follow long evenings. Although you were at work until 11 p.m., your adrenaline still runs high, as you are now on two live deals. One, a multibillion-dollar refinancing, was just mandated, and the second is in market with a lenders' meeting on Tuesday morning. There's always plenty going on in this job, which is exactly why you love it. You check e-mails and start to review the info memo shell that your topnotch analyst worked on late last night. That kid is definitely going places.

8:40 a.m. Realizing that you've got 20 minutes until your meeting, you run downstairs to grab a cup of coffee and a bagel.

9 a.m. You finish your bagel at your desk while reading the info memo, and head over to the meeting where the MD outlines the next tasks for the transaction. The MD is exceptionally pleased to know that the info memo was already started and you all talk about the next steps. You set a firm deadline for the info memo to be distributed to lenders, for a lenders' meeting to be held and for sit-downs with the sales and capital markets teams. The MD, always on the BlackBerry, forwards you all a note from senior management, which says how proud they are that the deal team pulled off another successful pitch. As you have been on quite a number of deals, you recognize that this is the calm before the storm and the crunch time before the deal launches.

Visit Vault at **www.vault.com** for insider company profiles, expert advice, career message boards, expert resume reviews, the Vault Job Board and more.

VAULT CAREER LIBRARY   187

10 a.m. With some clear deadlines in hand, you quickly debrief with the analyst, dividing up responsibilities. You agree to meet at the office at 10 a.m. tomorrow, to make sure that everything is on track and to review progress. Since the other analyst on your live transaction is out of the office for recruiting, you are doing all of the heavy lifting for the lenders' meeting and will need all of the help possible on this deal. With two live deals in market, things are busy right now. Thankfully your auctions have gone radio silent, while the owners review bids from the private equity shops and financing firms.

10:15 a.m. You return to your desk to find some investors have already called about the new transaction, even before the lenders' presentation has gone out. You call them back, giving them some information and passing the word along to your sales team. People are definitely excited about this deal.

10:45 a.m. As soon as you set down the phone, the VP for this deal comes over to your desk, checking in with you about the presentation. Almost on cue, the client calls, asking to review the lenders' presentation slides you sent last night. Since they will be traveling to New York on Monday for the presentation on Tuesday, they'd like to wrap up any major changes before the weekend.

11 a.m. On the call with the client, you are going slide-by-slide through your newest update to the presentation with the client. You discuss talking points, where you all should meet and any other changes. The client suggests updates to a few slides and you make note of them. Knowing these changes will be made to the info memo, you make note to change those as well. You promise to send them a soft copy of the slides by 4 p.m. so they can print them out before they leave for home.

12:30 p.m. Immediately after you get off the phone, you begin reviewing the changes. Recognizing that this will take you a few hours, you decide to grab a bite to eat from the cafeteria downstairs, since you know that you can get back to your desk quickly.

12:50 p.m. While eating lunch at your desk, you start cranking on changes. The VP stops by periodically to ask questions, but otherwise you spend most of the afternoon cranking on the changes and double-checking everything. Since hundreds of investors will be scrutinizing this deck of slides, you want it to be as perfect as possible. Also, since this is going back to the client, you want the work to be topnotch.

3 p.m. With the changes made, you circulate the presentation to the VP and MD to show them what you are sending. Often, the CFO and treasurer will call you directly and vice versa, but you still like to touch base with your deal team. Once you have final approval from them, you send over a copy of the lenders' meeting slides.

3:30 p.m. Your e-mail to the client has been sent, so now it is time to check in with your other deal team. Meanwhile, the analyst is cranking on the transaction overview section of the info memo and making good progress. You both grab some coffee to take a break, while you discuss the weekend and career stuff.

4 p.m. Once back at your desk, you check e-mails and voicemails. You make some calls to friends, check CNN and *The Wall Street Journal*, and catch up on the rest of your day. About this time, the analyst from your deal has arrived back in the office from the high-yield bond roadshow, completely exhausted. You both sit down to update on what has happened with the lenders' presentation, while you strategize what needs to happen before Tuesday's meeting. However, since the final approval for the deck of slides has not yet been given, you are really in a holding pattern on that front. Yet, updates need to be made to that info memo so that it can be sent to investors immediately after the meeting. This will definitely be your weekend work.

5 p.m. Before your MDs leave for the weekend, you check in with each of them to make sure they know where everything stands. The lenders' slides for the first transaction look great, the shell of the info memo for the refinancing transaction is underway and your auctions still remain quiet with no news. From the looks of it, you might actually have something of a weekend. You also make sure to check in with the VPs, since they are leaving shortly too. As one of them is drafting part of a credit agreement this weekend, she invites you to hop on a conference call tomorrow morning at 11 a.m. Since you will be in the office anyhow, this is fine by you.

6 p.m. You stop by both analysts' desks to see how they are doing. You divide up some minor tasks, so that everyone can get out of the office tonight, since it is a nice evening outside. With only a few hours of work on Saturday, you feel great about this weekend.

7 p.m. You shut down the laptop, remind the analysts not to stay late since a lot of that work can be done tomorrow, and you head home. As for a 7 p.m. departure on a Friday, you have seen a lot worse!

Visit Vault at **www.vault.com** for insider company profiles, expert advice, career message boards, expert resume reviews, the Vault Job Board and more.

VAULT CAREER LIBRARY 189

Employer Directory

ABN AMRO
Gustav Mahlerlaan 10
1082 PP Amsterdam
Netherlands
Phone: +31-20-628-9393
Fax: +31-20-629-9111
www.abnamro.com

Bank of America Leveraged Finance
100 North Tryon Street
Bank of America Corporate Center
Charlotte, NC 28255
Phone: (704) 386-5681
Fax: (704) 386-6699
www.bankofamerica.com

The Carlyle Group
1001 Pennsylvania Avenue NW
Washington, DC 20004-2505
Phone: (202) 729-5626
Fax: (202) 347-1818
www.thecarlylegroup.com

Citigroup
399 Park Avenue
New York, NY 10043
Phone: (212) 559-1000
Fax: (212) 793-3946
Toll free: (800) 285-3000
www.citigroup.com

Credit Suisse
11 Madison Avenue
New York, NY 10010
Phone: (212) 325-2000
Fax: (212) 325-8057
www.csfb.com

Deutsche Bank
Taunusanlage 12
60262 Frankfurt
Germany
Phone: +49-69-910-00
Fax: +49-69-910-34-225
www.deutsche-bank.de

Goldman Sachs
85 Broad Street
New York, NY 10004
Phone: (212) 902-1000
Fax: (212) 902-3000
www.goldmansachs.com

Goodwin Procter LLP
Exchange Place, 53 State Street
Boston, MA 02109
Phone: (617) 570-1000
Fax: (617) 523-1231
www.goodwinprocter.com

Jefferies & Co
212 East 47th Street, Apartment 15F
New York, NY 10017-2124
Phone: (212) 284-2550

JPMorgan Chase
270 Park Avenue
New York, NY 10017
Phone: (212) 270-6000
Fax: (212) 270-1648
www.jpmorganchase.com

KeyBank
202 South Michigan Street
South Bend, IN 46601-2021
Phone: (574) 237-5200

National City
1900 East 9th Street
Cleveland, OH 44114-3484
Phone: (216) 222-2000
Fax: (216) 222-9957
www.nationalcity.com

PNC
1 PNC Plaza, 249 5th Avenue
Pittsburgh, PA 15222-2707
Phone: (412) 762-2000
Toll Free: (888) 762-2265
Fax: (412) 762-7829
www.pnc.com

The Royal Bank of Scotland Group Leveraged Finance
36 St Andrew Square
Edinburgh, EH2 2YB
Scotland
Phone: +44-13-15-56-85-55
Fax: +44-13-15-57-61-40
www.rbs.com

SunTrust
303 Peachtree Street NE
Atlanta, GA 30308
Phone: (404) 588-7711
Fax: (404) 332-3875
Toll free: (800) 786-8787
www.suntrust.com

UBS
101 Park Avenue
New York, NY 10178
www.ubs.com

Wells Fargo & Company
420 Montgomery Street
San Francisco, CA 94163
Phone: (866) 878-5865
Fax: (626) 312-3015
Toll free: (800) 869-3557
www.wellsfargo.com

Managment Consulting

What is Consulting?

Strategy holding steady

2007 marked the consulting industry's third consecutive year of growth. The robust economy had clients interested in implementing improvements—and willing to spend top dollar to get the right advice. Positive economic conditions, such as the boom in private equity, set the stage for clients to focus on profit lines and to find savvy ways to cut costs. Consulting firms also benefited from an all-time high in M&A activity, as strategy shops were called on to help with due diligence projects or postmerger integration. In the U.S., which accounts for almost 50 percent of the worldwide consulting market, revenue hit $160 billion, up from $156 billion in 2006.

Though business was strong throughout most of 2007, by its end, the subprime mortgage crisis had changed the economic climate dramatically. Fallout from years of dubious lending policies motivated corporations across the industry spectrum to rein in their strategy spending. As a result, and in marked contrast to the double-digit growth of previous years, the consulting industry grew modestly in 2007, up just 6 percent for the year. And while analysts aren't yet predicting an all-out crisis for 2008, they are nevertheless forecasting tighter budgets and fewer engagements overall. The credit debacle hasn't meant only doom and gloom for the industry, however: In the short term, it is providing work, as financial services firms look to consultants for help with crisis management and recovery strategies. FTI Consulting, for example, has been especially prosperous of late, seeing a surge in demand in the face of the credit crunch. The firm focuses on services for companies that are facing trouble—whether economic, legal or regulatory—and its forensic accounting division, especially, has shown marked growth since 2007.

Weathering the storm

One thing is for certain—consultancies are better prepared this time around. After the dot-com trauma of the early 21st century, clients became more sophisticated buyers, demanding more value, deeper expertise and targeted solutions. Many now insist that their projects be staffed by senior level consultants—industry experts who really know their sector—rather than fresh-out-of-school generalists. In response to such client selectivity, over the last decade consulting firms have shifted strategies, offering specific industry knowledge and emphasizing quantifiable results. To differentiate themselves in the marketplace, many firms are now focused on niche areas such as economic consulting, security or globalization strategy. And rather than honing in solely on strategy, firms have also started offering a wider range of services, including IT, restructuring and compliance.

Anybody's game

With clients demanding targeted services, more niche firms (many spun off from larger consultancies after the dot-com bust and its ensuing layoffs) have entered the landscape, jousting with the larger, well-established consulting shops for projects. Competition in the consulting world has no doubt gotten tougher, since small firms are often able to undercut the fees of blue-chip houses by keeping overhead and staff expenses low. Smaller firms may also get a foot in the door by accepting projects that aren't as "sexy," such as implementation or data migration, before taking on actual strategy work.

Further heating up competition are the Big Four accounting firms that have re-entered the consulting arena. After the Enron scandal, the Securities and Exchange Commission tightened independence requirements, prompting several of the Big Four to separate their consulting divisions from their audit and accounting wings. 2007 saw the end of the five-year noncompete agreements that Ernst & Young, PricewaterhouseCoopers and KPMG signed with their spin-offs. The companies were

Visit Vault at www.vault.com for insider company profiles, expert advice, career message boards, expert resume reviews, the Vault Job Board and more.

VAULT CAREER LIBRARY   191

effectively released back into the consulting fold, and cranked up their business advisory services and financial and risk consulting divisions accordingly.

The hiatus has not diminished their brand value in clients' eyes, however: In 2007, consulting and advisory services were the fastest growing service lines for all three firms, and all posted impressive financial results. Ernst & Young posted a 29 percent revenue share coming from its transaction advisory services division in 2007, while KPMG's advisory division accounted for 32 percent of revenue and PwC's advisory service line brought in 22 percent. Deloitte, the only of the Big Four firms not to cast off its consulting practice, also enjoyed success in this area, with its advisory and consulting divisions comprising 31 percent of total revenue in 2007.

Servicing financial services

A large part of the past two years' strategy consulting growth was propelled by record-level M&A activity. Strong profits and cheaper debt drove up corporate demand for deals, while private equity firms rife with cash were eager to get in on the action. In 2007, the value of the global M&A market was $4.3 trillion (of which $1.4 trillion came from the U.S.), up 20 percent over 2006, and the frenzy created a new client base for consulting firms. As these transactions increased in value and grew more complex, consultants were called in to evaluate potential deals, analyze markets, conduct due diligence and smooth postmerger wrinkles. Bain & Company's mergers and acquisitions practice, for example, provides acquisition screening, due diligence, integration advisory and other M&A strategies aimed at growth and facilitation. Bain reported that 2007 M&A activity was strongest during the second and third quarters.

In 2008, however, with M&A and private equity activity dropping off, a range of other financial services has pumped demand for consulting services. As the market becomes more dynamic and more global, businesses are placing higher priority on risk management, raising demand for risk and security consulting. Another hot area is regulatory consulting, as banks navigate Basel II requirements and Sarbanes-Oxley compliance issues. Kennedy Information forecasts that financial services consulting spending will increase from $60 billion in 2007 to $74 billion in 2008.

America's got talent

Despite the shaky economic conditions, there are no signs of consulting firms slowing their recruiting plans. According to Kennedy Research, 75 percent of consulting firms plan to hire as many new recruits in 2008 as they did in 2007, when hiring at the junior level was at its peak. This aggressive hiring stance indicates that most firms are confident that the credit crunch won't stifle business growth in the long term. Some companies are also raising target hiring numbers to keep up with the slightly higher turnover that has resulted from competition for experienced consultants. Due to the war for talent, many U.S. firms saw 20 to 35 percent attrition in 2007.

In 2008, top graduates just entering the consulting field will be able to choose from a spectrum of options. Some will no doubt be attracted to the name and prestige of a blue-chip firm or a public entity that can offer stock options. Smaller, niche firms, on the other hand, may appeal to candidates who wish to accrue specialized experience. Although large public companies are typically able to offer higher salaries, smaller or private firms can lure candidates with the promise of more client exposure, faster career progression or profit sharing from an early stage in their career.

Recruiters are also scouring campuses for MBA candidates who have particular industry expertise, rather than a broad, generalist background. As firms seek to add value in a business climate where engagements are more complex and clients are pickier about whom they work with, specialist consultants are in high demand. Candidates with a track record in the public sector, compliance or risk management will likely have their choice of firms. Consultants with a few years' experience are also in demand, as companies seek out hires who can hit the ground running. And even with the financial services industry taking a beating, companies that specialize in this sector, such as Oliver Wyman and The Boston Consulting Group, are still hiring at a steady pace.

Cashing in

Though demand for talent is high, pay levels within the industry—both in terms of base salary and bonuses—have remained relatively flat. Some firms do offer an incentive-based compensation structure, tying bonuses to individual and group performance, and to that of the firm as a whole. As consultancies still aren't able to compete with the lucrative bonuses offered by hedge funds or private equity groups, many are sweetening employment packages with lifestyle perks like flexible schedules, work-from-home options, sabbaticals or part-time career tracks. The strategy seems to be working: Despite the unimpressive salary increases, the consulting industry remains one of the top picks for new MBA grads (and the stream of layoffs in the financial sector has no doubt enhanced the industry's allure for students).

Outsourcing's second wave

Well after the first wave of business process outsourcing projects first took customer service and software development overseas, the BPO market is still providing loads of work. In an ongoing effort to boost efficiency and save money, companies are now outsourcing more complex operations like finance, payroll and human resources. In 2007, the National Outsourcing Association estimated the North American BPO market at over $127 billion—more than half of the $217 billion global market. Consulting firms are getting a piece of this lucrative pie by assisting clients with global sourcing strategies and helping to transform their business operations to a BPO model.

Although the BPO market is still going strong, the business is trending away from the mega-deals ($1 billion-plus engagements) of the past. In North America, total contract value in 2007 dropped, as did contract duration. As *Consulting Times* posits, 2007 was the first time total contract numbers declined—by 12 percent. Part of the drop is due to maturation of the market; businesses are increasingly using several specialist providers, and contracting each for just one piece of the whole BPO project, instead of using a single outsourcing provider for all. According to Gartner Research, the highest demand for BPO services comes from the financial services and multi-process markets.

India and beyond

India continues to be a hot spot for growth, both for outsourcing and for advisory service lines. Between 2005 and 2007, IBM doubled its employee numbers in India to over 53,000, and in 2008, KPMG announced plans to raise headcount in the country from 3,000 to 5,000 by 2010. Accenture has also taken a substantial interest in the Indian market—it employs 35,000 there, more than in any other region, and maintains 12 global delivery centers.

Though most consulting firms are still investing resources in the subcontinent, India's rising labor costs and shortage of talent have firms eyeing China. In fact, according to a 2007 report from research firm IDC, China is expected to overtake India as the top outsourcing destination by 2011. Deloitte aims to have 20,000 employees in China by 2015, up from 8,500 in 2007, and Ernst & Young plans to expand from 8,000 to 30,000 in the country over the next decade, adding two or three new branches in Asia annually within the next few years. Additional areas popping up as prime BPO centers include Vietnam, Singapore and the Philippines. In fact, IDC predicts that the Asia Pacific BPO market as a whole will expand to $14 billion by 2010.

The next big thing

Consulting firms are also seeing business take off in other developing economies, such as Eastern Europe. Outsourcing in the region has been ramping up, thanks to the availability of highly educated, multilingual workers who demand less in salary than their Western European counterparts. The region's outsourcing industry, estimated at $2 billion in 2007, is expected to grow 30 percent by 2010. But Eastern Europe is now more than just an outsourcing destination; it is becoming a strong market for strategy consulting. As more countries in the region meet European Union economic standards, and as formerly

Visit Vault at www.vault.com for insider company profiles, expert advice, career message boards, expert resume reviews, the Vault Job Board and more.

VAULT CAREER LIBRARY   193

state-owned industries—such as telecommunications—deregulate, multinational businesses are establishing a presence in Turkey, Romania, the Czech Republic and Russia. As such, consultants are being tapped by banks, financial services and telecom clients to help them navigate these new markets. Kennedy Information predicts that growth in the $4 billion Eastern European consulting market will outpace that of the Western European market through 2009.

Earthy efforts

Environmental awareness was an emerging focus for the consulting industry in 2007. The pitfalls of global warming prompted a number of firms to adopt long-term initiatives with the stated goal of reducing their carbon footprint—many even hoping to achieve carbon neutrality. L.E.K., Capgemini and A.T. Kearney, as well as others, launched formal green programs in 2007. Among their resolutions are increased use of recycled and recyclable office materials, reduced energy waste in daily operations and minimization of air travel to client sites. These firms and others also spearheaded environmental advisory practice areas, applying the lessons of conservation learned in their own programs toward assisting clients, especially those in industries such as oil and gas, chemicals and energy, that face increasingly stringent compliance standards.

Consulting Myths

All this might sound great, but before we go on, we should address some common misconceptions about consulting.

- **Implementation**—You might be thinking, "All consultants do is figure out problems at companies and explain them. Awesome. I'm going to be making great money for doing something really easy." Unfortunately, that's not true. Spotting a client's problems is a mere fraction of the battle. (Most people with a fair amount of common sense and an outsider's perspective can identify a client's problems. And in many cases, clients also understand where the problems lie.)

  The job of the consultant, therefore, isn't just about knowing what's wrong. It's about figuring out how to make it right. Even finding the solution isn't the end of the story. Consultants must make sure the solution isn't too expensive or impractical to implement. (Many consulting firms have what's called an 80 percent rule: it's better to put in place a solution that takes care of 80 percent of the problem than to strive for a perfect solution that can't be put into place.) A corollary to this is the 80/20 rule: 80 percent of a problem can be solved in 20 percent of the time. Consultants must also get buy-in from the clients. Not only does bureaucracy often make implementation tough, but consultants must also convince individual client employees to help them make solutions work. It's tough to solve problems—and that's why clients hire consultants.

- **Glamour**—Consulting can indeed be exciting and high profile, but this is the exception, not the rule. Chances are, you won't be sitting across from the CEO at your next project kickoff, and you probably won't be staying in four-star hotels in the coolest cities in the world (though both are possible). Depending on the industry and location of your client's business, your environment might be a mid-range hotel in a small city, and you might be working with the senior vice president of one of the company's many business units.

- **Prestige**—Consulting is widely thought of as a prestigious career among business circles, particularly MBAs. But you should realize that in contrast to work in investment banking, your work in consulting will probably never get mentioned in *The Wall Street Journal*. Very few consulting firms are publicly recognized for the help they give.

  As a result, few people outside of the industry really understand what consulting is. In fact, a running joke about consulting is that no one can explain it, no matter how hard or many times one tries. If you want a job you can explain to your grandmother, consulting isn't for you. Most "civilians" won't have heard of your firm—unless it has been involved in a scandal, that is.

- **Income**—The salary looks attractive on paper, but remember, it's not easy money. Divide your salary over the (large) number of hours, and the pay per hour isn't much better than other business careers.

So what does a consultant actually do, anyway?

Most "non-consultants" are mystified by the actual job and its day-to-day responsibilities. There are good reasons why this is so. While you're used to giving advice and solving problems, you may not understand how this translates into a career path. The problem is compounded because consultants tend to use a very distinctive vocabulary. You may not know what your skill set is, or how not to boil the ocean, or what the heck consultants mean when they talk about helicoptering. In addition, many consulting firms have their own specific philosophies and problem-attacking frameworks, which only raise the level of jargon.

The short answer is that you will be working on projects of varying lengths at varying sites for different clients. What you do will depend on your seniority, experience, phase of the project and your company. If you are a partner, you are selling work most of the time, whereas if you have a recent MBA degree, you are probably overseeing a couple of entry-level consultants doing research. For the most part, we'll describe the job that entry-level and midlevel (MBA or the equivalent) consultants do. Generally, projects follow the pitching/research/analysis/report writing cycle.

Depending where you are in the project lifecycle, here are some of the things you could be doing:

Pitching

- Helping to sell and market the firm (preparing documents and researching prospective clients in preparation for sales calls)
- Helping to write the proposal
- Presenting a sales pitch to a prospective client (usually with PowerPoint, Microsoft's presentation software)

Research

- Performing secondary research on the client and its industry using investment banking reports and other research sources (these include Bloomberg, OneSource, Hoover's Online, Yahoo! News and SEC filings)
- Interviewing the client's customers to gather viewpoints on the company
- Checking your firm's data banks for previous studies that it has done in the industry or with the client, and speaking to the project leads about their insights on the firm
- Facilitating a weekly client team discussion about the client company's business issues

Analysis

- Building Excel discounted cash flow (DCF) and/or other quantitative financial models
- Analyzing the gathered data and the model for insights
- Helping to generate recommendations

Reporting

- Preparing the final presentation (typically a "deck" of PowerPoint slides, though some firms write up longer reports in Microsoft Word format)
- Helping to present the findings and recommendations to the client

Implementation

- Acting as a project manager for the implementation of your strategy, if your firm is typically active during the implementation phase of a project
- Executing the coding, systems integration and testing of the recommended system, if you work for an IT consulting practice
- Documenting the team's work after the project is over

Administration

- Working on internal company research when your firm has no projects for you. (Being unstaffed is referred to as being "on the beach," a pleasant name for what is often a tedious time.)
- Filling out weekly time tracking and expense reports

Visit Vault at **www.vault.com** for insider company profiles, expert advice, career message boards, expert resume reviews, the Vault Job Board and more.

VAULT CAREER LIBRARY   195

Keep in mind that the analysis phase—usually the most interesting part—is probably the shortest part of any assignment. Consultants staffed on projects typically do a lot of research, financial analysis, Excel model building and presentation. You will attend lots of meetings in your quest to find the data, create the process and meet the people who will help you resolve the issues you've been hired to address. And, when you're not staffed, you will spend time "on the beach" doing research on prospective clients and helping with marketing efforts. (It's called "on the beach" because the time when you're not staffed on a paid engagement is usually less frenetic—though not always so!) Consulting firms spend a lot of time acquiring the work, and depending on how the firm is structured or how the economy is doing, you could spend significant amounts of time working on proposals. For you, this usually means lots of research, which is then elucidated on the omnipresent PowerPoint slides.

To some extent, though, the boundaries of the job are virtually limitless. Each project carries with it a new task, a new spreadsheet configuration, a new type of sales conference, or an entirely new way of thinking about business. To top it all off, you often must travel to your work assignment and work long hours in a pressurized environment. It's not easy.

Practice Areas

Operations and implementation

Operations consulting is what puts strategy into action. In years past, operations consulting focused on saving money and increasing efficiency. In the recent booming economy, however, clients were more focused on expansion and profit growth, so operations consulting now revolves around responding to market changes, globalization and customer interaction (though today, with clients taking a cautionary stance toward spending, there has been a slight shift back to earlier conventions). While strategy involves marking out clear goals, operations consulting focuses on the practical means of reaching these goals, which might include allocating resources, shifting value chain priorities, evaluating benefits of outsourcing or examining customer service and distribution—all to help clients alter processes in response to competition or react to shifts in the market. Kennedy Information estimates that the $45 billion operational consulting market will grow at a compound annual growth rate of 7.1 percent through 2010.

Typical engagements may include:

- Evaluating procurement, sourcing and supplier relationships for a manufacturer
- Developing a global financial reporting system for a multinational business
- Implementing a customer loyalty program to help a credit card company attract and retain customers

Human resources consulting

Even with fine-tuned strategies and streamlined operations, businesses won't succeed without the right people in place. HR consulting addresses the issue of maximizing the value of staff and placing the right employees in roles that suit them. HR consulting firms are also hired for organizational restructuring, talent management, HR systems implementation, benefits planning and compensation. This segment is expected to expand in 2008, and to continue growing at a compound annual rate of 83 percent through 2010, according to Kennedy Information. Increased demand for benefits consulting, due to revisions in the U.S. Pension Protection Act and Financial Accounting Standards Board changes to pension plans, is contributing to growth in the market.

An important subsection of HR consulting is HR outsourcing. Increasingly, clients are turning to HR consulting firms to manage their internal HR systems. Kennedy Information reports that the combined global market for HR outsourcing and HR BPO was worth $31 billion at the end of 2007.

Examples of typical human resources consulting engagements include:

• Helping a business devise a leadership development plan for its junior employees

• Evaluating the financial consequences of changing benefits plans

• Developing a retention strategy for a firm that has experienced high turnover

Health care/pharmaceuticals consulting

With a market worth over $20 billion, health care consulting continues to be a core growth area. As the U.S. population and that of other industrialized countries ages, as scientists make further advances in genetic engineering and as patents for blockbuster drugs expire, the health care industry thrives.

The National Coalition on Health Care reports that total U.S. health care expenditures were $2.3 trillion in 2007, and are expected to hit $4.2 trillion by 2016. Furthermore, health spending in the U.S., at 16 percent of GDP, accounts for a larger share of GDP than in any other major industrialized country. With so much cash at stake, the industry is predictably overrun with players. That's where health care and pharmaceutical consulting firms come into play—helping clients, such as life sciences firms, hospitals, HMOs and drug companies, navigate a complicated maze of legislation, tackle competition, manage costs on vendors and equipment, and implement new technology.

Examples of typical health care/pharmaceutical engagements include:

• Developing an electronic medical records system for a hospital

• Analyzing market competition for a new pharmaceutical product

• Helping an insurance company manage reimbursements

Economic consulting

With global economies growing progressively intertwined, businesses in the U.S. are no longer isolated from economic shifts in other parts of the world. Thus, clients often turn to think tank-like economic consulting firms for guidance. These firms, typically loaded with economics PhDs and MBAs, as well as industry experts, investigate the economic factors that help clients resolve competition, antitrust, public policy and regulation issues, both domestic and global. Quantitative analysis, statistical studies and modeling services often form the core of economic consulting engagements.

Examples of typical economic consulting engagements include:

• Helping a client comply with a multitude of tax regulations in the various countries in which it operates

• Projecting the financial impact of a new environmental regulation

• Assessing the implications of a proposed merger

Financial consulting

In 2007, consulting spending by the financial services industry topped $60 billion, and is projected to hit $74 billion by 2011, according to Kennedy Information. Growth in the sector is predicted to remain strong over the long term, despite (and largely due to) current credit woes. The market has gained momentum as consultants step in to assist companies manage crises, deal with global market competition, develop offshore establishments and find new markets and customers. Other financial service areas driving expansion are regulatory compliance, M&A, divestitures, private equity and risk.

Financial consulting firms tend toward two types of service offerings; either they work with financial services firms to enhance their strategies and performance, or they use a specific financial model to enhance client performance. In both cases, the focus is typically on boosting shareholder value.

Visit Vault at **www.vault.com** for insider company profiles, expert advice, career message boards, expert resume reviews, the Vault Job Board and more.

VAULT CAREER LIBRARY   197

Examples of typical financial consulting engagements include:

- Applying a proprietary financial model to improve performance
- Helping an investment firm identify a strategy to reach a new target market
- Evaluating liquidity for a private equity firm

Consulting Skill Sets

Consultants focus their energies in a wide variety of practice areas and industries. Their individual jobs, from a macro level, are as different as one could imagine. While a supply chain consultant advises a client about lead times in their production facility, another consultant is creating a training protocol for a new software package. What could be more different?

Despite the big picture differences, however, consultants' day-to-day skill sets are, by necessity, very similar. (Before we go any further: by skill set, we mean "your desirable attributes and skills that contribute value as a consultant." Skill set is a handy, abbreviated way to refer to same.)

Before we talk about the skill sets, keep in mind that there is a big difference between the job now and the job six to eight years from now, if and when you are a partner. We are going to talk about whether you would like the job now, but you should think about whether this might be a good long-term career for you. Is your goal to see it through to partner? If you would rather have an interesting job for six years, you just have to know you have the qualities to be a good consultant and manager. To be a partner, you have to be a persuasive salesperson. You will spend nearly 100 percent of your time selling expensive services to companies who don't think they need help. Your pay and job security will depend on your ability to make those sales.

Do you have the following characteristics in your skill set?

- **Do you work well in teams?** Consultants don't work alone. Not only do they frequently brainstorm with other consultants, but they also often work with employees at the client company, or even with consultants from other companies hired by the client. Consultants also frequently attend meetings and interview potential information sources. If you're the sort of person who prefers to work alone in quiet environments, you will not enjoy being a consultant.

- **Do you multitask well?** Not only can consulting assignments be frenetic, but consultants are often staffed on more than one assignment. Superior organizational skills and a good sense of prioritization are your friends. Would your friends describe you as a really busy person who's involved in a ton of activities, and still able to keep your personal life on track?

- **Speaking of friends, do you like talking to people?** Do you find yourself getting into interesting conversations over lunch and dinner? If you consider yourself a true introvert and find that speaking to people all day saps your energy, you will likely find consulting quite enervating. On the other hand, if you truly relish meetings, talking to experts, explaining your viewpoints, cajoling others to cooperate with you and making impromptu presentations, you've got some valuable talents in your consulting skill set.

- **Did you love school?** Did you really like going to class and doing your homework? There's a high correlation between academic curiosity and enjoyment of consulting.

- **Are you comfortable with math?** Consulting firms don't expect you to be a math professor, but you should be comfortable with figures, as well as commonly used programs like Excel, Access and PowerPoint. If you hate math, you will hate consulting. On a related note, you should also relish and be good at analysis and thinking creatively. Consultants have a term, now infiltrating popular culture, called "out of the box thinking." This means the ability to find solutions that are "outside the box"—not constrained by commonly accepted facts.

- **Are you willing to work 70, even 80 hours a week?** Consultants must fulfill client expectations. If you must work 80 hours a week to meet client expectations, then that will be your fate. If you have commitments outside work, for example, you may find consulting hours difficult. Even if you have no major commitments outside work, understand what such a schedule means to you. Try working from 8 a.m. to 10 p.m. one day. Now imagine doing so five days a week for months on end.

- **Last, but certainly not least, are you willing to travel frequently?** (See the sidebar on page 193 for a discussion of travel in consulting.)

Be truthful. If you can't answer most of these points with a resounding "yes," consulting is most likely not for you. The point is not just to get the job, but also to know what you're getting into—and to truly want to be a consultant.

Who Hires Consultants, and Why?

Corporations, governments and nonprofit institutions hire consultants for a number of reasons. Every consulting project springs from a client's need for help, or at least the kind of help that short-term, internal hiring can't solve. Some clients, for example, need to overhaul their entire IT infrastructure, yet they're out of touch with the latest back-end systems or don't have the staff resources for such a large project. Other clients may be merging, but lack any experience with post-merger staffing procedures and need a neutral party to mediate. Some clients may need an outsider's perspective on a plant shutdown. Perhaps a client wants to bring in extra industry knowledge.

Consultants get hired for political reasons too. Launching big projects can be very cumbersome, particularly at Fortune 500 companies. In order for a single dollar to be spent on such a project, most companies require senior executive approval. And without a major consultancy brand name attached to the project, approval can be hard to get. But once a consulting firm steps into the picture, everyone involved has plausible deniability in the event that the project fails. There is an old adage: "No one ever got fired for hiring McKinsey" (or a similarly prestigious consulting firm). Some clients still adhere to this as a rule of thumb.

Second, even if a giant project gets the green light, there's no guaranteeing it will be implemented. The reason? Simple bureaucratic inertia. Senior executives lose interest. Direct reports move on to other issues. In short, companies lose their focus. (An insider at a large private global corporation reports that steps from a major consulting report from 1996 were approved but, as of September 2002, had not yet been implemented.) By bringing in consultants to oversee large projects, companies ensure that someone is always watching the ball. In many cases, the correct solution may be quite evident to many, but having it confirmed by an outside party makes implementing a plan easier politically.

In the era of downsizing, consultants have another political use. Companies with an itch to fire a percentage of their workforce often like to bring in consultants. When the consultants recommend a workforce reduction, the company can fire at will, blaming their hired guns for the downsizing.

For some types of consulting (particularly outsourcing or IT), consultants are actually a form of cost-effective labor. It costs the firm less money to hire some outsiders to help them with a project, rather than hire some folks full time at the expense of a competitive salary and benefits package. Consultants may also get the job done faster, not because they are necessarily better, but because the company might not get away with forcing regular employees to adhere to a compressed time frame by staying late hours. By definition, consultants are hired to work not at the pace of the corporation but at a differently prescribed pace. A contingency performance basis makes this an even better deal for the client.

Whatever the reasons for hiring consultants, they're bound to be compelling—because, even despite the cost-effectiveness argument in some cases, consultants are very costly on average. Given travel expenses, hotel bills and actual project fees, hourly prices for consultants can easily climb into the $500 per hour range.

The worker behind the curtain

Consultants are a backroom breed of professional. In joint projects with their clients, they do much of the work and can expect none of the recognition. All consultants must deliver bottom-line value, and often spend countless hours huddled in

Visit Vault at **www.vault.com** for insider company profiles, expert advice, career message boards, expert resume reviews, the Vault Job Board and more.

V/\ULT CAREER LIBRARY 199

cramped spaces to do just that. If you do a great job, chances are your client will thank you, but you may never hear about it again. In some cases, you will leave your project before its completion and may never know whether it succeeded or failed.

If you enjoy recognition and completion, you will want to consider the type of consulting firm you join. Does your firm have a history of repeat business? If so, you will have a better chance of seeing the client through different projects and business cycles; you may even work with the same client on different engagements. (Marakon Associates, for example, boasts that 90 percent of its work comes from engagements with previous clients.) Other firms might offer a methodology that isn't as repeatable. If your firm focuses solely on competitive analysis studies, chances are good that, if your client stays in the same industry, you won't need to sell that service to them again.

Economic consulting firms, like Charles River Associates and the Brattle Group, often help law firms with litigation support, including research, economic analysis and testimonies. This can be very interesting work, and since you're supporting one side or the other of a public dispute, you will certainly know how the fruits of your labor will turn out. Depending on the size of the dispute, so might everyone else who follows the business news.

Another example is M&A consulting. Some firms, like L.E.K. Consulting, have practice areas specifically focused on due diligence, company analysis and transaction support. The bad news is that on such projects, you are subject to the even longer and more erratic hours suffered by other M&A professionals. On the bright side, you will eventually read in *The Wall Street Journal* about any triumph enjoyed by your client. Your firm may not be mentioned, but at least you will be able to see the results of your hard work become a reality. (It'll also be easier for you to transition to other financial work in the future, if that is your wish.)

So, think about the level of recognition and completion you need for your work, and look for a firm that does the type of work that suits your level. If you find that you require higher levels of recognition and completion than any type of consulting can offer, then you may want to look into other professions.

The Traveling Salesman Problem

A lot of people go into the consulting field with the notion that travel is fun. "Traveling four days a week? No problem! My last vacation to Italy was a blast!" However, many soon find the traveling consultant's life to be a nightmare. Many consultants leave the field solely because of travel requirements.

Here's what we mean by consulting travel. Different consulting firms have different travel models, but there are two basic ones:

- A number of consulting firms (the larger ones) spend four days on the client site. This means traveling to the destination city Monday morning, spending three nights in a hotel near the client site, and flying home late Thursday night. (This will, of course, vary depending on client preference and flight times.) The same firms often try to staff "regionally" to reduce flying time for consultants.

- The other popular travel model is to go to the client site "as needed." This generally means traveling at the beginning of the project for a few days, at the end of the project for the presentation, and a couple of times during the project. There is less regularity and predictability with this travel model, but there is also less overall time on the road.

Here are some variations of these travel modes that pop up frequently:

- International projects involve a longer-term stay on the client site. (Flying consultants to and from the home country every week can get expensive.) For example, the consultant might stay two or three weeks on or near the client site (the client might put you up in a corporate apartment instead of a hotel to save costs) and then go home for a week, repeating the process until the end of the project.

- Then, there is the "local" project that is really a long commute into a suburb, sometimes involving up to two hours in a car. Examples of this include consulting to Motorola (based in not-so-convenient Schaumburg, Ill.)

while living in Chicago, or consulting to a Silicon Valley client while living in San Francisco. In these cases, you might opt to stay at a local hotel after working late, instead of taking the long drive home. This is not very different from nonlocal travel, and it can be more grueling, due to the car commute.

You need to ask yourself a number of questions to see if you are travel-phobic. For example, when you pack to go on vacation, do you stress about it? Do you always underpack or overpack? Do you hate flying? Do you hate to drive? Do you mind sleeping in hotel rooms for long periods of time? Are you comfortable with the idea of traveling to remote cities and staying there for three or four nights every week for 10 weeks? If you're married, do you mind being away from your spouse (and children if you have them) for up to three nights a week? Does your family mind? Will your spouse understand and not hold it against you if you have to cancel your anniversary dinner because the client wants you to stay a day later? If you and your spouse both travel for work, who will take care of the pets? Does the idea of managing your weekly finances and to-do lists from the road bother you?

If these questions make your stomach churn, look for consulting companies that promise a more stable work environment. For example, if you work in financial consulting and live in New York City, most of your clients may be local. But because consulting firms don't always have the luxury of choosing their clients, they can't guarantee that you won't travel. Moreover, many large companies build their corporate campus where they can find cost-effective space, often in the suburbs or large corporate parks. (If you absolutely cannot travel, some of the largest consulting firms, such as Accenture, have certain business units that can guarantee a non-traveling schedule—ask.)

Note that travel is common in the consulting field, but not all consultants travel. And not all clients expect you to be on site all the time. It absolutely depends on the firm's travel model, industry, your location and, most importantly, your project.

A Day in the Life: Associate Strategy Consultant

Greg Schneider is an associate at the Boston office of a top strategy consulting firm office. He kindly agreed to share a "typical" workday with Vault, noting that no day at any consulting firm can be called typical.

6:15 a.m. Alarm goes off. I wake up asking myself why I put "run three times per week" into the team charter. I meet another member of the team, and we hobble out for a jog. At least it's warm out—another advantage of having a project in Miami.

7:15 a.m. Check voicemail. Someone in London wants a copy of my knowledge building document on managing hypergrowth. A co-worker is looking for information about what the partner from my last team is like to work with.

7:30 a.m. Breakfast with the team. We discuss sports, Letterman and a morning meeting we have with the client team (not necessarily in that order). We then head out to the client.

9 a.m. Meet with the client team. We've got an important progress review with the CEO next week, so there's a lot going on. We're helping the client to assess the market potential of an emerging technology. Today's meeting concerns what kind of presentation would be most effective, although we have trouble staying off tangents about the various analyses that we've all been working on. The discussion is complicated by the fact that some key data is not yet available. We elect to go with a computer-based slide show and begin the debate on the content.

10:53 a.m. Check voicemail. The office is looking for an interviewer for the Harvard Business School hell weekend. The partner will be arriving in time for dinner and wants to meet to discuss the progress review. A headhunter looking for a divisional VP. My wife reminding me to mail off the insurance forms.

11 a.m. I depart with my teammate for an interview. We meet with an industry expert (a professor from a local university) to discuss industry trends and in particular what the prospects are for the type of technology we're looking at. As this is the

Visit Vault at **www.vault.com** for insider company profiles, expert advice, career message boards, expert resume reviews, the Vault Job Board and more.

VAULT CAREER LIBRARY 201

last interview we plan to do, we are able to check many of our hypotheses. The woman is amazing—we luck out and get some data we need. The bad news is, now we have to figure out what it means.

12:28 p.m. As I walk back in to the client, a division head I've been working with grabs me and we head to lunch. He wanted to discuss an analysis he'd given me some information for, and in the process I get some interesting perspectives about the difficulties in moving the technology into full production and how much it could cost.

1:30 p.m. I jump on a quick conference call about an internal knowledge building project I'm working on for the marketing practice. I successfully avoid taking on any additional responsibility.

2:04 p.m. Begin to work through new data. After discussing the plan of attack with the engagement manager, I dive in. It's a very busy afternoon, but the data is great. I get a couple "a-ha"s—always a good feeling.

3 p.m. Short call with someone from legal to get an update on the patent search.

6 p.m. Team meeting. The engagement manager pulls the team together to check progress on various fronts and debate some issues prior to heading to dinner with the partner. A quick poll determines that Italian food wins—we leave a voicemail with the details.

6:35 p.m. Call home and check in with the family. Confirm plans for weekend trip to Vermont. Apologize for forgetting to mail the insurance forms.

7:15 p.m. The team packs up and heads out to dinner. We meet the partner at the restaurant and have a productive (and calorific) meal working through our plans for the progress review, the new data, what's going on with the client team, and other areas of interest. She suggests some additional uses for the new data, adds her take on our debates and agrees to raise a couple issues with the CFO, whom she's known for years. She takes a copy of our draft presentation to read after dinner.

9:15 p.m. Return to hotel. Plug in computer and check e-mail, since I hadn't had a chance all day. While I'm logged in, I download two documents I need from the company database, check the Red Sox score, and see how the client's stock did.

10:10 p.m. Presleep voicemail check. A client from a previous study is looking for one of the appendices, since he lost his copy. The server will be down for an hour tomorrow night.

10:30 p.m. Watch *SportsCenter* instead of going right to sleep, as I know I probably should.

Note: Had this been an in-town study, the following things would have been different: I wouldn't have run with another member of my team, and we'd have substituted a conference call for the dinner meeting, so we could go home instead. Also, I probably wouldn't have watched *SportsCenter*.

Vault Q&A: Heather Eberle, Deutsche Post World Net Inhouse Consulting

Before attending Thunderbird, the Garvin School of International Management, Heather Eberle worked as an external consultant. Once at business school, she focused her job search on lesser known internal consulting opportunities. After graduating, she joined the in-house consulting division of international shipping giant Deutsche Post World Net (DPWN). She spoke with Vault about her experience with internal consulting at DPWN, especially in light of her previous experience as an external consultant.

Vault: Tell me about your background prior to getting your MBA.

Eberle: I was in consulting for five years at a smaller HRIS/strategy implementation firm.

Vault: So when you went to get your MBA, were you specifically looking for internal consulting positions?

Eberle: Yes, consulting or operations. Internal consulting had always appealed to me because it seemed like the work/life balance was better than the external consulting opportunities.

With external consulting, the travel is difficult. Maybe you are home on a Thursday night, but then leave Sunday night—every week. You are lucky if you get 48 hours at your house every week.

Vault: How did you find the position at DPWN?

Eberle: Alumni recruiting at school. We also had alumni postings for other in-house consulting positions, which opened my eyes to the size and scope of this job market. In my experience, these in-house jobs were often referred to as "in-house consulting" or "strategic projects group" along with some other key phrases. PMOs—project management organizations—which plan and manage projects are also an option and can be similar to consulting organizations.

Vault: How large is the DPWN InHouse Consulting group?

Eberle: In total around 150 people with about 20 each in our Fort Lauderdale and Singapore offices and the remainder in Bonn, Germany.

There is quite a bit of movement between offices as projects change. The organization is large enough to accommodate those who choose not to travel, but offers the opportunity for those who would like to work in another office. In addition, because of the group's worldwide footprint, there are project opportunities in many different countries and regions.

The consulting practice started in 1999 in Germany and the U.S. group was incorporated a year ago. We just returned from the annual InHouse Consulting conference in Germany where one of the main goals was to build up the ties between the groups and networking.

Vault: Is it mostly MBAs or also undergrad analysts?

Eberle: Mostly MBAs.

Vault: How does the work at DPWN compare to your previous experience in consulting?

Eberle: I would say that it is pretty similar to what you would expect with respect to the typical consulting engagement—all projects differ based on client needs.

Within DPWN there are organizational strategy projects that last six to nine months, operations projects that last three months and incremental improvement projects that last a month or two such as sales force optimization. It all depends on the scope of the project.

Vault: How is staffing done?

Eberle: Staffing is based on availability and skill set. DPWN probably does a better job than some eternal consultancies, which have a tendency to move consultants around frequently. At DPWN you would not be pulled off your project and moved to a new project unless you have some very specific expertise that is needed and unavailable elsewhere within the group.

Vault: So who are your "clients" when you're working on an engagement?

Eberle: We only accept projects that are sponsored by a member of the management board. However, the client may be a director, SVP or EVP with P&L ownership. In these cases we add them into the discussion regarding the consulting approach in-house consulting will employ. If there is no agreement, we decline to take the project.

Vault: And how are the projects requested? Or is it that they're not requested but that the CEO or some other high-level manager wants your group to go in and work with a group?

Eberle: In many cases, the business is requesting assistance either because they lack the project expertise or need someone from outside their department who is better able to identify key issues or manage pressure from disparate stakeholders.

Visit Vault at **www.vault.com** for insider company profiles, expert advice, career message boards, expert resume reviews, the Vault Job Board and more.

VAULT CAREER LIBRARY   **203**

In other cases, we identify a business issue that appears to be similar to another project we have worked on. If we felt that the methodology and expertise of InHouse Consulting could help the business, we would prepare a proposal—however, this is less common.

Vault: And so it's not often that it's because of poor performance that you're there and they don't actually want you to be there?

Eberle: I think that it is less the case that the business does not want us to be there for two reasons. One, InHouse Consulting does not engage in projects that are unlikely to secure buy-in and therefore success. Two, as DPWN employees our goal is to increase the success of the group—not get paid a fat bonus for a solution that won't work, and I think others in the business recognize this.

This is reflected in the amount of information you can get regarding the problem and solutions. I have found that it is really fun to get into the nitty-gritty because it is much more challenging to say here's 10 general best-practice recommendations versus here's 10 extremely detailed recommendations you can begin implementing tomorrow.

Vault: Why are you able to get into more detail?

Eberle: Because we are part of the company, there is zero likelihood we, as a consulting group, would data mine information from one project and use it for a competitor's project. For example, the five-year strategic operations roadmap for a business is not going to be shared with other consulting groups due to security concerns. By having access to the roadmap we may find out about an acquisition target that would change our recommendations.

The other great thing about InHouse Consulting is all the specialized knowledge we have within the group. It is enormously helpful to have a network to rely on if you have a question about anything logistics related. If you worked at an outside consulting firm unless you had a large logistics practice, it could take you days to come up with answers to some of the specialized logistics questions.

At InHouse Consulting everyone is extremely supportive and friendly. The best part is that we all work together, working towards the same goal of increasing the organizational effectiveness of DPWN. I didn't always get that feeling as an external consultant.

Vault: What sort of projects have you worked on?

Eberle: I worked on a project investigating market opportunities, which was great fun. I have worked on project working on sales force optimization and I am currently on a project looking at finance and accounting. The projects are quite different but each has been very interesting.

Vault: Were all these projects in Florida?

Eberle: They were all based in Fort Lauderdale but have included components from all regions of the world. The great thing about DPWN is that every project has a high degree of internationalization to it.

Vault: What are your hours like?

Eberle: Usually, 9 to 7. The group generally does not work weekends, which has been nice. There may be some travel, but it is not the weekly grind and usually you get to come home to sleep in your own bed—which means you are pretty much guaranteed to get a good night's sleep.

Vault: What are some other advantages of in-house consulting versus external consulting?

Eberle: One of the key advantages is that many in-house consulting groups have strong ties within the management level of the organization, which often allows for movement directly from the consulting group into the management track.

In this respect in-house consulting is similar to project based management development programs, but in-house consulting groups typically have a higher degree of project diversity. Because you have worked on projects for a variety of functions within the organization, you can often follow an accelerated career path.

In-house consulting also allows you to build a really strong network due to the number of clients you work with. With external consulting, while there are opportunities to join the companies you're consulting with, you probably don't have experience working with a number of functions within the client organization.

Visit Vault at **www.vault.com** for insider company profiles, expert advice, career message boards, expert resume reviews, the Vault Job Board and more.

VAULT CAREER LIBRARY   205

Employer Directory

A.T. Kearney
222 West Adams Street
Chicago, IL 60606
Phone: (312) 648-0111
www.atkearney.com

Accenture
1345 Avenue of the Americas
New York, NY 10105
Phone: (917) 452-4400
Fax: (917) 527-9915
www.accenture.com

The Advisory Board Company
2445 M Street NW
Washington, DC 20037
Phone: (202) 266-5600
Fax: (202) 266-5700
www.advisoryboardcompany.com

AlixPartners
2000 Town Center, Suite 2400
Southfield, MI 48075
Phone: (248) 358-4420
Fax: (248) 358-1969
www.alixpartners.com

Alvarez & Marsal
600 Lexington Avenue, 6th Floor
New York, NY 10022
Phone: (212) 759-4433
Fax: (212) 759-5532
www.alvarezandmarsal.com

Analysis Group, Inc.
111 Huntington Avenue, 10th Floor
Boston, MA 02199
Phone: (617) 425-8000
Fax: (617) 425-8001
www.analysisgroup.com

Aon Consulting Worldwide
Aon Center
200 East Randolph Street, 10th Floor
Chicago, IL 60601
Phone: (312) 381-4844
Fax: (312) 381-0240
www.aon.com/hcc

Archstone Consulting
4 Stamford Plaza
107 Elm Street, 6th Floor
Stamford, CT 06902
Phone: (203) 940-8200
Fax: (203) 940-8201
www.archstoneconsulting.com

Arthur D. Little
125 High Street
High Street Tower, 28th Floor
Boston, MA 02110
Phone: (617) 532-9550
Fax: (617) 261-6630
www.adlittle-us.com

Bain & Company
131 Dartmouth Street
Boston, MA 02116
Phone: (617) 572-2000
Fax: (617) 572-2427
www.bain.com

**BearingPoint Inc.
Management & Technology
Consultants**
1676 International Drive
McLean, VA 22102
Phone: (703) 747-3000
Fax: (703) 747-8500
www.bearingpoint.com

Booz & Company
101 Park Avenue, 18th Floor
New York, NY 10178
Phone: (212) 697-1900
Fax: (212) 551-6732
www.booz.com

The Boston Consulting Group
1 Beacon Street
Boston, MA 02108
Phone: (617) 973-1200
Fax: (617) 973-1339
www.bcg.com

Cambridge Associates LLC
100 Summer Street
Boston, MA 02110
Phone: (617) 457-7500
Fax: (617) 457-7501
www.cambridgeassociates.com

CRA International, Inc.
John Hancock Tower
200 Clarendon Street, T-33
Boston, MA 02116
Phone: (617) 425-3000
Fax: (617) 425-3132
www.crai.com

Cornerstone Research
353 Sacramento Street, 23rd Floor
San Francisco, CA 94111
Phone: (415) 229-8100
Fax: (415) 229-8199

599 Lexington Avenue, 43rd Floor
New York, NY 10022
Phone: (212) 605-5000
Fax: (212) 759-3045
www.cornerstone.com

Corporate Executive Board
1919 North Lynn Street
Arlington, VA 22209
Phone: (571) 303-3000
Fax: (571) 303-3100
www.executiveboard.com

Deloitte
1633 Broadway, 35th Floor
New York, NY 10019
Phone: (212) 492-4500
Fax: (212) 492-4743
www.deloitte.com

**Diamond Management &
Technology Consultants, Inc.**
John Hancock Center, Suite 3000
875 North Michigan Avenue
Chicago, IL 60611
Phone: (312) 255-5000
Fax: (312) 255-6000
www.diamondconsultants.com

Employer Directory, cont.

Deutsche Post World Net Inhouse Consulting
1200 S Pine Island Road
Suite 210
Plantation, FL 33324
Phone: (954) 888-7000
www.dhl.com

Ernst & Young LLP
5 Times Square
New York, NY 10036
Phone: (212) 773-3000
Fax: (212) 773-6350
www.ey.com

First Manhattan Consulting Group
90 Park Avenue
New York, NY 10016
Phone: (212) 557-0500
www.fmcg.com

FTI Consulting, Inc.
500 East Pratt Street, Suite 1400
Baltimore, MD 21202
Phone: (410) 951-4800
Fax: (410) 224-8378
www.fticonsulting.com

Gallup Consulting
The Gallup Building
901 F Street NW
Wasington, DC 20004
Phone: (202) 715-3030
Fax: (202) 715-3041
www.gallupconsulting.com

Gartner, Inc.
56 Top Gallant Road
Stamford, CT 06902
Phone: (203) 964-0096
www.gartner.com

Giuliani Partners LLC
5 Times Square
New York, NY 10036
Phone: (212) 931-7300
Fax: (212) 931-7310
www.giulianipartners.com

Hay Group
The Wanamaker Building
100 Penn Square East
Philadelphia, PA 19107
Phone: (215) 861-2000
Fax: (215) 861-2111
www.haygroup.com

Hewitt Associates
100 Half Day Road
Lincolnshire, IL 60069
Phone: (847) 295-5000
Fax: (847) 295-7634
www.hewitt.com

Huron Consulting Group
550 West Van Buren
Chicago, IL 60607
Phone: (312) 583-8700
Fax: (312) 583-8701
www.huronconsultinggroup.com

IBM Global Business Services
New Orchard Road
Armonk, NY 10017
Phone: (914) 499-1900
Fax: (914) 765-7382
www.ibm.com/consulting

IMS Health Incorporated
901 Main Avenue, Suite 612
Norwalk, CT 06851
Phone: (203) 845-5200
www.imshealth.com

Katzenbach Partners LLC
381 Park Avenue South
New York, NY 10016
Phone: (212) 213-5505
Fax: (212) 213-5024
www.katzenbach.com

KPMG LLP
345 Park Avenue
New York, NY 10154
Phone: (212) 758-9700
Fax: (212) 758-9819
www.kpmg.com

Kurt Salmon Associates
1355 Peachtree Street NE, Suite 900
Atlanta, GA 30309
Phone: (404) 892-0321
Fax: (404) 898-9590
www.kurtsalmon.com

L.E.K. Consulting
28 State Street, 16th Floor
Boston, MA 02109
Phone: (617) 951-9500
Fax: (617) 951-9392
www.lek.com

LECG
2000 Powell Street, Suite 600
Emeryville, CA 94608
Phone: (510) 985-6700
www.lecg.com

Lippincott
499 Park Avenue
New York, NY 10022
Phone: (212) 521-0000
Fax: (212) 308-8952
www.lippincott.com

Mars & Co
124 Mason Street
Greenwich, CT 06830
Phone: (203) 629-9292
Fax: (203) 629-9432
www.marsandco.com

Marakon Associates
245 Park Avenue, 44th Floor
New York, NY 10167
Phone: (212) 377-5000
Fax: (212) 377-6000
www.marakon.com

McKinsey & Company
55 East 52nd Street
New York, NY 10022
Phone: (212) 446-7000
Fax: (212) 446-8575
www.mckinsey.com

Visit Vault at **www.vault.com** for insider company profiles, expert advice, career message boards, expert resume reviews, the Vault Job Board and more.

VAULT CAREER LIBRARY   207

Employer Directory, cont.

Mercer LLC
1166 Avenue of the Americas
New York, NY 10036
Phone: (212) 345-7000
Fax (212) 345-7414
www.mercer.com

Mitchell Madison Group LLC
17 State Street, 22nd Floor
New York, NY 10004
Phone: (646) 873-4100
Fax: (212) 742-9719
www.mitchellmadison.com

Monitor Group
2 Canal Park
Cambridge, MA 02141
Phone: (617) 252-2000
Fax: (617) 252-2100
www.monitor.com

Navigant Consulting, Inc.
30 South Wacker Drive, Suite 3100
Chicago, IL 60606
Phone: (312) 583-5700
Fax: (312) 583-5701
www.navigantconsulting.com

NERA Economic Consulting
50 Main Street, 14th Floor
White Plains, NY 10606
Phone: (914) 448-4000
Fax: (914) 448-4040
www.nera.com

Oliver Wyman
1166 Avenue of the Americas
New York, NY 10036
Phone: (212) 345-8000
www.oliverwyman.com

The Parthenon Group
200 State Street, 14th Floor
Boston, MA 02109
Phone: (617) 478-2550
Fax: (617) 478-2555
www.parthenon.com

PricewaterhouseCoopers LLP
300 Madison Avenue, 24th Floor
New York, NY 10017
Phone: (646) 471-4000
Fax: (813) 286-6000
www.pwc.com
www.pwc.tv

PRTM
444 Castro Street, Suite 600
Mountain View, CA 94041
Phone: (650) 967-2900
Fax: (650) 967-6367
www.prtm.com

Putnam Associates
25 Burlington Mall Road
Burlington, MA 01803
Phone: (781) 273-5480
Fax: (781) 273-5484
www.putassoc.com

Roland Berger Strategy Consultants
230 Park Avenue, Suite 112
New York, NY 10022
Phone: (212) 651-9660
Fax: (212) 756-8750
www.rolandberger.com

Towers Perrin
One Stamford Plaza
263 Tresser Boulevard
Stamford, CT 06901
Phone: (203) 326-5400
Fax: (203) 326-5499
www.towersperrin.com

Watson Wyatt Worldwide
901 North Glebe Road
Arlington, VA 22203
Phone: (703) 258-8000
Fax: (703) 258-8585
www.watsonwyatt.com

ZS Associates
1800 Sherman Avenue, 7th Floor
Evanston, IL 60201
Phone: (888) 972-4173
Fax: (888) 972-7329
www.zsassociates.com

Manufacturing

Industry Overview

Got the motor running ...

America's manufacturing industry is a powerful engine that drives the nation's economy, making up 11 percent of employment and 12 percent of the U.S. gross domestic product (GDP) in 2006. In the past decade, the industry contributed 22 percent of the country's economic growth, or 28 percent with the addition of software production. Through a phenomenon known as the multiplier effect, manufacturing actually creates economic output in other industries by using intermediate goods and services in its production process—so that, according to the National Association of Manufacturers (NAM), every $1 of a manufacturing product sold to a final user has created an additional $1.37 in intermediate economic output, more than from any other economic group. The U.S. continues to lead the world in many manufacturing areas, including automobiles, aerospace, steel, telecommunications and consumer goods. In addition, it's the No. 2 country in terms of exports of manufactured products, and its total manufacturing output in dollars (close to $1.5 trillion in 2006) surpasses the GDP of all but eight of the world's countries. The manufacturing and exporting of goods is critical to maintaining a strong currency and economy, so it's no wonder economists pay close attention to manufacturing stats and figures.

The manufacturing process is a part of a wide array of businesses, from mineral products, metals, chemicals, plastics, machinery, computers and electronics to motor vehicles, furniture, paper, textiles and clothing. Several of the more important sectors are discussed in the paragraphs below; the Vault profile of the consumer products industry contains information about the manufacturing and marketing of food.

Greener pastures

The current media focus on global warming and greenhouse gases has begun to trickle down to manufacturers' corporate officers, who (in some cases) look forward to devising environmentally-friendly policies and products. DuPont chief Chad Holliday has made no secret of his decade-long involvement with eco-positive projects, and estimates that $5 billion of DuPont's annual $29 billion revenue comes from items that either energy-efficient or non-harmful to the planet. His company's pet projects include biofuels and a miracle fiber called bio-PDO (made from genetically-adjusted corn sugar). DuPont, Alcoa, Caterpillar and other firms are part of the U.S. Climate Action Partnership (USCAP), which proposes a market system that would lower the cost of cutting greenhouse-gas emissions, giving companies an incentive to do so. And in April 2007, Ford CEO Alan Mullaly said that he clearly believed in the reality of global warming, and created an executive slot devoted to environmentally-friendly strategies, the first such staff position for an automaker.

Auto manufacturing for the people

Manufacturing has long been closely tied to automobile production, and big-ticket purchases like cars are closely tied to consumer confidence. Indeed, a Michigan assembly line may be what many people think of when they hear the word "manufacturing." The U.S. has been able to weather the competition from Japanese companies, but just barely. General Motors remains the world's largest auto manufacturer, but its share of the U.S. market hit an 80-year low (24.6 percent) in 2006. It also faces a big threat in Toyota, which overtook Ford Motors as the No. 2 manufacturer and seller for several months in 2007 by continuously, and thoughtfully, improving product quality. (Toyota is expected to maintain that ranking in the year-end tabulations.) The so-called "Big Three" automakers—General Motors, DaimlerChrysler and Ford—claim about 55 percent of the U.S. passenger car market, though American-made staples like the Ford Excursion and Chevy Tahoe have witnessed an ongoing decline in sales. The main culprits in the auto industry slump include the hike in gas prices to record-high levels per gallon and the rapidly increasing price of steel per ton, which more than doubled from $260 in midyear 2003

Visit Vault at **www.vault.com** for insider company profiles, expert advice, career message boards, expert resume reviews, the Vault Job Board and more.

VAULT CAREER LIBRARY   209

to $580 in 2006 (according to purchasingdata.com). In turn, the steel industry and other automotive-related sectors experience a negative ripple effect from manufacturing slowdowns.

As the auto industry has attempted to rebound in the face of crashing demand for trucks and sport utility vehicles—sales of Ford's F-series pickup trucks, reportedly the company's most important product, were down by more than 45 percent in June 2006 from the previous year—analysts warned that U.S. companies need to look to the east as Asian markets improve and manufacturers like Toyota and Honda pick up the pace. To pique public interest, automotive companies are increasingly combining with major electronics manufacturers to provide a variety of in-vehicle add-ons like satellite radio, crash avoidance systems and iPods; the percentage of electronic content in automobiles is expected to increase to 40 percent by 2010. At the same time, though, such developments also increase automotive warranty costs and the possibility of vehicle recalls. Furthermore, expected changes in regulation of emissions and fuel efficiency (and consumer leanings away from gas-guzzlers in these times of lofty gasoline prices) are forcing the larger U.S. automakers to more seriously consider their contributions to the global warming problem. GM is toying with a battery-powered car (the Chevrolet Volt) and Ford has created an executive position devoted to environmentally-friendly strategies.

Vehicle manufacturing is also coming from a new source: auto makers such as BMW, Honda, Hyundai and Toyota have moved manufacturing plants to the Southeast U.S. In the past 20 years, these companies have quietly cut down on imports and increased domestic production by seven times—in fact, 2005 was the first year that Japanese car makers made more cars in the U.S. than in Japan. The Association of International Automobile Manufacturers estimates that by 2009 these foreign auto makers will have invested $3.3 billion and have hired 10,000 additional workers.

Steely resolve

Steel, demand for which has been bolstered by the developing economies of India and China (which was responsible for 30 percent of the world's demand in 2005), is another U.S. manufacturing mainstay. In addition, the destruction caused by hurricanes Katrina and Rita destroyed many steel structures in the Southeast, such as bridges, barges and oil rigs, which needed to be replaced or extensively repaired. The steel market hasn't always been so strong, however. Prices in 2002 were low, with seven companies controlling nearly half of American steel production. Along with rising prices and increased efficiency, a spate of acquisitions revived the industry; in 2006 alone, 241 buyouts or mergers were announced, to the tune of $82.3 billion (with another 129 agreements signed in the first half of 2007) and the Standard and Poor's Supercomposite Steel Index soared 63 percent. The largest domestic manufacturer, U.S. Steel, purchased Lone Star Technologies for $2.1 billion in early 2007 to command the top spot as producer of pipes for gas and oil interests, and intrigued speculators by talking with Germany's ThyssenKrupp (the world's 10th-largest steel concern according to the International Iron and Steel Institute) in June 2007.

Chemically altered

Besides representing the largest single slice—4 percent—of the manufacturing pie, chemical production is perhaps the most important segment of the industry, since it produces the solvents, dyes and other compounds used in all manner of other manufacturing industries: automobile production, paper processing, pharmaceuticals, electronics and agricultural. (Over 55 percent of all manufacturers say that their production is significantly, directly dependent on chemicals.) In addition, it makes soaps, bleaches and cleaners purchased by consumers for use at home. The hurricanes of 2004 and 2005 in the Southeastern U.S. hurt this segment by destroying a number of factories. Also, high oil prices drove up the cost of many petrochemical-derived products, and rising prices for natural gas, used as part of many manufacturing processes, have added costs as well. This has resulted in decreased revenues along with an increased drive toward mergers and acquisitions—like the June 2006 BASF purchase of the Engelhard Corp., a maker of pigments and chemical catalysts, for $5 billion. Analysts see specialty chemicals such as these as perhaps the best avenue for growth; manufacturers can keep a competitive edge by producing agents used for highly specific purposes.

Despite estimates of higher production, the BLS expects employment within the chemical manufacturing segment of the manufacturing industry to decline by 14 percent by 2014, due to increased efficiency, production outsourcing and more stringent regulation, among other factors. Three sectors—basic chemicals, other chemical products and synthetics—are projected to be the hardest hit, losing a total of 80,000 workers.

All roads lead to tech

Electronics manufacturing covers companies engaged in manufacturing power distribution equipment, communications devices, semiconductors, industrial electronics and household appliances, among other things. Above all, the sector plays a vital role in a number of other industries, including telecommunications, medical and automotive. Electronics demand is thus inextricably tied to the rise and fall of dependent industries. Innovative new consumer products and advancing digital technology have opened up new markets and avenues of revenue. Despite this, the BLS expects that employment in this sector will decrease by 7 percent through 2014 due to increased efficiency and jobs being moved overseas.

Cruising the skies

Aerospace is another sector that contributes significantly to U.S. manufacturing. In the commercial sphere, airplane manufacturing is dominated by Boeing and European rival Airbus. These companies and others, like Lockheed Martin, Northrop Grumman and Raytheon, are also involved in the production of military aircraft, missiles and space equipment. The commercial airline sector saw a severe downturn following September 11, but the past several years have seen a rebound. During 2005 and 2006, aerospace sales, orders, exports and employment all increased significantly, across all sectors of the industry, according to the Aerospace Industries Association (AIA). The civil aircraft segment, with a 21 percent sales boom, was particularly robust. Total sales in 2006 of $184 billion represented an increase of 8 percent over the previous year, and the AIA's predictions for 2007 remain on the positive side, with another 6 percent surge.

Production grab-bag

Other manufacturing sectors include textiles, apparel, forestry products (furniture and paper), rubber and minerals; together these hold claim to roughly 22 percent of all U.S. manufacturing output. Here again, employment figures have plummeted in recent years due to a convergence of unfavorable economic conditions and changes in demand due to the new "paperless" business environment as well as manufacturing techniques for furniture and cabinetry that use less wood. For a while, the industry expected solid profits due to the increasing demand for lumber driven by a rise in housing and construction activity in the hurricane-damaged Southeast. But the good news didn't last long. A severe depression in the housing market settled in, demand for lumber declined, and predictions for new home construction in 2007 came in at a nine-year low.

Work hard for the money

Though the industry as a whole enjoys higher wages than private industry as a whole (by nearly 25 percent), its component sectors vary wildly. Nonsupervisory workers at apparel manufacturers have average weekly earnings considerably lower ($351) than the average for all manufacturing ($659)—and worse, the textile sector projects a loss of 46 percent of its staff due to imports and technological advancements in the coming years. Steel workers and manufacturers of autos and aerospace products have the highest salaries in the group.

Nonetheless, the industry finds a great deal of pricing pressure in the mid-2000s. The price of natural gas, used in many processes, has jumped, and a combination of higher costs (corporate taxes, insurance and legal costs, pollution abatement fees and employee benefit programs) has put the U.S. at a significant disadvantage. In a report, the NAM and AMR Research calculate that these "add 31.7 percent to the cost of doing business in the United States compared to our nine (-largest) trading

Visit Vault at www.vault.com for insider company profiles, expert advice, career message boards, expert resume reviews, the Vault Job Board and more.

VAULT CAREER LIBRARY   211

competitors." And as the proportion of goods exported has risen, passing these costs along to the consumer has become extremely difficult. These facts point to possible escalating encroachment on the manufacturing industry by foreign firms.

A shifting outlook

Following a boom that spanned most of the 20th century, manufacturing employment declined sharply during the 2001-2003 economic downturn. Despite the economy's general resurgence from 2003 to 2006, industry employment has, according to the Bureau of Labor Statistics (BLS), only begun to level off. A number of circumstances led to the slump, including increased oil and energy prices. And like many industries, manufacturing has seen a steady push toward technologies that promise greater efficiency and productivity while reducing the need for manpower. It's likely that many of the factory jobs lost since the beginning of the century will never return, signaling a fundamental shift in the industry as a whole. The BLS predicts total manufacturing employment will decrease by 0.6 percent through 2014. Statistics from the Labor Department released in June 2007 showed a decline in manufacturing jobs for the eleventh straight month, placing employment at just above 14 million—the lowest total since the 1950s. As of midyear 2007, the auto sector accounted for about one million jobs, according to seasonally-adjusted data from the BLS. However, this represents 80,000 less than at the prior year's midpoint, the latest evidence of years of major job cuts.

Despite the forecasts of general decline, however, the job market is remarkably vibrant. According to a 2005 survey done by Deloitte with NAM, 90 percent of employers in the industry reported a demand for skilled workers, and 65 percent needed scientists and engineers. In another finding from the same report, about 83 percent of manufacturers thought that shortages were affecting their service to customers.

On the other hand, those statistics are just where some insiders see an upcoming crisis. At a 2005 trade show, NAM President John Engler said, "The emerging problem in manufacturing is not a shortage of jobs, but rather a shortage of qualified applicants." Companies and trade groups are developing initiatives (manufacturing certification programs, school and community career information sessions) to address the gap before the problem becomes critical.

What is the Supply Chain?

Suppliers and vendors

A simple definition of supply chain is the network of vendors that provides materials for a company's products, but in reality, the supply chain is more complicated. There is a stream of flows from supplier to supplier until a product reaches an end user. For example, oil is rigged from the ground, sent to a refinery, plastic is made, an injection molding shop buys plastic pellets, makes plastics components, ships the components to a customer, the customer assembles the plastic parts into their machine, and then sells the machine to their customer. The farther away from the customer, the farther "upstream" a supplier is considered to be.

The network of vendors in a supply chain often includes tiered suppliers (meaning a company does not receive materials directly from the supplier, but is involved in getting materials or parts from an upstream supplier to a downstream supplier). The more complex a product, the more significant the upstream supplier's roles are. From a supply chain manager's perspective, his suppliers are primarily responsible for managing their own supply chain but he should have some involvement.

Oftentimes, a manufacturing facility acts as a supplier to a downstream manufacturing facility. For example, a company could have their manufacturing plant in the U.S. and their assembly plant in Mexico. The U.S. plant would be considered an internal supplier, since it's part of the same company. The transportation of materials throughout the supply chain is often called logistics. This includes air, land and sea shipping, as well as customs processing to allow materials to cross borders. The supply chain does not end until the product reaches the consumer. For this reason, distribution centers, distributors and wholesalers are all part of the supply chain. It is not rare for a supply chain to involve a dozen parties.

The relationship between a supplier and a manufacturing company is not as simple as a supply chain manager ordering parts and the supplier shipping them. There are continuous flows between the supplier and the customer. The Supply Chain Flow Process Chart on page 336 shows these flows in chronological order from top to bottom. (Note that this figure is for an already established supplier and material.) In the case of a new supplier, a supplier audit (a verification that a supplier has the potential to meet the manufacturer's needs) should be conducted first to determine if the supplier is appropriate for the work.

In the case of new material, the customer must first supply the anticipated number of units required, along with all of the drawings and specifications, to the supplier to get a quotation of unit price and lead time. After the quotes are received and a supplier is chosen, a purchase order should be done for the setup costs and samples. Setup costs can be a few hundred to hundreds of thousands of dollars (mostly tooling costs). A supply chain manager should always present the setup costs along with the piece price quote when working with engineers (so manufacturing methods are not specified solely on unit cost). For example, making a simple part by thermoforming would cost about $50 each, whereas making it by injection molding would cost $5 each. However, injection molding requires a $10,000 mold. If you only need 20 pieces annually, you are better off using thermoforming.

Depending on whether prototypes or the component have already been made or not, the samples ordered may be just to verify the ability of the supplier to make the parts, or to verify the design of the finished product. In other words, the supplier may fabricate a part correctly, but a manufacturer's engineering department may determine that the part needs to be redesigned. This would start the process over.

A manufacturing company has to furnish a forecast (usually annually) so the supplier can then go through his supply chain and make sure that all the materials needed (e.g., material, lubricant, machine capacity, labor resources) for the component the supplier provides will be available. A manufacturer then issues a purchase order, which serves as a commitment to purchase a defined number of units. A purchase order must have terms and conditions accompanying it to protect your company. Usually, a customer will not want to receive the entire forecast amount at once. Instead, a manufacturer could issue multiple purchase orders throughout the year, or do what is called a blanket purchase order for a large number and then make releases against that purchase order for small numbers when they actually want it.

For example, a company uses 1,000 rods of aluminum in a year. They may lock into a price for the entire year (the price of aluminum changes daily), but not take delivery of all 1,000 rods at once. Instead, the supply chain manager would request economic order quantity (EOQ) releases. An EOQ is the optimal balance between taking delivery for the entire 1,000 rods at once and paying for material that will not be used for months, and paying transportation, inspection and transaction costs for receiving frequent smaller shipments. The formula for EOQ is:

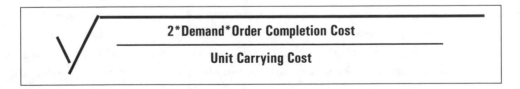

$$\sqrt{\frac{2*Demand*Order\ Completion\ Cost}{Unit\ Carrying\ Cost}}$$

The Order Completion Cost is the total cost of placing the purchase order, paying for a setup at the vendor (if applicable), and paying the transportation and in-house handling to get the components to the production floor. The unit carrying cost is the cost of holding inventory (insurance, warehouse lease, shrinkage costs, security, cost of capital, etc.).

Customers can do releases to the supplier at specific time intervals or specific inventory intervals. With inventory intervals, when a customer gets to a certain number of rods left, they would issue a release for the next shipment of rods.

A supplier should send a confirmation to the customer acknowledging they have received the purchase order and agreed to the terms and conditions described therein. The supplier sends the material per the purchase order and then sends an invoice for the number shipped. Once the goods have been accepted by the customer, a payment is sent to the supplier equal to the amount of the invoice.

Visit Vault at www.vault.com for insider company profiles, expert advice, career message boards, expert resume reviews, the Vault Job Board and more.

VAULT CAREER LIBRARY   213

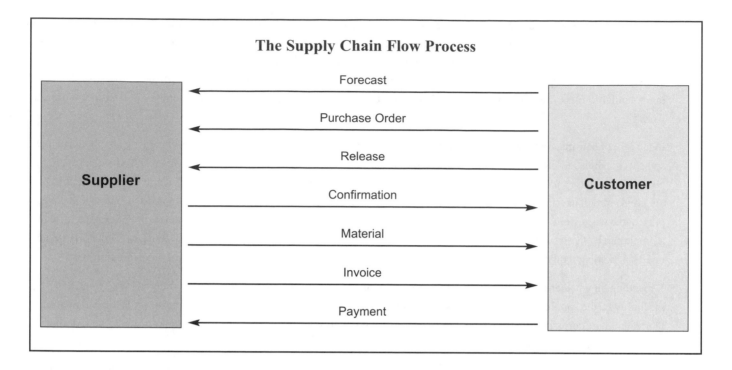

The Supply Chain Flow Process

Supplier

Customer

Forecast

Purchase Order

Release

Confirmation

Material

Invoice

Payment

OEM suppliers

There are basically three types of suppliers. In the first, or most conventional scenario, a company provides a design for what they want the supplier to furnish and the supplier makes it to the company's specifications. The second is the original equipment manufacturer (OEM) supplier. In this case, the company does not specify the design for a custom product, but in fact buys a product that the supplier sells to many customers. These products are called off-the-shelf (a screw is an example of a component that is usually purchased as an off-the-shelf product rather than being custom designed).

Contract manufacturers

Contract manufacturers are the third type of suppliers, in which formal contracts between the supplier (the contract manufacturer) and your manufacturing company are relied upon. The contract manufacturer purchases or makes all of the components, assembles the product, tests it, and ships the finished product either directly to the customer or to a warehouse. Companies that want to get out of the manufacturing aspect of their products turn to contract manufacturers. The supply chain manager finds suitable contract manufacturers and manages the relationship after a contract has been signed. A company has to put a huge amount of trust into the contract manufacturer, since the customer does not have the same level of visibility or control over the manufacturing of the product as they do when they are making the product themselves. Contract manufacturing is an option in almost every industry from food processing to semiconductors.

Freight forwarders and transportation providers

Transportation providers and freight forwarders are also controlled by a supply chain management practitioner. Transportation providers pick up product from one location and deliver them to another. Obviously, it is very costly to pick up some cargo in Los Angeles and drive it all the way to New York for delivery. For this reason, these companies consolidate shipments from different places in a departing hub (whether it be a port, a warehouse or an airport), send them to an arriving hub, and then deliver them to their final destination. It is quite common for a transportation provider to hand off a shipment to another company to carry out some or all of the transportation. This is called subcontracting or third party carriers. Specialty transportation providers also exist (i.e., for transporting explosive materials, refrigerated cargo, etc.). Some manufacturing companies have traffic, transportation, or logistics departments that take care of most of this work so a supply chain manager can concentrate on suppliers only.

Freight forwarders specialize in transportation across borders. They coordinate the paperwork, book the space with a transportation provider, and track the goods from pickup to delivery. Because of the complexity of customs requirements, tariff codes and language barriers for different countries, it is better to have freight forwarders involved if a company is dealing with more than a few countries or commodities.

Supply Chain Careers

Supply chain management occupations

Below are brief summaries of the duties for supply chain management occupations. Not every organization will have all of these positions and the duties of the positions will not be limited to those described here.

Buyer: Buyers do purchasing just like supply chain managers. The difference is that supply chain managers buy parts and materials for the company's products, whereas buyers purchase everything else. Some examples of items that buyers procure are desktop computers, office supplies and hand tools.

Planner: A planner takes the forecast from marketing/sales and breaks that into a build schedule of what products should be built and when they should be built to meet inventory goals. Planners also work with supply chain managers to control inventory of parts and materials.

Purchasing administrative assistant: A purchasing administrative assistant takes care of the filing of paperwork for the purchasing department. He/she will also coordinate travel arrangements.

Logistics manager: A logistics manager is responsible for the traffic of goods coming to and going from the factory. This encompasses air, land, and ocean traffic, both domestic and international.

Supply chain engineer: A supply chain engineer works on technical issues with the supplier. This involves working with suppliers to improve their quality, helping them to analyze failures, and developing new products.

Commodity manager: A commodity manager is similar to a supply chain manager. Some companies separate the ownership of parts and materials for the supply chain managers by product line. For example, if a company makes binoculars, telescopes, cameras and microscopes, and they have four supply chain managers, they might assign one supply chain manager for each product family. Another approach is to distribute the work by commodity. One supply chain manager would be responsible for the optics on all of the product families and one supply chain manager would be responsible for the plastic parts on all of the product families. When this is the case, the supply chain managers can be called commodity managers.

Receiving inspector: A receiving inspector is responsible for checking the quality of the parts and materials that come from the vendor before they get moved to the production floor for consumption and before the supplier gets paid. There are statistics charts that define the number of samples from a shipment that need to be checked to meet the desired confidence level that the entire lot received is acceptable, so a receiving inspector does not check 100 percent of the incoming items.

Procurement manager: A procurement manager is in charge of the buyers and supply chain managers. The procurement manager sets the goals for the department and provides a level of escalation when a supply chain manager is having trouble managing a supplier.

Receiving coordinator: The receiving coordinator processes the parts and materials delivered. This includes doing a receiving transaction in ERP, moving the parts to their location, and making sure the paperwork the supplier sends matches what was received.

Visit Vault at **www.vault.com** for insider company profiles, expert advice, career message boards, expert resume reviews, the Vault Job Board and more.

VAULT CAREER LIBRARY 215

Receiving supervisor: The receiving supervisor is responsible for the receiving department. Besides supervising receiving department workers, the receiving supervisor is in charge of creating and improving department processes.

Accounts payable coordinator: The accounts payable coordinator works in the accounting department and processes the invoices from the suppliers. After verifying the invoices match what was actually received, the accounts payable coordinator sends a payment to the supplier.

The MBA in Supply Chain Management

MBA graduates seeking opportunities in supply chain management usually pursue either a project manager or director of materials position. Both of these vocations require previous experience in supply chain management, so the likelihood of a new graduate landing one of these positions is low.

A project manager is responsible for large transitions related to supply chain management. One example of these transitions is a plant shutdown. A company may decide that it is more cost-effective to stop manufacturing their products themselves, and instead have a vendor do it for them. The management of a plant shutdown project requires cross-functional teamwork between accounting (working out the costs), engineering (helping the vendors get up and running), human resources (laying off the production workers), and manufacturing (managing the inventory to make a seamless transition). Another example of a transition is a large scale vendor change. A company may have a contract manufacturer in Mexico making its products. In an effort to reduce costs, the company may want to partner with a contract manufacturer in Vietnam instead. Making this transition can be even harder than a plant shutdown, because the existing supplier may become bitter and refuse to cooperate. Most often, these transitions are done without notifying the existing supplier until the new supplier is running at the required capacity.

A director of materials is responsible for the strategy of the purchasing group. He does not get involved in the details of the day-to-day operations of the supply chain management department, but will assume the reins when issues get out of control or need upper-management attention. A director of materials also sets the practices of his departments and approves large dollar item purchases. Similarly, the director of materials participates in vendor relationship management for the suppliers with whom the company spends the most money. In addition to providing strategic direction to the purchasing group, the director of materials spends significant time meeting with the other executives in the company, sharing expertise, championing causes, and staying abreast of issues facing the company. A director of materials also spends a lot of time networking with people outside of the company (i.e., industry experts, competitors and prospective vendors).

Employer Directory

AAR Corporation
1100 North Wood Dale Road
Wood Dale, IL 60191
Phone: (630) 227-2000
Fax: (630) 227-2019
Toll free: (800) 422-2213
www.aacorp.com

ABB Limited
Affolternstrasse 44
8050 Zürich
Switzerland
Phone: +41-43-317-71-11
Fax: +41-43-317-44-20
www.abb.com

Airbus S.A.S.
1, Rond point Maurice Bellonte
31707 Blagnac Cedex
France
Phone: +33-5-6193-33-33
Fax: +33-5-6193-49-55
www.airbus.com

Alcoa Incorporated
201 Isabella Street
Pittsburgh, PA 15212-5858
Phone: (412) 553-4545
Fax: (412) 553-4498
www.alcoa.com

Amcor Limited
679 Victoria Street
Abbotsford, VIC 3067
Australia
Phone: +61-3-9226-90-00
Fax: +61-3-9226-90-50
www.amcor.com

Amphenol Corporation
358 Hall Avenue
Wallingford, CT 06492
Phone: (203) 265-8900
Fax: (203) 265-8516
Toll free: (877) 267-4366
www.amphenol.com

Apogee Enterprises Inc.
7900 Xerxes Avenue South
Suite 1800
Minneapolis, MN 55431
Phone: (952) 835-1874
Fax: (952) 835-3196
Toll free: (877) 752-3432
www.apog.com

Armstrong World Industries, Inc.
2500 Columbia Avenue
Lancaster, PA 17603
Phone: (717) 397-0611
Fax: (717) 396-6133
www.armstrong.com

BAE Systems plc
Stirling Square
Carlton Gardens
London, SW1Y 5AD
United Kingdom
Phone: +44-12-52-37-32-32
Fax: +44-12-52-38-30-00
www.baesystems.com

BASF Group
Carl-Bosch-Straße 38
67056 Ludwigshafen
Germany
Phone: +49-621-60-0
Fax: +49-621-60-425-25
www.basf.com

BE&K, Inc.
2000 International Park Drive
Birmingham, AL 35243
Phone: (205) 972-6000
Fax: (205) 972-6651
www.bek.com

Bell Microproducts Inc.
1941 Ringwood Avenue
San Jose, CA 95131
Phone: (408) 451-9400
Fax: (408) 451-1600
Toll free: (800) 800-1513
www.bellmicro.com

BHP Billiton Finance Limited
L 27 180 Lonsdale Street
Melbourne 3000
Australia
Phone: +61-13-00-55-47-57
Fax: +61-3-96-09-30-15
www.bhpbilliton.com

The Black & Decker Corporation
701 East Joppa Road
Towson, MD 21286
Phone: (410) 716-3900
Fax: (410) 716-2933
Toll free: (800) 544-6986
www.bdk.com

BMW Group
Petuelring 130
Munich 80788
Germany
Phone: +49-89-3820
Fax: +49-89-382-258-58
www.bmwgroup.com

Boeing Company
100 North Riverside Plaza
Chicago, IL 60606-1596
Phone: (312) 544-2000
Fax: (312) 544-2082
www.boeing.com

Boise Cascade Holdings LLC
1111 West Jefferson Street
Boise, ID 83702
Phone: (208) 384-6161
www.bc.com

Caterpillar Inc.
100 NE Adams Street
Peoria, IL 61629
Phone: (309) 675-1000
Fax: (309) 675-1182
www.cat.com

Visit Vault at **www.vault.com** for insider company profiles, expert advice,
career message boards, expert resume reviews, the Vault Job Board and more.

VAULT CAREER LIBRARY   217

Employer Directory, cont.

Chevron Phillips Chemical Company LLC
10001 Six Pines Drive
The Woodlands, TX 77380-1498
Phone: (800) 231-1212
Fax: (800) 231-3890
www.cpchem.com

Chrysler LLC
1000 Chrysler Drive
Auburn Hills, MI 48326-2766
Phone: (248) 576-5741
Toll free: (800) 992-1997
www.chryslerllc.com

Cintas Corporation
6800 Cintas Boulevard
Cincinnati, OH 45262
Phone: (513) 459-1200
Fax: (513) 573-4130
Toll free: (800) 246-8271
www.cintas.com

Commercial Metals Company
6565 North MacArthur Boulevard
Suite 800
Irving, TX 75039
Phone: (214) 689-4300
Fax: (214) 689-5886
www.commercialmetals.com

Cooper Tire & Rubber Company
701 Lima Avenue
Findlay, OH 45840
Phone: (419) 423-1321
Fax: (419) 424-4108
Toll free: (800) 854-6288
www.coopertire.com

Corning Incorporated
1 Riverfront Plaza
Corning, NY 14831-0001
Phone: (607) 974-9000
Fax: (607) 974-8091
www.corning.com

Crown Holdings, Inc.
1 Crown Way
Philadelphia, PA 19154-4599
Phone: (215) 698-5100
Fax: (215) 676-7245
www.crowncork.com

Cummins, Inc.
500 Jackson Street
Columbus, IN 47202
Phone: (812) 377-5000
Fax: (812) 377-3334
www.cummins.com

Daimler AG
Mercedesstraße 137
70546 Stuttgart
Germany
Phone: +49-711-17-0
Fax: +49-711-17-94116
www.daimler.com

Dana Holding Corporation
4500 Dorr Street
Toledo, OH 43615
Phone: (419) 535-4500
Fax: (419) 535-4643
Toll free: (800) 472-8810
www.dana.com

Deere & Company
1 John Deere Place
Moline, IL 61265
Phone: (309) 765-8000
Fax: (309) 765-5671
www.deere.com

Delphi Corporation
5725 Delphi Drive
Troy, MI 48098
Phone: (248) 813-2000
Fax: (248) 813-2670
www.delphi.com

Donaldson Company, Inc.
1400 West 94th Street
Minneapolis, MN 55431
Phone: (952) 887-3131
Fax: (952) 887-3155
www.donaldson.com

The Dow Chemical Company
2030 Dow Center
Midland, MI 48674
Phone: (989) 636-1000
Fax: (989) 989-1556
Toll free: (800) 258-2436
www.dow.com

Dril-Quip, Inc.
13550 Hempstead Highway
Houston, TX 77040
Phone: (713) 939-7711
Fax: (713) 939-8063
www.dril-quip.com

DuPont
1007 Market Street
Wilmington, DE 19898
Phone: (302) 774-1000
Fax: (302) 999-4399
Toll free: (800) 441-7515
www.dupont.com

Eaton Corporation
Eaton Center
1111 Superior Avenue
Cleveland, OH 44114-2584
Phone: (216) 523-5000
Fax: (216) 523-3787
www.eaton.com

Ecolab Inc.
370 Wabasha Street North
St. Paul, MN 55102
Phone: (651) 293-2233
Fax: (651) 293-2092
www.ecolab.com

Emerson Electric Co.
8000 West Florissant Avenue
St. Louis, MO 63136
Phone: (314) 553-2000
Fax: (314) 553-3527
www.gotoemerson.com

Employer Directory, cont.

Federal-Mogul Corporation
26555 Northwestern Highway
Southfield, MI 48034
Phone: (248) 354-7700
Fax: (248) 354-8950
www.federal-mogul.com

Foamex International Inc.
1000 Columbia Avenue
Linwood, PA 19061-3997
Phone: (610) 859-3000
Fax: (610) 859-3035
Toll free: (800) 776-3626
www.foamex.com

Ford Motor Company
1 American Road
Dearborn, MI 48126-2798
Phone: (313) 322-3000
Fax: (313) 845-6073
www.ford.com

General Dynamics Corporation
2941 Fairview Park Drive, Suite 100
Falls Church, VA 22042-4513
Phone: (703) 876-3000
Fax: (703) 876-3125
www.gd.com

General Motors Corporation
300 Renaissance Center
Detroit, MI 48265-3000
Phone: (313) 556-5000
www.gm.com

Georgia Gulf Corporation
115 Perimeter Center Place, Suite 460
Atlanta, GA 30346
Phone: (770) 395-4500
Fax: (770) 395-4529
www.ggc.com

Georgia-Pacific Corporation
133 Peachtree Street NE
Atlanta, GA 30303
Phone: (404) 652-4000
Fax: (404) 749-2454
www.gp.com

Goodrich Corporation
Four Coliseum Centre
2730 West Tyvola Road
Charlotte, NC 28217-4578
Phone: (704) 423-7000
Fax: (704) 423-5540
www.goodrich.com

The Goodyear Tire & Rubber Company
1144 East Market Street
Akron, OH 44316-0001
Phone: (330) 796-2121
Fax: (330) 796-2222
www.goodyear.com

Hamilton Sundstrand Corporation
1 Hamilton Road
Windsor Locks, CT 06096
Phone: (860) 654-6000
www.hamiltonsundstrandcorp.com

Handy & Harman
555 Theodore Fremd Avenue
Rye, NY 10580
Phone: (914) 921-5200
Fax: (914) 925-4496
www.handyharman.com

Harley-Davidson, Inc.
3700 West Juneau Avenue
Milwaukee, WI 53208
Phone: (414) 342-4680
Fax: (414) 343-8230
www.harley-davidson.com

Herman Miller, Inc.
855 East Main Avenue
Zeeland, MI 49464-0302
Phone: (616) 654-3000
Fax: (616) 654-5234
www.hermanmiller.com

HNI Corporation
408 East 2nd Street
Muscatine, IA 52761-0071
Phone: (563) 272-7400
Fax: (563) 272-7655
www.hnicorp.com

Honeywell International Inc.
101 Columbia Road
Morristown, NJ 07962-1219
Phone: (973) 455-2000
Fax: (973) 455-4807
Toll free: (800) 601-3099
www.honeywell.com

Hyundai Motor America
10550 Talbert Avenue
Fountain Valley, CA 92728-0850
Phone: (714) 965-3000
Fax: (714) 965-3149
www.hyundaiusa.com

Ingersoll-Rand Company Limited
Clarendon House
2 Church Street
Hamilton HM 11
Bermuda
Phone: (441) 295-2838
www.irco.com

International Paper Company
6400 Poplar Avenue
Memphis, TN 38197
Phone: (901) 419-7000
Fax: (901) 214-9682
Toll free: (800) 223-1268
www.ipaper.com

Jaguar Cars Limited
Browns Lane, Allesley Coventry
West Midlands CV5 9DR
United Kingdom
Phone: +44-24-76-40-21-21
Fax: +44-24-76-20-21-01
www.jaguarvehicles.com

Johnson Controls, Inc.
5757 North Green Bay Avenue
Milwaukee, WI 53209
Phone: (414) 524-1200
Fax: (414) 524-2077
www.johnsoncontrols.com

Visit Vault at **www.vault.com** for insider company profiles, expert advice, career message boards, expert resume reviews, the Vault Job Board and more.

VAULT CAREER LIBRARY 219

Employer Directory, cont.

Lockheed Martin Corporation
6801 Rockledge Drive
Bethesda, MD 20817-1877
Phone: (301) 897-6000
Fax: (301) 897-6704
www.lockheedmartin.com

MeadWestvaco Corporation
11013 West Broad Street
Glen Allen, VA 23060
Phone: (804) 327-5200
Fax: (804) 897-6383
www.meadwestvaco.com

Monsanto Company
800 North Lindbergh Boulevard
St. Louis, MO 63167
Phone: (314) 694-1000
Fax: (314) 694-8394
www.monsanto.com

Moog Inc.
Plant 4, Jamison Road
East Aurora, NY 14052
Phone: (716) 687-4567
Fax: (716) 687-5969
www.moog.com

National Oilwell Varco, Inc.
7909 Parkwood Circle Drive
Houston, TX 77036
Phone: (713) 346-7500
Fax: (713) 435-2195
Toll free: (888) 262-8645
www.natoil.com

Northrop Grumman Corporation
1840 Century Park East
Los Angeles, CA 90067-2199
Phone: (310) 553-6262
Fax: (310) 553-4561
www.northropgrumman.com

Nucor Corporation
1915 Rexford Road
Charlotte, NC 28211
Phone: (704) 366-7000
Fax: (704) 362-4208
www.nucor.com

OSRAM SYLVANIA Inc.
100 Endicott Street
Danvers, MA 01923
Phone: (978) 777-1900
Fax: (978) 750-2152

Owens Corning
1 Owens Corning Parkway
Toledo, OH 43659
Phone: (419) 248-8000
www.owenscorning.com

PACCAR Inc.
777 106th Avenue NE
Bellevue, WA 98004
Phone: (425) 468-7400
Fax: (425) 468-8216
www.paccar.com

Parker Hannifin Corporation
6035 Parkland Boulevard
Cleveland, OH 44124
Phone: (216) 896-3000
Fax: (216) 896-4000
www.parker.com

Pella Corporation
102 Main Street
Pella, IA 50219
Phone: (641) 628-1000
Fax: (641) 628-6070
Toll free: (800) 374-4758
www.pella.com

Pitney Bowes Incorporated
1 Elmcroft Road
Stamford, CT 06926-0700
Phone: (203) 356-5000
Fax: (203) 351-7336
www.pb.com

Plum Creek Timber Company, Inc.
999 Third Avenue, Suite 4300
Seattle, WA 98104-4096
Phone: (206) 467-3600
Fax: (206) 467-3795
Toll free: (800) 858-5347
www.plumcreek.com

PolyOne Corporation
33587 Walker Road
Avon Lake, OH 44012
Phone: (440) 930-1000
Fax: (440) 930-3799
Toll free: (866) 765-9663
www.polyone.com

PPG Industries, Inc.
One PPG Place
Pittsburgh, PA 15272
Phone: (412) 434-3131
Fax: (412) 434-2011
www.ppg.com

Quanex Building Products Corporation
1900 South Loop West, Suite 1500
Houston, TX 77027
Phone: (713) 961-4600
Fax: (713) 439-1016
Toll free: (800) 231-8176
www.quanex.com

Rayonier Inc.
50 North Laura Street
Jacksonville, FL 32202
Phone: (904) 357-9100
Fax: (904) 357-9101
Toll free: (800) 243-2590
www.rayonier.com

Raytheon Company
870 Winter Street
Waltham, MA 02451-1449
Phone: (781) 522-3000
Fax: (781) 522-3001
www.raytheon.com

Rockwell Automation, Inc.
1201 South Second Street
Milwaukee, WI 53204-2496
Phone: (414) 382-2000
Fax: (414) 382-4444
www.rockwellautomation.com

Employer Directory, cont.

Rolls-Royce plc
65 Buckingham Gate
London, SW1E 6AT
United Kingdom
Phone: +44-20-72-22-90-20
Fax: +44-20-72-27 91-78
www.rolls-royce.com

Sanmina-SCI Corporation
2700 North 1st Street
San Jose, CA 95134
Phone: (408) 964-3555
Fax: (408) 964-3636
www.sanmina-sci.com

Shanghai Automotive Industry Corporation (Group)
489 WeiHai Road
Shanghai, 200041
China
Phone: +86-21-22-01-16-88
Fax: +86-21-22-01-11-188
www.saicmotor.com

Shaw Industries, Inc.
616 East Walnut Avenue
Dalton, GA 30722
Phone: (706) 278-3812
Toll free: (800) 441-7429
www.shawfloors.com

The Sherwin-Williams Company
101 Prospect Avenue NW
Cleveland, OH 44115-1075
Phone: (216) 566-2000
Fax: (216) 566-2947
www.sherwin-williams.com

The Stanley Works
1000 Stanley Drive
New Britain, CT 06053
Phone: (860) 225-5111
Fax: (860) 827-3895
www.stanleyworks.com

Tenneco Inc.
500 North Field Drive
Lake Forest, IL 60045
Phone: (847) 482-5000
Fax: (847) 482-5940
www.tenneco.com

Textron Inc.
40 Westminster Street
Providence, RI 02903-2591
Phone: (401) 421-2800
Fax: (401) 457-2220
www.textron.com

Toyota Motor Corporation
1, Toyota-cho
Toyota, Aichi
Japan
Phone: +81-565-28-21-21
Fax: +81-565-23-58-00
www.toyota.co.jp
www.toyota.com

TRW Automotive Holdings Corp.
12001 Tech Center Drive
Livonia, MI 48150
Phone: (734) 855-2600
Fax: (734) 855-2999
www.trw.com

Tyco International Ltd.
9 Roszel Road
Princeton, NJ 08540
Phone: (609)720-4200
Fax: (609) 720-4208
www.tyco.com

United States Steel Corporation
600 Grant Street
Pittsburgh, PA 15219-2800
Phone: (412) 433-1121
Fax: (412) 433-5733
www.ussteel.com

United Technologies Corporation
One Financial Plaza
Hartford, CT 06103
Phone: (860) 728-7000
Fax: (860) 565-5400
www.utc.com

Universal Forest Products, Inc.
2801 East Beltline Avenue NE
Grand Rapids, MI 49525
Phone: (616) 364-6161
Fax: (616) 361-8302
Toll free: (800) 598-9663
www.ufpi.com

The Valspar Corporation
1101 Third Street South
Minneapolis, MN 55415-1211
Phone: (612) 332-7371
Fax: (612) 375-7723
www.valspar.com

Vitro America Inc.
965 Ridge Lake Boulevard
Memphis, TN 38187
Phone: (901) 767-7111
Fax: (901) 682-3062
Toll free: (800) 238-6057
www.vitroamerica.com

Volkswagen AG
Brieffach 1849
Wolfsburg 38436
Germany
Phone: +49-53-61-9-0
Fax: +49-53-61-92-82-82
www.vw.com

Vulcan Materials Company
1200 Urban Center Drive
Birmingham, AL 35242
Phone: (205) 298-3000
Fax: (205) 298-2960
www.vulcanmaterials.com

Visit Vault at **www.vault.com** for insider company profiles, expert advice, career message boards, expert resume reviews, the Vault Job Board and more.

VAULT CAREER LIBRARY 221

Employer Directory, cont.

W.L. Gore & Associates, Inc.
555 Papermill Road
Newark, DE 19711
Phone: (410) 506-7787
Fax: (410) 996-8585
Toll free: (888) 914-4673
www.gore.com

Walter Industries, Inc.
4211 West Boy Scout Boulevard
Tampa, FL 33607-2551
Phone: (813) 871-4811
Fax: (813) 871-4399
www.walterind.com

Weyerhaeuser Company
33663 Weyerhaeuser Way South
Federal Way, WA 98003
Phone: (253) 924-2345
Fax: (253) 924-2685
Toll free: (800) 525-5440
www.weyerhaeuser.com

Worthington Industries, Inc.
200 Old Wilson Bridge Road
Columbus, OH 43085
Phone: (614) 438-3210
Fax: (614) 438-7948
www.worthingtonindustries.com

Media and Entertainment

Media and Entertainment MBAs

Not long ago, the creative types in media kept a wary eye on the suits or the bean counters, as the business side of media is known. For years, Wall Street paid little attention to the media biz, an industry it didn't take that seriously. Now, with the rise of the global conglomerates and the aftermath of dot-com meltdown, many media professionals, both on the creative and business sides, are finding it necessary to pursue an MBA.

A new order

"When we started, I had two courses and we had about 40 people in each. Today, in any given semester we have about 400 to 500 students taking one or more classes," says Al Lieberman, executive director of NYU Stern's Entertainment, Media and Technology Initiative. Started in 1996, Stern's EMT program awards a certificate to those students who complete at least nine credits in courses like Entertainment Finance and The Business of Sports Marketing. Over at Fordham Business School, Dr. Everette Dennis, chair of the communications and media management program has also seen an increased interest over the last couple of years, "We have a relatively small program, but we've had probably a 20 to 25 percent increase in applications." Fordham's program, believed to be one of the first in the country, began in the mid-1980s when Arthur Taylor, a former president of CBS, arrived as the business school's new dean and brought in William Small, another CBS executive, to head up the program.

So why are more and more media professionals interested in an MBA? Of course, many can argue that a wave of dot-com dropouts have decided to hide out in business school in the wake of the collapse of the dot-coms and the weak ad market. Lieberman argues that this is no trend. "It's a fundamental change because the competitive factors that are driving this are not going away. They are intensifying." He is talking about the shakeup of the media landscape. Deregulation and mergers have given rise to media behemoths.

Technology, without a doubt, has wrought havoc in the industry, forcing firms to rethink their business strategies. That's one reason why Jason Oberlander, a first-year student at Columbia Business School, finds the business side of media so attractive. "The technology that comes out, it's coming out so quickly that it requires people who are able to adapt and think on their feet and are able to pursue new opportunities in order to be successful and compete effectively."

Consumers today have a rainbow of media products to choose from. Dennis says the media industry has become an important economic engine and Wall Street has taken notice. "All of the sudden this was an industry to be reckoned with." Lieberman points to a shift towards cooperation and the building of alliances as well, in an industry that has been notoriously competitive. The current negotiations between CNN and *ABC News* would have been unheard of just 10 years ago. Not only has media seen enormous domestic growth, but abroad as well; says Lieberman, "For every dollar that is generated in the United States, 15 years ago the most they could look for was maybe 25 cents outside, as an export. Now it is dollar for dollar."

What does an MBA really offer?

"A few years ago, I would have said, 'An MBA—that would be nice, but it really isn't necessary.' Now, I think an MBA, or at least some exposure to business practices, is probably essential," says Dennis. He cites a growing need for better understanding of market research, audiences, how to manage change and the cash position of a company. In the mid 1980s, Lieberman started a marketing firm focused on entertainment and media. At the time, he couldn't find enough qualified candidates to keep pace with the growth of the firm. He ended up recruiting people right out of one of the courses he was teaching at NYU. "I taught this course that I created, called the Marketing of Entertainment Industries at the NYU School of Continuing Education. Out of the 40 or 45 adults that would come in from all kinds of industries to learn about this, I'd pick one or two that were the best and offer them jobs."

Visit Vault at www.vault.com for insider company profiles, expert advice, career message boards, expert resume reviews, the Vault Job Board and more.

VAULT CAREER LIBRARY 223

Oberland left Showtime as a communications manager in sports and event programming, but felt an MBA was the only way to increase his chances for advancement. "I felt that doing the transition within the company would have been difficult. I certainly would have had to take a significant step down in title and in compensation." Dennis concurs that an MBA is increasingly becoming a requirement for management in media companies. "I think people on the creative side are not going to move into major management and executive roles unless they either get this kind of background and experience on their own in some way, or they go to a business school and get it where it is taught systematically."

Bridging the gap

"One of the biggest problems was the business people who stepped into this world of creativity, didn't understand the creative product, didn't understand how it made money, didn't understand how to apply the basic strategic thinking, therefore there was a huge disconnect," says Lieberman. It takes two to tango, and the creative side has also contributed to the disconnect. Fordham, recognizing the interest by some creative folks to bridge this gap, will be launching a new MS program soon, "It's really tailored to the people from the creative side who do need to know and understand more about business." Stern is also helping the business types better understand the creative process by encouraging Stern students to take courses in filmmaking at the Tisch School of the Arts. "They're not going to make films, but at least they understand the skills, so they don't come on a set and make complete idiots of themselves." At the end of the day, Oberland argues that you need the overall package to get ahead. "I think someone who balances the creative skills with business skills is the most suitable person to run a business from a general management standpoint."

Media Business Positions

Strategic planning

Strategic planning groups are small groups of about five to 40 professionals that serve as in-house consulting and investment banking arms. Not coincidentally, most employees are ex-consultants and bankers. Strategists are involved in valuation and negotiation decisions for acquisitions, business plans for new ventures, the expansion of the current business lines (and sometimes creating new ones), forward-looking financial plans to provide budgeting and overall prognosis for the health of all divisions of the company, and any other high-level issues that the company as a whole may be facing.

Because these projects affect the overall health of the company, meetings are often power sessions in the corporate dining room or top-floor board rooms with the company's senior executives, including the CEO, COO and CFO. While exposure to these individuals is one of the perks of this position, the jobs also tend to be incredibly challenging and taxing, as inordinate amounts of background data, research and information are synthesized and spun into a story prior to the presentation of findings. This group's job is all the more challenging, given that the recommendations that strategic planning groups deliver must necessarily be at odds with decisions that have already been made. Strategic planners, after all, are constantly trying to maximize the returns on the company's capital, which means analyzing and dismissing many current projects.

This function is also sometimes called corporate development, business development or in-house consulting. Because of the frequent exposure to high-level executives, the overall clout of the group and its impact in the major decisions of media conglomerates, these tend to be highly sought-after jobs, mostly filled by top-notch MBAs.

Corporate finance

Corporate finance is a sister group to strategic planning. Corporate financiers are the people who work in concert with investment bankers (or in lieu of them) to price deals, investigate options and plot the course of the company's growth through acquisitions of other companies.

Nearly all the major entertainment companies have grown through major acquisitions in the past two decades, increasing the importance of their corporate financiers. Corporate finance professionals investigate acquisition opportunities, gather competitive intelligence on other companies, determine synergies and negotiate deals. Likewise, they also divest businesses that may be undesirable in exchange for cash.

Most individuals in the corporate finance function are former investment bankers, accounting wizards and CFOs-to-be who bring their expertise in finance and public company performance to the entertainment industry.

Corporate marketing

Corporate marketing assesses consumer reaction to new projects, initiatives and endeavors. Often these groups are direct reports of business units (where each division has its own marketing group), but there are also many cases in which these groups are centralized under corporate and provide their services on an as-needed basis. The benefit of centralized marketing is that it enables the sharing of data across the company since the information is compiled by one group that can then spread the information. It also provides leverage with outside vendors (advertising agencies, media placement agencies, market research firms) when negotiating fees: the more money a company plans on spending with one deal, the better its negotiating position when choosing among competing agencies.

Corporate marketing encompasses many objectives:

- Market research and the execution of both quantitative and qualitative research
- The management of outside vendors who oversee new software, focus groups or large research studies
- Determining revenue projections for new products
- Soliciting consumer feedback on new and existing products
- Creating pricing models
- Estimating market penetration and rollout strategies
- Authoring marketing plans
- Supervising advertising and direct mail
- Overseeing overall brand equity and elements of brand differentiation like logo and identity
- Overseeing product-specific public relations efforts that drive coverage in the media

Corporate marketers often have an extensive background with advertising agencies or marketing consultancy firms.

Corporate public relations

For years, corporate PR was considered to be exclusively for damage control during events like the Exxon Valdez or the Tylenol cyanide scare. Whenever a CEO had problems with the press, the white knights of corporate PR came to the rescue to help avert a worse catastrophe. Corporate PR groups still perform this function. However, the work of corporate PR groups is much broader than just handling crisis management. Corporate PR groups now manage corporate spokespersons, serve as experts on media training and public appearances and coach CEOs as they prepare for media appearances and event marketing.

The corporate PR group is also known for initiating major press coverage in industry and business trade publications, as well as corporate-focused articles in general interest magazines like *Time*, *Newsweek* or *Vanity Fair*. PR professionals also develop relationships with government officials and lobbying groups that may have influence over legislation affecting the company's growth and development. Often, this group works with outside public relations agencies like Edelman Worldwide, Bozell or Hill & Knowlton.

Visit Vault at **www.vault.com** for insider company profiles, expert advice, career message boards, expert resume reviews, the Vault Job Board and more.

VAULT CAREER LIBRARY   225

Internet strategy

As content becomes increasingly commoditized due to the fact that so much on the Internet is free, there are challenges in protecting the hallowed material that entertainment companies create. While studios would love to use the Internet to hoard their content and prevent anyone else from distributing and profiting from it (sort of a preemptive strike against companies like Napster), the Internet is also an incredibly seductive resource for marketing, mainly because information can be communicated broadly and cheaply—much more inexpensively than TV commercials, billboards and bus shelters. The popularity of *The Blair Witch Project*, a surprise hit, was partially attributed to a very effective web site.

This tension (to promote our properties or protect them?) feeds the very complex and critical role that Internet strategy plays in the growth of media and entertainment companies. Because of the constantly evolving and still uncertain nature of the business, there are hundreds of individuals at nearly all major entertainment companies, tracking evolving technologies, coding pages, maintaining fresh web site content and otherwise marketing via the Web. Media companies with Internet strategy groups include Walt Disney/ABC and AOL Time Warner.

Real estate development

Real estate development within an entertainment company involves not only theme parks, but also extensions of an entertainment empire's brands, including themed restaurants (Hard Rock Café), sports stadiums, entertainment complexes (Sony Metreon) and other destinations that involve large tracts of land that can both provide steady revenue streams and impress an entertainment-seeking audience. The major entertainment companies often have proprietary lots of their own land that were either part of the company's origin (as Disney does with its land in Florida and Southern California, now managed under the aegis of the Disney Development Corporation), were results of acquisitions or were acquired over time.

As real estate development is its own unique business with special financing rules and its own intrinsic rewards, the field generally attracts individuals from outside the entertainment industry. The most successful individuals in these divisions are those with substantial experience managing vendors, contractors and landscape architects, working with community development offices, leveraging tax benefits and executing visionary blueprints. Real estate development is a particularly exciting division for individuals wishing to combine interests in the hospitality industry, finance and real estate.

Our Survey Says: Lifestyle and Pay

Hours

Like so many industries, there is a work/life trade-off that comes in the entertainment industry. "There are tons of trade-offs," says one longtime employee in the strategic planning group of a studio. "The entertainment industry definitely doesn't come to mind when I think about a balanced lifestyle. It's a rare day I don't put in 12 hours."

But that's not always the case. There are many individuals that report (mostly outside of strategic planning and other corporate groups) consistently being home by 6 p.m. While the career trajectory is slower and the compensation is lower in the "business units" (versus the "corporate side"), the hours and the requirements are less demanding. There are always exceptions. Says one theme park executive: "Hours are usually 9 to 6, but every year for a few weeks in the spring during our five-year planning process, it's not uncommon for us to put in 12 hours a day, seven days a week."

One rule of thumb: Corporate jobs that report to the CEO typically face "fire drills" (i.e., urgent deadlines imposed at the last minute) on a regular basis. Jobs that are more predictable (i.e., positions with business units rather than corporate-level positions) generally have more predictable hours.

Pay

"The pay in corporate jobs is usually up there with investment banking and management consulting," reports one former consultant-turned-analyst at a publishing house. The business units, however, are typically known for paying less, both because they are responsible for profit and loss (high salaries come straight out of the topline) and because of the less grueling hours.

At the corporate level, beginning-level analysts out of college typically start at around $40,000, with several thousand dollars in bonuses and a 15 percent raise after a year. Managers make at least $80,000 and directors usually crack six figures. VPs earn in the low $100K range.

In business units, the pay can be anywhere from 10 to 30 percent lower.

Other perks

Entertainment is attractive partly because of its perks. "Let's face it, I got into the industry hoping to hang out with rock stars," confesses one record industry insider. Employees get discounts on products, invitations to advance screenings of movies and tickets to movie premieres and gala parties. That said, the perks are not nearly as lavish as the expense accounts and freebies that come on the creative side of the business. There are the stories of the business folks who occasionally get free lunches, tickets to movie premieres and celebrity wedding invitations, but these are mostly the result of a person's personal connections.

Another practice, widely considered a perk, is that many within the industry itemize taxes and deduct all their entertainment expenses in the name of the job. "I itemized everything from my stereo to my movie tickets," boasts one corporate finance manager.

Promotions and competition

There is indeed jockeying for certain roles and positions, as there is in any industry, but the business side is not as ugly as the creative side when it comes to competition. Promotion decisions are not based on whether people like you, or on how your last film did, but rather on the body of your professional work. Even though there is an oversupply of people vying for the available jobs, it is a largely meritocratic industry.

Visit Vault at **www.vault.com** for insider company profiles, expert advice, career message boards, expert resume reviews, the Vault Job Board and more.

VAULT CAREER LIBRARY   227

A Day in the Life: Strategic Planning Executive

While there's no "typical" day in strat planning at a media company, below are some of the most common day-to-day tasks:

- Interfacing with other business units, domestically and abroad, either in calls or in meetings (25 percent)
- Presentations to the senior executive team on key decisions (25 percent)
- Presentations from the business units on growth initiatives within other groups (10 percent)
- Responding to requests from senior management (25 percent)
- Managing junior team members (15 percent)

If this sounds murky or unclear, read on for an illustration of the specifics. Overall, the hours are long. There are often stories of many executives who do not have families or children, or often forsake them for their careers.

7 a.m. Arrive at work, make conference calls to Europe to discuss progress on a major new initiative to expand in Europe.

8 a.m. Breakfast meeting with a manager in another business unit to update one another on work and "keep both ears close to the ground."

9 a.m. Review a subordinate's presentation, assigned last night. The presentation is due early tomorrow for the CEO— revisions must be made with haste.

10 a.m. Return some morning phone calls. Glance at e-mail for anything urgent.

10:30 a.m. Leave for an off-site meeting to discuss what to do with a waning division in which the top chief just left.

10:45 a.m. Call my assistant. Have her type up e-mail responses to some new e-mails and send them off on my behalf.

10:55 a.m. Arrive at off-site meeting. Listen to presentations from key leaders on what to do next.

12 p.m. Depart for lunch meeting with a senior VP at another small entertainment company to propose an acquisition.

1:30 p.m. Return to office to debrief with CFO on the numbers needed for a five-year plan.

3 p.m. Answer e-mails, review daily trade publications, *The Hollywood Reporter* and *Daily Variety*.

3:45 p.m. For fun and to build team morale, respond to office pool on what the weekend's box office will be.

3:47 p.m. Spontaneous meeting with CEO in the hallway—turns out the presentation originally due tomorrow is not that urgent.

4 p.m. Tell junior manager to call off work and go home since she's been pulling all-nighters for a couple of days.

4:10 p.m. Start reviewing budget requests and expense reports of department employees.

5 p.m. Peruse the proposals from three top management consulting firms, all vying for a piece of a major project.

6:30 p.m. Make a conference call to Asia executives to discuss progress on their latest initiative.

7:30 p.m. Answer all outstanding e-mails.

8:30 p.m. Leave the office.

Employer Directory

ABC, Inc.
77 West 66th Street
New York, NY 10023-6298
Phone: (212) 456-7777
Fax: (212) 456-1424
www.abc.com

Activision
3100 Ocean Park Boulevard
Santa Monica, CA 90405
Phone: (310) 255-2000
Fax: (310) 255-2100
www.activision.com

AMC Entertainment Holdings, Inc.
920 Main Street
Kansas City, MO 64105
Phone: (816) 221-4000
Fax: (816) 480-4617
www.amctheatres.com

Bad Boy Entertainment
1710 Broadway
New York, NY 10019
Phone: (212) 381-1540
Fax: (212) 381-1599
www.badboyonline.com

Bertelsmann AG
Carl-Bertelsmann-Strasse 270
33311 Gütersloh
Germany
Phone: +49-52-41-80-0
Fax: +49-52-41-80-96-62
www.bertelsmann.com

Black Entertainment Television
One BET Plaza
1235 West Street NE
Washington, DC 20018
Phone: (202) 608-2000
Fax: (202) 608-2589
www.bet.com

Bloomberg L.P.
731 Lexington Avenue
New York, NY 10022
Phone: (212) 318-2000
Fax: (917) 369-5000
www.bloomberg.com

British Broadcasting Corporation
Broadcasting House
Portland Place
London, W1A 1AA
United Kingdom
Phone: +44-20-75-80-44-68
Fax: +44-20-76-37-16-30
www.bbc.co.uk

Cable Satellite Public Affairs Network
400 North Capitol Street NW
Suite 650
Washington, DC 20001
Phone: (202) 737-3220
Fax: (202) 737-6226
www.c-span.org

CBS, Inc.
51 West 52nd Street
New York, NY 10019
Phone: (212) 975-4321
Fax: (212) 975-4516
www.cbs.com

Clear Channel Communications
200 East Basse Road
San Antonio, TX 78209
Phone: (210) 822-2828
Fax: (210) 822-2299
www.clearchannel.com

Comcast Corporation
1500 Market Street
Philadelphia, PA 19102-2148
Phone: (215) 665-1700
Fax: (215) 981-7790
www.comcast.com

Cox Communications, Inc.
1400 Lake Hearn Drive
Atlanta, GA 30319
Phone: (404) 843-5000
www.cox.com

Creative Artists Agency
2000 Avenue of the Stars
Los Angeles, CA 90067
Phone: (424) 288-2000
Fax: (424) 288-2900
www.caa.com

The DIRECTV Group, Inc.
2230 East Imperial Highway
El Segundo, CA 90245
Phone: (310) 964-5000
Fax: (310) 535-5225
www.directv.com

Discovery Communications, Inc.
1 Discovery Place
Silver Spring, MD 20910
Phone: (240) 662-2000
Fax: (240) 662-1868
www.discovery.com

DreamWorks Animation SKG Inc.
1000 Flower Street
Glendale, CA 91201
Phone: (818) 695-5000
Fax: (818) 695-9944
www.dreamworksanimation.com

Electronic Arts
209 Redwood Shores Parkway
Redwood City, CA 94065
Phone: (650) 628-1500
Fax: (650) 628-1422
www.ea.com

EMI Group plc
27 Wrights Lane
London, W8 5SW
United Kingdom
Phone: +44-20-77-95-70-00
Fax: +44-20-77-95-72-96
www.emigroup.com

Visit Vault at **www.vault.com** for insider company profiles, expert advice, career message boards, expert resume reviews, the Vault Job Board and more.

VAULT CAREER LIBRARY   229

Employer Directory, cont.

Fox Entertainment Group
10201 West Pico Boulevard
Building 100, Suite 3220
Los Angeles, CA 90035
Phone: (310) 369-1000
Fax: (310) 969-3300
www.fox.com

Gannett Company, Inc.
7950 Jones Branch Drive
McLean, VA 22107-0910
Phone: (703) 854-6000
Fax: (703) 854-2046
www.gannett.com

Group Televisa SA
Avenida Vasco de Quiroga, No. 2000
Colonia Santa Fe
Delegación Álvaro Obregón
01210 México, D.F.
Mexico
Phone: +52-55-5261-2445
Fax: +52-55-5261-2494
www.televisa.com

Home Box Office (HBO)
1100 Avenue of the Americas
New York, NY 10036
Phone: (212) 512-1000
Fax: (212) 512-1182
www.hbo.com

International Data Group, Inc.
1 Exeter Plaza, 15th Floor
Boston, MA 02116-2851
Phone: (617) 534-1200
Fax: (617) 423-0240
www.idg.com

Liberty Media
12300 Liberty Boulevard
Englewood, CO 80112
Phone: (720) 875-5400
Fax: (720) 875-5401
www.libertymedia.com

Live Nation, Ltd
9348 Civic Center Drive
Beverly Hills, CA 90210
Phone: (310) 867-7000
Fax: (310) 867-7001
www.livenation.com

Lucasfilm Limited
1110 Gorgas Avenue
San Francisco, CA 94129
Phone: (415) 662-1800
Fax: (415) 448-2495
www.lucasfilm.com

Martha Stewart Living Omnimedia, Inc.
11 West 42nd Street
New York, NY 10036
Phone: (212) 827-8000
Fax: (212) 827-8204
www.marthastewart.com

Metro-Goldwyn-Mayer Inc.
10250 Constellation Boulevard
Los Angeles, CA 90067
Phone: (310) 449-3000
Fax: (310) 449-8857
www.mgm.com

MTV Networks Company
1515 Broadway
New York, NY 10036
Phone: (212) 258-8000
Fax: (212) 258-6175
www.mtv.com

NBC Universal
30 Rockefeller Plaza
New York, NY 10112
Phone: (212) 664-4444
Fax: (212) 664-4085
www.nbcuni.com

News Corp.
1211 Avenue of the Americas
8th Floor
New York, NY 10036
Phone: (212) 852-7000
Fax: (212) 852-7147
www.newscorp.com

Nintendo of America, Inc.
4820 150th Avenue NE
Redmond, WA 98052
Phone: (425) 882-2040
Fax: (425) 882-3585
www.nintendo.com

Paramount Pictures Corporation
5555 Melrose Avenue, Suite 121
Hollywood, CA 90038
Phone: (323) 956-5000
www.paramount.com

Pixar Animation Studios
1200 Park Avenue
Emeryville, CA 94608
Phone: (510) 922-3000
Fax: (510) 922-3151
www.pixar.com

Public Broadcasting Service
2100 Crystal Drive
Arlington, VA 22202-3785
Phone: (703) 739-5000
Fax: (703) 739-8495
www.pbs.org

Reed Elsevier Group PLC
1-3 Strand
London, WC2N 5JR
United Kingdom
Phone: +44-20-79-30-70-77
Fax: +44-20-71-66-57-99
www.reedelsevier.com

Reed Elsevier NV
Raderweg 29
1043 NX Amsterdam
The Netherlands
Phone: +31-20-485-2222
Fax: +31-20-618-0325
www.reedelsevier.com

Employer Directory, cont.

Reuters Group Limited
The Reuters Building
Canary Wharf
London, E14 5EP
United Kingdom
Phone: +44-20-72-50-11-22
Fax: +44-20-75-42-40-64
www.reuters.com

Regal Entertainment Group
7132 Regal Lane
Knoxville, TN 37918
Phone: (865) 922-1123
Fax: (865) 922-3188
www.regalcinemas.com

Sirius Satellite Radio Inc.
1221 Avenue of the Americas
36th Floor
New York, NY 10020
Phone: (212) 584-5100
Fax: (212) 584-5200
www.sirius.com

Sony BMG Music Entertainment
550 Madison Avenue
New York, NY 10022-3211
Phone: (212) 833-7100
Fax: (212) 833-7416
www.sonybmg.com

Sony Corporation of America
550 Madison Avenue
New York, NY 10022
Phone: (212) 833-6800
Fax: (212) 833-6938
Toll free: (800) 556-3411
www.sony.com

SourceMedia
One State Street
27th Floor
New York, NY 10004
Phone: (212) 8030-8200
www.sourcemedia.com

Take-Two Interactive Software, Inc.
622 Broadway
New York, NY 10012
Phone: (646) 536-2842
Fax: (646) 536-2926
www.take2games.com

Time Warner
1 Time Warner Center
New York, NY 10019
Phone: (212) 484-8000
www.timewarner.com

Universal Music Group
1755 Broadway
New York, NY 10019
Phone: (212) 841-8000
Fax: (212) 331-2580
www.umusic.com

Univision Communications Inc.
1999 Avenue of the Stars, Suite 3050
Los Angeles, CA 90067
Phone: (310) 556-7665
Fax: (310) 556-7615
www.univision.com

USA Network, Inc.
30 Rockefeller Plaza
New York, NY 10112
Phone: (212) 664-4444
Fax: (212) 664-6365
www.usanetwork.com

Viacom Inc.
1515 Broadway
New York, NY 10036
Phone: (212) 258-6000
Fax: (212) 258-6464
www.viacom.com

Virgin Group, Ltd.
120 Campden Hill Road
London W8 7AR
United Kingdom
Phone: +44-20-72-29-12-82
Fax: +44-20-77-27-82-00
www.virgin.com

Vivendi SA
42 avenue de Friedland
75380 Paris Cedex 08
France
Phone: +33-1-71-71-10-00
Fax: +33-1-71-71-10-01
www.vivendiuniversal.com

The Walt Disney Company
500 South Buena Vista Street
Burbank, CA 91521-9722
Phone: (818) 560-1000
Fax: (818) 560-1930
disney.go.com

Warner Music Group Corp
75 Rockefeller Plaza
New York, NY 10019
Phone: (212) 275-2000
Fax: (212) 757-3985
www.wmg.com

William Morris Agency
1 William Morris Place
Beverly Hills, CA 90212
Phone: (310) 859-4000
Fax: (310) 859-4462
www.wma.com

Visit Vault at **www.vault.com** for insider company profiles, expert advice, career message boards, expert resume reviews, the Vault Job Board and more.

VAULT CAREER LIBRARY   231

Nonprofit

Imagine what it might be like to say:

> "Today at work I helped to provide a safe place for 100 teens in my community to go after school to receive tutoring and homework assistance."

> "This year at work I raised $1.5 million to fund a program that promotes better early education for young children."

> "Throughout the course of my career I helped to clean up my city's most depressed neighborhoods and developed hundreds of new affordable homes for disadvantaged families."

If being able to do this type of work in the course of your career appeals to you, you may want to consider a career in the nonprofit/philanthropy world. It won't be easygoing, though. In recent years, and especially since the September 11 terrorist attacks, the U.S. has seen a jump in its number of registered charitable organizations. All of these organizations are in need of strong leaders as many in the sector are concerned that our country is not prepared to financially support this recent influx of newly registered charities. It is clear that only the strongest and savviest organizations are certain to survive.

This is where your MBA jumps in. As more and more MBA programs integrate nonprofit management, social entrepreneurship and socially responsible business practices focuses into their curriculum, going into a career in the nonprofit world becomes more viable. Most nonprofit organizations employ wide-eyed and ambitious youth who are striving to save the world, one puppy at a time. With your business and management skills, you can make sure they can. After all, the New York Stock Exchange is a nonprofit!

The rewards can be quite satisfying for professionals who succeed. Such positions come with, at times, a tremendous amount of prestige and respect, interactions with a broad array of people from all class levels and at executive levels, a satisfying salary. Many organizations represent the lifeblood of their communities and are in the daily eye of the local, and sometimes national, public and media.

Nonprofit Doesn't Mean Money Doesn't Matter

Today's nonprofit organization is a very different institution than it was only a decade ago. In a nutshell, the nonprofit corporate culture has become more professional. An increased emphasis on efficient management has enhanced the sector's approach to program implementation or problem solving through the development of better, more cost-effective strategies for providing services. Just as important, nonprofit organizations have also greatly improved their approach to cultivating and accessing stronger financial support. Many unpredictable variables impact our national economy and subsequently philanthropic donations to nonprofits. The nonprofit/philanthropy field is learning how to protect itself from financial fluctuations.

One common approach to this challenge is to diversify funding sources. An extreme example of this is a church in Jamaica, N.Y. that is running and staffing its own charter bus company, essentially running its own for-profit venture and "donating" the income to the church's operational funds. More commonly, however, nonprofits are branching out into other areas of service in hopes of attracting new donors. This is programmatically justified as a way of making a more comprehensive impact on a single area of service or issue.

Other nonprofits are developing entirely new competencies in hopes of introducing the organization to an entirely new pool of supporters. One example of this is an early education advocacy group, Child Care Action Campaign, which has served as a facilitator and communicator of research and best practices for 20 years. Recently, however, it developed and implemented an early literacy child care provider training program, sending trainers out into neighborhoods to teach providers how to encourage literacy with the young children in their care. This decision was responsible for nearly $300,000 in new support from donors who only fund "direct service" programs (nonprofits that work directly with those it seeks to serve, rather than

Visit Vault at www.vault.com for insider company profiles, expert advice, career message boards, expert resume reviews, the Vault Job Board and more.

VAULT CAREER LIBRARY 233

just training workers who work with them or conducting research), essentially opening a door to a new revenue stream. In this instance, the organization jumped into community or direct service while continuing its work in advocacy and research.

Nonprofit Organizations

In the largest sense, philanthropy refers to any activity to improve society—to make communities safer, to shelter the unfortunate, to heal the sick, to give voice to the underserved, to feed the needy, among other important goals. Government agencies—from city-run homeless shelters to state art commissions, to federal welfare programs—play an enormously important philanthropic role. But from the perspective of most Americans today, the wide variety of nonprofit or not-for-profit institutions is the heart of modern philanthropy. This guide focuses almost exclusively on careers associated with these institutions, specifically those having the responsibility of raising the money to keep the organizations going. To avoid confusion, we will use the term *philanthropic giving* from this point forward to describe the work of the professionals who give money away to worthy causes, rather than the more general term of *philanthropy*, which is associated with the good works of nonprofit organizations to address a social problem or cause.

As direct descendents of the organizations first created by Benjamin Franklin, modern nonprofit organizations are, in the simplest of terms, entities with some formal structure that do not distribute any profits to its owners or leadership, but rather devote all resources toward a cause. As you can imagine, such a definition covers a staggeringly broad range of organizations—youth clubs, churches, schools, trade associations, free clinics, homeless shelters, hospitals, libraries, museums, advocacy groups, dance and theater troupes, to name just a few. While it is not required, most of these groups incorporate themselves under the laws of the state in which they operate, primarily to prevent lawsuits against individual staff members, volunteers and directors when someone claims negligence or other wrongdoing on the part of the organization itself. Nonprofit groups vary widely in size and shape, but most are required under state law to establish a board of directors ultimately responsible for the policies, practices and overall direction of the organization. The vast majority of these governing boards are comprised of volunteers, as was true in the days of Benjamin Franklin. And also as was true then, savvy organizations try to recruit board members with political and/or financial clout. Most nonprofits also have a formal leadership structure (an executive director or president at the very least) responsible for overseeing day-to-day operations.

Tax exemptions

Generally, nonprofit organizations also apply for tax-exempt status under the federal tax code. Such exemptions have been in place since the modern tax code was in enacted, but today's tax-exempt designations emerged in 1954, when Congress approved the first major overhaul of the code. Under current federal law, there are several tax exemption categories for nonprofit groups, depending on their activities. Most groups are public-serving organizations, as outlined in section 501(c)(3) of the Internal Revenue Code. As defined in section 501(c)(3), such as a group must be "a public charity or private foundation, which is established for purposes that are religious, educational, charitable, scientific, literary, testing for public safety, fostering of national or international amateur sports or prevention of cruelty to animals and children." A 501(c)(3) nonprofit organization is not only exempt from federal taxes (and in most cases state taxes as well), but they are also allowed to receive donations that individuals can deduct from their personal income taxes. It is important to note that the 501(c)(3) category covers both charitable organizations that provide services or advocate for a cause and the foundations and other institutions that fund these groups. You should also be aware that there are other tax exempt designations for nonprofit groups; for example, organizations exclusively devoted to lobbying and political activities can apply for tax exempt status under section 501(c)(4) of the Internal Revenue Code. Such groups can also seek donations, but these gifts are not tax deductible.

According to the National Center for Charitable Statistics, nearly 1.5 million registered, tax-exempt, nonprofit organizations operate throughout the country, including 501(c)(3) charities (from homeless shelters to grant-giving foundations), political advocacy groups, and membership organizations (such as trade associations, chambers of commerce and churches). This number does not account for the scores of smaller, informal groups (including many individual church groups and congregations) serving every population, every community and every cause that exists. The nonprofit or independent sector has evolved into a vibrant part of American life and its economy, regarded as separate from but in balance with public agencies and private, for-profit businesses.

Many Choices

The sheer size and diversity of the nonprofit sector can be daunting to contemplate. With so many different groups taking different approaches to different causes, it's more than a little difficult to talk about the general character or personality of nonprofit organizations.

The IRS, the U.S. Bureau of Labor Statistics and numerous universities and think tanks that study the sector do lump nonprofit organizations into several different categories largely based on approach and purpose. The most common categories used are health, education, social or human services, religious, civic and advocacy, international relief and development, arts and culture and funders. It's a crude kind of taxonomy and definitely not infallible, since many nonprofits fall into more than one category. (The IRS and Bureau of Labor Statistics use a more complicated classification system to capture specific information about the number and kinds of nonprofits; for instance, they try to determine how many community hospitals there are or how many nonprofit theater groups.) But organizations that exemplify one category or another do share with one another characteristics in size, infrastructure, and to some extent, the kinds of people who work there.

Here's a bit more information about the kinds of groups in each category that might help you make some decisions about where you would like to work. Again, the descriptions here are very general and cannot be applied to every organization in any particular category. Moreover, no one kind of nonprofit has cornered the market on efficiency and dynamic leadership, nor mismanagement and dysfunction.

Health organizations

Health organizations—such as hospitals, clinics, nursing homes, hospice facilities and drug rehabilitation centers—take up the largest piece of the nonprofit pie, in terms of revenue, expenses and the number of people they employ. According to the latest version of the Nonprofit Almanac published by the Urban Institute, more than half the revenue earned by or contributed to the entire nonprofit sector goes to organizations providing health services. Perhaps because of their relative wealth, or the demands of physicians, salaries at health organizations (especially hospitals) tend to be among the highest in the nonprofit world. Along with healing the sick, health organizations nurture extensive bureaucracies to deal with stringent state and federal regulations, concerns about patient privacy and the need to navigate complicated health insurance programs—including Medicare and Medicaid—which provide the lion's share of revenue. So as a fundraiser, you are just as likely to work with a hospital administrator of some sort as you are a doctor or nurse. In some health organizations, politics may go hand in hand with treatment of the sick; hospital associated with universities will have interns, residents and researchers vying for the best residencies, teaching and administrative positions. You may also see different departments at a hospital competing with one another for funding, especially for clinical research. Facilities focused on community health (including hospice care and community hospitals) are known to have warmer, friendlier environments. It's important to remember that even if you are squirreled away in the administrative offices as a fundraiser, sickness and death will be a part of your everyday existence. Some find that fulfilling; others find it depressing.

Visit Vault at www.vault.com for insider company profiles, expert advice, career message boards, expert resume reviews, the Vault Job Board and more.

VAULT CAREER LIBRARY 235

Educational institutions

Primarily universities, colleges and private, independent schools (meaning those that are not part of the system of public schools), educational institutions are the second-largest category based on revenue and employment. For the most part, universities and schools rely heavily on tuitions, as well as funding from individuals, foundations, and state and federal agencies. Schools are also among the oldest American nonprofit institutions; indeed Harvard University, founded in 1638, is considered to be the first nonprofit in the U.S. Thu, many schools have a strong sense of history of which staff and alumni are rather proud. There is, however, a big difference in the size, infrastructure and organizational culture between a university and an independent school. Universities are large (employing hundreds of people), hierarchical and extremely political places, exacerbated by the fact that professor/scholars tend to have strong personalities. So associate professors jockey for tenure, tenured professors squabble among themselves about their scholarly pursuits and publishing opportunities and different departments fiercely compete for dollars. Given their size and the myriad demands for resources, universities maintain large fundraising programs with well-paid staff. Independent schools—ranging from Montessori to Catholic, to boarding—are considerably smaller. Some mimic universities in style and structure, but most are far less formal. Fundraising teams are also small with as little as two staff. Salaries are also considerable smaller than at universities. Many independent schools have religious affiliations, which you may be expected to uphold as an employee. Both universities and independent schools focus most fundraising activities on alumni, and there may be opportunities to meet distinguished former students who have gone on to Hollywood or politics. Most fundraisers for schools and universities find interactions with students, parents and alumni to be the best part of their jobs.

The social or human service category

This category encompasses a broad array of groups that provide resources and services for the disabled and disenfranchised, including legal aid societies, housing assistance programs and homeless shelters, soup kitchens, job training centers, child welfare groups, day care operations, immigrant assistance organizations, rape crisis centers and mental health counseling facilities, among many, many others. While this class of nonprofits places third in terms of total revenue for the sector, the sheer number of such groups far exceeds any other category. As a result, many scholars in the nonprofit field describe social service agencies as the face of the nonprofit world, the kind of group that most people think of when they hear the word "nonprofit." The size and scope of work for these organizations is extraordinarily diverse, ranging from the Salvation Army's multi-faceted programs for the poor to a soup kitchen. Most social service operations heavily rely on state and federal funding, either through grants or contracts and are therefore subject to myriad regulations from those for food preparation to client privacy. Social service agencies must also wrestle with establishing rigorous and somewhat cumbersome self-evaluation processes, since many government agencies and private foundations award contracts and grants based on performance. This is an issue that the entire nonprofit sector contends with, but it's a particular challenge for social service groups because of their heavy reliance on public funding. Moreover, the United Way (a major funder for social services groups) also requires that its beneficiaries establish benchmarks and performance outcomes. Aside from organizations like the Salvation Army, Catholic Charities or the YMCA, most social services groups are small and lean without much of infrastructure beyond what is required of them by state agencies and the federal government. As a result, fundraising teams are often small and are not paid top dollar. As a fundraiser, you are most likely to work with social workers and clinicians, who are generally a compassionate and caring bunch. They are not, however, necessarily very educated about or interested in fundraising.

The category of religious organizations

Congregations of various religious sects (Christian, Muslim, Jewish, Buddhist, etc.) and any denominations or associations under which congregations may organize constitute the category of religious organizations. There are many hospitals, schools, social services agencies and advocacy groups with religious affiliations (such as the Salvation Army or Catholics for

Free Choice), but these organizations fall under the category of the cause that they serve or the assistance they provide. The primary purpose of a congregation is to offer religious guidance and education to the individuals that belong to it, while denominations are regional or national associations that provide additional leadership and support services to individual congregations. It is important to note that a congregation in any given community may be completely independent from a particular denomination. While there are a few large congregations with several paid staff (including fundraisers), most are very small and run entirely by volunteers, aside from the priest, pastors, ministers, rabbis, etc. providing religious instruction. Likewise, any social services that a congregation provides (such as clothes or housing to the needy) are almost entirely volunteer operations. And as you would expect, congregations are almost entirely reliant on donations from its members. There are therefore few opportunities to work for a congregation or denomination as a professional fundraiser. However, there are many opportunities with other nonprofit organizations with religious ties. As you would expect, the character of congregations and denominations is determined by the structure and culture of the faith, the religious leadership and the individual members.

Civic and advocacy organizations

These organizations comprise a relatively small (in terms of revenue and number of people they employ) category of nonprofits focused on changing policies around a particular issue or problem. Such prominent groups as the Sierra Club, National Organization for Women, American Civil Liberties Union, National Association for the Advancement of Colored People, American Association of Retired People and the Christian Coalition fall into this category, as well as a range of smaller groups focused on specific issues in their communities. Generally these groups engage in four basic activities: (1) educating and organizing people to engage their local policy-makers (county commissioners, state agencies, Members of Congress, etc.); (2) generating interest in an issue with the media; (3) analyzing changes in policy and educating the general public on their impact; and, (4) directly advocating for policy changes with local, state and federal officials. Many of these groups are centered in major metropolitan areas near seats of government. As you would expect, the largest groups have headquarters in Washington, D.C. Advocacy organizations are not political action committees or private lobbying firms, and as public institutions are subject to strict regulations regarding direct lobbying of policy-makers. Most receive very little support from government agencies. Rather, the major sources of funding are individuals, corporations and foundations (although foundations have requirements on what kind of advocacy activities they can support). The largest advocacy groups will pay top-dollar for experienced fundraisers; smaller groups in communities often employ one fundraiser who relies heavily on program staff for assistance, especially in foundation relations, proposal development and report writing. Core staff at advocacy groups is usually comprised of some combination of lawyers, public relations and communications specialists, and organizers who tend to be passionate, driven and somewhat aggressive. The pace at advocacy groups can be more intense, especially when Congress and state legislatures are in session. Some find it energizing, while others quickly burn out.

International relief and development groups

Known abroad as non-governmental organizations (NGOs), international relief and development groups focus on activities to improve the quality of life for communities outside of the United States, primarily in developing countries. Groups like the American Red Cross and Oxfam provide immediate, direct relief in the wake of war and natural disasters, while other groups devote time and energy to education and building local economies. This category of nonprofits also includes organizations who do not provide direct assistance to communities but peripherally impact quality of life—environmental organizations like the Ocean Conservancy and Conservation International are examples. Most groups also have a dual focus on direct relief activities and advocacy. According to the *Nonprofit Almanac*, more than 5,000 such groups are incorporated in the United States. The majority of the United Nation's and U.S. government's humanitarian relief funds are funneled through these international groups, which usually have headquarters in Washington, D.C. or New York (to connect more directly to the United Nations), as well as field offices in the countries where they work. Fundraising teams usually work

Visit Vault at **www.vault.com** for insider company profiles, expert advice, career message boards, expert resume reviews, the Vault Job Board and more.

VAULT CAREER LIBRARY   237

from headquarters with opportunities to travel abroad. Like advocacy groups, the largest of the international relief agencies will pay their fundraising staff well. Since there's a heavy reliance on government funding, there's also a heavy focus on proposal and report writing, so fundraisers are usually strong writers. The rest of the staff is usually comprised of policy experts from the U.S. and abroad with field staff who are largely from the country in which they are working. The work is rewarding, exciting, dangerous and stressful. In some countries, field staff are at considerable risk from terrorism and civil strife, and most are used to living without much luxury. With a truly global workforce, cultural difference is a challenge, especially in navigating different communication styles.

The category of "arts and culture" organizations

These organizations include community and professional theaters, dance companies, nonprofit art galleries and museums, orchestras and symphonies, literary and cultural magazines, as well as a range of arts appreciation groups. While there are almost as many arts groups in the country as there are in health care, the arts community is far less wealthy. Revenue to health care groups is in fact 25 times greater than what goes to the arts. Salaries are therefore considerably smaller at arts organizations, although there are many cases where a development director is paid more than the artistic director. Most revenue comes from ticket sales, so marketing and audience development is an important concern and a constant challenge. Arts groups in fact are always looking for ways to engage new constituents, especially the Generation X'ers who have accumulated some wealth by now. Art organizations also tend to work in close partnership with schools to support arts education programs. They also try to foster relationships with corporate interests that see a variety of opportunities to elevate their profile through the arts. Most arts groups struggle to keep qualified and experienced administrative staff because of the lower salaries, long hours (especially when working for a performance group) and the strong temperament of artistic directors and boards. It is not at all unusual for highly public and bitter fights to break out between boards and organizational leadership over the artistic direction of an organization. That said, the passion, dedication and talent of artists involved with these organizations is intoxicating.

Grant-giving organizations

Like private foundations and federated charities, grant-giving organizations fall into the "funders" category. These groups generally do not engage in any other activity other than giving away money, although there are exceptions, such as the Pew Charitable Trusts, which provides grants and is also involved in advocacy work. While private foundations like the Ford Foundation are the most commonly known, there are in fact a variety of nonprofit organizations that function as grant givers. Federated charities are organizations that collect donations from individuals and distribute them to a chosen group of nonprofit organizations. Those charities that wish to receive funds usually go through an application process to demonstrate that they are legal and viable nonprofits. Most people are familiar with the United Way, but there are other such groups, such as Jewish federations and societies that raise funds for research and treatment of diseases—an example is the Leukemia and Lymphoma Society. Investment firms can also establish donor-advised funds that are registered as nonprofit organizations. These funds are comprised of donations from wealthy individuals and are managed by a financial advisor who may either follow the instructions of the donor on which charities to support or may make those decisions on their own. Most community foundations also create donor-advised funds to help donors in any given location be effective in their philanthropy. Like other nonprofit organizations, a board of directors (usually known as the board of trustees) oversees the general direction of grant-giving. A professional staff of financial advisors, policy experts and those with expertise in nonprofit management make day-to-day decisions about how to wisely invest the pool of funds and how to distribute grants. Like the rest of the nonprofit sector, there are far more small family foundations and donor-advised funds run by one or two staff than large, professional foundations run by many. The larger foundations and federated charities generally pay well and provide rather generous benefits. As we will discuss later in the guide, jobs at foundations are among the most competitive in the fundraising and philanthropic giving field.

Philanthropy and Fundraising

Interested in a career in fundraising and/or philanthropy? You are in good company. You are, in fact, entering the ranks of Christian saints and Buddhist monks, the world's greatest thinkers (Plato and Benjamin Franklin, for example), industry giants like Andrew Carnegie, Bill Gates and Warren Buffett, leaders of social change like Booker T. Washington, and celebrities of all sorts, from Robert Redford to Angelina Jolie, to Bono.

It is a profession honored throughout time and a practice undertaken by every kind of society and institution—from the Lakota tribe of North America to the villages of Sub-Saharan Africa, to the Buddhist temples of Japan, to Ghengis Khan's Middle Eastern empire. The fundamental principle of the profession—that one should give one's wealth to help the less fortunate and improve the conditions in which we all live—is deeply woven into the fabric of religious doctrine and codified in the earliest laws.

As such, the field of fundraising and philanthropy is truly global with opportunity to interact with any and every strata of society. And it is a field that in America alone generates nearly $300 billion a year for social causes and over a million different charitable organizations in America afloat. The role of fundraising and philanthropy in American society has never been so prominent, as foundations grow larger, the wealthy grow wealthier, and the nonprofit community grows into an influential sector of the overall economy. In fact, *U.S. News & World Report* recently named fundraising as one of the 25 best careers to enter.

Professional fundraising

It would seem that from either side of the fence—as the philanthropic giving professional looking out to the sea of nonprofits or as the fundraiser looking to land the big fish donor—the primary focus is money, either asking for it or distributing it. Well, let's throw that notion back out to sea, for most professionals in the business will quickly let you know that the focus of their work is fundamentally different.

People generally have one of two reactions to the whole notion of professional fundraising. It's either, "God, how awful to beg people for money all day," or "How hard can it be to ask people for money all day?"

Here's the most worst-kept secret among fundraisers: you actually spend very little time "begging" for money. In fact, if you are asking every person you meet to write a check (and you've seen those eager young folks on street corners with their clipboards), or running through a list of telephone numbers like a telemarketer, you are unlikely to have much success.

The mantra of the professional fundraiser is very simple: people give to people. So in order to get someone to invest in your organization, you need to help that person get invested in you and that organization. And that's about establishing and strengthening a relationship with people who care about your cause. As one fundraising consultant puts it, "No matter if you're creating an individual donor campaign or writing a letter of inquiry to a foundation or meeting with a possible major donor to your organization, it's all about nurturing and building relationships for the long haul."

So asking for money from someone who deeply cares about your organization is the easiest thing in the world. The hard part is finding those people, establishing a rapport with them, and giving them the right information and arguments to convince them that their support of your organization over time will make a fundamental difference in the world. Therefore, a fundraiser's daily activities (no matter what his or her particular specialty) revolve around five basic strategies:

Identify the right people—If you surround yourself with wealthy people, this may seem obvious and easy. As one fundraiser for a national environmental group states, "If you happen to be best friends with Bill Gates, sure, chances are he'd support your cause." But if your best friend with a trust fund doesn't care about the issue that your organization addresses, then you actually don't know the right people. In fact, identifying potential donors, also known as "prospects," takes careful research. A successful fundraiser develops a list of potential donors who (1) have the ability to give, (2) the interest in your issue, and,

Visit Vault at **www.vault.com** for insider company profiles, expert advice, career message boards, expert resume reviews, the Vault Job Board and more.

VAULT CAREER LIBRARY 239

(3) feel connected to your organization. Most large nonprofit organizations (those with budgets of $10 million or more) employ either a part-time or full-time prospect researcher solely responsible for identifying likely prospects and keeping fundraisers apprised of changes in people's finances and their giving habits. The more information you have, the more likely you are to get someone interested in your organization.

Establish a relationship—Fundraisers spend the vast majority of their time finding ways to get to know and engage potential and existing donors, whether they are program officers at a foundation or people writing up their wills. They meet with donors, invite them to events and informational presentations, alert them to important events, inform them of major victories and simply thank them for their support. Like any good friendship, a strong relationship with a donor is open, honest and warm. As described by a fundraiser:

"One of the best moments I've ever had in fundraising was when a major funder told me that she had worked with hundreds of nonprofits and had 'never seen it done better' than by us. Her accolade spelled out everything I work for: not only was she donating at a major level, but she completely believed in us and the organization, and in turn, we could be completely open with her, use her expertise and, of course, count on her for continued funding. She has even helped get us new funders."

This is the kind of relationship a fundraiser hopes to have with every donor.

Ask at the right time—Yes, there comes a time when you need to sit down with a donor and ask for that check, or in the case of a foundation, submit that proposal for support. But it's all in the timing. You may have the most enthusiastic donors in the world, but if they are in the midst of starting a new business, they may not have the money to spare. And if that foundation's assets have been hit by a bad break in the stock market, they may not be able to fund a six-figure grant request. You also need to know if these donors have already given or are about to give to another organization with a similar mission, and are therefore tapped out, or if a foundation board is about to undergo strategic planning and fundamentally changes the direction of their giving interests. Again, you need to know your donors to know when to ask for money.

Thank the donor—This may seem like another obvious step in fundraising, but the importance of a prompt and proper thank you for a gift cannot be overemphasized. Every donor—whether he or she has given $5 or $5 million—wants to know that his or her gift has made a difference, and that you as a fundraiser appreciate the person behind the gift. Indeed, that thank you alone can guarantee another gift in the future. Most development operations have a rule of thanking major donors (including foundation officers and corporate community relations directors) within 48 hours with a personalized thank you letter from the executive director, often coming on the heels of a phone call from the development staff person. The process of thanking members for their donation is often more elaborate than the membership drive itself, for the staff must generate personalized thank you letters for hundreds or thousands of donors and send out the membership gifts. The procedures for generating these thank you letters is also known in the business as the "acknowledgement process" and is often supervised by the development assistant, with input from other development staff that have been involved in cultivating the relationship with the donor.

Strengthen the relationship—To paraphrase The Carpenters' classic ballad, you've only just begun when your donor writes that check or that grant comes in. Your donor needs just as much time and attention afterwards, especially if you think he or she is capable of giving more money in the future. A good fundraiser reports back regularly to donors, telling them how their money was spent, informing them of new activities or directions, and engaging them with others in the organization. A fundraiser is also likely to be the one to discuss problems and challenges with donors, which can be just as important as outlining the opportunities that an organization is pursuing. For example, many fundraisers need to explain how shrinking state and federal budgets impact the organization, both positively and negatively.

Professional philanthropy

The same basic framework for relationship building holds true for the professional philanthropist who gives money away, the only real difference being that you are looking to give (rather than ask) at the right time and to the right charitable cause.

Whether you are advising someone with a charitable trust or supervising a grant-giving program at a foundation, you want the money to make the most impact as possible. Therefore you need to identify the organizations that fit the interests of the donor or the guidelines of the foundation and that you believe are effective in what they do. You also need to build a relationship with those groups, understand their unique role in the nonprofit community, their challenges and capacity needs, and their strategies for addressing an issue. And you need to track the progress of the groups to whom you donate, both to assess the effectiveness of your gift or grant and to better understand the challenges and opportunities that they face.

As was true 140 years ago when the first foundations invested in education for freed slaves, philanthropists are active participants, and more than ever want to build long-lasting partnerships with the nonprofit organizations that they care about. Moreover, donors at all levels look for creative ways to support communities, causes and organizations, and this means that partnerships take many different forms and include many different players. Giving institutions often establish and drive these partnership—community foundations in particular bring together wealthy individuals, community leaders, policy experts, mayors, county commissioners, Members of Congress, businesses, activists and nonprofit organizations to address the problems of a community, such as immigration, homelessness or health care coverage. But sophisticated donors also deeply invest in organizations and issues to become important partners for social change.

So in truth, fundraising and philanthropy boils down to people and the relationships between donors, organizations and causes. Money is the means to an end and not to be forgotten. But most fundraisers and philanthropic giving professionals would describe themselves as more than money managers or salespeople. A good fundraiser may be able to work a cocktail party, chatting up the entrepreneur who just sold his company or the socialite with the big inheritance. And an effective philanthropic giving professional is keenly aware of his or her responsibility to make sound investment decisions to grow foundation endowments and donor-advised funds. He is also perfectly willing to use money as an incentive to ensure cooperation from nonprofit organizations. But the best in the field consider themselves advocates for a cause, a calling beyond schmoozing and sound investment portfolios. They are mediators and facilitators, building crucial relationships toward successful philanthropy in that larger sense of serving people, communities and causes.

Is this a higher calling? Many in the field will say yes. The director of development at a breast cancer awareness group describes the most successful fundraisers and giving professionals as possessing the same qualities of great social leaders and thinkers. They have Martin Luther King Jr.'s passion about a cause; President Clinton's charm and confidence to make a case for someone to donate; Stephen Hawking's deep knowledge about an organization, its programs, its fundraising practices, its financial health; Sigmund Freud's listening skills; and Lance Armstrong's resilience when the inevitable "no" comes your way.

Foundation/Program Officer

Perhaps the most prestigious job in the philanthropic giving world is that of a foundation officer, also known as a program officer. At the largest foundations, program officers are the elite, intellectual powerhouses behind philanthropy in America and the world. They are admired, courted and feared by fundraisers and nonprofit executive directors alike.

In the simplest terms, a foundation officer is the gatekeeper at a foundation, determining how to distribute a pool of grant funds each year to worthy nonprofit organizations. Foundations are themselves nonprofit organizations but with the single purpose of supporting other nonprofits through grant-making programs. A foundation is built from a pool of assets carefully invested over time. Those assets can come from a variety of places—from the pocket of a wealthy individual (in the case of a family foundation), a percentage of corporate profits (in the case of a corporate foundation) or from a group of different funds of varying size (as is true for the community foundation). Foundations with a single source of assets are referred to as private foundations; those with multiple sources are known as public foundations. By law, foundations are required to distribute 5 percent of their assets in any given year, and most give away about that much. However, some foundations are set up to dissolve at a point in the future and therefore program officers are tasked with spending down assets in a more

Visit Vault at www.vault.com for insider company profiles, expert advice, career message boards, expert resume reviews, the Vault Job Board and more.

VAULT CAREER LIBRARY 241

aggressive manner. Like all other nonprofit organizations, foundations must establish a board of trustees to oversee operations. A foundation's board of trustees is ultimately responsible for the financial health of the foundation and the effective distribution of grant funds.

What does the foundation officer do?

As a gatekeeper, the foundation officer is the primary contact to nonprofit organizations seeking grants and the key coordinator of the foundation's grant-making process. Every foundation has a different way of doing business. Foundations that employ program officers—and this is a very small percentage of foundations, since the vast majority of foundations are run by volunteer boards of trustees—usually establish a formal and rigorous process for reviewing grant applications.

Most foundations today will not accept unsolicited grant proposals; there are simply too many groups seeking grant funding for program officers to keep up with requests. So the grant-making process usually begins as a series of conversations between foundation officers and the staff of grant-seeking organizations. Most of the time, initial contact is made by the grant-seeker. An executive director meets a program officer at a meeting, a board member at a grant-seeking nonprofit has a business or personal relationship with a board member at a foundation or a fundraiser writes a compelling introduction letter to a program officer.

A foundation officer then must evaluate potential grantees, determining if they are a good fit for the foundation. The evaluation process usually involves interviewing staff at a grant-seeking organization, visiting the organization's facilities and/or the communities that the grant-seeker serves, as well as meeting with leaders at other nonprofit organizations providing similar or complementary services. Program officers are also guided by the foundation's giving priorities, usually established by the person or corporation that established the foundation, and by strategic planning initiated by the board of trustees. It's not uncommon for a foundation to change its mission and giving priorities over time, especially if founding members pass on. For example, a wealthy entrepreneur may establish a foundation to fund nonprofit organizations in a particular community, such as his/her hometown, but not provide any other guidance on what kind of nonprofit organizations to support. But as that foundation matures, the board of trustees may survey the community and further refine the foundation's mission to meet particular challenges and needs.

If a foundation officer believes that a nonprofit organization is a strong candidate for funding, he/she will ask for some kind of proposal that makes the case for support. The proposal review process at each foundation is different; in some cases, foundation officers have the authority to approve or reject grant proposals with minimal interference from the board of trustees. At other foundations, there are lengthy and complicated review procedures, where the foundation officer serves as the advocate for the grant-seeking nonprofit organization at a series of meetings and presentations with foundation staff and the board. If approved, the foundation officer is then charged with monitoring the progress of the grantee; that may merely mean that they require the foundation to send along periodic progress reports. It can also mean more direct involvement; the foundation officer may want to help the organization further shape program activities and campaigns.

To be in a position to evaluate the potential of nonprofit organizations, you need expertise and experience. Foundation officers are therefore highly educated with a background in a particular issue, such as urban planning, reproductive rights policy or performing arts. They have also spent time working at nonprofit organizations in some capacity. It's important to note that the largest foundations are now looking to the corporate world for leadership, as evidenced by the recent change in guard at the Ford Foundation, the second largest foundation in the country (the largest is the Bill and Melinda Gates Foundation). The foundation recently hired a management consultant from McKinsey to take over as president.

A Day in the Life: Foundation Officer

This is the day in the life of a fictional foundation officer at one of the top-100 largest foundations in the country, with a mission to serve nonprofit organizations in an urban region crossing three states along the East Coast. In total, the foundation gives away $50 million a year. The foundation officer is part of a three-person team charged with giving $11 million in grants annually to arts and culture organizations in the region.

8:15 a.m. Arrive at the office a bit early so that you can answer e-mails before the phone starts ringing. You've been tied up in so many meetings this week that you have a mountain of messages you haven't even opened yet. About a dozen are from grantees that have sent interim reports due at the six-month point of their grant terms. You shoot them all quick e-mails thanking them for the report and telling them you will get back to them with any questions. You scan through another six or seven e-mails with news clippings on various topics—reviews of local theater productions, a profile of the new executive director of the city's chamber orchestra and a feature article in the *Enquirer* (the primary newspaper for the region) on the status of performing arts in the region. You take a minute to read this article in full. It's centered on a report that the foundation funded and that you helped develop, a survey of performing arts organizations with commentary from several economists on the many ways in which arts and culture activities bolster local economies. You're glad to see that one of the economists that you brought on board to the project, a professor from New York University, is quoted in the article.

You also respond to an e-mail from your boss, the director of the arts and culture program, confirming that you are available for lunch. There's also an e-mail from him asking for a list of the letters of inquiry to be considered at the next review meeting to occur at the end of the month. You quickly tick off the 13 organizations that have sent you letters, a three-page request summary that serves as the first step in the proposal submission process for the foundation. You also let your boss know that you have invited two other organizations to submit letters, and you expect to receive them by next week.

9:20 a.m. Start returning phone messages; you had five from yesterday from various grantees. You call the grant writer at the natural history museum, who had a question about how to update outcome measures in the letter of intent that the museum is about to submit to you. You tell her it's not necessary to update them at all, that the ones submitted last year provided a lot of information to the foundation's board on how the museum was evaluating the impact of new programs on audience attendance. You leave a message for the director of development for a dance company giving her three days next month when you would be available for a site visit. You also ask that she send you a copy of the company's latest marketing plan to review before the visit; the grant the foundation gave last year was to help the company hire a new marketing director and a contract publicist. You're curious to see how the new hires are working out. Then you speak with the executive director of a small puppet theater, assuring him that it's perfectly fine to submit a letter of intent some time next week. He is extraordinarily apologetic that the letter will come several days later than anticipated, explaining that the director of development and her assistant are both out with the flu.

10:15 a.m. Join the monthly conference call for the Cultural Alliance, a consortium of arts organizations across the region focused on audience development. Your foundation is one of three funders that have invested in an online ticketing and audience management system to be managed by the Cultural Alliance that will allow a broad range of nonprofit arts organizations to manage tickets sales and demographic information. The software developer has set up these monthly calls to discuss progress on the system. Today, the developer is taking the group through an online presentation to introduce the web site and interface for the system. It's impressive and seems easy to use. The developer declares he is confident that the system will be up and running in time for three performing arts groups to use it for ticket sales next season.

11:35 a.m. Step out the door with your boss for a meal at the Chinese restaurant down the block. This is a periodic lunch he schedules so that the two of you can catch up on things outside of weekly staff meetings. You spend most of the lunch describing the presentation by the software developer. Your boss asks if you could arrange a one-on-one meeting with him and the developer so that he can see the system for himself.

Visit Vault at **www.vault.com** for insider company profiles, expert advice, career message boards, expert resume reviews, the Vault Job Board and more.

VAULT CAREER LIBRARY   243

You two also discuss the upcoming planning retreat with the board of trustees. The foundation is entering the third year of its five-year strategic plan and the board has asked each of the four program teams to schedule a daylong retreat to discuss progress toward goals and lessons learned. Your boss wants you to give a presentation focused on various projects you are managing, including the performing arts report and various efforts to assist groups with audience development and marketing.

1:15 p.m. Get back to your office to make a few more phone calls. You catch up with the development directors for two different organizations—a youth orchestra and an art gallery focused on displaying work by at-risk children—and schedule site visits. You also get in touch with the professor from New York University, who is about to catch the train down for a town hall meeting you have helped organize. The meeting is an outgrowth of the report project and is meant to bring urban planning experts and economists, city officials and leaders from the arts community together to discuss the impact of urban revitalization efforts on arts and culture institutions in the city. You assure the professor that he does not need to prepare extensive opening remarks but rather should be prepared to answer questions from the audience. He asks if you can join him for dinner beforehand, but you decline. You just don't think you have time today, especially since you need to try and review a couple of letters of inquiry today and tomorrow.

You notice that while you have been on the phone, you've received three voicemail messages. You don't have time to review them now, since you're a little late for a meeting.

2:05 p.m. Run down the stairs for a meeting in the conference room on the Regional Arts and Culture Information Project. A group of five funders, including your foundation, have joined officials at local art councils and state cultural agencies to create a new mechanism for capturing demographic information about audiences that attend art events, as well as financial data from arts organization to gauge their health and growth. Unfortunately, the project is going slowly. The group has spent many weeks deliberating on what kind of data to compile, a conversation that you think should happen later once you have hired a contractor to design the system. And now the group is struggling to put together a request for proposals in order to hire the contractor. Once again, the team reviews the draft request, which has gone through at least 10 iterations. It looks like everyone is finally ready to sign off on it, and you now hope the project can now move along at a faster pace.

3:45 p.m. Return to your office and review your voicemail messages. None of them are urgent, so you decide to focus on the draft letter of intent you received yesterday. It's from a fledgling performing arts groups focused on incubating new theater and dance pieces. Six months ago, you read a glowing review in the local paper of one of their workshop productions and attended. You were impressed with the quality of the work and the sophistication of the production. You spoke to the artistic director after the performance and again, you were impressed by her level of sophistication, especially since you guessed she wasn't yet 30. After inviting her to your office for a longer conversation about the direction she wants to take the organization, you asked her to submit a letter of intent.

The basic concept described in the letter is exciting; the organization wants to link up with the local theater fringe festival to showcase new work and then promote those productions that are successful at the festival to other local theater and dance companies. Unfortunately, the letter is poorly written and riddled with typos. And the artistic director doesn't seem to quite understand what an outcome measure is. You just don't think the letter will make it through the first step of the review process. You decide to give the artistic director a call to talk about the possibility of a small planning grant for the organization; perhaps you can help them hire some contractors to help with fundraising efforts. You also make a note to talk with your colleague at another foundation with a technical assistance fund for small arts organizations.

4:35 p.m. Leave the office in order to grab the train to the city. You should be able to get to the central library, where the town meeting is to be held, with just enough time to grab a sandwich beforehand.

5:30 p.m. Arrive at the library full from a triple-decker sandwich from a nearby deli. The meeting starts in a half-hour, and you see that the panelists and a number of your colleagues from other foundations have arrived. You chitchat outside the meeting hall for a bit with your professor friend from New York University and a colleague from a community foundation. The primary host of the meeting, the president of the Cultural Alliance, takes the professor away to get fitted for a microphone. You and your friend from the community foundation complain a bit about the meeting earlier this afternoon. She is part of the team leading the Regional Arts and Cultural Information Project and is just as frustrated as you that it's taking so long just to hire a contractor. As more people arrive, you two separate to shake hands with various participants, most of whom are grantees. But you're pleased to see that members of the local actor's union have come, as well as some local store owners and one of the big real estate developers in the area.

6:15 p.m. Sit down as the town meeting gets underway. It's starting a bit late, but that's largely to accommodate a large crowd who came in at the last minute. The large meeting hall is three-quarters full. The discussion is lively and there's some strong statements made against real estate developers. You're glad that the facilitator, the director of the arts administration program at the University of Pittsburgh, is strong and unflappable. There's a rich conversation about the importance of festivals in creating a sense of unity in neighborhoods. The theatre fringe festival and the Get on your Feet Dance Jamboree are mentioned repeatedly—two festivals that your foundation has funded since their start.

7:50 p.m. Grab a bottle of sparkling water at the drinks table and join the reception. You catch your boss' eye, and he wanders over. He joined the meeting about a half-hour late. He's very excited about the discussion of the theater fringe festival; it's one of his pet projects. You talk to him about the letter of intent you read this afternoon from the small theater group focused on new work. You all discuss ways that the foundation might find some mentoring opportunities for the artistic director around fundraising.

As your boss heads out the door, you catch up with the professor and congratulate him. You two talk a bit about how to build better relations between arts groups and real estate developers. He mentions an initiative in Chicago where the city arts commission worked with local foundations and bankers to convince a real estate developer to set aside a few units of artist housing in a new apartment complex on the south side of the city. The professor wonders out loud if it would be possible to replicate that model elsewhere. You make a mental note to continue this conversation with your boss; perhaps the foundation can find a little money for a study to determine the viability of such a project in this region.

9:15 p.m. Arrive home after the reception. You're quite full (the hors d'oeuvres were tasty and you had one too many bruschetta) and quite tired. You send a quick e-mail to your boss to remind him that you will be working from home in the morning. You want a little quiet time to review letters of intent without interruption.

Visit Vault at **www.vault.com** for insider company profiles, expert advice, career message boards, expert resume reviews, the Vault Job Board and more.

VAULT CAREER LIBRARY   245

Employer Directory

AARP
601 E Street NW
Washington, DC 20049
Phone: (202) 434-2277
Fax: (202) 434-6548
www.aarp.org

American Cancer Society, Inc.
1599 Clifton Road NE
Atlanta, GA 30329
Phone: (404) 320-3333
Fax: (404) 982-3677
www.cancer.org

American Civil Liberties Union (ACLU)
125 Broad Street, 18th Floor
New York, NY 10004-2400
Phone: (212) 549-2500
Fax: (212) 549-2646
www.aclu.org

American Heart Association, Inc.
7272 Greenville Avenue
Dallas, TX 75231
Phone: (214) 373-6300
Fax: (214) 706-1191
www.americanheart.org

American Red Cross
2025 E Street NW
Washington, DC 20006
Phone: (202) 303-4498
www.redcross.org

American Society for the Prevention of Cruelty to Animals (ASPCA)
424 East 92nd Street
New York, NY 10128-6804
Phone: (212) 876-7700
Fax: (212) 423-9813
www.aspca.org

AmeriCares Foundation, Inc.
88 Hamilton Avenue
Stamford, CT 06902
Phone: (203) 658-9500
Fax: (203) 966-6028
www.americares.org

America's Second Harvest
35 East Wacker Drive, Suite 2000
Chicago, IL 60601
Phone: (312) 263-2302
Fax: (312)263-5626

AmeriCorps
1201 New York Avenue NW
Washington, DC 20525
Phone: (202) 606-5000
www.americorps.org

Amnesty International USA
Five Penn Plaza
New York, NY 10001
Phone: (212) 807-8400
Fax: (212) 627-1451
www.amnestyusa.org

Big Brothers Big Sisters of America
230 North 13th Street
Philadelphia, PA 19107
Phone: (215) 567-7000
Fax: (215) 567-0394
www.bbbsa.org

The Bill & Melinda Gates Foundation
1551 Eastlake Avenue East
Seattle, WA 98102
Phone: (206) 709-3100
Fax: (206) 709-9180
www.gatesfoundation.org

The Boy Scouts of America
1325 West Walnut Hill Lane
Irving, TX 75015
Phone: (972) 580-2401
Fax: (972) 580-2413
www.scouting.org

Boys & Girls Clubs of America
1275 Peachtree Street NE
Atlanta, GA 30309
Phone: (404) 487-5700
Fax: (404) 487-5705
www.bgca.org

Carnegie Corporation
437 Madison Avenue
New York, NY 10022
Phone: (212) 371-3200
Fax: (212) 754-4073
www.carnegie.org

Corporation for Public Broadcasting
402 Ninth Street NW
Washington, DC 20004
Phone: (202) 879-9600
Fax: (202) 879-9700
www.cpb.org

The Ford Foundation
320 East 43rd Street
New York, NY 10017
Phone: (212) 573-5000
Fax: (212) 351-3677
www.fordfound.org

Girl Scouts of the United States of America
420 Fifth Avenue
New York, NY 10018
Phone: (212) 852-8000
Fax: (212) 852-6514
www.girlscouts.org

Goodwill Industries International
15810 Indianola Avenue
Rockville, MD 20855
Phone: (301) 530-6500
Fax: (301) 530-1516
www.goodwill.org

Habitat for Humanity International
121 Habitat Street
Americus, GA 31709
Phone: (229) 924-6935
Fax: (229) 924-6541
www.habitat.org

Employer Directory, cont.

Human Rights Watch
350 5th Avenue, 34th Floor
New York, NY 10118-3299
Phone: (212) 290-4700
Fax: (212) 736-1300
www.hrw.org

The Humane Society of the United States
2100 L Street NW
Washington, DC 20037
Phone: (202) 452-1100
Fax: (202) 778-6132
www.hsus.org

March of Dimes Foundation
1275 Mamaroneck Avenue
White Plains, NY 10605
Phone: (914) 428-7100
Fax: (914) 428-8203
www.marchofdimes.com

Médecins Sans Frontières
Rue de la Tourelle, 39
1040 Brussels
Belgium
Phone: +32-2-280-1881
Fax: +32-2-280-0173
www.msf.org

National Women's Law Center
11 Dupont Circle NW, Suite 800
Washington, DC 20036
Phone: (202) 588-5180
www.nwlc.org

Open Society Institute
400 West 59th Street
New York, NY 10019
Phone: (212) 548-0600
Fax: (212) 548-4679
www.soros.org

The Peace Corps
1111 20th Street NW
Washington, DC 20526
Phone: (202) 692-2230
Fax: (202) 692-2901
www.peacecorps.gov

Planned Parenthood Federation of America, Inc.
434 West 33rd Street
New York, NY 10001
Phone: (212) 541-7800
Fax: (212) 245-1845
www.plannedparenthood.org

The Rockefeller Foundation
420 5th Avenue
New York, NY 10018
Phone: (212) 869-8500
Fax: (212) 764-3468
www.rockfound.org

Rotary International
1 Rotary Center
1560 Sherman Avenue
Evanston, IL 60201-3698
Phone: (847) 866-3000
Fax: (847) 328-8281
www.rotary.org

The Salvation Army
615 Slaters Lane
Alexandria, VA 22313
Phone: (703) 684-5500
Fax: (703) 684-3478
www.salvationarmyusa.org

Smithsonian Institution
1000 Jefferson Drive SW
Washington, DC 20560
Phone: (202) 633-1000
Fax: (202) 786-2377
www.si.edu

Teach for America, Inc.
315 West 36th Street, 7th Floor
New York, NY 10018
Phone: (212) 279-2080
Fax: (212) 279-2081
www.teachforamerica.org

UNICEF
3 United Nations Plaza
New York, NY 10017
Phone: (212) 326-7000
Fax: (212) 887-7465
www.unicef.com

United Nations
First Avenue at 46th Street
New York, NY 10017
Phone: (212) 963-1234
Fax: (212) 963-3133
www.un.org

United Way of America
701 North Fairfax Street
Alexandria, VA 22314
Phone: (703) 836-7100
Fax: (703) 683-7840
national.unitedway.org

YMCA of the USA
202 North Wacker Drive
Chicago, IL 60606
Phone: (312) 977-0031
Fax: (312) 977-9063
www.ymca.net

Visit Vault at **www.vault.com** for insider company profiles, expert advice, career message boards, expert resume reviews, the Vault Job Board and more.

V\ULT CAREER LIBRARY   247

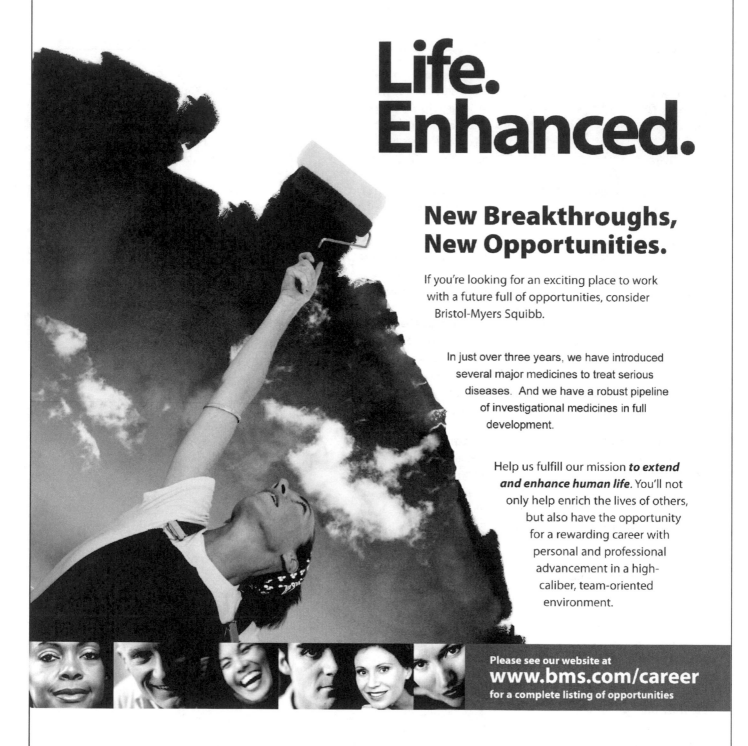

Life. Enhanced.

New Breakthroughs, New Opportunities.

If you're looking for an exciting place to work with a future full of opportunities, consider Bristol-Myers Squibb.

In just over three years, we have introduced several major medicines to treat serious diseases. And we have a robust pipeline of investigational medicines in full development.

Help us fulfill our mission *to extend and enhance human life*. You'll not only help enrich the lives of others, but also have the opportunity for a rewarding career with personal and professional advancement in a high-caliber, team-oriented environment.

Please see our website at
www.bms.com/career
for a complete listing of opportunities

BMS offers opportunities for MBA students and graduates to join Summer and Full-Time Associate Programs in the following areas: Marketing, Finance, Information Management, and Technical Operations.

Undergraduate-level students and other advanced-degree graduates may also pursue internship, co-op and permanent job opportunities in many business divisions and functions across BMS and its family of companies.

 Bristol-Myers Squibb

Bristol-Myers Squibb
P.O. Box 4000, Princeton, NJ 08543-4000

Bristol-Myers Squibb is an equal opportunity employer.

© 2007 Bristol-Myers Squibb Company   ZN-K0112 11/07

Pharmaceuticals and Biotech

What's in a Name: Big Pharma, Big Biotech and Biopharma

Small molecules and large companies

Strictly speaking, the term "pharmaceuticals" refers to medicines composed of small, synthetically produced molecules, which are sold by large, fully integrated drug manufacturers. The largest of these players—companies like Pfizer, GlaxoSmithKline and Merck—as well as a handful of others are known as "Big Pharma" because they are huge research, development and manufacturing companies with subsidiaries around the globe. Indeed, Big Pharma is where most of the industry's sales are generated. During 2007 the industry racked up $712 billion in global sales and that number is predicted to grow to $735 billion in 2008, a five to six percent uptick from 2007.

A profitable business

According to the Kaiser Family Foundation, from 1995 to 2002, the pharmaceutical business was the most lucrative industry in America. Pharmaceutical manufacturers didn't fare as well in later years, however. In 2003, the pharmaceutical industry ranked third; and in 2005, it ranked fifth. However, in 2006, the pharmaceutical industry ranked second in the country.

From aspirin to Herceptin: a brief history of the industry

Many of today's big pharmaceutical firms have roots that go back to the late 19th or early 20th century. Not all of these companies started out as drug manufacturers. For instance, Frederich Bayer founded Bayer in Germany in 1863 to make synthetic dyes. In the 1920s and 1930s, scientists discovered miracle drugs such as insulin and penicillin, and pharmaceutical companies began to market researchers' life-saving inventions. During the 1950s and 1960s, companies started to mass produce and market new drugs, such as blood-pressure medications, birth control pills and Valium. Pharmaceutical companies researched and developed new cancer treatments, including chemotherapy, in the 1970s. The modern biotech business was born when Herbert Boyer and Robert Swanson founded Genentech, which would eventually make breast cancer biologic Herceptin. In the 1980s, drug companies faced new environmental and safety regulations and mounting economic pressures. For Big Pharma, the 1990s was a time of turmoil. There were lots of mergers and acquisitions in the industry during that decade, and pharmaceutical companies also began to use contract research organizations for more of their R&D efforts.

Big Pharma

In 2006, large pharmaceutical companies launched several high-profile products, including the HPV vaccine, Gardasil; oral diabetes drug, Januvia; and cancer treatment, Sutent.

Big Pharma is responsible for all those television commercials urging us to contact our doctors if we suspect we suffer from restless leg syndrome or social anxiety disorder. Yet despite life-saving, cancer-fighting drugs and significant corporate philanthropy, Big Pharma's recent product recalls and concerns over drug safety have made it the industry many people love to hate. In 2007, diabetes medication Avandia made the headlines after researchers found it increased patients' risk of heart attack.

Before we help you chart a career in the industry, we should point out that both the scope of players and the types of products the industry produces are moving targets. This is because the pharmaceutical and biotech industries are gradually integrating into one industry.

Visit Vault at **www.vault.com** for insider company profiles, expert advice, career message boards, expert resume reviews, the Vault Job Board and more.

VAULT CAREER LIBRARY   249

Most of the largest Big Pharma players are either gobbling up small biotechs through outright acquisitions or, alternatively, are entering licensing agreements. For example, in 2006, AstraZeneca acquired small biotech firm Cambridge Antibody Technology Group and Merck purchased GlycoFi and Abmaxis. In 2008, U.K. pharma stalwart GlaxoSmithKline forked over $1.65 billion to purchase privately-held specialty pharmaceutical company Reliant, the maker of Lovaza, a heart drug that is the only prescription omega-3 med approved by the FDA to treat very high triglyceride levels. This trend is likely to continue throughout the rest of this decade, since it's increasingly difficult to find innovative new drugs through traditional science.

In fact, innovation is the industry's biggest current challenge. Companies are using acquisitions and alliances to round out their product pipelines and meet investor expectations. Big drug manufacturers can now claim to research, manufacture and sell both types of drugs: synthetic small molecules (or old chemistry) and injectable large molecules (or biologics).

Big Pharma

In 2006, large pharmaceutical companies launched several high-profile products, including the HPV vaccine, Gardasil; oral diabetes drug, Januvia; and cancer treatment, Sutent.

Big Pharma is responsible for all those television commercials urging us to contact our doctors if we suspect we suffer from restless leg syndrome or social anxiety disorder. Yet despite life-saving, cancer-fighting drugs and significant corporate philanthropy, Big Pharma's recent product recalls and concerns over drug safety have made it the industry many people love to hate. In 2007, diabetes medication Avandia made the headlines after researchers found it increased patients' risk of heart attack.

Before we help you chart a career in the industry, we should point out that both the scope of players and the types of products the industry produces are moving targets. This is because the pharmaceutical and biotech industries are gradually integrating into one industry.

Most of the largest Big Pharma players are either gobbling up small biotechs through outright acquisitions or, alternatively, are entering licensing agreements. For example, in 2006, AstraZeneca acquired small biotech firm Cambridge Antibody Technology Group and Merck purchased GlycoFi and Abmaxis. In 2008, U.K. pharma stalwart GlaxoSmithKline forked over $1.65 billion to purchase privately-held specialty pharmaceutical company Reliant, the maker of Lovaza, a heart drug that is the only prescription omega-3 med approved by the FDA to treat very high triglyceride levels. This trend is likely to continue throughout the rest of this decade, since it's increasingly difficult to find innovative new drugs through traditional science.

In fact, innovation is the industry's biggest current challenge. Companies are using acquisitions and alliances to round out their product pipelines and meet investor expectations. Big drug manufacturers can now claim to research, manufacture and sell both types of drugs: synthetic small molecules (or old chemistry) and injectable large molecules (or biologics).

The Global Pharmaceutical Industry

Three major market segments dominate the global industry. North America is the largest and comprises about 46 percent of the total market, Europe is second with some 31 percent. Japan comes in third at about 9 percent in 2007 sales. Although these combined markets account for nearly 86 percent of global sales, the remaining emerging market segments—other Asian countries, Africa, Australia and Latin America—are growing rapidly. According to IMS Health, Inc., a health care research and information company, sales in Asia, Africa and Australia were $62 billion in 2007, a 13.1 percent increase from 2006. Global pharmaceutical sales in Latin America in 2007 were $32 billion, a 12 percent increase from the previous year.

Although a handful of super-large companies rake in most of the pharmaceutical industry's revenue, the global industry is actually highly fragmented. More than 2,000 pharmaceutical and biotech companies exist worldwide. In the top tier are the large, multinational companies that dominate the market, or Big Pharma. In the middle tier are the specialty companies.

Many large companies have tended to absorb second-tier companies before they can grow enough to pose a competitive threat. That trend has a contracting effect on the number of firms. The opposite happens on the third and lowest tier, which is composed of an ever-increasing group of startups mostly focused on discovery research.

According to IMS Health, Inc., as recently as 1999, the global pharmaceutical market was valued at $334 billion. By 2007, total global sales had nearly doubled to $663 billion, or more than half a trillion dollars! (IMS derived this figure from retail sales in major global markets.) This astonishing growth reflects the increasing role of pharmaceuticals as a first-line treatment option for many disease conditions in the developed world. The term "first-line" means that physicians opt to prescribe a pharmaceutical first in lieu of a more invasive procedure, such as surgery. In some cancers, physicians now have the option of recommending a tumor-shrinking drug, for example, before surgery to minimize the level of invasiveness to the body.

In the U.S.

The U.S. pharmaceutical industry is comprised of approximately 100 companies—according to the Pharmaceutical Research and Manufacturers of America (PhRMA), a leading industry trade and lobbying organization—with the top 10 companies referred to as Big Pharma. According to the Biotechnology Industry Organization (BIO), there were also 1,452 biotech companies in the United States at the end of 2006.

The U.S. has not only the largest pharmaceutical market in the world but also the only one without government price controls. This is a consequence of the privately-owned system prevalent in the U.S. and a strong industry lobby, which has resisted government incursions into its market-based pricing. On the other hand, developed economies with universal health care access (European Union, U.K., Japan) exert stringent controls on the prices companies can charge. A big consequence is that, with thin profit margins, the incentive for innovation is curbed, and former leaders, especially in the EU (German and French companies, in particular) lost the lead in innovation in the 1990s. Standard & Poor's expects the U.S. to continue to be the largest of the top 10 pharmaceutical markets for the foreseeable future, as well as the fastest growing.

Although pharmaceutical companies are scattered throughout the continental United States, the industry is geographically concentrated in the Mid-Atlantic states, New York, New Jersey and Pennsylvania, and on the West Coast in California. A handful of companies can also be found in Massachusetts, Illinois and North Carolina. New Jersey is the heart of the industry and has by far the largest number of companies within a single state. According to the California Healthcare Institute, roughly a quarter of U.S. biotech jobs are in sunny California.

Medicare change boosts drugs sales

Before January 1, 2006, Medicare, the federal health program for the disabled and elderly, didn't pay for outpatient prescription drugs. The Medicare Prescription Drug, Improvement and Modernization Act—known as Part D—gave Medicare beneficiaries the option to enroll in private drug plans. Due to the changes, Medicare became the country's largest public customer of prescription medications in 2006. The change to Medicare helped boost prescription sales in the United States in 2006, but the U.S. Department of Health and Human Services doesn't think it will have a huge impact on drug spending in the future.

Growth in generics

In 1984 the passage of the Drug Price Competition and Patent Term Restoration Act, also called the Hatch-Waxman Act, increased generic drug manufacturers' access to the marketplace. One recent trend in the industry has been a boom in generic drug sales. The biggest generic drug manufacturers, such as the Israeli firm Teva and U.S.-based companies Mylan and Barr, have thousands of employees and boasted more than a billion dollars in revenue in 2006. According to the Kaiser Family

Visit Vault at **www.vault.com** for insider company profiles, expert advice, career message boards, expert resume reviews, the Vault Job Board and more.

VAULT CAREER LIBRARY   251

Foundation, in 2006 more than 60 percent of prescriptions dispensed and 20 percent of prescription drug sales were generics, and sales of generic drugs grew 22 percent from 2005 to 2006.

In the United States, managed health care has contributed to the rise in generic drugs. Managed care programs such as HMOs often ask their doctors to prescribe generic drugs in place of more expensive brand-name products. Recent changes to the Medicare program in the United States are also likely to lead to an increase in generic drug sales. Under Medicare Part D, through "multitiered pricing," plans can charge patients more for brand-name drugs than generics. In addition, plans can ask doctors to fill out prior authorization forms in order for patients to obtain branded drugs.

The expiration of patents on branded pharmaceuticals has also increased generic drug companies' revenues. As more brand-name drugs go off patents in coming years, generic drug manufacturers' profits are likely to increase. Big pharmaceutical companies that make brand-name drugs usually attempt to extend their drugs' exclusivity and prevent generic competition. They do this in various ways, including litigation. Some big pharmaceutical companies have responded to generic competition by entering into licensing agreements with generic drug manufacturers.

To complicate things further, not all pharmaceutical companies make just generics or only branded drugs. For example, Novartis has a generics division, called Sandoz. Due to strong growth and two major acquisitions in 2005, Sandoz is currently the second-largest generics company in the world based on sales after Teva. Sandoz raked in $7.2 billion in pharmaceutical sales in 2007 alone. Some generic companies also sell branded pharmaceuticals. For instance, generic drug manufacturer Barr's subsidiary Duramed Pharmaceuticals develops, makes and sells the firm's proprietary pharmaceuticals, mostly female healthcare products, such as Seasonale and Seasonique oral contraceptives.

Generic drug companies are also branching out into generic versions of biologic drugs. In 2005, Barr Pharmaceuticals announced a deal to license Croatian pharmaceutical company Pliva's version of Neupogen, a white-blood-cell booster made by Amgen. In 2006, Barr and Iceland's Actavis Group battled for Pliva. Barr outbid Actavis, and—in a deal worth $2.5 billion—the company acquired Pliva. The Croatian company is working on a copycat version of Amgen's Epogen, a protein that boosts red blood cells. Barr has also broken ground on a $25 million biotech factory in Croatia.

A rise in CROs

Increasingly, pharmaceutical companies have been outsourcing drug research and development. As a result, contract research organizations (or CROs) have been on the rise. In 2005, a survey by Cambridge Healthtech Advisors found that 45 percent of pharmaceutical companies expected to outsource at least 60 percent of their clinical development work by 2008. Examples of CROs include New Jersey-based Covance and North Carolina's Quintiles Transnational Corporation. In 2006, Covance worked with more than 300 biopharmaceutical companies, ranging from small and startup organizations to the world's largest pharmaceutical companies. Quintiles has helped develop or commercialize the world's 30 best-selling drugs.

MBA Level Sales and Marketing Jobs

Most companies consider sales and marketing to be one function, but with two basic areas of activity. Within the sales function, you can typically find three career tracks: field sales, sales management and managed markets. A fourth track, sales training is closely associated with sales and is distinct from the broader training and development function, which is usually associated with human resource departments. Sales training groups bridge the sales and marketing function: in some companies, they are considered part of marketing support, and hence part of the marketing function. The main point, however, is that all companies that have field sales forces have rigorous sales training departments.

Within the marketing function are two main areas of activity: marketing management and marketing support. The latter is actually composed of several distinct groups, some of which are quite large, but all of which serve essentially the same purpose: to provide support services for marketing managers. Depending on the size of the company, the distinction between the two areas may be either blurred or nonexistent. Typical groups include training and development, advertising and promotion, market analysis, customer call center, e-business, and commercialization and strategic planning.

Fully integrated Big Biotech companies have their own sales and marketing infrastructure and essentially the same job classifications. The main difference from their Big Pharma cousins is that biotech sales reps are specialty reps, who market products to specific and highly defined patient groups. On an experiential level, the big difference is that that very focus prevents the overreaching to the mass market that is now plaguing the marketers of broadly acting agents.

The good thing about the sales and marketing function in the biopharmaceutical industry is that, once you get hired in a particular work area, it is possible, and even encouraged, to gain experience in other areas.

Sales management

Managing a sales force can be one of the most lucrative tracks in the pharmaceutical industry. District sales manager is the first rung on the management ladder, followed by regional sales manager, area sales director and vice president of sales. Each level has increasing responsibility for the sales of a broader geographic area. This is not an entry-level job and usually requires several years of direct sales experience plus evidence of leadership potential. In particular, the first level, district sales manager, is a position people from several areas of activity can move in and out of to get perspective on sales activity.

Like field reps, the responsibilities of a sales manager fall into three distinct categories. Management responsibilities require a sales manager to lead assigned sales district in meeting upper management goals; recruit, hire and train sales reps; ensure efficient coverage of their assigned geographic area; plan and lead meetings to review sales achievements; and manage reps' activities when coordinating educational events (e.g., symposia, speakers bureaus, seminars, etc.). Administrative responsibilities require sales managers to develop business plans and plans of action (POAs), implement market strategies, monitor progress of ongoing sales activity, stay current on industry and company issues that impact the sales force, ensure optimal distribution and consistent stocking of product samples, monitor the district's budget, and control its expenses. Professional development responsibilities require the sales manager to maintain a work environment that maximizes motivation, act as a coach and mentor to the sales reps, and create individualized development plans for each direct report.

Marketing management

Marketing management is the core work of the marketing function and is where strategy is formulated and implemented. Many companies organize marketing management according to therapeutic areas (i.e., oncology drugs, cardiovascular drugs, anti-hypertensives, etc.). Until recent years, marketing had a single upward path to senior positions. With large companies merging into mega-companies (e.g., Pfizer acquired both Warner-Lambert and Pharmacia to become the largest company in the industry), some companies have opted to organize therapeutic areas and their associated products into separate business units, so that marketing management decisions get made with fewer layers of oversight and with closer contact with customer physicians and targeted patient groups.

The main job title in marketing management is product manager and is consistent throughout the industry. From there, titles like product director, group product manager, and vice president of marketing represent higher level marketing management jobs. None of these are entry-level positions at the BS level, although MBAs with previous marketing experience can work in product management groups, as assistant or associate product managers.

Visit Vault at www.vault.com for insider company profiles, expert advice, career message boards, expert resume reviews, the Vault Job Board and more.

VAULT CAREER LIBRARY 253

A product manager's responsibilities fall into two main categories. Product management responsibilities require the product manager to develop and manage the short-term product strategy and marketing plans for assigned products, oversee development of business plans, specify the positioning of a product among its competitors, monitor those competitor products, acquire both a quantitative and intuitive feel for customer needs, and act as an in-house champion for a product or brand. From an administrative perspective, a product manager must develop budgets, maintain records of expenses, and manage and develop entry-level support staff.

In companies organized as business units, product managers effectively become mini-CEOs and are involved in virtually every aspect of getting a product to market. Most product managers also have substantial communication and negotiation skills, as they are required to interact with professionals from every part of the organization.

Marketing support: market analysis

Market analysis groups are responsible for gathering and analyzing business information in specific geographic areas to understand the economic profile of specific disease conditions in which the company specializes, the associated targeted patient populations—including demographic trends and shifts and progression of disease conditions—and the competitive landscape for the products under development. Jobs have titles like market analyst or regional analyst. Although these jobs are usually not entry-level with only a bachelor's degree, many MBAs target market analyst jobs after graduation and can land them if they have basic science education and can demonstrate evidence of some understanding of the industry's marketing issues.

A market analyst has primarily analytical responsibilities, which are consistent throughout the industry. Typical tasks are to perform local health care marketplace assessments, provide analysis and consulting support to sales and marketing management, develop and implement tools and processes for standard sales performance measurement, identify opportunities and assess threats for the company's products, measure financial ratios (e.g., return on investment or ROI, market share, etc.), and analyze tactical plans based on historic performance.

Business Development in Biotech

On the business development side, research analysts provide the extensive research and analysis needed to determine how and with whom a biotech company should partner with. Analysts generate the assessments that help business development management determine how to meet its goals. Analysts answer such questions as, "Should we expand organically or acquire other companies to grow?" and "Who should we partner with to become more competitive?" Research analysts work with attorneys to assess intellectual property and licensing issues, help develop and enforce agreements, and secure licenses for ongoing operations. Many companies have senior analyst positions with the same responsibilities, but operating more autonomously. Analysts can bring home salaries ranging from $90,000 to $110,000.

It's a significant step up to manager of corporate planning, a job that generally appears at the larger companies. They prepare long-range and strategic plans (usually several years out) and short-range/tactical plans (up to a year out). Other activities include designing and executing financial planning processes, setting targets and planning guidelines. The manager of corporate planning works closely with the CFO to develop the company's financial plans for senior management, industry analysts and investors. They complete competitive analysis and continually assess the prospects for the company. This senior position usually has salaries ranging from $110,000 to $120,000.

At the head of the group is the vice president of business development, a very important position in most biotech companies. The VP of biz dev oversees all efforts to identify, evaluate and pursue potential strategic partners, joint ventures and alliances. This person also directs the assessment of the licensing potential of targets, leads and drug candidates as well as the managing of all collaborations. They maintain partnership agreements and address the inevitable issues that arise in any relationship.

Most companies ask for impressive credentials to reach this level: an MBA, a science degree and nearly a decade of experience that includes knowledge of due diligence, asset valuation, alliance integration, and portfolio management. As an executive, the VP can expect to earn a salary ranging from $160,000 to $190,000 and also receive additional incentive compensation.

Visit Vault at **www.vault.com** for insider company profiles, expert advice, career message boards, expert resume reviews, the Vault Job Board and more.

VAULT CAREER LIBRARY

255

Employer Directory

Bristol-Myers Squibb Co

Bristol-Myers Squibb
P.O. Box 4000
Princeton, NJ 08543-4000
Phone: (609) 252-4000
www.bms.com/career

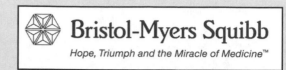

BMS offers opportunities for MBA students and graduates to join summer and full-time associate programs in the following areas: marketing, finance, information management and technical operations.

Business Schools Firm Recruits From: Columbia University, Cornell University, Dartmouth College, Duke University, NYU, University of Michigan, University of North Carolina, Thunderbird.

Employer Directory, cont

Abbott
100 Abbott Park Road
Abbott Park, IL 60064
Phone: (847) 937-6100
Fax: (847) 937-1511
www.abbott.com

Acambis PLC
Peterhouse Technology Park
100 Fulbourn Road
Cambridge CB1 9PT
United Kingdom
Phone: +44-12-23-27-53-00
Fax: +44-12-23-41-63-00
www.acambis.com

Advanced Cell Technology, Inc.
1201 Harbor Bay Parkway, Suite 120
Alameda, CA 94502
Phone: (510) 748-4900
Fax: (510) 748-4950
www.advancedcell.com

Allergan, Inc.
2525 Dupont Drive
Irvine, CA 92612
Phone: (714) 246-4500
Fax: (714) 246-4971
www.allergan.com

Amgen, Inc.
One Amgen Center Drive
Thousand Oaks, CA 91320-1799
Phone: (805) 447-1000
Fax: (805) 447-1010
www.amgen.com

Amylin Pharmaceuticals, Inc.
9360 Towne Centre Drive
San Diego, CA 92121
Phone: (858) 552-2200
Fax: (858) 552-2212
www.amylin.com

Applera Corporation
301 Merritt 7
P.O. Box 5435
Norwalk, CT 06856-5435
Phone: (203) 840-2000
Fax: (203) 840-2312
www.applera.com

AstraZeneca PLC
15 Stanhope Gate
London, W1K 1LN
United Kingdom
Phone: +44-20-73-04-50-00
Fax: +44-20-73-04-51-83

P.O. Box 15437
Wilmington, DE 19850-5437
Phone: (302)-886-3000
Fax: (302) 886-2972
www.astrazeneca.com

Barr Pharmaceuticals, Inc.
223 Quaker Road
Pomona, NY 10970
Phone: (845) 362-1100
Fax: (845) 362-2774
www.barrlabs.com

Baxter International
1 Baxter Parkway
Deerfield, IL 60015-4625
Phone: (847) 948-2000
Fax: (847) 948-2016
www.baxter.com

Bayer AG
Bayerwerk, Gebäude W11
Kaiser-Wilhelm-Allee
51368 Leverkusen
Germany
Phone: +49-214-30-1
Fax: +49-214-30-66328
www.bayer.de

Becton, Dickinson and Company
1 Becton Drive
Franklin Lakes, NJ 07147-1880
Phone: (201) 847-6800
Fax: (201) 847-6475
www.bd.com

Biogen Idec Inc.
14 Cambridge Center
Cambridge, MA 02142
Phone: (617) 679-2000
Fax: (617) 679-2617
www.biogenidec.com

Boehringer Ingelheim corporation
Binger Strasse 173
55216 Ingelheim
Germany
Phone: +49-61-32-770
Fax: +49-61-32-720

900 Ridgebury Road
Ridgefield, CT 06877
Phone: (203) 798-9988
Fax: (203) 791-6234
www.boehringer-ingelheim.com

Bristol-Myers Squibb Company
345 Park Avenue
New York, NY 10154-0037
Princeton, NJ 08543
Phone: (212) 546-4000
Fax: (212) 546-4020
www.bms.com

Celgene Corporation
86 Morris Avenue
Summit, NJ 07901
Phone: (908) 673-9000
www.celgene.com

Cephalon, Inc.
41 Moores Road
Frazer, PA 19355
Phone: (610) 344-0200
Fax: (610) 738-6590
www.cephalon.com

Visit Vault at **www.vault.com** for insider company profiles, expert advice, career message boards, expert resume reviews, the Vault Job Board and more.

VAULT CAREER LIBRARY   257

Employer Directory, cont.

Charles River Laboratories International, Inc.
251 Ballardvale Street
Wilmington, MA 01887-1000
Phone: (978) 658-6000
Fax: (978) 658-7132
www.criver.com

Covance
210 Carnegie Center
Princeton, NJ 08540
Phone: (609) 452-4440
Fax: (609) 452-9375
Toll Free: (888) 268-2623
www.covance.com

CSL Limited
45 Poplar Road
Parkville, Victoria 3052
Australia
Phone: +61-3-93-89-19-11
Fax: +61-3-93-89-14-34
www.csl.com.au

Eli Lilly and Company
Lilly Corporate Center
893 South Delaware
Indianapolis, IN 46285
Phone: (317) 276-2000
Fax: (317) 277-6579
www.lilly.com

Exelixis, Inc.
170 Harbor Way
South San Francisco, CA 94083
Phone: (650) 837-7000
Fax: (650) 837-8300
www.exelixis.com

Forest Laboratories
909 3rd Avenue
New York, NY 10022
Phone: (212) 421-7850
Fax: (212) 750-9152
www.frx.com

Genentech, Inc.
1 DNA Way
South San Francisco, CA 94080
Phone: (650) 225-1000
Fax: (650) 225-6000
www.gene.com

Genzyme Corporation
500 Kendall Street
Cambridge, MA 02142
Phone: (617) 252-7500
Fax: (617) 252-7600
www.genzyme.com

Gilead Sciences, Inc.
333 Lakeside Drive
Foster City, CA 94404
Phone: (650) 574-3000
Fax: (650) 578-9264
www.gilead.com

GlaxoSmithKline
980 Great West Road, Brentford
London, TW8 9GS
United Kingdom
Phone: +44-20-80-47-50-00
Fax: +44-20-80-47-78-07
www.gsk.com

Hospira, Inc.
275 North Field Drive
Lake Forest, IL 60045
Phone: (224) 212-2000
Fax: (224) 212-3350
Toll Free: (877) 946-7747
www.hospira.com

Human Genome Sciences, Inc.
14200 Shady Grove Road
Rockville, MD 20850
Phone: (301) 309-8504
Fax: (301) 309-8512
www.hgsi.com

ImmunoGen, Inc.
128 Sidney Street
Cambridge, MA 02139
Phone: (617) 995-2500
Fax: (617) 995-2510
www.immunogen.com

Incyte Corporation
Experimental Station
Route 141 and Henry Clay Road
Building E336
Wilmington, DE 19880
Phone: (302) 498-6944
Fax: (302) 425-2707
www.incyte.com

Infinity Pharmaceuticals, Inc.
780 Memorial Drive
Cambridge, MA 02139
Phone: (617) 453-1000
Fax: (617) 453-1001
www.ipi.com

Inspire Pharmaceuticals, Inc.
4222 Emperor Boulevard, Suite 200
Durham, NC 27703-8466
Phone: (919) 941-9777
Fax: (919)-941-9797
www.inspirepharm.com

Invitrogen Corporation
1600 Faraday Avenue
Carlsbad, CA 92008
Phone: (760) 603-7200
Fax: (760) 602-6500
www.invitrogen.com

Johnson & Johnson Inc.
1 Johnson & Johnson Plaza
New Brunswick, NJ 08933
Phone: (732) 524-0400
Fax: (732) 524-3300
www.jnj.com

King Pharmaceuticals
501 5th Street
Bristol, TN 37620
Phone: (423) 989-8000
Fax: (423) 274-8677
www.kingpharm.com

Employer Directory, cont.

Laboratory Corporation of America Holdings
358 South Main Street
Burlington, NC 27215
Phone: (336) 229-1127
Fax: (336) 436-1205
www.labcorp.com

Lexicon Pharmaceuticals, Inc.
8800 Technology Forest Place
The Woodlands, TX 77381-1160
Phone: (281) 863-3000
Fax: (281) 863-8088
www.lexpharma.com

McKesson Corporation
1 Post Street
San Francisco, CA 94104
Phone: (415) 983-8300
Fax: (415) 983-7160
www.mckesson.com

Merck & Co., Inc.
One Merck Drive
P.O. Box 100
Whitehouse Station, NJ 08889
Phone: (908) 423-1000
Fax: (908) 735-1253
www.merck.com

Millennium Pharmaceuticals, Inc.
40 Landsdown Street
Cambridge, MA 02139
Phone: (617) 679-7000
Fax: (617) 374-7788
www.mlnm.com

Monsanto Company
800 North Lindbergh Boulevard
St. Louis, MO 63137
Phone: (314) 694-1000
Fax: (314) 694-8394
www.monsanto.com

Mylan Inc.
1500 Corporate Drive, Suite 400
Canonsburg, PA 15317
Phone: (724) 514-1800
Fax: (724) 514-1870
www.mylan.com

Novartis AG
Lichtstrasse 35
CH-4056 Basel
Switzerland
Phone: +41-61-324-1111
Fax: +41-61-324-8001
www.novartis.com

Novo Nordisk A/S
Novo Allé
2880 Bagsværd
Denmark
Phone: +45-44-44-88-88
Fax: +45-44-49-05-55

Nuvelo, Inc.
201 Industrial Road, Suite 310
San Carlos, CA 94070-6211
Phone: (650) 517-8000
Fax: (650) 517-8001
www.nuvelo.com

Perrigo Company
515 Eastern Avenue
Allegan, MI 49010
Phone: (269) 673-8451
Fax: (269) 673-9128
www.perrigo.com

Pfizer Inc.
235 East 42nd Street
New York, NY 10017
Phone: (212) 573-2323
Fax: (212) 573-7851
www.pfizer.com

Promega Corporation
2800 Woods Hollow Road
Madison, WI 53711-5300
Phone: (608) 274-4330
Fax: (608) 277-2601
Toll Free: (800) 356-9526
www.promega.com

Quintile Transnational Corp.
4709 Creekstone Drive, Suite 200
Durham, NC 27703
Phone: (919) 998-2000
Fax: (919) 998-9113
www.qtrn.com

Roche Group
Grenzacherstrasse 124
CH-4070 Basel
Switzerland
Phone: +41-61-688-1111
Fax: +41-61-691-9391
www.roche.com

Sanofi-Aventis
174 Avenue de France
Paris 75013
France
Phone: +33-1-53-77-40-00
Fax: +33-1-53-77-42-96
www.sanofi-aventis.com

Schering-Plough Corporation
2000 Galloping Hill Road
Kenilworth, NJ 07033
Phone: (908) 298-4000
Fax: (908) 298-7653
www.schering-plough.com

Shire PLC
Hampshire International Business Park
Chineham, Basingstoke
Hampshire RG24 8EP
United Kingdom
Phone: +44-12-56-89-40-00
Fax: +44-12-56-89-47-08
www.shire.com

Visit Vault at **www.vault.com** for insider company profiles, expert advice, career message boards, expert resume reviews, the Vault Job Board and more.

VAULT CAREER LIBRARY   259

Employer Directory, cont.

Takeda Pharmaceutical Company Limited
1-1, Doshomachi 4-chome
Chuo-ku, Osaka 540-8645
Japan
Phone: +81-6-62-04-21-11
Fax: +81-6-62-04-28-80
www.takeda.com

1 Takeda Parkway
Deerfield, IL 60015
Phone: (847) 383-3000

Teva Pharmaceutical Industries Limited
5 Basel Street
Petach, Tikva 49131
Israel
Phone: +972-3-926-7267
Fax: +972-3-923-4050
www.tevapharm.com

UCB S.A.
60 Allée de la Recherche
B-1070, Brussels
Belgium
Phone: +32-2-559-9999
Fax: +32-2-559-9900
www.ucb-group.com

Vectura Group PLC
One Prospect West
Chippenham, Wiltshire SN14 6FH
United Kingdom
Phone: +44-12-49-66-77-00
Fax: +44-12-49-66-77-01
www.vectura.com

Verenium Corporation
55 Cambridge Parkway
Cambridge, MA 02142
Phone: (617) 674-5300
www.verenium.com

Watson Pharmaceuticals, Inc.
311 Bonnie Circle
Corona, CA 92880
Phone: (951) 493-5300
Fax: (973) 355-8301
www.watsonpharm.com

Wyeth
5 Giralda Farms
Madison, NJ 07940
Phone: (973) 660-5000
Fax: (973) 660-7026
www.wyeth.com

Private Equity

What is Private Equity?

In its broadest sense, private equity is an investment derived from a nonpublic entity. Of course, under that definition, any individual who owns a single share of stock is, indeed, a private equity investor. The kind of private equity we're talking about is much bigger; these individuals don't just invest in stock—they buy whole companies.

In modern private equity, a pool of capital is created from private investors, ranging from university endowments and pension funds to hedge funds, Wall Street investment banks and high-net-worth individuals. The managers of these private equity pools, or funds, then try to put that capital to work, generally by purchasing private or public companies, "fixing" them so they generate more revenue, cash and earnings, and then "flipping" them by selling the improved company to another buyer or taking it public on the equity markets.

Private equity investments aren't just about buying and selling companies, however. Many private equity firms invest in debt, helping a company salvage itself by loaning it money in exchange for an equity position or another form of return. Some private equity firms target funds at startup companies—these are called venture capital firms, though a diversified private equity management company will often include venture capital activity alongside acquisitions and debt purchases. Venture capital investments are often made in exchange for equity in the private company that, the firm hopes, will turn into big profits should the startup go public or get sold.

Who are private equity investors?

The institutions and people who invest in private equity funds are some of the wealthiest in the world. Major pension funds, such as the California Public Employees Retirement Systems (CalPERS), place some of their money with private equity funds to boost returns. Major Wall Street investment banks also place investments in private equity funds—unless, of course, they create their own in-house private equity funds as did Goldman Sachs and Morgan Stanley. Hedge funds often invest in private equity funds due to the outstanding performance these funds have amassed through the years. Indeed, a few hedge funds have blurred the line between themselves and private equity firms by taking part in public company buyouts either on their own or in partnership with more traditional private equity firms.

And finally, the firms themselves are often heavily invested in their own private equity funds. The private—and, recently, public—companies that manage private equity pools ensure their interests are aligned with those of their investors by placing a large chunk of their own wealth in the mix. This has, of course, resulted in the creation of a breed of private equity deal makers that have joined the billionaires' club, most famously Henry Kravis at KKR or current industry poster boy Steve Schwarzman of Blackstone.

The Modern Private Equity Firm

Today, private equity firms are primarily dedicated to the purchase of companies or stakes therein. Yet some, including Bain Capital and The Blackstone Group most notably, have entered other businesses, including distressed debt and real estate. At the same time, hedge funds have started dabbling in private equity as well, mostly through placements, but occasionally through their own, active efforts as well.

Yet the average private equity firm remains dedicated to the concept of the buyout. Over the long haul, the returns from a private equity placement have yet to be rivaled consistently by any other asset class, including hedge funds. There simply aren't any other investments where returns can reasonably be as high. And even with questions arising about the current M&A and LBO environments, private equity funds have proven their worth to investors time and again.

Visit Vault at **www.vault.com** for insider company profiles, expert advice, career message boards, expert resume reviews, the Vault Job Board and more.

VAULT CAREER LIBRARY 261

Private equity in the U.S.

There are only about 200 private equity companies operating at any one time in the United States, and that number can vary due to openings and closures on the small end of the scale. But the money they manage is impressive. According to the Private Equity Council—formed by firms in response to increasing pressure from Washington on their activities and profits—private equity firms were responsible for $406 billion in transactions in 2006. They had already eclipsed that mark by mid-2007.

Like their venture capital cousins, private equity firms generally find specialties within the industry. Some firms will focus on middle-market, mid-cap transactions, while others take aim at overseas purchases. Still others look at small, public companies or those within a specific sector.

And then there are the big ones. They have the money and clout to go after the biggest deals in a variety of sectors. Here's a list of the biggest and most noteworthy firms in private equity today:

> Apollo Advisors
>
> Bain Capital
>
> The Blackstone Group
>
> The Carlyle Group
>
> Cerberus Capital Management
>
> Kohlberg Kravis Roberts & Co. (KKR)
>
> Providence Equity Partners
>
> Texas Pacific Group
>
> Thomas H. Lee Partners
>
> Warburg Pincus

The Players in Private Equity

So who's doing all of this? Who makes the private equity industry run? Like the rest of the financial sector—and really, much of the American economy these days—private equity is fueled by human capital. And when an industry has as many moving parts as private equity does, it takes a breadth and depth of experience unmatched by nearly any other business today.

From finding investors and researching companies, to making the deal and executing exit strategies, a private equity firm relies on a diverse group of players. The following is a look at the various roles in a typical private equity firm.

The fund raisers and investor relations

A private equity firm won't get anywhere without money. To that end, private equity firms employ fund raisers to help attract the capital needed. These roles are quite similar to investor relations positions at public companies, institutional banks and mutual funds. Their job is to sell the ideas behind the firm's latest private equity fund, convincing major institutions—hedge funds, banks, pension funds and the like—to give the firm hundreds of millions of dollars to manage.

These people also serve as investors' point of contact. They help manage investors' accounts, let them know when they can expect returns and assuage any fears they may have. For major accounts, they also bring in some of the firm's top leadership as needed to help close major investments.

Naturally, those in these roles are exceptional salespeople with experience in dealing with major financial institutions.

The researchers

The key to unlocking value is knowing where to look, and that falls to the researchers at the private equity firm. These are the people who comb through volumes of analyst reports, news releases and articles, looking for opportunity. They investigate potential targets thoroughly for signs of possible value. They're tenacious and determined, with the ability not only to crunch numbers but also to get a "feel" for a company in admittedly subjective ways.

First, researchers identify targets. Again, some companies make it easy by putting themselves on the block or having a proxy, like an investment bank, contact the private equity firm. Other times, an article or research report on a company highlights a potential problem that the firm's experts are known for fixing, or an analyst may simply note that a company's share price has been flat for a long time. That can trigger an intensive and somewhat covert investigation into the company's fortunes. The firm's researchers gather and collate all existing Wall Street research and media reports on the company. They'll contact the company's suppliers and clients. They may even reach out to a handful of key people within the company on an informal basis.

Then, the researchers coordinate with the deal makers to agree on whether the company is a potential target. Once the company is approached and enters into negotiations, there's a whole new set of data that needs to be explored. The would-be target opens its books and operations to the firm's researchers. At that point, the firm's overall investment thesis is tested and, hopefully, proven. Some avenues of potential value are discovered, and others are abandoned.

Finally, the researchers come up with a final investment thesis for the company that serves as not only the basis for negotiations, but the agenda for the company's entire ownership. This thesis outlines areas of savings, cost-cutting plans, new ventures, the state of the company's balance sheet and how much debt it can take on—everything. The researchers come up with the plan that will ultimately be executed.

Needless to say, it takes someone with an incredible depth of knowledge to engage in this kind of work. Most have a strong financial bent, and some have spent time in corporate finance, Wall Street buy-side or sell-side research shops, or both. A few actuaries have found themselves crunching numbers for private equity firms as well.

The deal-makers

Once a target has been identified and the investment thesis proven, the deal-makers go to work. They're the ones responsible for obtaining the company at the best possible terms. In many cases, they work not only with the target company, but also with sources of financing, including investment banks and hedge funds, to obtain the necessary leverage at low enough rates to make the deal work. They are the old-school Masters of the Universe, making deals worth billions that can affect the lives of thousands. This is heady stuff, to be sure.

In most firms, the chief deal-maker and the head of the firm are often one and the same. Deals don't get done, after all, until the top guy signs off on them, and men like KKR's Henry Kravis and Blackstone's Steve Schwarzman are renowned deal-makers. That's not to say that they're the ones sitting at the table—though sometimes they are if the deal's big enough. But they're directing the firm's negotiations and making sure that the deal jives with the overall investment thesis.

Some firms employ their own negotiators who answer to the company's top leadership. Other firms don't—like any other would-be buyer, many simply hire an investment bank to do the negotiating. But at most private equity firms, at least one of the firm's top managers, if not the founder, is really calling the shots at the table, while the I-bankers are there in more of a research and advisory role.

Visit Vault at www.vault.com for insider company profiles, expert advice, career message boards, expert resume reviews, the Vault Job Board and more.

VAULT CAREER LIBRARY   263

The operators

Once a deal is done and the target becomes a portfolio company, the firm's operators go to work. Few are actually full-time employees of the private equity firm, though each portfolio company is supervised by one or more managing directors and their accompanying staffs. The private equity firm's staff acts as both top-level managers and consultants, making sure the portfolio company meets its targets, as outlined by the investment thesis, and offering advice on how to get there.

There's also a whole other level of operators that firms use: established corporate executives who go from company to company on behalf of the private equity firm. They take on top leadership roles at the newly acquired company and get things done. These "hired guns" are generally successful C-level executives noted for their turnaround expertise and willingness to do whatever it takes to get the company where the private equity firm wants it to be.

To put it in another perspective, the private equity firm's representatives are the portfolio company's board of directors, and the hired guns take over the top-level positions and get the job done.

The in-house operators and hired guns must work together, though there have been times when the CEO installed by the private equity firm sees things differently than the researchers who came up with the investment thesis or the firm's assigned in-house operator. This is particularly true if the hired gun has more experience than the firm's assigned supervisor. This can generally be ironed out, though only after a managing director or a member of the firm's executive committee gets involved.

Hitting a moving target

All of the roles and people within a private equity firm continue to interact throughout the investment's lifespan. The researchers are often revisiting their thesis with input from operators on the ground, and the deal-makers are often pulled in to iron out the investment's exit strategy, especially if it involves a direct sale. Investor relations personnel answer questions, provide updates on investments, assuage disgruntled stakeholders and make sure everyone gets their money in the end—and can often assist in IPO road shows, too.

And of course, these are positions in firms that, generally, have fewer than 500 full-time employees around the globe. Each person at your typical private equity firm can fit into one of these roles, but they're handling multiple funds, targets, deals and/or portfolio companies. And the top managers are often shuttling between different roles—approving the investment thesis, sealing the deal, ensuring operations go smoothly and glad-handing the firm's fund investors.

A Day in the Life: The Deal Maker

6 a.m. Up and reading the presentation books drawn up by the associates the night before. Phone calls to the associates ("to wake them up") to get some changes going before the day's meetings begin.

7:30 a.m. Picked up by the car. More e-mails and phone calls.

8:30 a.m. At the office. Check in with the managing director for an update of the previous day's negotiations and what's planned for today.

9 a.m. Meeting with the team. We'll have the updates in the presentation book done, we'll have a strategy mapped out. This is simply kind of a double check before we head over.

9:40 a.m. In the cars and heading to the investment bank. We have a war room set up there, too, but we're only 15 minutes away, so we do a lot of work back at the office.

10 a.m. First negotiating session. The target company always tends to come up with a new wrinkle over night, as do we. So we spend the first few hours going through those. Sometimes we can just call each other on our B.S. and move on, but sometimes we have to retrench and figure out what they're saying.

12:30 p.m. Break for lunch. Hit the phones to figure out countermoves based on the morning's presentations.

1:30 p.m. The real session. This is where stuff gets done. Today we drilled down and agreed upon a value for their major business arm, which was key. We got a lot more than they did out of it.

6 p.m. Have dinner sent over. Informal chatting between the two sides over dinner.

7 p.m. Wrap up the day's talks.

7:30 p.m. Convene with the team in the war room and dole out assignments for the overnight. Make a few phone calls to key people and update the MD again.

9 p.m. Call the car and go home.

Visit Vault at **www.vault.com** for insider company profiles, expert advice, career message boards, expert resume reviews, the Vault Job Board and more.

VAULT CAREER LIBRARY   265

Employer Directory

Advent International Corporation
75 State Street
Boston, MA 02109
Phone: (617) 951-9400
Fax: (617) 951-0566
www.adventinternational.com

Allied Capital Corporation
1919 Pennsylvania Avenue NW
Washington, DC 20006
Phone: (202) 721-6100
Fax: (202) 721-6101
Toll free: (888) 818-5298
www.alliedcapital.com

Anschutz Company
555 17th Street, Suite 2400
Denver, CO 80202
Phone: (303) 298-1000
Fax: (303) 298-8881

Apax Partners
153 East 53rd Street, 53rd Floor
New York, NY 10022
Phone: (212) 753-6300
Fax: (212) 319-6155
www.apax.com

Apollo Investments
9 West 57th Street, 41st Floor
New York, NY 10019
Phone: (212) 515-3520

Aurora Capital Group
10877 Wilshire Boulevard, Suite 2100
Los Angeles, CA 90024
Phone: (310) 551-0101
Fax: (310) 277-5591

Bain Capital
111 Huntington Avenue
Boston, MA 02199
Phone: (617) 516-2000
Fax: (617) 516-2010
www.baincapital.com

Berkshire Hathaway Inc.
1440 Kiewit Plaza
Omaha, NE 68131
Phone: (402) 346-1400
Fax: (402) 346-3375
www.berkshirehathaway.com

The Blackstone Group L.P.
345 Park Avenue
New York, NY 10154
Phone: (212) 583-5000
Fax: (212) 583-5712
www.blackstone.com

Bruckmann, Rosser, Sherrill & Co., L.L.C.
126 East 56th Street, 29th Floor
New York, NY 10022
Phone: (212) 521-3700
Fax: (212) 521-3799
www.brs.com

The Carlyle Group
1001 Pennsylvania Avenue NW
Washington, DC 20004
Phone: (202) 729-5626
Fax: (202) 347-1818
www.carlyle.com

Castle Harlan, Inc.
150 East 58th Street
New York, NY 10155
Phone: (212) 644-8600
Fax: (212) 207-8042
www.castleharlan.com

Cerberus Capital Management, L.P.
299 Park Avenue
New York, NY 10171
Phone: (212) 891-2100
Fax: (212) 891-1540
www.cerberuscapital.com

Clayton, Dubilier & Rice, Inc.
375 Park Avenue, 18th Floor
New York, NY 10152
Phone: (212) 407-5200
Fax: (212) 407-5252
www.cdr-inc.com

D. E. Shaw & Co., L.P.
120 West 45th Street, 19th Floor
Tower 45
New York, NY 10036
Phone: (212) 478-0000
Fax: (212) 478-0100
www.deshaw.com

Everett Smith Group, Ltd.
330 Kilbourn Avenue, Suite 750
Milwaukee, WI 53202
Phone: (414) 223-1560
Fax: (414) 225-0025
www.esmithgroup.com

Forstmann, Little & Co.
767 5th Avenue
New York, NY 10153
Phone: (212) 355-5656
Fax: (212) 759-9059

Fortress Investment Group LLC
1345 Avenue of the Americas
New York, NY 10105
Phone: (212) 798-6100
www.fortressinv.com

Freeman Spogli & Co. Incorporated
11100 Santa Monica Boulevard
Suite 1900
Los Angeles, CA 90025
Phone: (310) 444-1822
Fax: (310) 444-1870
www.freemanspogli.com

Gladstone Capital Corporation
1521 Westbranch Drive, Suite 200
McLean, VA 22102
Phone: (703) 287-5800
Fax: (703) 287-5801
www.gladstonecapital.com

Employer Directory, cont.

Heico Companies LLC
70 West Madison Street, Suite 5600
Chicago, IL 60602
Phone: (312) 419-8220
Fax: (312) 419-9417

Icahn Enterprises L.P.
767 5th Avenue, Suite 4700
New York, NY 10153
Phone: (212) 702-4300
www.icahnenterprises.com

J.W. Childs Associates, L.P.
111 Huntington Avenue, Suite 2900
Boston, MA 02199
Phone: (617) 753-1100
Fax: (617) 753-1101
www.jwchilds.com

Jupiter Partners LLC
12 East 49th Street, 36th Floor
New York, NY 10017
Phone: (212) 300-1000
Fax: (212) 300-1001
www.jupiterpartners.com

Kelso & Company
320 Park Avenue
New York, NY 10022
Phone: (212) 751-3939
Fax: (212) 223-2379
www.kelso.com

KKR & Co. L.P.
9 West 57th Street, Suite 4200
New York, NY 10019
Phone: (212) 750-8300
www.kkr.com

Leonard Green & Partners, L.P.
11111 Santa Monica Boulevard
Suite 2000
Los Angeles, CA 90025
Phone: (310) 954-0444
Fax: (310) 954-0404
www.leonardgreen.com

Lone Star Funds
2711 North Haskell Avenue
Suite 1700
Dallas, TX 75204
Phone: (214) 754-8300
www.lonestarfunds.com

Madison Dearborn Partners, LLC
3 First National Plaza, Suite 3800
Chicago, IL 60602
Phone: (312) 895-1000
Fax: (312) 895-1001
www.mdcp.com

MVC Capital, Inc.
287 Bowman Avenue, 2nd Floor
Purchase, NY 10577
Phone: (914) 701-0310
Fax: (914) 701-0315
www.mvccapital.com

Oak Hill Capital Partners
1 Stamford Plaza
263 Tresser Boulevard, 15th Floor
Stamford, CAT 06901-3236
Phone: (203) 328-1600
www.oakhillcapital.com

Oaktree Capital Management, L.P.
333 South Grand Avenue, 28th Floor
Los Angeles, CA 90071
Phone: (213) 830-6300
Fax: (213) 830-6293
www.oaktreecapital.com

Sentinel Capital Partners
330 Madison Avenue, 27th Floor
New York, NY 10017
Phone: (212) 688-3100
Fax: (212) 388-6513
www.sentinelpartners.com

Silver Lake Partners, L.P.
2775 Sand Hill Road, Suite 100
Menlo Park, CA 94025
Phone: (650) 233-8120
Fax: (650) 233-8125
www.silverlake.com

Stonehenge Partners, Inc.
191 West Nationwide Boulevard
Suite 600
Columbus, OH 43215
Phone: (614) 246-2500
Fax: (614) 246-2431
www.stonehengepartners.com

Sun Capital Partners, Inc.
5200 Town Center Circle, Suite 600
Boca Raton, FL 33486
Phone: (561) 394-0550
Fax: (561) 394-0540
www.suncappart.com

Thomas H. Lee Partners L.P.
100 Federal Street
Boston, MA 02110
Phone: (617) 227-1050
Fax: (617) 227-3514
www.thl.com

Tracinda Corporation
150 Rodeo Drive, Suite 250
Beverly Hills, CA 90212
Phone: (310) 271-0638
Fax: (310) 271-3416

The Veritas Capital Fund, L.P.
590 Madison Avenue, 41st Floor
New York, NY 10021
Phone: (212) 688-0020
Fax: (212) 688-9411
www.veritascapital.com

Veronis Suhler Stevenson LLC
350 Park Avenue
New York, NY 10022
Phone: (212) 935-4990
Fax: (212) 381-8168
www.vss.com

Warburg Pincus LLC
466 Lexington Avenue
New York, NY 10017
Phone: (212) 878-0600
Fax: (212) 878-9351
www.warbugpincus.com

Visit Vault at **www.vault.com** for insider company profiles, expert advice, career message boards, expert resume reviews, the Vault Job Board and more.

VAULT CAREER LIBRARY   267

Employer Directory, cont.

Welsh, Carson, Anderson & Stowe
320 Park Avenue, Suite 2500
New York, NY 10022
Phone: (212) 893-9500
Fax: (212) 893-9575
www.welshcarson.com

Westar Capital LLC
949 South Coast Drive, Suite 650
Costa Mesa, CA 92626
Phone: (714) 481-5160
Fax: (714) 481-5166
www.westarcapital.com

Wingate Partners
750 North St. Paul Street, Suite 1200
Dallas, TX 75201
Phone: (214) 720-1313
Fax: (214) 871-8799
www.wingatepartners.com

The Yucaipa Companies LLC
9130 West Sunset Boulevard
Los Angeles, CA 90069
Phone: (310)789-7200
Fax: (310) 228-2873

Private Wealth Management

What do Private Wealth Managers Do?

The private wealth management industry integrates the varied and complex business of managing wealth by accounting for income needs, taxes, estate preservation and asset protection for the wealthy. Typically, private wealth management is a smaller division of a much larger investment firm or bank. The private wealth manager leverages the expertise of the various departments inside the firm (such as the trust department) to present clients with solutions to wealth management issues. Though not required to be expert in one particular area of wealth management, private wealth managers must know enough about each area to represent their clients' best interests and, where appropriate, offer advice.

Creating income

It is the first job of private wealth managers to help create, from among various investment strategies, income or growth sufficient for the everyday needs of their clients. In addition, they must provide enough excess growth to account for inflation in order that their client's purchasing power does become eroded over time. Let's face it, $1 doesn't buy as much as it used to for Jed and Granny. In addition, hopefully the wealth manager will continue to grow the clients' assets so that they become richer.

Because the rich wealthy often need to live solely off of their investments, today's private wealth managers must use a variety of investment techniques to help clients create enough income every year to live off of. Sounds easy enough right? Not really. When you consider that someone who invests $1 million in a conservative corporate bond returning 5 percent creates a modest $50,000 a year in income, it becomes obvious that having a million dollars or so just isn't as a big a deal as it used to be. Sure $50,000 is a lot of money for doing nothing. But living on champagne and caviar is out of the question. With average wages in the U.S. at a little over $38,000 per year as of 2006, according to the Social Security Administration, the average typical family with two income-earners can earn more than someone with $1 million in the bank who lives off of his or her investments. Indeed, because of inflation, the portfolio with a $1 million must return in excess of 7.5 percent just to keep up with the two-worker household that can possibly expect to get raises every year. With rates of return in the stock market sometimes as high 20 percent or more, 7.5 percent may not seem a very high return, but when you consider that the S&P 500 over the last six years has returned less than 1 percent annually, you'll see that the job of private wealth managers in creating income for their clients isn't always easy.

Paying taxes

Another problem wealthy clients often encounter is taxes. None of us like paying taxes. For most of us, however, we would willingly pay additional taxes if it meant that we were making additional income. For the wealthy, it isn't quite as simple. When managing large pools of assets, small differences in tax rates can translate into big changes in after-tax returns. Various types of investments used by the wealthy are treated and taxed differently by the IRS. For example, income derived from the interest rates of bonds is taxed differently than long-term capital gains derived from selling stock. It is the private wealth manager's job to balance assorted types of investments to create the most tax efficient combination for the client.

Asset protection

In today's society, people with money are sometimes targeted with lawsuits just because they happen to have money. So, an increasingly popular area of practice for private wealth managers is called "asset protection," which helps the wealthy guard against losing their money in civil lawsuits. There are several techniques used to protect assets, including U.S. trusts laws and foreign, offshore banks. Advocates of asset protection methods contend that making their clients impervious to lawsuits doesn't just protect assets, but also prevents lawsuits from even happening.

Visit Vault at **www.vault.com** for insider company profiles, expert advice, career message boards, expert resume reviews, the Vault Job Board and more.

VAULT CAREER LIBRARY   269

Career Paths

The primary role in private wealth management is the private banker, also called the investment or financial advisor. This is the person who evaluates a client's financial position, recommends solid investments, helps with the fiduciary aspects of their client's accounts (regularly consulting tax and accounting experts within the firm), and even sets up a family office for wealthier clients to pay bills, staff and make sure family members are appropriately taken care of, or "given their allowances" as one banker put it.

Analysts

The career track for the private banker is fairly cut and dry at the major corporate banks and Wall Street brokerage firms. Undergrads coming in are called analysts, just as they are in the sales and trading division and the investment banking arm and everywhere else within the corporation. They're the ones who do all the researching, number crunching, report writing, and yes, coffee fetching on occasion, for the higher ups who are actually working for the clients.

Associates

The next rank up is associate, or just plain old private banker at the smaller firms. These are the guys who work with the clients and attract new business, the real face of the private bank for most clients. This is considered a very entrepreneurial job, in that you'll be expected to not only serve clients, but attract new clients as well. At many firms, you'll also be expected to attempt to sell your clients on the company's proprietary financial products, though the practice is starting to be curtailed at some firms.

Associates will work closely with clients to create an overall financial strategy that encompasses not only investment, but also income management, budget, real estate holdings, taxes, small business partnerships, estate planning and even paying the day-to-day bills of the household, all depending on the level of service the client wants (and the fees he or she is willing to pay, but at this level, fees are a secondary consideration to impeccable service and peace of mind).

Associate pay generally mirrors other Wall Street positions, with a newly minted associate making about $75,000 to $85,000 per year. Bonuses can vary, however, depending on how the firm structures compensation. Some private bankers receive bonuses solely on selling the client new services and the company's investment products, getting a percentage of the business the private bank brings in from that client. Others have more complex metrics, measuring performance against the client's stated goals. For example, some private wealth management clients may not want anything more complex than safe fixed-income investments that generate income with little or no risk, with a stated goal of five percent yield each year. If the private banker reached that goal, he would get a larger bonus than he would have if the investment only yielded 4.85 percent. Or if the banker managed to get 5.35 percent—without altering the client's risk profile or otherwise deviating from the state goals—the bonus would be higher.

Some private wealth managements eschew commission bonuses altogether, preferring to grant bonuses that do not give clients the appearance that their banker is simply interested in selling them on products. These firms' bonus metrics are primarily based on fulfilling the clients' goals—a few firms even ask clients to review their bankers each year. Of course, firms will always appreciate it when associates convince their clients to use the private bank's estate planning services instead of someone else's, and in that sense, selling a non-investment service is seen as very bonus-worthy.

Likewise, associates are expected to drum up new business, and bonuses can come if you manage to gain new clients. Sometimes this will come from word-of-mouth, as current clients recommend the associate to their high-net-worth peers. It also comes from good old-fashioned networking, which means an investment on the associate's part in both time and, at times, money—especially when belonging to the right club or attending the right charitable event can mean a room full of potential clients. Some private banking firms organize cultural events or sports outings for their clients as well, with the hopes that they'll bring well-moneyed colleagues or friends for associates to network with.

Vice presidents

In time, salaries and bonus money for motivated, skilled and trusted associates can top $500,000, usually anywhere from five to eight years, depending on the firm and opportunities that have presented themselves, and up to $1 million within 10 to 13 years of private banking. At that level, however, an associate has often already been promoted to the level of vice president. As such, he or she can be placed in a position overseeing a number of associates, or even a regional office. Alternatively, an associate that has specialized in spotting unique investment opportunities or has helped come up with new products can branch off from the client business and into an investment specialty. They may end up as market strategist or in-house portfolio consultants, gaining a smaller piece of individual clients' business, but making up for it by consulting with larger numbers of clients.

Managing directors

Finally, after years of service-and income that can top $2 million or more for the best performing vice presidents—a successful, entrepreneurial, client-driven VP can be named a managing director. In these positions, an MD can expect to be in charge of associates in a major branch office, or even in the headquarters city. They can be given the highest-net-worth clients, or the problem clients whose money is just too valuable for the firm to lose. In specialty positions, they may end up as the private bank's chief investment officer, chief fiduciary officer or general counsel. There are generally only a handful of MDs within any private wealth management firm, and they are often on the executive committees of the firm. At this level, salaries enter a realm in which the MD may want to find a private banker of his own—and are generally high enough that firms don't discuss them, though still nowhere near the level where they have to be reported to the Securities and Exchange Commission!

Job Responsibilities

Do wealth managers need to be good at sales? Marketing? Investing? Schmoozing?

The answer to all of these questions is yes. A private wealth manager must be good at many things—he or she must be as skilled at developing relationships as investing.

Sales

Among the responsibilities of a private wealth manager are sales and prospecting for sales. If your heart fell a little when you read that you'd have to, gasp, gulp … s … s … sell, then hold on for just a minute. The first stop on the road to success for any private wealth manager (or any other salesperson or manager for that matter) is to improve his or her listening skills. A good private wealth manager will be able to draw out a client's needs by asking the right questions then actively listening to the answers for cues and clues as to what the client might be thinking.

Money can be a very uncomfortable subject for people. Studies have shown that many people are more uncomfortable talking about money then they are about being naked in front of a strange doctor. Like a doctor, a private wealth manager's bedside manner, so to speak, will go a long way to identifying a client's needs.

When you improve your listening skills, you will find that you become a true professional salesperson. Such a professional salesperson is not someone who can simply talk another person into anything. A professional salesperson, rather, is an expert at listening to what clients need and filling that need by identifying a product or service appropriate for them. This means that often you are not selling anyone anything at all. Rather, you are listening to clients, building relationships with them, and understanding what their goals are. That's what sales is really all about. If you let it, it can be one of the best parts of your job.

Visit Vault at **www.vault.com** for insider company profiles, expert advice, career message boards, expert resume reviews, the Vault Job Board and more.

VAULT CAREER LIBRARY   271

Marketing

Marketing is the art of telling people who you are—whether you're a product or service—and why people should want to do business with you. This last part (why people should want to do business with you) is the most important aspect of promoting your business. And since private wealth management is a highly regulated industry, there are some notable challenges to marketing.

When it comes to marketing itself, the private wealth management industry has more restrictions on what it can lawfully claim than some other industries. For example, if you had owned an oil company and sold gasoline, like Jed Clampett, you could say that your gasoline made cars more fun to drive to promote your particular brand of gasoline. In the private wealth management business, though, it's a little more difficult to make claims of being "the best," or being "better than" something or someone else. Generally, the marketing is pretty standard, with some notable exceptions. Private wealth management companies might say they offer some sort of superior service quality or a degree of caring that may be missing from a competing firm. For instance, Raymond James and Associates offers BIO (by invitation only) visits to clients meeting certain liquid net-worth thresholds. These potential clients are flown down to Raymond James corporate headquarters and given a tour of the firm's four-acre campus in St. Petersburg, Florida. Clients then can meet with various departments of the firm, including the senior management, right up to the CEO.

What some firms lack in old-fashioned marketing, they allow (and expect) you to make up. Some wealth managers may use newsletters to promote themselves, others network in their community. How you market yourself will be a decision to make after thoroughly evaluating what strengths you can bring to your clients.

Many managers spend time on the golf course to meet prospective clients. But golfing isn't a marketing strategy that can replace the hard work of meeting or calling prospects. It might be one component of a networking plan, which may also include volunteering on community boards, doing charity work and getting involved in other activities that allow a wealth manager to have more contact with wealthy individuals.

Investing

Private management firms provide their wealth managers with professionals to help them handle their clients' day-to-day investment decisions. This does not mean that wealth managers won't have a lot of input about those decisions or that they could not make those types of decisions themselves given the time. But think for a moment about how their time should be best spent? Talking to clients? Prospecting for new clients? Meeting new contacts? Learning about new estate planning techniques? Or keeping a close eye on the market?

Certainly they need to develop well-informed opinions about investing and various investment strategies. And the most important function of a wealth manager in the investment process will be explaining the implications of the various strategies presented, thereby helping his or her clients select the most appropriate strategy.

Uppers and Downers

Like any job, there are pros and cons to a career in private wealth management. The vast majority of private bankers are quite content in their jobs—but then again, they wouldn't be there if they weren't. Here are some uppers and downers that private bankers experience every day.

Uppers

- **Clients.** You'll be helping people realize their hopes and dreams, manage the results of a lifetime of hard work and plan for their futures. They're generally interesting people with fascinating life experiences, and you may end up becoming very close to them.

- **Entrepreneurship.** Once you're an associate or higher, you'll be ultimately responsible for your clients' performance, and you'll have the opportunity to build your own client base. You'll have quite a bit of input into how much money you make, based on your drive and your investment savvy.

- **On-the-job knowledge.** It's not just stocks and bonds. While you'll have backing from experts or consultants made available to you by your firm, you'll end up learning quite a bit about a variety of investments and financial planning tools. From real estate to hedge funds, from prenups to estate planning, you'll only get smarter as time goes on.

- **Philanthropy.** Many private bankers find particular joy from helping their clients give their money away. While it's not a high-commission activity by any stretch, it's certainly good for the soul. And as one banker pointed out, it can lead to more business contacts and potential clients!

- **Lifestyle.** For the most part, you can actually have a life outside of work if you manage your time and client accounts properly. You won't have many eight-hour days, but you can reasonably expect to have weekends free, and you'll be able to take vacations like the rest of humanity.

- **Money.** While you'll never receive multimillion-dollar checks for leading a merger deal, you'll certainly be making plenty of money, enough to easily become a high-net-worth individual in your own right.

Downers

- **Clients.** While the majority of your clients will fall into the "uppers" category, a few will most certainly drive you nuts. They'll ignore your advice, do stupid things with their money, and then blame you for it. A few will call constantly with each tick of the market, and many will need hand-holding or supremely well-thought-out arguments for each move you think they should make. Even your best clients will make you want to pull your hair out every now and again.

- **Conservatism.** Many of your clients will be risk adverse, and investments that could make them (and you) a pretty penny could be summarily rejected despite your best arguments.

- **Income fluctuations.** Feeding into the above, you may end up having a run of low bonuses or commissions due to uncertainty in the markets or a conservative investing trend. Just as your clients can fall prey to the vagaries of the market, your own income will as well.

- **Always on.** While the majority of your clients will leave you alone on weekends, holidays and vacations, you'll constantly have to be ready to spring into action at a moment's notice. Don't think of even heading to the grocery store without your BlackBerry on, and if you're going on vacation, a laptop with a reliable wireless connection is essential. An understanding domestic partner is also important should a client call in the middle of a honeymoon or family holiday.

- **Limited geographic potential.** You're going to have to live where high-net-worth individuals live, which means a major U.S. or world city, with all the expense and headaches that comes along with it. You can certainly live in the suburbs, but if you're hankering for a small town lifestyle, you won't get it—at least not without a major commute.

Visit Vault at **www.vault.com** for insider company profiles, expert advice, career message boards, expert resume reviews, the Vault Job Board and more.

V/\ULT CAREER LIBRARY   273

Employer Directory

The Bank of New York Mellon Wealth Management
1 Wall Street
New York, NY 10286
Phone: (212) 495-1784
Fax: (212) 809-9528
www.bankofny.com/privatebank/index.htm

Barclays Private Bank
1 Churchill Place
London E14 5HP
United Kingdom
www.barclayswealth.com/private-banking.htm

Brown Brothers Harriman Private Wealth Management
140 Broadway
New York, NY 10005-1101
Phone: (212) 483-1818
Fax: (212) 493-7287
www.bbh.com

Citigroup Private Bank
399 Park Avenue
New York, NY 10043
Phone: (212) 559-1000
Fax: (212) 793-3946
www.citigroup.com

Commerce Bank Private Banking
Commerce Atrium
1701 Route 70 East
Cherry Hill, NJ 08034-5400
Phone: (856) 751-9000
Fax: (856) 751-9260
www.commercebank.com

Credit Suisse Private Banking
11 Madison Avenue
New York, NY 10010
Phone: (212) 325-2000
www.credit-suisse.com

Deutsche Bank Private Wealth Management
Deutsche Bank AG
Theodor-Heuss-Allee 70
60486 Frankfurt
Germany
Phone: +49-69-910-00
Fax: +49-69-910-34-225
www.db.com

Fifth Third Asset Management
Fifth Third Bancorp
Fifth Third Center
Cincinnati, OH 45263
Phone: (513) 534-5300
Fax: (513) 579-6246
www.53.com

Friedman Billings Ramsey Investment Management
1001 19th Street
North Arlington, VA 22209
Phone: (703) 312-9500
Fax: (703) 312-9501
www.fbr.com

Goldman Sachs Private Wealth Management
85 Broad Street
New York, NY 10004
Phone: (212) 902-1000
Fax: (212) 902-3000
www.gs.com

HSBC Private Bank
World Headquarters
8 Canada Square
London, E14 5HQ
United Kingdom
Phone: +44-20-79-91-88-88
Fax: +44-20-79-92-48-80

HSBC Bank USA
452 Fifth Avenue
New York, NY 10018
Phone: (212) 525-5000
www.us.hsbc.com

Jefferies Private Client Services
520 Madison Avenue, 12th Floor
New York, NY 10022
Phone: (212) 284-2300
Fax: (212) 284-2111
www.jefferies.com

JPMorgan Private Bank
270 Park Avenue
New York, NY 10017
Phone: (212) 270-6000
Fax: (212) 270-1648
www.jpmorganchase.com

Lazard Private Client Group
30 Rockefeller Plaza
New York, NY 10020
Phone: (212) 632-6000
www.lazardnet.com

Legg Mason Wealth Management
100 Light Street
Baltimore, MD 21202-1099
Phone: (877) 534-4627
www.leggmason.com

Morgan Keegan Private Client Group
Morgan Keegan Tower
50 North Front Street
Memphis, TN 38103
Phone: (901) 524-4100
www.morgankeegan.com

Morgan Stanley Private Wealth Management
1585 Broadway
New York, NY 10036
Phone: (212) 761-4000
www.morganstanley.com

Northern Trust Private Banking
50 South La Salle Street
Chicago, IL 60603
Phone: (312) 630-6000
www.northerntrust.com

Employer Directory, cont.

Raymond James Financial Private Client Group

880 Carillon Parkway
St Petersburg, FL 33702
Phone: (727) 567-1000
Fax: (727) 573-8365
www.raymondjames.com

Royal Bank of Canada Global Private Banking

200 Bay Street
Toronto, Ontario
Canada
Phone: (416) 974-5151
Fax: (416) 955-7800
www.rbcprivatebanking.com

Thomas Weisel Partners Private Client Services

1 Montgomery Tower
1 Montgomery Street
San Francisco, CA 94104
Phone: (415) 364-2500
Fax: (415) 364-6295
www.tweisel.com

UBS Wealth Management

101 Park Avenue
New York, NY 10178
www.ubs.com

U.S. Bank Private Client Group

U.S. Bancorp Center
800 Nicollet Mall
Minneapolis, MN 55402
Phone: (651) 466-3000
www.usbank.com

U.S. Trust

(Bank of America Private Wealth Management)
114 West 47th Street
New York, NY 10036
Phone: (212) 852-1000
Fax: (212) 852-1140
Toll free: (800) 878-7878
www.bankofamerica.com/ustrust

Wells Fargo Private Client Services/Private Banking

420 Montgomery Street
San Francisco, CA 94104
Phone: (866) 249-3302
www.wellsfargo.com

William Blair Wealth Management

222 West Adams Street
Chicago, IL 60606
Phone: (312) 236-1600
www.willliamblair.com

Visit Vault at **www.vault.com** for insider company profiles, expert advice, career message boards, expert resume reviews, the Vault Job Board and more.

V/\ULT CAREER LIBRARY   275

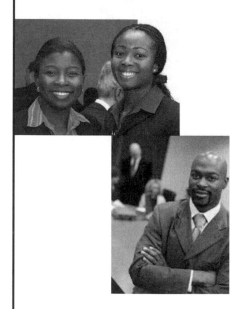

Real Estate

A concrete business

Real estate is tangible. It's a piece of land and any building or structures on it, as well as the air above and the ground below. Everyone comes into direct contact with real estate; the places where we live, work, vacation, shop and exercise are all assets to be bought, sold and rented. The real estate industry is usually considered one of the most dynamic sectors in the American economy—people may sell their stocks, but they always need a place to buy groceries and somewhere to sleep.

Yes, it's for real

The real estate sector depends on a number of economic factors; small shifts can turn trends significantly. For example, the technology industry boom helped the real estate industry in Silicon Valley in the 1990s. There was more demand for space—both commercial and residential—and asset values skyrocketed. The subsequent technology bust had a dramatic effect on some parts of the sector, too. Commercial real estate firms that deal with office and retail development projects found the market glutted with available space, driving prices down. Residential is affected by economic swings as well, in addition to changes in the federal interest rate (which affects mortgage interest rates) and the unemployment rate (which affects both consumer confidence and buying power). In turn, these have effects on mortgage lenders and housing construction companies (such as Lennar, Pulte Homes, Beazer Homes and KB Homes).

Most residential real estate offices are small and focus on properties in their immediate location. But their brand names come from just a few industry leaders. Realogy, a 2006 spin-off of Cendant, has several big names in its stable, including Sotheby's International, ERA, Century 21 and Coldwell Banker. The company claims it was involved in one in four U.S. residential real estate transactions in 2007. During that year, Apollo Management acquired Realogy, and the company signed a licensing deal with Meredith Corporation to use the Better Homes and Gardens brand. Realogy's competition includes RE/MAX and HomeServices of America. Firms that only handle commercial real estate are frequently larger and employ more brokers and salespeople than residential firms; they may also manage properties or administer real estate investment trusts (REITs). Most of the residential companies also deal in commercial sales.

Real estate rollercoaster

In the early part of the decade, the topic of real estate frequently popped up in the news media, as housing prices on both coasts and in urban areas skyrocketed. The reasons for this were numerous: following the market crash of 2000, the Federal Reserve rolled back interest rates from 6.5 percent to 1 percent over a three-year period, and a loosening of lending regulations made getting money to buy a house easier than ever. The influx of cheaper money fueled the boom: housing prices on the coasts shot up 55 to 100 percent, accounting for inflation, in five years. According to an article in *BusinessWeek*, in the first half of 2005, real estate accounted for 50 percent of the growth of the GDP; in less overheated markets it usually accounts for a tenth of that amount.

Since then, the sales market has fallen hard—and fast. Newly-constructed properties, which had been built up rather optimistically over those five years, began to be offered cheap to fill up empty units. By June 2006, the National Association of Realtors said the annual rate of residential sales was down nearly 9 percent compared to a year before. One year later, that figure was down another 10 percent to just under six million, the lowest seasonally-adjusted total in four years. The number of homes listed for sale at that point (4.4 million, the largest amount since 1992) was enough to last almost nine months at current sales rates. The situation in Florida was especially bad, compounded by huge property taxes, the hurricanes of 2004 and 2005 and the resultant spiral in insurance costs.

Visit Vault at **www.vault.com** for insider company profiles, expert advice, career message boards, expert resume reviews, the Vault Job Board and more.

VAULT CAREER LIBRARY   277

Prices leveled off, and then inched down for 10 straight months, dropping a total of 4 percent since October 2005. In a June 2007 article in *The New York Times*, Mark Zandi (chief economist at Moody's Economy.com) indicated that price declines were occurring in over 40 percent of metro areas in the United States, some by 8 to 12 percent. After the housing bubble burst, the subprime mortgage crisis emerged as a problem in 2007 and 2008, when borrowers started having trouble making payments on adjustable-rate loans with interest rates that had shifted upwards. To make matters worse, many people's homes were now worth less than what they had paid for them. Foreclosure filings increased because homeowners couldn't resort to options such as selling their homes or taking out other loans.

From bad to worse

The situation became more abysmal in 2008, when banks and other financial institutions suffered huge losses related to increasing mortgage payment defaults and falling real estate values. The Housing and Economic Recovery Act of 2008, which attempted to restore confidence in the U.S. mortgage industry, was passed in July 2008. The act lets the Federal Housing Administration guarantee as much as $300 billion in new 30-year fixed rate mortgages for homeowners with subprime loans. In addition, during 2008 the federal government bailed out mortgage lenders Fannie May and Freddie Mac, and the Fed also made massive loans to fund J.P. Morgan Chase's acquisition of Bear Stearns and to keep massive insurance firm AIG solvent.

After investment bank Lehman Brothers filed for bankruptcy, stock markets plummeted on September 15, 2008, a day the news media dubbed "Meltdown Monday." The following week, Federal Reserve Chairman Ben Bernanke and Treasury Secretary Henry Paulson urged Congress to pass a $700 billion bailout package, which would let the federal government purchase bad mortgages and other assets. While testifying on Capitol Hill, Bernanke said that the world's financial markets were under "severe stress." Bernanke added, "Action by Congress is urgently required to stabilize the situation and avert what otherwise could be very serious consequences for our financial markets and for our economy."

Some opponents to the legislation say the government (and, hence, the taxpayer) shouldn't be bailing out private companies. Other individuals approve of the plan but think it needs to include adequate safeguards, such as requiring that troubled financial firms don't give "golden parachutes" and big bonuses to executives. The National Association of Realtors has said that it supports the government's attempts to stabilize the financial markets.

Next on the real estate horizon

The subprime mortgage crisis has had an obvious impact on residential real estate, but it's also creating problems in the commercial real estate market. In August 2008, the National Association of Realtors said it expected poor economic conditions to have an impact on commercial real estate over the coming six to nine months. In New York, the financial crisis is expected to slow big construction projects such as Atlantic Yards in Brooklyn and the World Trade Center, and office buildings might have trouble renting out space if companies downsize.

If the economic downturn continues for an extended time, the results would be horrendous; bringing to mind the last time housing prices took a large fall: the Great Depression of the 1930s. Even if the economy and the real estate market recover, it's unlikely that housing prices will hit the historic highs that they saw in 2005 any time soon.

Valuing Real Estate

There are three generally accepted approaches to valuing real estate: the sales approach, the cost approach and the income approach. Professional appraisers will reach a valuation after carefully considering each approach. You should make sure to review all three approaches before any real estate interview.

The sales approach

The sales approach arrives at a value for a property based on recent sales of similar properties. This approach can be used for both residential and commercial properties. There are proprietary databases that track home and commercial building sales, which make it easier for real estate professionals to access market information used in valuing properties. One of the most popular databases is the Multilisting Service (MLS), which is used to track residential properties. The MLS contains useful information about homes, such as the sales history, tax records and property amenities that can be accessed for an annual fee. In the sales approach, appraisers will use databases, such as the MLS, to look for homes with similar characteristics (e.g., location and house specifics), as the subject property. For example, when valuing a four-bedroom, two-bathroom house in the Pacific Heights section of San Francisco, it is logical to value that property based on the most recent sales information for properties in the same area with similar characteristics. Bear in mind that no two properties are alike, so when valuing a property using the sales approach you must adjust for differences between the properties.

The cost approach

In markets where it is difficult to find similar properties, an appraiser can value a property based on the cost approach. This approach focuses on a few steps. First, you must determine the cost of replacing or reconstructing the improvements or building. Next, the age of the improvements must be considered and an appropriate amount of depreciation is subtracted from the value of improvements. Finally, the value of the land must be taken into consideration. The land value is added to the improvements minus the estimated property depreciation. The cost approach is used for truly unique properties like churches, which cannot use either the sales or income approach to arrive at a valuation.

The income approach

The income approach is the most quantitative of the three approaches. The income approach involves the use of net operating income (NOI) in calculating the value of the property. Think of NOI as the reason most investors buy a building. The investment community talks about NOI incessantly, so make sure to understand this concept if you plan on being involved with real estate investing.

There are two forms of the income approach. One form involves isolating NOI for one year, while the other form involves a longer time horizon. Both forms use a capitalization (cap) rate to calculate a value. The cap rate is a market mechanism, so don't worry about what goes in the calculation. Just be concerned with how it is used. In practice the cap rate is generally used in a formula with the NOI to arrive at a property value. For example, suppose you were buying an industrial facility whose net operating income in the following year was projected to be $500,000. If you knew the market cap rate for similar properties, you could arrive an estimated value of the property. Assume the market cap rate for industrial facilities was 10 percent. To arrive at the value of the building, divide NOI by the cap rate. In our example, the value of the building would be:

$$\text{Value} = \frac{\text{NOI}}{\text{Cap Rate}} = \frac{\$500,000}{.10} = \$5,000,000$$

The yield capitalization form uses a longer time horizon. It involves calculating a discounted cash flow to arrive a property value.

$$\text{Value} = \frac{\text{NOI year n}}{(1+\text{discount rate})^n} + \frac{\text{NOI year n}+1}{(1+\text{discount rate})^{n+1}} + \frac{\text{residual value}}{(1+\text{discount rate})^{n+1}}$$

In the example above, the numerator represents the cash flows that the building generates today and in the coming years, which theoretically provides a value for the asset. Note, that there is also a future residual value listed in

Visit Vault at www.vault.com for insider company profiles, expert advice, career message boards, expert resume reviews, the Vault Job Board and more.

VAULT CAREER LIBRARY   279

the formula. The discount rate reflects the cost of capital. Your client may provide this cost, or you may have to estimate the discount rate based on similar transactions and knowledge of the market. The discount rate is necessary because it allows you to bring all the future cash flows back to today's dollars or present value (PV). The discount rate factors in the opportunity cost of money or the return that you could expect elsewhere with the cash flows. The exponent "n" in the denominator represents the period or number of years in the future that you would receive that cash flow. The DCF is calculated based on a stated number of years and adds up the PVs. At some point in the future cash flows you have a residual value because it is assumed the property is eventually sold. The residual value is calculated by taking the NOI of the year after the assumed time horizon and then dividing that year's NOI by an assumed cap rate. Some investors use different time periods when calculating the DCF but 10 years is the generally accepted period to value an asset. The DCF is normally used for income-producing property, while a single-family house is typically valued by the sales comparison approach.

Although there are different ways to value real estate, there are a few common variables such as location, the property's condition and market demand that make real estate valuable regardless of the asset type. There is a popular industry saying, "The three most important things in real estate are location, location, location." You simply cannot underestimate the importance of location. While you can restore and upgrade a property as much as you want, there is no substitute for being located close to: transportation, good schools, attractive retail and an aesthetically pleasing area. While location is important, keeping the property in good working order also creates value because it lessens the need to make improvements or contribute capital to the property. In addition, fundamental macroeconomics plays a major role in real estate values. For example, when interest rates offered by lenders are low, people will rush to buy a house to take advantage of the low financing costs. If this new market demand is greater than the market supply, property prices will increase.

The Real Estate MBA

One possible educational route into real estate is to get an MBA at an inttution with a specific real estate program. Some of the best programs, based on *U.S. News & World Report* rankings, are Wharton, University of California-Berkeley's Haas Business School, MIT's Sloan School of Management, University of Wisconsin-Madison and Ohio State University's Fisher School of Business. These schools also have strong real estate clubs that produce annual conferences and other activities.

Job Seeking Advice for Real Estate MBAs

Joseph Pagliari, a clinical assistant professor and director of the Real Estate Center at the Kellogg School of Management, says, "There are host of opportunities in real estate for MBAs. The issue is identifying the best fit for the candidate. Positions that are good fits for MBAs are with firms that supply capital to the industry. Typically these are large, sophisticated, financially-oriented firms. MBAs should identify these institutions and aggressively pursue them for employment. In today's marketplace, this means looking at REITs, mezzanine funds (funds built around mezzanine financing, which combines equity and fixed income investments) and private equity firms.

"In general, the high-profile real estate positions and financially rewarding jobs are on the capital side," adds Pagliari, who is also a principal of a real estate investment firm. "These jobs are almost self-selecting because they are tough to get and you have to be smart and aggressive to succeed. Given that positions in the capital side of the business are reserved for the elite, MBAs should pursue these positions because many of them possess the necessary qualities for these roles."

Employers look for a variety of skill sets. "It is difficult to narrow it to just a few things," he says. "Some positions are very quantitative while others emphasize strong interpersonal skills. Having a combination of both is a competitive advantage. In general, I tell all my students to look for roles that speak to their skill sets. It is going to be hard enough to get the interview, so don't blow it by going after a job that probably doesn't fit your background. MBAs should do their homework on the types of roles out there and match their background and interest with the best fit. However, you still want to shoot for the sky and leverage your MBA."

Job seekers shouldn't be shy about using their contacts "This industry is very tough for outsiders or newcomers to break into and students should be ready to accept that," he advises. "Get in the hunt as soon as possible and network, network, network. Using alums or anyone else you know in the industry is something I always recommend." When you have the interview, be prepared to talk about the local market—or any other in which the company operates. If it's a public firm, check *The Wall Street Journal* for the scuttlebutt. Also, be certain they'll welcome your MBA.

"In the interview you will most likely be asked about why you are interested in real estate and a few technical questions," Pagliari warns. "Be ready to describe a cap rate and market specifics like rental rates and general economic conditions."

To MBA students just starting a real estate program who know they want to enter the industry, he stresses, "Don't rely on simply taking real estate classes, especially if you have no prior real estate experience." You need to demonstrate passion by joining a real estate club or getting active in real estate-related activities at school. "Do whatever it takes to be able to demonstrate your enthusiasm for the industry," he adds. "If it takes starting a real estate club or being the driving force behind an event, then so be it."

The professor also advises individuals who are evaluating MBA programs that offer real estate curriculums to: make sure the professors have some practical experience and the curriculum will give you a skill set that will meet your end goal. Don't sacrifice the overall MBA experience for a school that simply offers a strong real estate curriculum and is lacking in other areas.

For MBA students who are interested in real estate but whose programs do not offer real estate classes, Pagliari offers a solution. "Classes related to finance and economic principles that help you price risks are very useful," he says, noting that the ability to price risk is a strong differentiating factor. Pagliari also recommends taking business law classes because there are many legal issues involved in the industry. "Which is why you should not be surprised to find so many attorneys in the business," he says.

"I was a career switcher and was repeatedly asked in interviews about why I was interested in real estate," says Rich Monopoli, a recent graduate from business school. "Many of the interviewers wanted an explanation of how my background tied to my interest in real estate. I can't emphasize enough how important it is to be prepared to answer the question of why you are interested in real estate."

Visit Vault at **www.vault.com** for insider company profiles, expert advice, career message boards, expert resume reviews, the Vault Job Board and more.

VAULT CAREER LIBRARY   281

Employer Directory

7MB Property Corporation
Pier 1, Bay 1
San Francisco, CA 94111
Phone: (415) 394-9000
Fax: (415) 394-9001
www.amb.com

Apartment Investment and Management Company
4582 South Ulster Street Parkway
Suite 1100
Denver, CO 80237
Phone: (303) 757-8101
Fax: (303) 759-3226
Toll free: (888) 789-8600
www.aimco.com

Archstone
9200 East Panorama Circle, Suite 400
Englewood, CO 80112
Phone: (303) 708-5959
Fax: (303) 708-5999
www.archstonesmith.com

AvalonBay Communities, Inc.
2900 Eisenhower Avenue, Suite 300
Alexandria, VA 22314
Phone: (703) 329-6300
Fax: (703) 329-1459
www.avalonbay.com

Beazer Homes
1000 Abernathy Road, Suite 1200
Atlanta, GA 30328
Phone: (770) 829-3700
Fax: (770) 481-2808
www.beazer.com

Boston Capital Corporation
1 Boston Place
Boston, MA 02108-4406
Phone: (617) 624-8900
Fax: (617) 624-8999
www.bostoncapital.com

Boston Properties, Inc.
111 Huntington Avenue
Boston, MA 02199-7610
Phone: (617) 236-3300
Fax: (617) 536-5087
www.bostonproperties.com

Brookfield Properties Corporation
BCE Place, 181 Bay Street, Suite 330
Toronto, Ontario M5J 2T3
Canada
Phone: (416) 369-2300
Fax: (416) 369-2301
www.brookfieldproperties.com

Catellus - A ProLogis Company
4545 Airport Way
Denver, CO 80239
Phone: (303) 567-5700
www.catellus.com

CB Richard Ellis Group, Inc.
100 North Sepulveda Boulevard
Suite 1050
El Segundo, CA 90245
Phone: (310) 606-4700
Fax: (310) 606-4701
www.cbre.com

CBL & Associates Properties
2030 Hamilton Place Boulevard
Suite 500
Chattanooga, TN 37421-6000
Phone: (423) 855-0001
Fax: (423) 490-8390
Toll free: (800) 333-7310
www.cblproperties.com

Centex Corporation
2728 North Harwood Street
Dallas, TX 75201-1516
Phone: (214) 981-5000
Fax: (214) 981-6859
www.centex.com

Century 21 Real Estate LLC
1 Campus Drive
Parsippany, NJ 07054
Phone: (877) 221-2765
Fax: (973) 496-7564
www.century21.com

Coldwell Banker Real Estate Corporation
1 Campus Drive
Parsippany, NJ 07054
Phone: (973) 407-2000
Fax: (973) 496-7217
Toll free: (877) 373-3829
www.coldwellbanker.com

Day & Zimmermann Group
1500 Spring Garden Street
Philadelphia, PA 19103
Phone: (215) 299-8000
Fax: (215) 299-8030
www.dayzim.com

Developers Diversified Realty
3300 Enterprise Parkway
Beachwood, OH 44122
Phone: (216) 755-5500
Fax: (216) 755-1500
www.ddrc.com

Duke Realty Corporation
600 East 96th Street, Suite 100
Indianapolis, IN 46240
Phone: (317) 808-6000
Fax: (317) 808-6794
Toll free: (800) 875-3366
www.dukerealty.com

Equity Office Properties Trust
2 North Riverside Plaza, Suite 2100
Chicago, IL 60606
Phone: (312) 466-3300
Fax: (312) 454-0332
www.equityoffice.com

Employer Directory, cont.

Equity Residential
2 North Riverside Plaza, Suite 450
Chicago, IL 60606
Phone: (312) 474-1300
Fax: (312) 454-8703
www.equityresidential.com

FelCor Lodging Trust Incorporated
545 East John Carpenter Freeway
Suite 1300
Irving, TX 75062
Phone: (972) 444-4900
Fax: (972) 444-4949
www.felcor.com

Forest City Enterprises, Inc.
1100 Terminal Tower 50 Public Square
Cleveland, OH 44113-2203
Phone: (216) 621-6060
Fax: (216) 263-4808
www.forestcity.net

General Growth Properties, Inc.
110 North Wacker Drive
Chicago, IL 60606
Phone: (312) 960-5000
Fax: (312) 960-5475
www.generalgrowth.com

Heitman LLC
191 North Wacker Drive, Suite 2500
Chicago, IL 60606
Phone: (312) 855-5700
www.heitman.com

Hilton Hotels Corporation
9336 Civic Center Drive
Beverly Hills, CA 90210
Phone: (310) 278-4321
Fax: (310) 205-7678
www.hiltonworldwide.com

Hines
Williams Tower
2800 Post Oak Boulevard
Houston, TX 77056-6118
Phone: (713) 621-8000
Fax: (713) 966-2053
www.hines.com

Hospitality Properties Trust
400 Centre Street
Newton, MA 02458
Phone: (617) 964-8389
Fax: (617) 969-5730
www.hptreit.com

Host Hotels & Resorts, Inc.
6903 Rockledge Drive, Suite 1500
Bethesda, MD 20817
Phone: (240) 744-1000
Fax: (240) 744-5125
www.hosthotels.com

Hovnanian Enterprises, Inc.
110 West Front Street
Red Bank, NJ 07701
Phone: (732) 747-7800
Fax: (732) 747-7159
www.khov.com

HRPT Properties Trust
400 Centre Street
Newton, MA 02458-2076
Phone: (617) 332-3990
Fax: (617) 332-2261
www.hrpreit.com

Jones Lang LaSalle
200 East Randolph Drive
Chicago, IL 60601
Phone: (312) 782-5800
Fax: (312) 782-4339
www.joneslanglasalle.com

KB Home
10990 Wilshire Boulevard, 7th Floor
Los Angeles, CA 90024
Phone: (310) 231-4000
Fax: (310) 231-4222
www.kbhome.com

Kimco Realty Corporation
3333 New Hyde Park Road
New Hyde Park, NY 11042-0020
Phone: (516) 869-9000
Fax: (516) 869-9001
www.kimcorealty.com

Menard, Inc.
4777 Menard Drive
Eau Claire, WI 54703
Phone: (715) 876-5911
Fax: (715) 876-2868
www.menard-inc.com

TheMcCormick Group
1440 Central Park Boulevard
Suite 207
Fredericksburg, VA 22401
Phone: (540) 786-9777
Fax: (540) 786-9355
www.mccormickgroup.com

MetroList, Inc.
7100 East Belleview Avenue
Englewood, CO 80111-1632
Phone: (303) 850-9576
www.metrolistmls.com

Morgan Stanley Real Estate
1585 Broadway
New York, NY 10036
Phone: (212) 761-4000
www.morganstanley.com/realestate

Murdock Holding Company
10900 Wilshire Boulevard, Suite 1600
Los Angeles, CA 90024
Phone: (310) 208-3636
Fax: (310) 824-7756
www.castlecooke.net

NRT Incorporated
339 Jefferson Road
Parsipanny, NJ 07054
Phone: (973) 240-5000
Fax: (973) 240-5241
www.nrtllc.com

Visit Vault at www.vault.com for insider company profiles, expert advice, career message boards, expert resume reviews, the Vault Job Board and more.

VAULT CAREER LIBRARY   283

Employer Directory, cont.

Parkway Properties, Inc.
1 Jackson Place
188 East Capitol Street, Suite 1000
Jackson, MS 39201-2195
Phone: (601) 948-4091
Fax: (601) 949-4077
Toll free: (800) 748-1667
www.pky.com

ProLogis
4545 Airport Way
Denver, CO 80239
Phone: (303) 567-5000
Fax: (303) 567-5605
Toll free: (800) 566-2706
www.prologis.com

Public Storage, Inc.
701 Western Avenue
Glendale, CA 91201-2349
Phone: (818) 244-8080
Fax: (818) 553-2376
www.publicstorage.com

Rayonier Inc.
50 North Laura Street
Jacksonville, FL 32202
Phone: (904) 357-9100
Fax: (904) 357-9101
www.rayonier.com

RE/MAX International, Inc.
5075 S. Syracuse Street
Denver, CO 80237-2712
Phone: (303) 770-5531

Fax: (303) 796-3599
Toll free: (800) 525-7452
www.remax.com

RREEF America L.L.C.
875 N Michigan Avenue
Chicago, IL 60611-1803
Phone: (312) 266-9300
www.dbrealestate.com/rreef

Tishman Speyer Properties
45 Rockefeller Plaza
New York, NY 10111
Phone: (212) 715-0300
Fax: (212) 895-0326
www.tishmanspeyer.com

Trammell Crow Residential
2 Buckhead Plaza
3050 Peachtree Road NW, Suite 500
Atlanta, GA 30305
Phone: (770) 801-1600
Fax: (770) 801-1256
www.tcresidential.com

The Trump Organization
725 5th Avenue
New York, NY 10022
Phone: (212) 832-2000
Fax: (212) 935-0141
www.trump.com

URS Corporation
600 Montgomery Street, 26th Floor
San Francisco, CA 94111
Phone: (415) 774-2700

Fax: (415) 398-1905
www.urscorp.com

USG Corporation
550 West Adams Street
Chicago, IL 60661-3676
Phone: (312) 436-4000
Fax: (312) 436-4093
www.usg.com

Vornado Realty Trust
888 7th Avenue
New York, NY 10019
Phone: (212) 894-7000
Fax: (212) 894-7070
www.vno.com

Walton Street Capital L.L.C.
900 North Michigan Avenue
Suite 1900
Chicago, IL 60611
Phone: (312) 915-2800
Fax: (312) 915-2881
www.waltonst.com

Weyerhaeuser Company
33663 Weyerhaeuser Way South
Federal Way, WA 98003
Phone: (253) 924-2345
Fax: (253) 924-2685
Toll free: (800) 525-5440
www.weyerhauser.com

Sales and Trading

The War Zone

If you've ever been to an investment banking trading floor, you've witnessed the chaos. It's usually a lot of swearing, yelling and flashing computer screens: a pressure cooker of stress. Sometimes the floor is a quiet rumble of activity, but when the market takes a nosedive, panic ensues and the volume kicks up a notch. Traders must rely on their market instincts, and salespeople yell for bids when the market tumbles. Deciding what to buy or sell, and at what price to buy and sell, is difficult when millions of dollars are at stake.

However, salespeople and traders work much more reasonable hours than research analysts or corporate finance bankers. Rarely does a salesperson or trader venture into the office on a Saturday or Sunday; the trading floor is completely devoid of life on weekends. Any corporate finance analyst who has crossed a trading floor on a Saturday will tell you that the only noise to be heard on the floor is the clocks ticking every minute and the whir of the air conditioner.

Shop Talk

Here's a quick example of how a salesperson and a trader interact on an emerging market bond trade.

Salesperson: Receives a call from a buy-side firm (say, a large mutual fund). The buy-side firm wishes to sell $10 million of a particular Mexican Par government-issued bond (denominated in U.S. dollars). The emerging markets bond salesperson, seated next to the emerging markets traders, stands up in his chair and yells to the relevant trader, "Give me a bid on $10 million Mex Par, six and a quarter, 19s."

Trader: "I got 'em at 73 and an eighth."

Translation: I am willing to buy them at a price of $73.125 per $100 of face value. As mentioned, the $10 million represents amount of par value the client wanted to sell, meaning the trader will buy the bonds, paying 73.125 percent of $10 million plus accrued interest (to factor in interest earned between interest payments).

Salesperson: "Can't you do any better than that?"

Translation: Please buy at a higher price, as I will get a higher commission.

Trader: "That's the best I can do. The market is falling right now. You want to sell?"

Salesperson: "Done. $10 million."

S&T: A Symbiotic Relationship?

Institutional sales and trading are highly dependent on one another. The propaganda that you read in glossy firm brochures portrays those in sales and trading as a shiny, happy integrated team environment of professionals working for the client's interests. While often that is true, salespeople and traders frequently clash, disagree and bicker.

Simply put, salespeople provide the clients for traders, and traders provide the products for sales. Traders would have nobody to trade for without sales, but sales would have nothing to sell without traders. Understanding how a trader makes money and how a salesperson makes money should explain how conflicts can arise.

Traders make money by selling high and buying low (this difference is called the spread). They are buying stocks or bonds for clients, and these clients filter in through sales. A trader faced with a buy order for a buy-side firm couldn't care less about

Visit Vault at **www.vault.com** for insider company profiles, expert advice, career message boards, expert resume reviews, the Vault Job Board and more.

VAULT CAREER LIBRARY   285

the performance of the securities once they are sold. He or she just cares about making the spread. In a sell trade, this means selling at the highest price possible. In a buy trade, this means buying at the lowest price possible.

The salesperson, however, has a different incentive. The total return on the trade often determines the money a salesperson makes, so he wants the trader to sell at a low price. The salesperson also wants to be able to offer the client a better price than competing firms in order to get the trade and earn a commission. This of course leads to many interesting situations, and at the extreme, salespeople and traders who eye one another suspiciously.

The personalities

Salespeople possess remarkable communication skills, including outgoing personalities and a smoothness not often seen in traders. Traders sometimes call them bullshit artists while salespeople counter by calling traders quant guys with no personality. Traders are tough, quick and often consider themselves smarter than salespeople. The salespeople probably know better how to have fun, but the traders win the prize for mental sharpness and the ability to handle stress.

The MBA in S&T

Do I need an MBA to be promoted on a sales and trading desk?

Generally, sales and trading is a much less hierarchical work environment than investment banking. For this reason, it is widely believed that you don't need an MBA to get promoted on sales and trading desks. This view is often perpetuated be people who work on trading desks, but just because you hear this once or twice, don't accept it as truth. Whether you need an MBA or not is really a function of the firm you work for and the desk you're on. If the firm you're considering hires both associates and analysts, but you notice that associates are offered twice as much pay as analysts, then this is certainly an indication that MBAs are better paid. This doesn't mean that you can't be promoted without an MBA; you'll just have to work much harder to get recognized. When it's time for a promotion, you may also be somewhat behind in the pecking order. Some firms, on the other hand, don't want MBAs. This may result from budgetary constraints, or explicit firm policy. Some firms also hold the view that it's hard to teach an old dog new tricks, so they will hire exclusively out of undergraduate programs.

A more subtle point to discern are the desk dynamics. A lot about being on a trading desk is about fitting in, and if everyone else, including the boss, doesn't have an MBA, then chances are that having an MBA won't add too much value in this environment. In fact, an MBA degree may even hurt your career prospects if there's a downright disdain for MBA-types. Alternatively, if the desk you're on is populated with MBAs, then not having an MBA could potentially limit your career advancement. Alternatively, you can be in a situation where you're the only MBA and everyone thinks that you're the brain, which can work to your advantage even if the boss has no personal biases about the value of the degree.

The bottom line is that there are no hard and fast rules. Depending on the particular firm and desk, an MBA may not advance your career. Be aware of the aforementioned issues, and ask some good questions to get a better feel for whether an extra degree is a benefit.

What are some of the tangible benefits of an MBA?

The pay is better and you will generally have a faster track for promotion to salesperson or trader. The MBA associate will typically have to do the same demeaning things that an undergraduate analyst does, but mercifully for a shorter period of time. In some cases, MBAs are also more likely to be assigned the desk that they'd like to work for. Undergraduate sales and trading recruiting programs, on the other hand, may hire you as part of a generalist pool and place you on a desk that isn't your top choice.

Another tangible benefit for the MBA candidate is the availability of more exit options.

A Day in the Life: Sales-Trader

Here's a look at a day in the life of a sales-trader, given to us by an associate in the equities division.

6:30 a.m. Get into work. Check voicemail and e-mail. Chat with some people at your desk about the headlines in the *Journal*.

7:15 a.m. Equities morning call. You find out what's up to sell. ("I'm sort of a liaison between the accounts [clients] and the block traders. What I do is help traders execute their trading strategies, give them market color. If they want something I try to find the other side of the trade. Or if I have stuff available, I get info out, without exposing what we have.")

9:30 a.m. Markets open. You hit the phones. ("You want to make outgoing calls, you don't really want people to call you. I'm calling my clients, telling them what research is relevant to them, and what merchandise I have, if there's any news on any of their positions.")

10 a.m. More calls. ("I usually have about 35 different clients. It's always listed equities, but it's a huge range of equities. The client can be a buyer or seller—there's one sales-trader representing a buyer, another representing the seller.")

10:30 a.m. On the phone with another trader, trying to satisfy a client. ("If they have questions in another product, I'll try to help them out.")

11 a.m. Calling another client. ("It's a trader at the other end, receiving discussions from portfolio manager; their discretion varies from client to client.")

12 p.m. You hear a call for the sale for a stock that several of your clients are keen on acquiring. ("It's usually a block trader, although sometimes it's another sales-trader. The announcement comes 'over the top,'—over the speaker. It also comes on my computer.")

12:30 p.m. Food from the deli comes in. ("You can't go to the bathroom sometimes, say you're working 10 orders, you want to see every stock. We don't leave to get our lunch, we order lunch in.")

1 p.m. Watching your terminal ("There's a lot of action. If there's 200,000 shares trade in your name [a stock that a client has a position in or wants] and it's not you, you want to go back to your client and say who it was.)

2 p.m. Taking a call from a client. ("You can't miss a beat, you are literally in your seat all day.")

2:05 p.m. You tell the client that you have some stock he had indicated interest in previously, but you don't let him know how much you can unload. ("It's a lot of how to get a trade done without disclosing anything that's going to hurt the account. If you have one stock up you don't want the whole Street to know, or it'll drive down the price.")

4:30 p.m. Head home to rest a bit before going out. ("I leave at 4:30 p.m. or sometimes 5 p.m. It depends.")

7 p.m. Meet a buy-side trader, one of your clients, at a bar. ("We entertain a lot of buy-side traders—dinner, we go to baseball games, we go to bars. Maybe this happens once or twice a week.")

MBA Career Path

First-year MBA students and recent MBA graduates are eligible for summer associate and full-time associate positions respectively. Associates start with similar responsibilities as analysts, but add more responsibility quickly and are typically on a faster track for promotion.

MBAs are also more likely to have the opportunity to get staffed abroad. For example, Goldman Sachs and Morgan Stanley have recently hired MBAs from American business schools directly into their European trading desks. MBAs interested in

Visit Vault at **www.vault.com** for insider company profiles, expert advice, career message boards, expert resume reviews, the Vault Job Board and more.

VAULT CAREER LIBRARY

287

pursuing sales and trading opportunities abroad must be able to demonstrate local language proficiency, and a strong desire to make a long-term commitment to the region. Each of these firms has recently also offered summer internship opportunities, but these programs are less established than the New York-based opportunities, and therefore shouldn't be counted on as a stable source of MBA hiring demand.

Associate pay: to infinity and beyond

Sales and trading associates will start at about the same base pay as their investment banking counterparts. The going rate has held up around $80,000 to $85,000 per year plus an end of year bonus of $20,000 to $30,000. While signing bonuses were the norm during the bull market of the late 1990s, they are now rare. Salaries increase primarily through performance bonuses, especially if you've become a position trader for the firm. Bonuses are normally computed as a percentage of the trading revenue you generate (or commission dollars that you generate if you're a salesperson), so depending on how cheap or generous your firm is, this number can be normally expected to fluctuate between 0 percent and 10 percent in any given year.

If you make $10 million for the firm, however, don't expect to receive a cool million for your efforts. Wall Street firms are highly conscious of expense control, and the largest expense item is compensation. To keep compensation expense at or below 50 percent of revenue, investment banks hand out compensation packages that include among other things, cash, stock options and restricted stock. Generous stock option grants are a non-cash form of compensation that doesn't hit the income statement, but aren't quite as motivating as cash. Another game in the compensation is the granting of restricted stock. This is a major component of pay as you move up the ladder, and you can only convert this compensation into cash according to a vesting schedule that stretches out for years.

Finally, keep in mind that investment banks are operating across all markets and products sectors. In a simplified world, the investment bank operates a bond desk and an equity desk. The bond traders make more money and the salespeople sell more bonds when the economy is in recession. On the other hand, the stock-traders make more money and the sales-traders sell more stock when the economy is robust. What happens at the end of the year when the compensation committee is determining how big the bond bonus pool and the equity bonus pool should be? Most firms tend to cross-subsidize the equity desk with the bond desk's revenue when the stock market falls on hard times, and to return the favor to the bond desk when the bond market falls on hard times. This makes sense at the corporate level (preventing mass defections, for example), but the immediate consequence to the stock-trader that generated $10 million in revenue and is expecting a $1 million check is that he'll see a lot less than $1 million. The small consolation to the expectant stock-trader is that when he makes substantially less than his budget, maybe the bond desk will stuff his stocking.

The winding promotion road in S&T

The path to promotion on a sales and trading desk is less standard than it is in investment banking. Investment banking analysts really don't have much too look forward to except perhaps a third year and then back to business school or some other career. By contrast, undergraduate analysts who have a demonstrated ability to add value to a desk have the potential to move up without an MBA.

One common scenario that unfolds is that after several years, the restless undergraduate analyst decides to apply to business school and gets accepted. If this analyst is a prized employee, then the boss might offer the analyst a promotion to associate in order to keep the analyst on the desk.

Promotions on trading desks are generally not much to celebrate, except that it leads to potentially higher pay. Investment banking associates can look forward to moving out of the bullpen and into a real office with a secretary. Salespeople and traders settle for better accounts and more trading responsibility. The focus of promotions shouldn't be to achieve a particular title (vice president, director, managing director, etc.), but rather, to earn real sales and trading responsibility. Of course, if you do your job well, you'll be duly compensated and promoted, but after reaching a level of significant responsibility, you shouldn't be expecting to get promoted every couple of years.

Employer Directory

Arnhold S. Bleichroeder
1345 Avenue of the Americas
44th Floor
New York, NY 10105-4300
Phone: (212) 698-3000
Fax: (212) 299-4360
Toll free: (800) 800-9006
www.asbai.com

Banc of America Investment Services, Inc.
Gateway Village, Building 900
900 West Trade Street
Charlotte, NC 28255
Phone: (800) 926-1111
www.baisidirect.com

Barclays Capital
The North Colonnade
Canary Wharf
London, E14 4BB
United Kingdom
Phone: +44-20-76-23-23-23
www.barcap.com

Bernard L. Madoff Securities
885 3rd Avenue
New York, NY 10022
Phone: (212) 230-2424
Fax: (212) 486-8178
www.madoff.com

BMO Capital Markets
100 King Street West
1 First Canadian Place
Toronto, Ontario M5X 1H3
Canada
Phone: (416) 359-4000
www.bmocm.com

Cantor Fitzgerald
110 East 59th Street
New York, NY 10022
Phone: (212) 938-5000
Fax: (212) 829-5280
www.cantor.com

Charles Schwab Corporation
120 Kearny Street
San Francisco, CA 94104
Phone: (415) 636-7000
Fax: (415) 636-9820
Toll free: (800) 648-5300
www.schwab.com

CIBC World Markets
161 Bay Street, BCE Place
Toronto, Ontario M5J 2S8
Canada
Phone: (416) 594-7000
Fax: (416) 956-6958
ww.cibcwm.com

Citigroup's Global Corporate and Investment Bank (formerly Salomon Smith Barney)
388 Greenwich Street
New York, NY 10013
Phone: (212) 816-6000
www.citigroupcib.com

Collins Stewart LLC
350 Madison Avenue
New York, NY 10017
Phone: (212) 389-8000
Fax: (212) 389-8810
www.collinsstweart.com/USBusiness

Crédit Agricole S.A.
91-93 Boulevard Pasteur
75015 Paris
France
Phone: +33-1-43-23-52-02
Fax: +33-1-43-23-34-48
www.credit-agricole-sa.fr

Credit Suisse
11 Madison Avenue
New York, NY 10010-3629
Phone: (212) 325-2000
Fax: (212) 325-6665
www.credit-suisse.com/us/en

Daiwa Securities Group Inc.
6-4, Otemachi 2-chome, Chiyoda-ku
Tokyo, 100-8101
Japan
Phone: +81-3-32-43-21-00
Fax: +81-3-32-42-09-55
www.daiwa.jp

Deutsche Bank
Theodor-Heuss-Allee 7-
60486 Frankfurt
Germany
Phone: +49-69-910-00
Fax: +49-69-910-34-225
www.deutsche-bank.de

Dresdner Bank AG
Jürgen-Ponto-Platz 1
D-60329 Frankfurt
Germany
Phone: +49-69-263-0
Fax: +49-69-263-15839
www.dresdner-bank.com

Ferris Baker Watts
100 Light Street
Baltimore, MD 21202
Phone: (410) 685-2600
Fax: (410) 468-2746
Toll free: (800) 436-2000
www.fbw.com

Fox-Pitt Kelton
420 Fifth Avenue, 5th Floor
New York, NY 10018
Phone: (212) 687-1105
Fax: (212) 599-2723
www.fpk.com

Friedman Billings Ramsey
1001 19th Street North
Arlington, VA 22209
Phone: (703) 312-9500
Fax: (703) 312-9501
Toll free: (800) 846-5050
www.fbr.com

Visit Vault at **www.vault.com** for insider company profiles, expert advice, career message boards, expert resume reviews, the Vault Job Board and more.

VAULT CAREER LIBRARY   289

Employer Directory, cont.

Goldman Sachs
85 Broad Street
New York, NY 10004
Phone: (212) 902-1000
Fax: (212) 902-3000
www.goldmansachs.com

Group One Trading
220 Bush Street, Suite 360
San Francisco, CA 94104-3533
Phone: (415) 283-3410

JP Morgan Chase
270 Park Avenue
New York, NY 10017
Phone: (212) 270-6000
Fax: (212) 270-2613
www.jpmorganchase.com

Janney Montgomery Scott
1801 Market Street
Philadelphia, PA 19103-1675
Phone: (215) 665-6000
Fax: (215) 564-9597
Toll free: (800) 526-6397
www.janneys.com

Jefferies & Co.
212 East 47th Street, Apartment 15F
New York, NY 10017-2124
Phone: (212) 284-2550
www.jefco.com

Johnson Rice & Co
639 Loyola Avenue, Suite 2775
New Orleans, LA 70113-7115
Phone: (504) 525-3767

Kaufman Bros., L.P.
800 Third Avenue, 30th Floor
New York, NY 10022
Phone: (212) 292-8100
Fax: (212) 292-8101
www.kbro.com

Ladenburg Thalmann
4400 Biscayne Boulevard, 12th Floor
Miami, FL 33137
Phone: (305) 572-4100
Fax: (305) 572-4199
Toll free: (800) 523-8425
www.ladenburg.com

Legg Mason
100 Light Street
Baltimore, MD 21202
Phone: (877) 534-4627
www.leggmason.com

Miller Tabak & Co
331 Madison Avenue, 12th Floor
New York, NY 10017-5107
Phone: (212) 370-0040

Morgan Stanley
1585 Broadway
New York, NY 10036
Phone: (212) 761-4000
www.morganstanley.com

Oscar Gruss & Son
74 Broad Street, 5th Floor
New York, NY 10004-2210
Phone: (212) 952-1100

Piper Jaffray & Co.
800 Nicollet Mall, Suite 800
Minneapolis, MN 55402-7020
Phone: (800) 333-6000
www.piperjaffray.com

Prudential Securities
751 Broad Street
Newark, NJ 07102-3777
Phone: (973) 802-6000
Fax: (973) 802-4479
Toll free: (800) 346-3778
www.prudential.com

RBC Capital Markets
1 Liberty Plaza, Room 300
New York, NY 10006-1404
Phone: (212) 858-7000
www.rbccm.com

Robert W. Baird
777 East Wisconsin Avenue
Milwaukee, WI 53201
Phone: (414) 765-3500
Toll free: (800) 792-2473
www.rwbaird.com

Sanders Morris Harris
600 Travis, Suite 3100
Houston, TX 77002
Phone: (713) 993-4610
Fax: (713) 224-1101
Toll free: (800) 900-4611
www.smhgroup.com

Sanford C. Bernstein
1345 Avenue of the Americas
New York, NY 10105
Phone: (212) 486-5800
Fax: (212) 969-6189
www.bernstein.com

SunTrust Banks, Inc
303 Peachtree Street NE
Atlanta, GA 30308
Phone: (404) 588-7711
Fax: (404) 332-3875
Toll free: (800) 786-8787
www.suntrust.com

Susquehanna International Group, LLP
401 City Avenue, Suite 220
Bala Cynwyd, PA 19004
Phone: (610) 617-2600
Fax: (610) 617-2689
www.sig.com

Thomas Weisel Partners
1 Montgomery Tower
1 Montgomery Street
San Francisco, CA 94104
Phone: (415) 364-2500
Fax: (415) 364-2695
www.tweisel.com

Employer Directory, cont.

UBS
Bahnhofstrasse 45
CH-8098 Zurich
Switzerland
Phone: +41-44-234-11-11
Fax: +41-44-239- 91-11
www.ubs.com

Van der Moolen Holding N.V.
Keizersgracht 307
1016 ED Amsterdam
Netherlands
Phone: +31-20-535-6789
Fax: +31-20-535-6788
www.vandermoolen.com

Wedbush Morgan Securities
1000 Wilshire Boulevard
Los Angeles, CA 90017
Phone: (213) 688-8000
Fax: (213) 688-6652
www.wedbush.com

William Blair & Co.
222 West Adams Street
Chicago, IL 60606
Phone: (312) 236-1600
Fax: (312) 368-9418
Toll free: (800) 621-0687
www.williamblair.com

Visit Vault at **www.vault.com** for insider company profiles, expert advice, career message boards, expert resume reviews, the Vault Job Board and more.

VAULT CAREER LIBRARY   291

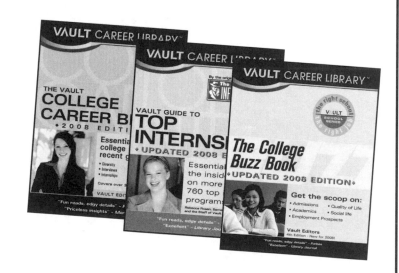

Technology Consulting

The State of Technology Consulting

IT services surge

For the past few years, the technology consulting industry has seen an upswing in spending. After a period of stagnation resulting from the stock market downturn of 2000 and 2001, the economy started to pick up again in 2004. The positive economic environment encouraged companies to invest in IT improvements to help boost profits and spur business growth. Over 2006 and 2007, tech consulting firms experienced a return to prosperity, thanks to clients with ample IT budgets. In addition, a wave of regulatory changes—like Basel II and China's State Administration of Foreign Exchange in 2006—opened up significant opportunities in the financial services and banking sectors, driving up demand for tech consulting services.

Cautious clients

Though work has remained steady at most consulting firms, a mild recession after 2007's subprime mortgage crisis once again put businesses in a precarious position. Sluggish economic growth and fears of a crash are forcing companies to be more cost-conscious about spending on "nonessentials" like upgraded data systems. In the short term, industry analysts estimate a slight year-over-year decline in the demand for IT services from 2007. Analysts also predict that more conservative budgets and the ability of providers to broaden their service offerings may push fee levels down in 2008.

Over the long term, however, the outlook is more favorable. Globalization, a growing postmerger integration market and increasing industry deregulation around the world are helping to keep demand for tech consulting consistent. The industry is expected to increase globally at a compound annual growth rate of 5.2 percent through 2010, according to research firm IDC. Consulting projects that support core business operations, such as infrastructure or regulatory requirements, are areas that will likely remain in high demand. Security consulting, custom application development and web services consulting are also promising areas for tech consultants.

Change is good

Facing a market that's sensitive to economic shifts, tech consulting firms must continually adapt their strategies to suit the current marketplace. With the gradual recovery of the consulting industry since 2004, clients have become more sophisticated and have specific demands relating to their industry sector, forcing consulting firms to really prove their worth. Clients also tend to be more price-sensitive, and want to know what the bottom-line savings will be before projects begin. As a result, consultancies have had to concentrate on services that add tangible value and boost profit margins. To protect profits, consulting firms have been aiming for short-term projects that require less labor and expense, like implementation, as well as higher profit margin services, like taking over a client's entire business processes in HR or finance.

In addition, consulting firms have gone to greater lengths to differentiate their services, positioning themselves as specialists on the cutting edge, rather that as generic software implementers. Adding new information technologies to their portfolio also helps larger firms extend their target client base. Instead of investing time and money into expensive R&D, consultancies can acquire smaller firms with a niche technology specialty. For example, in 2007, Accenture purchased California-based defense firm Maxim Systems to bulk up its services in that area. Cisco has proven to be a master of this maneuver, having snapped up over 120 smaller companies in its 24-year history.

Visit Vault at www.vault.com for insider company profiles, expert advice, career message boards, expert resume reviews, the Vault Job Board and more.

VAULT CAREER LIBRARY 293

EMEA takes the lead

The tech consulting client makeup is also undergoing a geographic shift. Today, the Europe, the Middle East and Africa region has emerged as a promising market, with the rate of demand quickly eclipsing that of North America. Industry observers predict that by 2009, EMEA will outpace the Americas as the largest IT services market in the world—in 2007, the region had already jumped ahead of the Americas in outsourcing activity.

Asia is also rising in prominence as a major market for tech consulting services. Springboard Research forecasts that the Asia Pacific IT services market will grow annually at 10.5 percent over the next five years, hitting $55 billion by 2011.

Outsourcing's steady climb

Outsourcing remains a core service offering that helps keep profit margins buoyant. While overall demand for IT consulting may slow, the need for IT outsourcing is expected to increase 9 percent in 2008, according to Forrester Research. When outsourcing took off in the late 1990s, these services revolved around cheap call centers and low-cost data services for clients that needed to find a way to cut costs. Now, outsourcing is an almost $400 billion industry, accounting for a major chunk of overall IT consulting revenue, and often involves more complex projects, such as supporting a company's entire IT infrastructure from an offshore location. Since 2006, consulting firms are also getting a boost from a second round of work resulting from mature outsourcing projects. Business process outsourcing is the fastest-growing services sector in the market, with clients also demanding applications development and maintenance.

Although the outsourcing industry is still expanding globally, 2007 saw a decrease in U.S. total contract value for the first time in five years, a result of both smaller contracts and the slowdown of outsourcing business from the Americas.

India dominates

Since the outsourcing craze began, India has dominated the market as the go-to location for lower cost labor. A McKinsey Global Institute report indicates that India's outsourcing industry revenue will expand to $60 billion by 2010. The country's skilled labor market and large English-speaking population have given India a distinct advantage over other developing countries, and American consulting firms continue to pour resources and talent into it to capitalize on the well-established market. In 2007, IBM announced its intention to invest $6 billion in India over the next three years, and in 2008, Cisco announced plans for a talent development program there, aiming to increase its staff in the country six-fold to 360,000 in the next five years. Currently, IBM has almost one-fifth of its employees—about 73,000—in the country, and Accenture has over 37,000 staff there, making India home to its largest workforce. EDS currently has about 32,000 employees in India, thanks in part to its acquisition of Bangalore-based BPO firm MphasiS in 2006.

The country's BPO market is still growing steadily, keeping tech consulting firms supplied with a stream of engagements. NASSCOM predicts that the BPO market will soar to $50 billion from its current $11 billion by 2012. But over the past few years, India has developed beyond its former reputation as strictly a BPO and call center location; recently, the country has experienced a surge in M&A activity, and has started to become a player in international acquisitions. In 2007, Indian firms made over 75 foreign acquisitions, creating a stream of postmerger work in the financial services sector for consultants.

Where will they go next?

While the labor market in India matures, salaries are inching upward at a rate of 15 percent per year, making it more expensive for consulting firms to hire local staff—at this rate, analysts say the country may soon price itself out of the offshoring market. In addition, India faces an impending shortage of workers with IT skills. A 2007 report from Dun & Bradstreet estimated that the country will need half-a-million more tech workers by 2009 to meet expected demand. China, which has also risen recently as an outsourcing hotspot, is facing a similar deficiency in skilled labor.

As such, Western firms have started looking beyond India and China, eyeing other emerging countries for outsourcing opportunities. Indonesia, Vietnam, the Philippines and Eastern European nations are gaining popularity as viable outsourcing centers. In fact, industry observers identify Vietnam as the real up-and-comer, and predict that the country will surpass India and China as a premier outsourcing site by 2012. Thanks to recent economic deregulation and access to the World Trade Organization, companies are now more able to take advantage of Vietnam's skilled labor and low costs.

The race to the States

As consulting firms compete for the most lucrative engagements, those that were once outsourcing shops are making inroads into the high-end IT consulting market. Outsourcing firms looking to move into higher-profit services are heading to the U.S. and Europe to gain regional and industry traction, and to get closer to their customers. Tata Consultancy Services recently increased its U.S. presence with a new development center in Cincinnati, Ohio, opened in March 2008. The firm has not been shy about its intention to steal business from the traditional consulting giants—like EDS and BearingPoint Inc. Management & Technology Consultants—and already has 50 U.S. offices and a headquarters in New York. In August 2007, India-based Wipro acquired U.S. infrastructure management vendor InfoCrossing. The firm also plans to recruit about 500 employees for a new development center in Atlanta, Ga., and it has two more U.S. development centers in the works. Satyam has also been hunting for acquisitions in the U.S., since about 60 percent of its business already comes from North America.

For the most profitable tech engagements, there's no doubt that American firms have the longstanding relationships it takes to establish client trust—which gives them a distinct advantage over newcomers. This could soon change as competitors willing to undercut these firms' prices establish a stronger presence in the West.

Software, strategy and more

Another rising trend in the tech consulting world is the merging of business consulting and IT services. Many companies are wising up to the fact that technology plays an essential role in meeting strategic goals; in searching for solutions to business problems, clients are increasingly turning to consulting firms that can offer nontechnical solutions as well as IT systems. To expand into business consulting, tech firms often acquire a strategy consulting firm. EDS was one of the first firms to start this trend when it purchased A.T. Kearney in 1995 (and subsequently sold it in a management buyout in January 2006). And until IBM took over PricewaterhouseCoopers' strategy consulting practice in 2002, it had focused primarily on systems integration.

Likewise, strategy firms are recently embracing services like outsourcing, formerly considered the domain of software implementers and tech shops. Bain, considered a strategy-heavy house, now offers IT business alignment and outsourcing. The firm also publishes research on technology trends to get the word out about its IT expertise. Even McKinsey, long established as an exclusive strategy player, is vying for a piece of the lucrative tech market by offering outsourcing, IT architecture and other business technology services. Though niche firms have their place in the technology industry, the biggest players have a leg up in winning clients who wish to deal with a firm that can seamlessly weave customized IT solutions and software into business strategy.

Tempting talent

Against the backdrop of a shaky economy, the IT consulting industry is moving forward with aggressive hiring—a clear sign of optimism that the demand for IT services will remain steady. Tech talent is in short supply, and new graduates with the right background are finding that they have their pick of the consulting litter. In many cases, employers competing for new MBAs have had to boost salary offers and relocation payouts, in addition to signing bonuses.

Visit Vault at **www.vault.com** for insider company profiles, expert advice, career message boards, expert resume reviews, the Vault Job Board and more.

VAULT CAREER LIBRARY   295

Though demand for talent is high, salary increases to are moderate, averaging about 4 to 5 percent. To compensate for these moderate bumps in compensation, consulting firms are becoming more competitive and creative with traditional benefits packages. And in an era of fewer IPOs than in previous decades, applicants are more concerned with overall compensation than with earning shares in a company. Employee-friendly options such as flexible work schedules or on-site conveniences (such as Tata's on-campus laundry service and gym) help win over the best candidates.

Realistic recruiting online

Consulting firms are also getting more creative in their recruiting practices to reel in the cream of the crop. Recently, the digital media world Second Life has become an outlet for firms to conduct "virtual recruiting," hold information sessions and even "meet" and interview candidates (or their avatars). PA Consulting Group implemented Second Life recruiting in 2007, and plans to increase its virtual recruiting presence in the future. IBM Global Services also uses Second Life in its recruiting efforts, as well as for new-hire training and orientation. Firms appreciate that Second Life broadens the candidate pool and provides a low-cost way to interact with potential new hires all over the world.

The combo candidate

While it is a job-seeker's market, IT consulting firms are very choosy about picking hires with the right set of skills. Particularly desirable candidates are those with experience in web development, database management, wireless networking and applications engineering. Firms are also more concerned now about applicants' business savvy, as the line between IT services and business consulting is becoming increasingly blurred. Candidates with a deep understanding of business concepts as well as IT skills are the top picks for the most selective consulting firms.

A Day in the Life: IT Consultant

Kristine is a consultant at a major consulting firm with many IT consulting engagements. Her role is team lead of the design and developer for eight web-based training modules. She has five analysts on her team.

4:30 a.m. It's Monday morning. Time to wake up. There's time for a shower this Monday morning—such luxury!

5:30 a.m. I am in a cab on the way to the airport, making a mental list of anything that could have been forgotten. I ask the cabbie to tune the radio to NPR.

6:10 a.m. At the airport I go up to the self check-in kiosk. I take the boarding pass and head down to the security line, laptop and small carry-on in hand.

6:25 a.m. At security, I remove my laptop from my bag and place it on the tray. I move through security quickly. No alarms beep.

6:35 a.m. After a quick stop at Starbucks, I arrive at the gate. I say hello to three other members of my project and check out the other passengers I see every week on this Monday morning flight. I board early along with the other premier fliers— one of the perks of being a frequent traveler.

7 a.m. The flight departs on time. Yay! I relish my window seat close to the front of the airplane.

8 a.m. The beverage cart wakes me up. I ask for coffee and scan *The Wall Street Journal* as I drink.

9:30 a.m. I arrive at my destination and share a ride with my fellow consultants to the project site.

10:30 a.m. At the project site. As I crawl underneath my desk to hook my laptop to the client LAN connection, one of my team members informs me that he still hasn't received feedback from his client reviewer. That's not good news.

11 a.m. After checking and responding to e-mail, I call my team member's client reviewer. The reviewer agrees to send me the team member feedback on the training material by noon tomorrow.

11:15 a.m. I remind the team of the 1 p.m. status meeting. I've got to start it on time—I have a meeting downtown at 3:15 p.m. I start to review the content outlines for the training modules.

12 p.m. I scurry, along with two teammates, to get sandwiches at a nearby eatery. Mine is turkey and cheddar.

12:20 p.m. Back at my desk, I get a call from the project manager, who is working at a client site in another state. He tells me that clients in the training department are nervous about their job security and asks that the entire team be sensitive to how the training changes may affect the training positions in the organization.

1 p.m. The team holds a status meeting. I pass on the message from the project manager. Each member discusses what has been completed and what he or she expects to complete that week. Two other team members are having difficulty obtaining feedback from their client reviewers. We all brainstorm ideas on how to obtain the feedback.

2 p.m. I finish up the meeting and get directions to my meeting downtown.

2:40 p.m. Off to the 3:15 p.m. meeting.

3:15 p.m. I meet the head of the training department to discuss the training courses. He calls in a close associate who has opinions on how the courses should be organized. The associate wants to add several more web-based training modules. I politely suggest that part of the additional subject matter could be covered in the modules that have been agreed to in the scope of the project. We all sketch out the course structure on a white board.

4:45 p.m. Back at the project site. I check in with my team members via e-mail.

5:45 p.m. I complete a draft of the course flow in PowerPoint and send it to the client and my manager for review.

7 p.m. I have reviewed 50 percent of the course outlines. It's time to head back to the hotel. I stop by a local diner for a quick dinner.

8:30 p.m. Time for a workout in the hotel gym.

9:15 p.m. I'm ready for bed. Clothes for the next day are hanging in the closet. The alarm clock is set to 6:30 a.m.

10:30 p.m. I go to sleep.

Visit Vault at **www.vault.com** for insider company profiles, expert advice, career message boards, expert resume reviews, the Vault Job Board and more.

VAULT CAREER LIBRARY 297

Employer Directory

Accenture
1345 Avenue of the Americas
New York, NY 10105
Phone: (917) 452-4400
Fax: (917) 527-9915
www.accenture.com

Affiliated Computer Services, Inc. (ACS)
2828 North Haskell Avenue
Dallas, TX 75204
Phone: (214) 841-6111
Fax: (214) 821-8315
www.acs-inc.com

Ajilon Consulting
210 West Pennsylvania Avenue
Suite 650
Towson, MD 21204
Phone: (410) 821-0435
Fax: (410) 828-0106
www.ajilonconsulting.com

Alliance Consulting Group
Six Tower Bridge
181 Washington Street, Suite 350
Conshohocken, PA 19428
Phone: (610) 234-4301
Fax: (610) 234-4302
www.allianceconsulting.com

Atos Origin
5599 San Felipe, Suite 300
Houston, TX 77056
Phone: (713) 513-3000
Fax: (713) 403-7204

Tour les Miroirs - Bat C
18, avenue d'Alsace
92926 Paris La Défense 3 Cedex
France
Phone: +33-1-55-91-20-00
Fax: +33-1-55-91-20-05
www.atosorigin.com/en-us

BearingPoint, Inc., Management and Technology Consultants
1676 International Drive
McLean, VA 22102
Phone: (703) 747-3000
Fax: (703) 747-8500
www.bearingpoint.com

Booz Allen Hamilton
8283 Greensboro Drive
McLean, VA 22102
Phone: (703) 902-5000
Fax: (703) 902-3333
www.boozallen.com

BT Global Services
350 Madison Avenue
New York, NY 10017
Phone: (646) 487-7400
Fax: (646) 487-3370
www.btglobalservices.com

Bull
296 Concord Road
Billerica, MA 01821
Phone: (978) 294-6000
Fax: (978) 294-7999
www.bull.com

Capgemini
623 Fifth Avenue, 33rd Floor
New York, NY 10022
Phone: (212) 314-8000
Fax: (212) 314-8001
www.us.capgemini.com

Place de l'Étoile
11 rue de Tilsitt
75017 Paris
France
Phone: +33-1-47-54-50-00
Fax: +33-1-47-54-50-25
www.apc.capgemini.com

CGI
4050 Legato Road
Fairfax, VA 22033
Phone: (703) 267-8000
Fax: (703) 267-5111

1130 Sherbrooke Street West
Montreal, Quebec H3A 2M8
Canada
Phone: (514) 841-3200
Fax: (514) 841-3299
www.cgi.com

CIBER, Inc.
5251 DTC Parkway, Suite 1400
Greenwood Village, CO 80111
Phone: (303) 220-0100
Toll free: (800) 242-3899
www.ciber.com

Cisco Systems, Inc.
170 West Tasman Drive
San Jose, CA 95134
Phone: (408) 526-4000
Toll free: (800) 553-NETS
www.cisco.com

Cognizant Technology Solutions
500 Frank W. Burr Boulevard
Teaneck, NJ 07666
Phone: (201) 801-0233
Fax: (201) 801-0243
www.cognizant.com

Computer Sciences Corporation
2100 East Grand Avenue
El Segundo, CA 90245
Phone: (310) 615-0311
www.csc.com

Covansys Corporation
32605 West Twelve Mile Road
Farmington Hills, MI 48334
Phone: (248) 688-2088
Fax: (248) 488-2089
www.covansys.com

Employer Directory, cont.

CTG
800 Delaware Avenue
Buffalo, NY 14209
Phone: (716) 882-8000
Fax: (716) 887-7464
www.ctg.com

Deloitte LLP
1633 Broadway, 35th Floor
New York, NY 10019
Phone: (212) 492-4500
Fax: (212) 492-4743
www.deloitte.com

Detica
Surrey Research Park
Guildford ,Surrey
GU2 7YP
United Kingdom
Phone: +44-14-83-81-60-00
Fax: +44-14-83-81-61-44
www.detica.com

**Diamond Management &
Technology Consultants, Inc.**
John Hancock Center
875 North Michigan Avenue
Suite 3000
Chicago, IL 60611
Phone: (312) 255-5000
Fax: (312) 255-6000
www.diamondconsultants.com

EDS
5400 Legacy Drive
Plano, TX 75024
Phone: (972) 605-6000
Toll free: (800) 566-9337
www.eds.com

Getronics
290 Concord Road
Billerica, MA 01821
Phone: (978) 625-5000
www.getronics.com

GFI Informatique
15, rue Beaujon
75008 Paris
France
Phone: +33-1-53-93-44-39
Fax: +33-1-53-93-44-91
www.gfi.fr

Fujitsu Consulting
343 Thornall Street, Suite 630
Edison, NJ 08837
Phone: (732) 549-4100
Fax: (732) 632-1826
www.fujitsu.com/us/services/consulting

HP Services
3000 Hanover Street
Palo Alto, CA 94304
Phone: (650) 857-1501
Fax: (650) 857-5518
www.hp.com/hps

**IBM Global Technology
Services**
New Orchard Road
Armonk, NY 10504
Phone: (914) 499-1900
Fax: (914) 765-7382
www.ibm.com/consulting/services

Infosys Consulting Inc.
6607 Kaiser Drive
Fremont, CA 94555
Phone: (510) 742-3000
Fax: (510) 742-3090
www.infosysconsulting.com

**Interactive Business Systems,
Inc.**
2625 Butterfield Road
Oak Brook, IL 60523
Phone: (630) 571-9100
Fax: (630) 571-9110
www.ibs.com

Keane, Inc.
210 Porter Drive, Suite 315
San Ramon, CA 94583
Phone: (925) 838-8600
Fax: (925) 838-7138
Toll free: (877) 88-KEANE
www.keane.com

Lockheed Martin Corporation
6801 Rockledge Drive
Bethesda, MD 20817
Phone: (301) 897-6000
Fax: (301) 897-6704
www.lockheedmartin.com

Logica
10375 Richmond Avenue, Suite 1000
Houston, TX 77042
Phone: (713) 954-7000
Fax: (713) 785-0880
www.logicacmg.com

McKinsey & Company
55 East 52nd Street
New York, NY 10022
Phone: (212) 446-7000
Fax: (212) 446-8575
www.mckinsey.com

Oracle Consulting
500 Oracle Parkway
Redwood Shores, CA 94065
Phone: (650) 506-7000
www.oracle.com/consulting/index.html

PA Consulting Group
4601 North Fairfax Drive, Suite 600
Arlington, VA 22203
Phone: (571) 227-9000
Fax: (571) 227-9001

123 Buckingham Palace Road
London, SW1W 9SR
United Kingdom
Phone: +44-20-77-30-90-00
Fax: +44-20-73-33-50-50
www.paconsulting.com

Visit Vault at **www.vault.com** for insider company profiles, expert advice,
career message boards, expert resume reviews, the Vault Job Board and more.

V/\ULT CAREER LIBRARY

299

Employer Directory, cont.

Perot Systems
2300 West Plano Parkway
Plano, TX 75075
Phone: (972) 577-0000
Fax: (972) 340-6100
Toll free: (888) 31-PEROT
www.perotsystems.com

The Revere Group
An NTT DATA Company
325 North LaSalle Street, Suite 325
Chicago, IL 60610
Phone: (312) 873-3400
Fax: (312) 873-3500
www.reveregroup.com

SAIC
10260 Campus Point Drive
San Diego, CA 92121
Phone: (858) 826-6000
www.saic.com

Sapient
25 First Street
Cambridge, MA 02141
Phone: (617) 621-0200
Fax: (617) 621-1300
www.sapient.com

Satyam Computer Services Ltd.
8500 Leesburg Pike, Suite 201
Vienna, VA 22182
Phone: (703) 734-2100
Fax: (703) 734-2110
www.satyam.com

Siemens IT Solutions and Services, Inc.
101 Merritt 7
Norwalk, CT 06851
Phone: (203) 642-2300
www.usa.siemens.com/it-solutions

Smartronix, Inc.
22685 Three Notch Road
California, MD 20619
Phone: (301) 737-2800
Fax: (301) 866-0528
www.smartronix.com

Tata Consultancy Services
101 Park Avenue, 26th Floor
New York, NY 10178
Phone: (212) 557-8038
Fax: (212) 867-8652
www.tcs.com

Telcordia
One Telcordia Drive
Piscataway, NJ 08854
Phone: (732) 699-2000
www.telcordia.com

Unisys
Unisys Way
Blue Bell, PA 19424
Phone: (215) 986-4011
www.unisys.com

Wipro Ltd.
Doddakannelli Sarjapur Road
Bangalore, Karnataka 560 035
India
Phone: +91-80-844-0011
Fax: +91-80-844-0256
www.wipro.com

Telecommunications

Industry Overview

We're all connected

In simpler times, the word "telecommunications" might have conjured up an image of a telephone—and not much else. These days, though, the telephone is less the shining symbol of the industry and more an antiquated relic of its humble beginnings. Telecom today is high-tech and mobile, encompassing wireless communication, broadband Internet access, and cable and digital TV; it's also (for now) landline phone service for those who have yet to enter the 21st century.

These varying forms of modern communication aren't even distinct services anymore. The lines have blurred considerably, so while your cell phone downloads the latest music video, you can call your best friend across the country (sans long distance charges) with a PC and an Internet connection. Due to this growing interrelation among telecom products, the sector's main players have spread their reach into Internet and digital television to offer bundled "triple-play" phone, Internet and cable TV subscription packages to customers.

A big (and broad) industry

According to the Telecommunications Industry Association (TIA), in the U.S., total telecom spending rose more than 8 percent during 2007 (to about $1 trillion), and the global telecom market is expected to reach $4.9 trillion by 2011. Much of this growth comes thanks to the ascendancy of the Internet and the accompanying need for high-speed connections. Big Telecom (namely, the three largest telecommunications firms: AT&T, Verizon and Sprint Nextel) holds the trump card with its control of the fiber-optic network that brings broadband and other services into millions of homes.

The sector also includes cable companies (Comcast, Cablevision, et. al.), mobile and network equipment manufacturers (Cisco, 3Com and Black Box, to name a few) and local telephone service providers, but other firms play less obvious roles in helping people share information electronically. Corporations like Loral Space & Communication make the satellites that are used for military communications as well as for broadcasting radio and TV. Other firms, such as Trimble Navigation, focus on GPS technology, which is increasingly being incorporated into mobile phones and other devices.

The bell tolls for AT&T

Established in 1877 as American Bell, AT&T enjoyed the largest share of the telecom industry pie for nearly a century, thanks to the government's belief that the utility constituted a "natural" monopoly. That monopoly crumbled in 1969, when the Federal Communications Commission (FCC) allowed other companies—such as MCI—to play in Ma Bell's sandbox. But monopolies don't disappear overnight. To encourage competition in the long-distance market, the Department of Justice followed up with an antitrust suit against AT&T in 1974, which resulted in the company's division into a long-distance retailer and seven regional Bell operating companies (RBOCs) that competed in the local call market as independent LECs, or local exchange carriers. Originally, these so-called "Baby Bells" consisted of Ameritech, Bell Atlantic, BellSouth, NYNEX, Pacific Telesis, Southwestern Bell (later SBC) and U.S. West. The dissolution of the "old" AT&T was completed in 1984.

The industry thrived after the breakup, exploding into hundreds of smaller competitors, lowering the cost of long-distance calling dramatically. AT&T, which held about 70 percent of the market in 1984, controlled only a third in 2005. (The company bounced back, however, to become the biggest kid on the playground as the "new" AT&T after its buyout by SBC in 2005 and subsequent union with Bell South and Cingular Wireless in 2006.)

Visit Vault at **www.vault.com** for insider company profiles, expert advice, career message boards, expert resume reviews, the Vault Job Board and more.

VAULT CAREER LIBRARY   301

Untangling the wires

As the long-distance market diversified, the local exchange market remained relatively homogenous. The Telecommunications Act of 1996 aimed to change that by deregulating entry into local markets and requiring that the Baby Bells, or incumbent local exchange carriers (ILECs), offer their network elements to smaller competitors (CLECs). The incumbents were required to unbundle their networks for reasonable prices, with the goal of decentralizing the system into a "network of networks." The act also temporarily blocked an RBOC from entering the long-distance market until it could prove sufficient competition in its local territory.

Another provision of the Telecom Act, which granted RBOCs the right to sell cable television services and phone equipment, proved to be a boon. Thanks to those services and the entry of the Baby Bells into long distance, the Act actually had the opposite of its intended effect, allowing the strongest RBOCs to solidify their positions and dominate the market through mergers and acquisitions. Today, just three RBOCs—Verizon, AT&T and Qwest—dominate both local phone service and the DSL (digital subscriber line) market. Until recently there were five such companies, but the market contracted with AT&T's SBC and BellSouth deals.

Meltdown on Wall Street

As mergers and acquisitions activity heated up, Wall Street took notice: investors poured $1.3 trillion into telecom companies in the five years following passage of the Telecom Act, according to Forbes magazine. But with this activity came increased scrutiny and risk. Ultimately, the industry was subject to the same meltdown that hit the rest of the tech sector beginning in late 2000. Again according to Forbes, the industry's market value plummeted by $1 trillion after the Dow took its dive. Mergers also fell by the wayside: in July 2000, a proposed merger between Sprint and WorldCom fell through when the Justice Department filed a lawsuit that attempted to block the deal.

Compounding the gloom, a number of major telecoms had high-profile problems in their accounting departments. About a half-dozen other providers of telecom services began Chapter 11 bankruptcy proceedings in 2002, dumping customers and employees as they went. The biggest by far was WorldCom. The company filed for the largest bankruptcy in U.S. history in July of that year, racking up $41 billion in debt and an estimated $11 billion in fraudulent expenses—leading to a $100 billion loss to shareholders. Even as the company attempted a rebound, it had to contend with scores of class-action lawsuits. Former CEO Bernard J. Ebbers also faced a growing list of federal fraud and conspiracy charges. Accounting firm Citigroup, which had conspired with WorldCom, announced in May 2004 that it would pay $2.65 billion to investors for its role in the scandal. In March 2005, Ebbers was found guilty on all counts and sentenced to 25 years in prison. A year after that, the beleaguered company was virtually disappeared, having been gobbled up by Verizon in a deal worth $8.5 billion.

For its part, in 2003, Sprint reorganized into separate business and consumer units in an effort to save itself $1 billion.

Honing in on each other

Competition that got rolling when telecom firms entered the cable game following the Telecommunications Act has only gained momentum since. In recent years, it's gotten downright ugly, with each industry reaching into the other's picnic basket of products to get at the goodies. Because of the onward and upward march of technology, the wires and signals that bring you cable TV can just as easily bring you phone service, and vice versa. Throw Internet access into the mix and you've got a subscriber feeding frenzy, with phone and cable companies all vying to sell consumers the same services.

In December 2006, the FCC stepped in to referee the melee. In a ruling that handed advantage to the phone companies, the FCC limited to 90 days the amount of time local municipalities could take to grant phone companies a video franchise in their area. Previously, local governments had historically been slow to grant approval of phone companies entering the cable television game.

Neutral tones

The FCC has also stepped into the ring on the issue of "net neutrality," a term that describes the indiscriminate nature of the web, where no sites are more readily accessible than others. The crux of the issue is whether or not broadband access providers (namely, telephone companies) can charge higher rates to certain Internet content providers—creating a toll-lane on the information superhighway and potentially favoring certain sites over others. The FCC launched an inquiry into the issue in May 2007, specifically looking to see if broadband companies had adhered to the "open Internet" principles laid out by the federal organization in 2005. The debate about "net neutrality" continues. In early January 2008, the FCC said it would launch three inquires into the blocking of certain text messages on cellular phone networks, the slowing of P-to-P (peer-to-peer) traffic and what constitutes acceptable broadband traffic management.

Can you hear me now?

It's practically a social norm that every person in possession of even a modest amount of spending money must have a cell phone. The wireless market outpaced long distance for the first time in 2003, according to TIA number crunchers (LD posted $78 billion in spending to the $89 billion spent on wireless services), the same year that the number of wireless users was estimated to be above one billion worldwide. By December 2007, industry analysts reckoned that 84 percent Americans had wireless phones, and it is projected that 100 percent of the adult population will tote cell phones by 2013. During 2007, total wireless revenue was nearly $139 billion, an increase from $113.5 billion the previous year. Americans used 2.1 trillion cell phone minutes in 2007, and they sent 363 billion SMS text messages. And more than 13 percent of U.S. households were wireless-only in 2007, up from 8.4 percent in 2006.

The wireless boom touched off renewed corporate activity within the industry. Competition began to sizzle in late 2003, as the first phase of a federal law allowing "portability"—aka, letting consumers retain their mobile phone numbers when switching carriers—took effect. One notable event was Cingular's $41 billion purchase of rival AT&T Wireless, announced in February 2004, following a fierce bidding war with Vodafone. Deals kept perking right along as Sprint merged with Nextel in August 2005, when the companies were, respectively, the No. 3 and No. 5 wireless carriers.

Down to the wire

Wireline companies have also been involved in M&A activity during recent years. One Communications was born in July 2006 through a merger between three telecom companies—Choice One, CTC and Conversent. And, in December 2006, the FCC approved a merger between AT&T and RBOC BellSouth. But while landlines were once seen as a source of dependable revenue and a way to spread risk, wireless companies have recently spun off their local phone units to function as independent companies. Sprint cleaved off its wireline business in May 2006 under the name Embarq, while Alltel, after beefing up its stock by acquiring Valor Communications, divested the landline unit under the name Windstream in July 2006. This may have something to do with conventional wisdom (and statistics, of course) that says consumer wireline business is on its way out, the victim of wireless cell phones which are convenient, practical, and for some, ultra fashionable. As evidence, Embarq saw its store of access lines shrink by 416,000 (6 percent of its total) in its first year of life, and the scenario has played out similarly over the past few years with scores of companies. While "wireline" companies are now fully invested in selling cable and wireless as well, they'll try to hold onto those customers as long as they can, either by rolling out new ways for home and mobile phones to interact, or by making a bundled package too affordable to pass up.

Off the hook and on the 'Net

Cell phones aren't the only way consumers are making calls these days—Voice over Internet Protocol (VoIP) service, offered by companies like Vonage and Skype, allows any user to turn a personal computer into a telephone by sending "packets" of voice data over a broadband connection, much the same way that other data is sent online. Growth in the VoIP market has

Visit Vault at **www.vault.com** for insider company profiles, expert advice, career message boards, expert resume reviews, the Vault Job Board and more.

VAULT CAREER LIBRARY 303

been exponential: in 2005, the number of Internet phone subscribers in the U.S. went from a mere 1.3 million to 4.5 million, according to industry research group TeleGeography. (The think tank also predicts that by 2010, about 19 million talkers will use VoIP on a regular basis.)

Bypassing questions of local and long distance networks entirely, VoIP providers allow complete number portability—a subscriber in Iowa, for instance, could have a Manhattan area code. (She would be all set if only the Chinatown restaurant with the good kung pao chicken would deliver that far.) The technology is also advantageous in terms of cost. Thanks to the FCC, VoIP is exempt from some of the taxes and regulations with which regular phone carriers are saddled. But—of course— the major telecoms petitioned Capitol Hill, trying to level the playing field.

In June 2005 the FCC ruled that VoIP companies had to contribute, just like any other phone company, to the Universal Service Fund (USF). The program disburses the funds as subsidies to carriers for providing service in rural and low-income areas where costs are high; needless to say, carrier fund contributions are mostly passed on to consumers. (The USF itself has been the source of some controversy—industry watchers note that the program has collected billions of dollars, but its subscriber gains are achieved quite inefficiently.) A panel of the U.S. Court of Appeals for the D.C. Circuit in June 2007 ordered cable companies that offer VoIP service to start paying up—specifically, 64.9 percent of their income is subject to the USF tax, which is usually around 10 percent.

Predators or prey?

During the past five years especially, many telecom firms have grown through acquisitions. In August 2006, Oregon-headquartered Integra purchased competitor Electric Lightwave, making Integra a West Coast powerhouse. Integra got even bigger when the company acquired Eschelon Telecom for $710 million in August 2007. That purchase turned Integra into one of the biggest CLECs in the United States.

At the same time, telecoms have become possible targets. Some analysts have suggested that the next step for Internet biggies such as Microsoft or Google could be the acquisition of telephone businesses (possible regulatory complications notwithstanding). For example, in late 2007 rumors circulated that Google could pick up Sprint Nextel to gain control of WiMax networks. Additionally, companies outside the U.S. have started to express an interest in American telecom businesses. In early 2008, for instance, after Motorola announced plans to spin off its mobile devices division, Videocon, an Indian manufacturer of appliances and electronics, expressed interest in Motorola's handset unit.

Mergers on the rise?

In late May of 2008, Verizon Wireless announced that it would buy Alltel for $5.9, and that it would also pick up $22.2 billion in debt. The merger will make the company the largest mobile phone operator in the United States. The deal is expected to be completed by the end of 2008. Other mergers might be in the works as well, as U.S. mobile phone carriers scramble for a greater share of the cell phone market. The Verizon-Alltel deal makes a merger between Sprint Nextel and TMobile USA more likely. Outside of the United States, Deutsche Telekom agreed to acquire Hellenic Telecommunications, which owns mobile assets in the Balkans, in May 2008. In addition, France Télécom and TeliaSonera, a Swedish-Finish telecom company, have talked about teaming up to form the fourth-largest mobile operator in the world.

Will the credit crunch hurt telecoms?

It's unclear how 2007's subprime mortgage mess will affect the sector. According to Deloitte & Touche's Telecommunications Predictions Report, a wide-reaching economic slowdown may have a negative impact on the industry during 2008 if consumers and businesses reduce tele-spending. However, the document adds that the impact of the subprime correction will likely vary from company to company. Individuals and enterprises may put off buying telecom equipment, but they probably won't stop buying Internet or voice services. Moreover, some businesses may actually invest more in telecommunications as a way to improve productivity. Pre-paid services—in the form of mobile phones and calling cards that are the domain of providers such as MetroPCS, Leap Wireless and IDT Corporation—is one segment of the telecom industry that could thrive during the tough times. The group already caters to lower-income consumers, whose ranks may grow if the economic downturn persists.

Working in the Telecom Industry

A job market roller coaster

The numbers are intimidating: telecom seems to thrive on sudden booms and equally rapid readjustments. By some estimates, the industry slashed 300,000 jobs during the troubled period beginning in late 2000. Telecom firms have started to cut jobs again during the recent economic slump. In January 2008, struggling Sprint Nextel announced that the company would close 125 retail stores and cut 4,000 jobs, some 7 percent of its workforce. Companies also feel compelled to trim excess fat when they merge—the 2006 MCI-Verizon merger, for example, resulted in the elimination of some 7,000 positions. Even with increased demand for telecom services, the U.S. Department of Labor's Bureau of Labor Statistics (BLS) says that employment in the industry is expected to grow by just 5 percent over the period between 2006 and 2016, compared with an 11 percent increase for all industries put together.

But there's still plenty of work out there. According to the BLS, telecom accounted for nearly one million wage and salary jobs in 2006, the latest year for which statistics are available. Of these employees, nearly two-thirds worked in office and administrative support or sales, while most of the rest toiled in maintenance, installation and repair. In 2006, wireline telecommunications carriers accounted for 49 percent of all telecommunications positions. Another 21 percent of jobs were with wireless carriers, and 15 percent were with cable companies and other program distributors. The rest were primarily with satellite telecommunications businesses and equipment and service resellers. The BLS insists that having a diverse and flexible skill set (and keeping it up to date) is crucial in this rapidly changing industry.

Talk the talk

Not surprisingly, excellent communication skills are necessary throughout the telecommunications industry. Customer service agents have to field calls from agitated subscribers with grace and good humor. Technicians have face-to-face contact with customers when installing or fixing network equipment in the field. And then there are the sales reps that pass out smiles and handshakes with aplomb in pursuit of corporate accounts. Communication serves workers well within the office, too, say insiders, because front-line field and call-center workers often serve as an intermediary between subscribers and management.

While job outsourcing continues to be a factor—customer service positions can be handled as easily in New Delhi, India as in Dayton, Ohio—many telecom positions are here to stay. Because all the industry's networks are based on some sort of physical component, whether its cell phone towers or fiber-optic cables, telecom companies will always need a staff to expand, update and maintain those networks. Accordingly, technical positions abound for those toting undergraduate or advanced degrees in electrical engineering and related fields.

Tough sell?

While call-center jobs are ubiquitous and open to those without college degrees (and can offer commission income on top of salary) insiders say there is no upward mobility for people entering the company from this route. Instead, those looking for a sales position in the telecom industry are encouraged to start with an internship after completing their degree. Once your foot is in the door, our sources stress, networking is crucial to rising through a company's ranks. In fact, networking is

Visit Vault at **www.vault.com** for insider company profiles, expert advice, career message boards, expert resume reviews, the Vault Job Board and more.

VAULT CAREER LIBRARY   305

MBA Career Bible • 2009 Edition

Telecommunications

important throughout the telecom world, regardless of your position. As one consultant in the industry puts it, "networking has to be built into your system because that man in the blue suit at that official gathering could well be your next lead for a $1 million consulting engagement."

Work free

In addition to the obvious perks involved with working in the telecom industry (free cable TV, anyone? How about free Internet access and cell phone service while we're at it?), many workers report that flexible scheduling is a valued attribute of their jobs. Salespeople, marketers and managers alike are allowed to budget their time as they see fit. As long as they're doing their part to push the company forward, no one in management usually bats an eye at those extra-long lunches or midday golf sessions. Additionally, telecommuting has become more and more acceptable throughout the industry—perhaps because it's these companies' products that are facilitating web conferences and work-from-home options for the rest of the business world.

This section was excerpted from the *Vault Guide to the Top Telecom Employers.* Get the inside scoop on on telecom careers with:

- **Vault Guides:** *Vault Guide to the Top Telecom Employers*
- **Employee Surveys:** Vault's exclusive employee surveys for Sprint, Verizon, BellSouth, Cingular and other top telecom employers
- **Employer Research:** Company snapshots providing business descriptions and the latest news on top telecom employers
- **Career Services:** Vault Resume and Cover Letter Reviews, rated the "Top Choice" by *The Wall Street Journal* for resume makeovers

Go to www.vault.com

or ask your bookstore or librarian for other Vault titles.

306   VAULT CAREER LIBRARY

© 2008 Vault.com, Inc.

Employer Directory

Alcatel-Lucent
54, rue La Boétie
75008 Paris
France
Phone: +33-1-40-76-10-10
Fax: +33-1-40-76-14-00
www.alcatel-lucent.com

Alltel Corporation
1 Allied Drive
Little Rock, AR 72202
Phone: (501) 905-8000
Fax: (501) 905-5444
www.alltel.com

AT&T Incorporated
175 East Houston Street
San Antonio, TX 78205-2233
Phone: (210) 821-4105
Fax: (210) 351-2187
www.att.com

BellSouth Corporation
1155 Peachtree Street NE
Atlanta, GA 30309-3610
Phone: (404) 249-2000
Fax: (404) 249-2071
www.bellsouth.com

BT Group plc
BT Centre
81 Newgate Street
London, EC1A 7AJ
United Kingdom
Phone: +44-20-73-56-50-00
Fax: +44-20-73-56-55-20
www.btplc.com

Cablevision Systems Corporation
12405 Powerscourt Drive, Suite 100
St. Louis, MO 63131
Phone: (314) 965-0555
Fax: (314) 965-9745
www.cablevision.com

Cellco Partnership
1 Verizon Way
Basking Ridge, NJ 07920
Phone: (908) 559-2000
www.verizonwireless.com

CenturyTel, Inc.
100 CenturyTel Drive
Monroe, LA 71203
Phone: (318) 388-9000
Fax: (318) 388-9064
Toll free: (800) 833-1188
www.centurytel.com

Charter Communications Inc.
12405 Powerscourt Drive, Suite 100
St. Louis, MO 63131-3660
Phone: (314) 965-0555
Fax: (314) 965-9745
www.charter.com

Cincinnati Bell Inc.
221 East 4th Street
Cincinatti, OH 45202
Phone: (513) 397-9900
Fax: (513) 397-5092
www.cincinattibell.com

Comcast Corporation
1 Comcast Center
Philadelphia, PA 19102
Phone: (215) 665-1700
Fax: (215) 981-7790
Toll free: (866) 281-2100
www.comcast.com

Corning Incorporated
1 Riverfront Plaza
Corning, NY 14831-0001
Phone: (607) 974-9000
Fax: (607) 974-5927
www.corning.com

Cox Communications Incorporated
1400 Lake Hearn Drive
Atlanta, GA 30319
Phone: (404) 843-5000
Fax: (404) 843-5975
www.cox.com

CSC Holdings, Inc.
1111 Stewart Avenue
Bethpage, NY 11714
Phone: (516) 803-2300
Fax: (516) 803-3134
www.cablevision.com

The DIRECTV Group, Inc.
2230 East Imperial Hightway
El Segundo, CA 90245
Phone: (310) 964-5000
Fax: (310) 535-5225
www.directv.com

DISH Network Corporation
9601 South Meridian Boulevard
Englewood, CO 80112
Phone: (303) 723-1000
Fax: (303) 723-1999
www.dishnetwork.com

Frontier Communications Company
3 High Ridge Park
Stamford, CT 06905
Phone: (203) 614-5600
Fax: (203) 614-4602
www.czn.com

Level 3 Communications, Inc.
1025 Eldorado Boulevard
Broomfield, CO 80021
Phone: (720) 888-1000
Fax: (720) 888-5085
Toll free: (877) 585-8266
www.level3.com

Mediacom Communications Corporation
100 Crystal Run Road
Middletown, NY 10941
Phone: (845) 695-2600
Fax: (845) 695-2699
www.medicomcc.com

Visit Vault at **www.vault.com** for insider company profiles, expert advice,
career message boards, expert resume reviews, the Vault Job Board and more.

VAULT CAREER LIBRARY   307

Employer Directory, cont.

Motorola, Inc.
1303 East Algonquin Road
Schaumburg, IL 60196
Phone: (847) 576-5000
Fax: (847) 576-5372
Toll free: (800) 262-8509
www.motorola.com

Nortel
195 The West Mall
Toronto, Ontario M9C 5K1
Canada
Phone: (905) 863-7000
www.nortel.com

Orange PLC
50 George Street
London, W1U 7DZ
United Kingdom
Phone: +44-87-03-76-88-88
Fax: +44-20-79-84-16-01
www.orange.co.uk

Qwest Communications International
1801 California Street
Denver, CO 80202
Phone: (800) 899-7780
Fax: (303) 992-1724
www.qwest.com

Scientific-Atlanta, Inc.
5030 Sugarloaf Parkway
Lawrenceville, GA 30044-2689
Phone: (770) 236-5000
Fax: (408) 526-4545
Toll free: (800) 433-6222
www.sciatl.com

Sprint Nextel Corporation
6200 Sprint Parkway
Overland Park, KS 66251
Phone: (703) 443-4000
Toll free: (800) 829-0965
www.sprint.com

T-Mobile USA, Inc.
12920 SE 38th Street
Bellevue, WA 98006
Phone: (425) 378-4000
Fax: (425) 378-4040
Toll free: (800) 318-9270
www.t-mobile.com

Telephone and Data Systems, Inc.
30 North LaSalle Street, Suite 4000
Chicago, IL 60602
Phone: (312) 630-1900
Fax: (312) 630-1908
www.teldta.com

Telephone Electronics Corporation
236 East Capitol Street, Suite 500
Jackson, MS 39201
Phone: (601) 354-9070
Fax: (601) 352-8830
www.tec.com

Time Warner Cable Inc.
One Time Warner Center, North Tower
New York, NY 10019
Phone: (212) 364-8200
Fax: (203) 328-0604
www.timewarnercable.com

United States Cellular Corporation
8410 West Bryn Mawr, Suite 700
Chicago, IL 60631
Phone: (773) 399-8900
Fax: (773) 399-8936
Toll free: (888) 944-9400
www.uscc.com

Verio Inc.
8005 South Chester Street, Suite 200
Englewood, CO 80112
Phone: (303) 645-1900
Fax: (303) 792-5644
www.verio.com

Verizon Communications
140 West Street
New York, NY 10007
Phone: (212) 395-1000
Fax: (212) 571-1897
Toll free: (800) 621-9900
www.verizon.com

Verizon New York Inc.
140 West Street
New York, NY 10007
Phone: (212) 395-2121
Fax: (212) 398-0951
www.verizon.com

Virgin Media Inc.
909 Third Avenue, Suite 2863
New York, NY 10022
Phone: (212) 906-8440
Fax: (212) 397-5943
www.virginmedia.com

Vodafone Group plc
Vodafone House
The Connection
Newbury, Berkshire RG14 2FN
United Kingdom
Phone: +44-1635-33-251
Fax: +44-1635-45-713
www.vodafone.com

Vonage Holdings Corporation
23 Main Street
Holmdel, NJ 07733
Phone: (732) 365-1328
Fax (732) 231-6783
www.vonage.com

XO Communications
11111 Sunset Hills Road
Reston, Virginia 20190-5327
Phone: (703) 547-2000
www.xo.com

Transportation and Airlines

Transportation Industry Overview

Planes, trains and automobiles

Transportation is a vast and dynamic business sector in which time and accuracy—getting people and products where they're going when they need to be there—are two of the crucial factors affecting success and failure. While it's tempting to view the industry as a collection of modes of transport (train, truck, plane and so on), there is much more happening within the sector than mere haulage or people-moving, and it pays to keep an eye on not only the movers, but the shakers (or facilitators) in the industry as well. Where, for example, would boats be without ports, trains without tracks, or planes without airports? Then, of course, there are the companies that merely facilitate transport for others—logistics groups, non-asset based shipping companies and the like, an industry by itself estimated to be worth over $300 billion. And last, but certainly not least, there is the individual to consider. The person who can't afford—or doesn't want—to pay someone else to move their possessions from one place to another but who is willing to do it themselves, given a big enough rental truck. According to Ryder, a firm most well-known for renting trucks to do-it-yourselfers, the U.S. commercial fleet leasing and rental market is worth over $25 billion annually. The case is clear, then; whichever way you turn in transport, from hauling your couch across town to routing a shipment of semiconductors across three continents by several modes of transport, there's money in this game. Squeezing out a profit margin may be getting harder (see below), but for the company that can manage all the variables, the rewards will be there for as long as stuff has somewhere it needs to be. In an increasingly globalized world, with more stuff finding more places to get to, that's shaping up to be a very long time indeed.

Legislating openness

In the last 50 years, there have been two major developments at a political level that have affected the transportation industry—or at least the portion of it that's dedicated to moving freight. Loosely summed up, those developments are deregulation, and NAFTA.

Between 1978 and 1986, the U.S. government passed a series of deregulation legislation (try saying that three times fast) that opened the skies, the railroads and the interstates to country-wide competition, sparking a series of acquisitions, mergers and a pattern of growth across the industry. Trucking companies such as J.B. Hunt found themselves perfectly positioned to take advantage of a glut of new routes, and swiftly established themselves as leading players in the field.

With the new routes, however, came increased logistical concerns, with companies hauling more freight further and further afield, and relying on an ever-increasing number of rigs and drivers to do the hauling—an option that didn't come cheap. Thus, the industry found itself faced with the challenge of finding a more (cost and time) effective way of doing business—by arranging, for example, larger shipments to regional hubs, which could then be distributed on a local basis by trucks. The answer to the conundrum lay in the railroads, and their ability to transport much larger volumes of cargo on a single train than the most ambitious trucker could think about hauling in their rig. A great deal of work lay in conquering the suspicion that naturally arose between two competing modes of transport, but once conquered, the concept of intermodal shipping began to take over from mere trucking alone, with several companies—again including J.B. Hunt—forming partnerships with privately-owned railroads around the company. The next step in the chain, obviously, was shipping and plane cargo to help with international delivery, and pretty soon there were companies that could arrange to ship something pretty much anywhere in the world, utilizing several modes of transport, and never have it leave their possession. That's where companies like the Hub Group and UTi Worldwide come in, posting 2007 revenues of $1.7 billion and $1.5 billion respectively from the logistics sector alone, living proof that there's more to haulage than point A to point B.

Visit Vault at **www.vault.com** for insider company profiles, expert advice, career message boards, expert resume reviews, the Vault Job Board and more.

VAULT CAREER LIBRARY   309

The NAFTA effect

As mentioned above, the passage into law of the North American Free Trade Agreement in 1994 had a significant effect on the U.S. transportation industry. Despite being a controversial piece of legislation (which brought fears that U.S. companies would pack up and head south to take advantage of lower labor rates), the agreement has been—broadly speaking—advantageous for the transportation industry. The increase in cargo rolling across both the Canadian and Mexican borders was a boon to U.S. haulage and logistics firms, some of whom partnered with, acquired, or set up firms in the other North American countries to achieve a cohesive transportation network. Schneider is an example of that, having set up a U.S-based operations center just north of the Mexican border, and partnered with a Mexican firm with a similar facility south of the border, in order to ensure smooth passage of goods between the two nations.

At the time of writing, there is a weighty debate raging at Congressional level about the future of a cross-border pilot program—launched in late 2007—that gives Mexican trucks access to U.S. roads and vice versa. The program, which could further streamline trade between the two nations, has met with some vociferous opposition, most notably in the form of Senator Byron Dorgan (D-N.D.), who has called for it to be abandoned, citing safety concerns. Fuel was added to the fire in the early days of 2008, as Congress voted to block funding to set up a program but did not include language that prevents funding for the current program from continuing. Mexico, meanwhile, has threatened to block U.S. imports if the program is halted, reasoning that the U.S. would be in violation of NAFTA if it did so.

Going private

Of all the trends in all the industries, one of the most notable has been the number of private equity buyouts of transportation firms in the last few years. As *Transport Topics* magazine pointed out midway through 2007, private equity firms acquired 16 for-hire carriers in just the first five months of 2007. Most notable among these was perhaps Swift Transportation's buyout by its founders for $2.7 billion—a deal that saw the largest publicly-traded trucking firm in the U.S. relinquish that title. Later in the year, meanwhile, the industry lost another publicly-traded firm, as $3 billion-a-year U.S. Xpress was taken private by its founders. *Transport Topics* notes that the private-equity moves are likely to increase the amount of capital flowing to those firms, which will in turn increase their competitiveness and market share—crucial factors as economic conditions point to slowdown (with recession a distinct possibility), and a likely short-to-medium term decrease in haulage volume. Those looking for a precedent for the carnage that can be wrought on the industry by a back-sliding economy need look no further than the losses and job cuts that followed the economic downturn at the start of the millennium.

Any port in a storm

Should the slowdown continue, it's not only the haulage companies that will suffer. While recession leading to fewer jobs leading to less spending is a fairly simple cycle that obviously affects consumers and producers, it can easily be extrapolated to less goods being shipped. Again, bad news for haulage companies, easy to identify, but the effect on the facilitators of the transportation industry shouldn't be overlooked either.

While airports such as Houston, Atlanta and LAX have spent heavily over the past few decades to keep up with the pace of change, and ports such as Boston and New York are routinely dealing in millions of tons of cargo every year, their respective balance sheets may also be affected by a downturn in trade—and without the luxury enjoyed by the haulage firms of expansion into emerging markets. Having said that, Dallas-Fort Worth Airport has begun increasing the number of passenger routes it serves, marketing the area in Central America as it seeks to increase its share of the aviation market.

Ordinary Joe

Of course, the beating heart of the transportation industry—its raison d'être—is the ordinary man and woman in the street. Without their (and our) needs, there would be no goods being shipped. No reason for all those trains and planes and trucks. Or public transportation, for that matter—one industry segment that is almost certain to ride out a recession with no loss of customer base. In fact, recession—coupled with rising oil prices and a desire for greener forms of transport—may even see ridership of subways and buses going up as more and more people resort to a cheaper method of getting around. This is great, as long as urban mass transit networks can handle the influx of passengers. New York's MTA, for example, has been running at capacity on some lines for quite some time, and yet is still several years away from opening its long-awaited (some would say mythical) Second Avenue line.

The road ahead

In its most recent report on the transportation and warehousing industry, the Bureau of Labor Statistics projected an increase in jobs of some 11.9 percent between 2004 and 2014, compared to 14.8 percent across all industry sectors. Of those jobs, more than 40 percent were held by truck drivers—a figure that represents the labor intensity of the industry. While technological advances may have increased miles per gallon, infrastructure and many other factors within the industry, the fact remains that one driver can still only cover so many miles per day.

At the end of 2007, mention anything to do with fuel consumption, and two elephants suddenly appear in the room, begging for attention. The first of these is the ever-increasing price of oil, which has consistently stayed at over $100 a barrel in during 2008. The second, of course, is the environment or—more specifically—CO_2 emissions, which global warming hawks claim are in large part responsible for the phenomenon. As one of the major users of gas, and therefore a major producer of CO_2, the transportation industry sits astride both problems, and under considerable pressure to find solutions to them. While many companies have made efforts to introduce more fuel-efficient machines and energy-efficient buildings, the greening of business practices is a long-term investment with high initial costs that may not be realized as savings on the balance sheets for some time to come.

Overall, the outlook for the industry is something of a mixed bag—slower anticipated job growth than other industries and a vulnerability in an uncertain economic climate come set against continued globalization, with many companies expanding into developing markets to keep the balance sheets ticking over. But that's the nature of the industry—be it people, cargo or the times, it just keeps moving.

Airlines Industry Overview

A volatile industry

The airline industry consists of companies that move people and cargo with planes. The International Air Transport Association (IATA) claims that this $470 billion worldwide industry stimulates 8 percent of global GDP through tourism, shipping and business travel. But despite its enormous contribution to world commerce, the industry has historically gone through dizzying booms and alarming busts as it reacts to regulatory changes and economic factors. Airlines are just starting to dig themselves out of the hole caused by September 11th. The IATA says the implementation of security measures has cost the industry $5.6 billion per year. Spats with labor unions, troubles with underfinanced pensions, high jet fuel prices and a string of bankruptcies, from which some carriers are still emerging, have caused further havoc. The July 2007 attack on Glasgow's airport is a reminder that the airline industry is still a target for terrorists. Nevertheless, *The Economist* thinks that once these issues have been resolved (no easy task), the airlines will be in a position to expand.

Visit Vault at **www.vault.com** for insider company profiles, expert advice, career message boards, expert resume reviews, the Vault Job Board and more.

VAULT CAREER LIBRARY   311

Cleared for takeoff

The airline industry took to the skies following the Wright brothers' first successful flight in 1905. As with many new technologies, airplanes were first used extensively by the military—namely, during World War I, for reconnaissance, bombing and aerial combat. Following the war, when the U.S. found itself with a surplus of military aircraft and pilots without much to do, the postal service opted in 1918 to start a transcontinental airmail service, which ran from New York to San Francisco. To keep costs down, 12 spur routes were spun off to independent contractors. Thus the familiar scions of the friendly skies— American Airlines, United Airlines, TWA and Northwest—were born.

Passenger flights didn't become a reality until Ford introduced a 12-seat plane in 1925. The Ford Trimotor made carrying people potentially profitable. Pan American Airways, the first airline with international destinations, was founded in 1927. Remarkably, airlines remained generally profitable during the Great Depression. Under the New Deal, the government subsidized airlines to carry mail. In 1934, however, postal reforms reduced the amount of money airlines earned for carrying the mail. By 1938, over a million Americans were flying on airplanes. This industry's rapid growth prompted new government policies. In 1938, Congress enacted the Civil Aeronautics Act. The airlines were happy that an independent agency was in charge of aviation policy. Before 1938 Civil Aeronautics Act passed, numerous government agencies and departments pushed and pulled airlines in many directions.

World War II brought many advances to the civilian air transport sector. Innovations initially intended for bombers made passenger planes larger, faster, and able to carry heavier payloads and to fly at higher altitudes. The 1970s saw the introduction of supersonic air travel with the advent of the Concorde. Due to the Concorde's only crash in 2000, as well as world economic effects after the September 11, 2001 attacks, the supersonic airliner stopped flying in October 2003.

Big trouble for the Big Six

After September 11th, Congress gave well over $20 billion to the airline industry in the form of reimbursements for losses incurred while planes were grounded following the attacks, monetary help for new passenger and plane security requirements, and pension funding relief. But many of the industry's major players were forced to shoulder massive debt loads to continue their operations; this was on top of debt they had been accumulating since even before the terrorist attacks. Of the "Big Six"—United, US Airways, American, Northwest, Continental and Delta—all but two, Continental and American, have been forced to file for Chapter 11. Smaller airlines, including Great Plains, Hawaiian, Midway, National, Sun Country and Vanguard, have also shown up in bankruptcy court.

Though passenger confidence continued to grow in the years following the terrorist attacks, the industry's red ink kept on flowing. The SARS scare in Asia, the Iraq war and a slowdown in the economy also hurt airlines. According to a June 2004 Senate report, the industry carried combined debts of more than $100 billion. Thus, major carriers continued to lobby the feds for financial support in the form of subsidies and loans.

Looking up?

The industry has struggled with profitability due to a combination of factors. Air carriers have been hit hard by rising fuel costs, with jet fuel prices in 2007 averaging about $80 per barrel. The high cost of oil remains a huge challenge to the airline industry. The IATA projected that in 2007, the industry's fuel bill will grow to $119 billion, an increase of $8 billion from 2005, when fuel costs totaled $111 billion. Labor disputes and underfinanced pensions have also been expensive problems for many carriers. Even JetBlue, which had strong profits for several years, suffered loses recently as it continues to grapple with rapid growth and rising expenses.

Overall, however, costs associated with air travel have dropped significantly over the past five years, resulting from price competition and attempts to keep ticket prices low despite high fuel costs. In early 2007, IATA Director General and CEO

Giovanni Bisignani said the industry's distribution costs (the cost of selling tickets, such as ticket processing, credit card processing fees, etc.) are down 13 percent. Bisignani added that non-fuel unit costs, the cost per seat mile excluding the price of fuel, have declined 15 percent. Industry belt-tightening seems to be working. The IATA reports that the industry break-even fuel price went from $22 per barrel in 2003 to $65 per barrel in 2006.

Recently, the airline industry has started to show other signs of recovery. According to the IATA, a stronger world economy saw passenger traffic rise by 7 percent between 2005 and 2006, and air freight experienced a 5 percent gain. In order to accommodate this increased demand for air travel and to lower their fuel expenditures, airlines began snapping up new, more fuel-efficient planes. The airline industry's profitability has improved, and the IATA predicts that the industry will see $5 billion in profits in 2007. However, IATA Director General Bisignani pointed out that the airlines still have $200 billion dollars of debt. Moreover, he warned that an event like another terrorist attack or a pandemic scare could put many carriers back in the red.

A global network

Around the world, many airlines still are heavily subsidized—or owned outright—by their home nations. While this has been a successful setup for many, others haven't been so lucky. Swissair and Belgium's airline, Sabena, both crumbled when their respective governments couldn't keep up with demands for subsidies. Subsidized international and U.S. carriers have formed global alliances to avoid some regulatory issues and to maximize profits by sharing resources, including routes and marketing strategies. Well-known alliances include Oneworld—an alliance between American Airlines, British Airways and several other carriers—and SkyTeam, a partnership made up of Delta Air Lines, Air France, AeroMexico and other airlines. Such partnerships aren't always successful. An alliance between Dutch carrier KLM and Alitalia fell apart, for instance, after the Italian airline had trouble securing funding from its government patrons.

Partnerships aside, the airline industry remains remarkably competitive, and in today's tough climate, it's everyone for themselves. Tight regulatory controls in the U.S. make it difficult for major domestic carriers to merge. For example, a plan to join United Airlines and US Airways was shot down due to antitrust regulations. The US Airways name showed up again in merger talks, linked to America West for $1.5 billion, and the two companies made it official in September 2005. Then, in November 2006, US Airways made an offer for Delta. However, in early 2007, Delta's creditors rejected US Airways' $10 billion bid. Even if US Airways had purchased Delta, size (large or small) is no guarantee of profit. Four of the Big Six have gone into bankruptcy since 2001, and smaller budget airlines have also started struggling to make a profit.

Going regional

Regional airlines, which benefit from smaller, newer jets and lower operating costs than the domestic giants, have gained ground in recent years, becoming the fastest growing segment of the airline market. Approximately 25 to 30 regional, or commuter, carriers operate in the industry today, according to the Bureau of Labor Statistics. Recent statistics from the Regional Airline Association reveal that one in five domestic airline passengers travel on a regional airline, and that planes serving regional markets make up one-third of the U.S. commercial airline fleet on the whole. The big carriers have taken notice, and many now have controlling interests in newer regional airlines—Delta controls Comair, for instance, while American has American Eagle. In April 2006, Compass Airlines became a subsidiary of Northwest. The trend is reflected in Europe, too. Both globally and domestically, alliances with major carriers give the upstart regionals access to major airport hubs. In some cases, however, regional and low-budget airlines have skirted the hub question altogether by choosing to operate out of slightly out-of-the-way airports—Southwest's use of Islip airport, in a suburb of New York, and JetBlue's adoption of Long Beach, near Los Angeles, are two examples. And in other instances, regional airlines have decided to spread their wings and join the burgeoning low-cost boom. Some regional airlines now do longer haul flights. For example, Midwest Airlines (formerly Midwest Express) connects several cities in the Midwest to destinations like Boston, New York and San Francisco.

Visit Vault at www.vault.com for insider company profiles, expert advice, career message boards, expert resume reviews, the Vault Job Board and more.

VAULT CAREER LIBRARY   313

The budget boom

The budget airline sector—consisting of top performers like Southwest Airlines and JetBlue, plus a growing number of upstarts—has gotten a good deal of attention lately. But budget flight isn't a new phenomenon in the industry. In fact, Southwest has been around since 1971. The difference is in the branding and public acceptance of these carriers, fueled in part by Southwest's customer-centric approach, and by customers' reduced service expectations post-September 11th. Expanded routes have helped, too. Where once low-budget carriers limited their flights to relatively short hauls in regional markets, today's top discount airlines regularly offer cross-country, and even international, flights.

The budget carrier phenomenon has rocked Europe, too, where about 60 low-cost carriers operated in 2006, compared to just four in 1999. European customers have warmed up to the budget boom as well. British-based easyJet increased its passenger flow more than eightfold between 1999 and 2004, while low-cost carrier Ryanair, operating out of Ireland, ranked as one of the top performers in the industry worldwide. Some of the larger airlines have decided to take advantage of the low-cost boom, such as United's Ted and Delta's Song, but to not much avail; Song, in fact, was reabsorbed into Delta in 2006, three years after its first plane took off.

The boom in low-budget carriers isn't limited to North America and Europe. There are also low-fare carriers in Asia, where there are now about 45 discount airlines. Examples are Singapore-based Tiger Airways, Pakistani carrier Aero Asia and Jakarta-headquartered Adam Air. In June 2007, South Korea's largest airline, Korean Air Lines, announced plans to start a low-fare unit to compete with discount carriers in Asia. Some budget airlines are also branching out into long-haul flights across the Atlantic and Pacific.

Cutting costs

Above all, cost-savings are seen as key to the success of low-budget carriers. One way air carriers measure their fiscal health through cost per available seat mile (or CASM), a complex formula involving airplane capacity, operating costs, route lengths and other factors. Whereas American Airlines spends about 9.4 cents for each seat on each mile flown, budget competitors like Southwest and JetBlue lighten their loads with CASMs of 7.6 cents and 6.4 cents, respectively, according to an MSNBC article from December 2003. Those pennies add up over time, and so-called "legacy" carriers are under pressure to pinch them ever harder. But with more liberal work rules and a less-senior workforce overall, low-cost carriers beat their established rivals in terms of labor costs.

Other cost-cutting measures in the airline industry overall include streamlining fleets and retiring older planes, canceling unprofitable routes, greater efficiency in procurement processes involving suppliers and slashing commissions once paid regularly to middlemen such as travel agencies. Airlines have saved money through online booking, and they encourage customers to book directly through airlines web sites by offering incentives such online bonus miles. According to a 2006 *International Herald Tribune* article, online booking saves the airline industry $2 billion a year.

These airlines have also realized that consumers prefer to pick and choose their perks. An in-flight cocktail on JetBlue will still set you back $5, but XM radio and DIRECTV are free. Charging for amenities that previously came gratis allows carriers to keep ticket prices low, yet still turn a profit. Many airlines now charge passengers for meals and snacks. On Air Canada, customers now pay $2 for a pillow and a blanket. Moreover, some airlines now charge people for extra legroom. On Northwest, a bigger exit-row seat costs an additional $15. United's flyers can sign up an Economy Plus subscription, which is $299 a year. Subscribers get seats with five inches of extra legroom.

How low can you go?

Low-fare carriers, such as Southwest and JetBlue, were once the darlings of the airline industry. Recently, however, Southwest and JetBlue have had troubles of their own. When an ice storm hit JetBlue's hub at JFK airport in New York in

February 2007, passengers were trapped on the tarmac for eight or more hours. It took JetBlue nearly a week to resume normal operations. JetBlue's founder and CEO David Neeleman apologized publicly for what happened and also introduced a "passenger's bill of rights." In May 2007, Neeleman stepped down as the airline's CEO.

In June 2007, *The Wall Street Journal* reported on a growing profit squeeze at Southwest. Over the past four years, Southwest's unit costs—the expenses to fly each seat one mile—have risen almost 20 percent due to increased labor costs and higher fuel prices. The airline's hedges to lock in low fuel prices have become less successful, and passengers have resisted increases in fares. Low-cost carriers are also facing greater competition from other airlines, which copied budget airlines' low-cost model during the post-September 11 industry downturn. Southwest has said it will respond to these pressures by reining in its rapid growth.

The lap of luxury

Some of the newest carriers attempt to attract the super-wealthy and business travelers instead of the budget-minded traveler. Upscale airlines MaxJet, SilverJet and Eos fly between New York and London. On Eos, which was launched in 2005, the airline's "guests" travel in style—they sleep on 6'6" beds and dine on gourmet meals. L'Avion, a business-class airline that offers service between Paris and New York, boasts that passengers can enjoy comfy seats and French food. In the Middle East, luxury airline Al Khayala aims to attract well-heeled customers by providing service that's somewhere between first class and a private jet. The airline uses specially modified Airbus A319s, which the company has configured to seat just 44 people instead of the usual 170 passengers. The wealthy also have the option of the Eclipse 500. Eclipse Aviation makes this "very light jet," which sells for about $1.5 million. Florida-based company DayJet owns several of the small jets and runs an air taxi service for business travelers.

Established airlines are also trying to cater to the luxury market. For example, Lufthansa is expanding the airline's first-class lounge in the Munich airport. New additions to the lounge will include day beds, showers, a gourmet restaurant and a bigger bar. Lufthansa is also spending millions of dollars to upgrade luxe lounges in Paris, New York's JFK, Berlin and Düsseldorf. In addition, Singapore Airlines is upgrading its business and first-class cabins on certain flights. The airline announced that, on some flights, it was rolling out 35-inch wide seats in first class. According to Singapore Air, the seats, which fold into beds, are "the largest seat in the sky" and are "exquisitely upholstered in fine-grained leather with mahogany wood trimming."

Investing in a dream(liner)

Major carriers hope to save money in the future by investing in new planes that offer a lower cost of ownership and operation. In late 2003, Boeing's board of directors gave the company the go-ahead to offer the 787 Dreamliner for sale. The following April, Japan's All Nippon was the first airline to order Boeing's new passenger jet, which promises fuel savings of up to 20 percent. By December 2006, Boeing had nearly 450 orders for the new Dreamliner, and the number had soared to more than 580 by June 2007.

Meanwhile, Airbus, the French firm and Boeing's rival for No. 1 aircraft maker in the world, unveiled a brand new high-scale jumbo-jet, the A380, at the start of 2005 at a gala event during the Le Bourget air show in Toulouse, France. Designed to comfortably seat 555, the A380 rocked the airline industry and represented a joint effort with France, Britain, Germany and Spain, all of whom contributed to the 10-year, $13 billion program that designed the plane. The double-decker leviathan, the largest plane ever built, boasts a 262-foot wingspan and extra space companies can use to install bedrooms, gyms, bars and lounges.

The conservation end, though, is where the A380 packs its biggest punch: its carbon fiber components and fuel-efficient technology are estimated to match or exceed Boeing's 20 percent fuel savings, and slash cost per passenger. However, in October 2006, Airbus announced that the delivery of the new jet would be delayed until the second half of 2007, with the

Visit Vault at **www.vault.com** for insider company profiles, expert advice, career message boards, expert resume reviews, the Vault Job Board and more.

VAULT CAREER LIBRARY 315

industrial ramp-up finished in 2010. As of June 2007, Airbus had 13 signed contracts from two airlines for the A350, and another five customers had agreed to purchase 148 A350s.

It's not easy being green

Global warming is a hot topic, and airplanes are one of the biggest contributors to carbon emissions. Environmentalists have also criticized the airline industry for planes' air pollution in general. In 2006, Al Gore's documentary *An Inconvenient Truth* was a surprise hit, and a number of businesses have started going "carbon-neutral." Members of the airline and aviation industries are finally starting to address concerns about airplanes' emissions. In June 2007, the IATA has asked the aerospace industry to build zero-emissions airplanes within the next 50 years. Later that month, Louis Gallois, the CEO of Airbus, called on aircraft makers to work together to invent more environmentally-friendly technology. In addition, the European Commission proposed a $2.13 billion public-private plan, dubbed the Clean Sky program. The program, which would start in 2008, would help Europe's air-transportation sector develop technologies to reduce planes' pollution.

Labor pains

According to the Bureau of Labor Statistics, labor costs make up roughly 38 percent of many airlines' operating costs—that's around 40 cents for every dollar spent by an air carrier. Passenger safety regulations and a workforce made up of highly specialized and rarely cross-trained professionals, half of whom are unionized, make it tough for airlines to trim costs from their labor budgets. One way they've done this is by cutting staffs to the bare bones. Following September 11th, Continental Airlines and US Airways were the first to make dramatic cuts, laying off about 20 percent of their respective workforces and paring flight schedules. Most other carriers followed suit.

Cuts in salaries and benefits

At many airlines, employees have agreed to salary and benefit cuts to help keep airlines from going bankrupt. For example, in June 2006, Delta's pilots union agreed to a 14 percent pay cut. Other employees at Delta also agreed to pay cuts, including CEO Gerald Grinstein, whose pay was chopped by 25 percent. In May 2007, Northwest Airlines departed bankruptcy protection following a 20-month reorganization. The restructuring attempted to make the airline competitive for future years. Among other things, Northwest's new labor contracts pay employees less. Flight attendants for the airline used to make as much as $44,190, but now their pay tops out at $35,400.

Although American Airlines posted an annual profit for the first time in six years, many workers were angry during the airline's annual stockholder meeting in May 2007. These employees, who agreed to salary cuts in recent years to keep the airline flying, were unhappy because top executives got bonuses worth millions of dollars. At Northwest, the airline cut pilots' wages by 40 percent and increased their hours. In protest, pilots regularly call in sick to take days off, which results in more cancelled flights.

In order to save money, airlines have also started outsourcing many jobs that used to be filled with airline employees. For example, in 2005, Alaska Airlines replaced its baggage handlers with lower-paid outside contractors. In 2006, Northwest hired non-union employees to clean airplanes. In some cases, airlines have also replaced people with machines—just think of the self-service check-in kiosks that have sprung up at airports in recent years.

Not just plane jobs

One manager for a major airline says, "This is not a place for the faint of heart. The airline industry is chaotic, and [it has been] particularly brutal for the traditional or legacy carriers since 2001." This source feels career development opportunities are extremely limited. The contact adds, "There is a glut of MBAs that have never moved up due to the incredibly heavy toll exacted by several world events (the dot-com bust, September 11th, SARS, the Iraq war). However, work hours are pretty light, and the travel benefits can be fantastic." An insider at American Airlines agrees that working for the airline industry is tough, explaining, "If making lots of money, getting big bonuses and securing promotion opportunities are important to you, AA may not be the best place to work. However, if you value work/life balance, enjoy solving challenging business problems and love flying first class to any destination across the globe, American really isn't that bad."

The airline industry hires a wide variety of employees ranging from pilots and flight attendants to ticket agents, sales people and managers. Although flight crews are the most visible in the industry, most airline employees don't fly the friendly skies. Rather, they work in airport terminals or in offices. Due to the fact the flights leave at all hours, many who work in the industry have schedules that are variable or irregular. Most jobs with the airline industry are in or near the cities that serve as major airlines hubs. For example, many of Northwest Airlines' jobs are in Minneapolis-St. Paul.

In the airline industry, most recieve standard benefits, such as health insurance and paid vacation—and many also have benefits like retirement plans and profit sharing. One perk that attracts many people to the industry is free or reduced-fare flights for airline employees and sometimes even their family members.

Many airline jobs are also unionized. Unions include the Air Line Pilots Association International (ALPA), the International Association of Machinists and Aerospace Workers (IAM), and the Association of Flight Attendants-CWA (AFA-CWA). The AFA, which represents 55,000 flight attendants at 20 airlines, claims it is the largest flight attendant union.

Navigating airline interviews

Most sources at airlines, regardless of their position, say the interview process can be long and usually involves multiple meetings. A reservations agent for Continental says, "The hiring process was very long. It took about six months from resume submitted to being hired." The contact says there were two rounds of interviews. One HR person with American Airlines says, "The interview process can be lengthy and meeting with a number of people the norm." A mechanic with Continental says getting the job entailed three interviews. Flight attendants for various airlines say a group interview is part of the hiring process.

An airline agent says interview questions included "Where do you see yourself 10 years from now?", "How do you deal with difficult people?", "Do you work better by yourself or in a group?", "Do you loose you temper easily?" and "How important it is to spend the holidays with your loved ones?" Another ticket agent says one question was, "Describe the most difficult problem you dealt with at a previous job and how you handled it." A manager says questions included "What is your greatest accomplishment?" Some say they also needed to pass a medical examination or psychological tests.

The future of airline careers

Industry employment is largely at the mercy of the economy, though the BLS expects jobs to increase somewhat independently due to a growing population and greater demand for air travel. The BLS predicts employment growth initially in low-cost and local carriers. After larger airlines recover from bankruptcy, the BLS says, larger airlines will start hiring again. However, the airline industry is often as turbulent as the skies it flies, and salaries and perks aren't what they used to be.

Visit Vault at **www.vault.com** for insider company profiles, expert advice, career message boards, expert resume reviews, the Vault Job Board and more.

VAULT CAREER LIBRARY 317

Employer Directory

ABF Freight System, Inc.
3801 Old Greenwood Road
Fort Smith, AR 72903
Phone: (479) 785-6000
Fax: (800) 599-2810
Toll free: (800) 610-5544
www.abfs.com

Air Tran Holdings, Inc.
9955 AirTran Boulevard
Orlando, FL 32827
Phone: (407) 318-5600
Fax: (407) 318-5900
Toll free: (800) 965-2107
www.airtran.com

Alaska Air Group, Inc.
19300 International Boulevard
Seattle, WA 98188
Phone: (206) 392-5040
Fax: (206) 392-2804
Toll free: (800) 252-7522
www.alaskaair.com

AMERCO (U-Haul International, Inc.)
1325 Airmotive Way, Suite 100
Reno, NV 89502
Phone: (775) 688-6300
Fax: (775) 688-6338
www.amerco.com

AMR Corporation (American Airlines)
4333 Amon Carter Boulevard
Fort Worth, TX 76155
Phone: (817) 963-1234
Fax: (817) 967-9641
www.aa.com

British Airways Plc
Waterside, Harmondsworth
London, UB7 0GB
United Kingdom
Phone: +44-87-08-50-85-03
Fax: +44-20-87-59-43-14
www.british-airways.com

Caterpillar Logistics Services, Inc.
500 North Morton Avenue
Morton, IL 60661
Phone: (312) 664-7200
www.catlogistics.com

C.H. Robinson Worldwide, Inc.
8100 Mitchell Road
Eden Prairie, MN 55344-2248
Phone: (952) 937-8500
Fax: (952) 937-6714
www.chrobinson.com

Chicago Transit Authority
567 West Lake Street
Chicago, IL 60661
Phone: (312) 664-7200
www.transitchicago.com

Continental Airlines, Inc
1600 Smith Street Department HQSEO
Houston, TX 77002
Phone: (713) 324-2950
Fax: (713) 324-2687
www.continental.com

Con-way Inc.
2855 Campus Drive, Suite 300
San Mateo, CA 94403
Phone: (650) 378-5200
Fax: (650) 357-9160
www.con-way.com

CSX Corporation
500 Water Street, 15th Floor
Jacksonville, FL 32202
Phone: (904) 359-3200
Fax: (904) 359-2459
www.csx.com

Delta Air Lines, Inc
1030 Delta Boulevard
Atlanta, GA 30320-6001
Phone: (404) 715-2600
Fax: (404) 715-5042
www.delta.com

Deutsche Lufthansa AG
Von-Gablenz-Straße 2-6
D-50679 Cologne, 21
Germany
Phone: +49-0221-826-3992
Fax: +49-221-826-3646
www.lufthansa.com

DHL Holdings (USA)
1200 South Pine Island Road
Plantation, FL 33324
Phone: (954) 888-7000
Fax: (954) 888-7310
www.dhl.com

Enterprise Rent-A-Car Company
600 Corporate Park Drive
St. Louis, MO 63105
Phone: (314) 512-5000
Fax: (314) 512-4706
www.enterprise.com

Estes Express Lines, Inc.
3901 West Broad Street
Richmond, VA 23230
Phone: (804) 353-1900
Fax: (804) 353-8001
www.estes-express.com

Expeditors International of Washington, Inc.
1015 3rd Avenue, 12th Floor
Seattle, WA 98104
Phone: (206) 674-3400
Fax: (206) 682-9777
www.expeditors.com

ExpressJet Holdings, Inc.
700 North Sam Houston Parkway
West, Suite 200
Houston, TX 77067
Phone: (832) 353-1000
Fax: (832) 353-1008
Toll free: (866) 958-3932
www.expressjet.com

Employer Directory, cont.

FedEx Corporation
942 South Shady Grove Road
Memphis, TN 38120
Phone: (901) 818-7500
Fax: (901) 395-2000
www.fedex.com

FirstGroup PLC
395 King Street
Aberdeen, AB24 5RP
Scotland
Phone: +44-12-24-65-01-00
Fax: +44-12-24-65-01-40
www.firstgroup.com

Hertz Global Holdings, Inc.
225 Brae Boulevard
Park Ridge, NJ 07656-0713
Phone: (201) 307-2000
Fax: (201) 307-2644
www.hertz.com

Houston Airport System
16930 JFK Boulevard
Houston, TX 77032
Phone: (281) 233-1800
Fax: (281) 233-1859
www.fly2houston.com

J.B. Hunt Transport Services, Inc.
615 J.B. Hunt Corporate Drive
Lowell, AR 74745
Phone: (479) 820-0000
Fax: (479) 820-3418
Toll free: (800) 643-3622
www.jbhunt.com

JetBlue Airways Corporation
118-29 Queens Boulevard
Forest Hills, NY 11375
Phone: (718) 286-7900
Fax: (718) 709-3621
www.jetblue.com

Kansas City Southern
427 West 12th Street
Kansas City, MO 64105
Phone: (816) 983-1303
Fax: (816) 983-1108
www.kcsi.com

Metropolitan Transportation Authority
347 Madison Avenue
New York, NY 10017
Phone: (212) 878-7000
Fax: (212) 878-0186
www.mta.info

National Railroad Passenger Corporation (Amtrak)
60 Massachusetts Avenue NE
Washington, DC 20002
Phone: (202) 906-3000
Fax: (202) 906-3306
www.amtrak.com

Norfolk Southern Corporation
3 Commercial Place
Norfolk, VA 23510-2191
Phone: (757) 629-2600
Fax: (757) 664-5069
www.nscorp.com

Northwest Airlines Corporation
2700 Lone Oak Parkway
Eagan, MN 55121
Phone: (612) 726-2111
Fax: (612) 726-7123
www.nwa.com

Pacer International
2300 Clayton Road, Suite 1200
Concord, CA 94520
Phone: (925) 887-1400
Fax: (925) 887-1503
Toll free: (877) 917-2237
www.pacer-international.com

Ryder
11690 NW 105th Street
Miami, FL 33178
Phone: (305) 500-3726
Fax: (305) 500-3203
www.ryder.com

Sabre Holdings Corp.
3150 Sabre Drive
Southlake, TX 76092
Phone: (682) 605-1000
Fax: (682) 605-8267
www.sabre-holdings.com

Schneider National, Inc.
3101 South Packerland Drive
Green Bay, WI 54306
Phone: (920) 592-2000
Fax: (920) 592-3063
Toll free: (800) 558-6767
www.schneider.com

SkyWest, Inc.
444 South River Road
St. George, UT 84790
Phone: (435) 634-3000
Fax: (435) 634-3105
www.skywest.com

Southwest Airlines Co.
2702 Love Field Drive
Dallas, TX 75235
Phone: (214) 792-4000
Fax: (214) 792-5015
www.southwest.com

SSA Marine
1131 SW Klickitat Way
Seattle, WA 98134
Phone: (206) 623-0304
Fax: (206) 623-0179
Toll free: (800) 422-3505
www.ssamarine.com

Visit Vault at **www.vault.com** for insider company profiles, expert advice,
career message boards, expert resume reviews, the Vault Job Board and more.

VAULT CAREER LIBRARY   319

Employer Directory, cont.

Swift Transportation Co., Inc.
2200 South 75th Avenue
Phoenix, AZ 85043
Phone: (602) 269-9700
Fax: (623) 907-7380
Toll free: (800) 800-2200
www.swifttrans.com

UAL Corporation (United Airlines)
77 West Wacker Drive
Chicago, IL 60601
Phone: (312) 997-8000
www.united.com

UniGroup, Inc.
1 Premier Drive
Fenton, MO 63026
Phone: (636) 305-5000
Fax: (636) 326-1106
www.unigroupinc.com

Union Pacific Corporation
1400 Douglas Street
Omaha, NE 68179
Phone: (402) 544-5000
Fax: (402) 271-6408
www.up.com

United Parcel Service, Inc.
55 Glenlake Parkway NE
Atlanta, GA 30328
Phone: (404) 828-6000
Fax: (404) 828-6562
Toll free: (800) 874-5877
www.ups.com

United States Postal Service
475 L'Enfant Plaza SW
Washington, DC 20260-3100
Phone: (202) 268-2500
Fax: (202) 268-4860
www.usps.com

US Airways Group, Inc.
111 West Rio Salado Parkway
Tempe, AZ 85281
Phone: (480) 693-0800
Fax: (480) 693-5546
www.usairways.com

Werner Enterprises, Inc.
14507 Frontier Road
Harrison, AR 72601
Phone: (870) 741-9000
Fax: (870) 741-7325
Toll free: (800) 874-4723
www.werner.com

WIS International
9265 Sky Park, Suite 100
San Diego, CA 92123
Phone: (858) 565-8111
Fax: (858) 492-2751
Toll free: (800) 888-8210
www.wisint.org

YRC Worldwide Inc.
10990 Roe Avenue
Overland Park, KS 66211
Phone: (913) 696-6100
Fax: (913) 696-6116
Toll free: (800) 846-4300
www.yrcw.com

Venture Capital

Venture Capital Today

It's no secret that the U.S. economy goes through cycles, and is now in the midst of another correction. Everything from housing prices to stock valuations tend to get overheated, or overly depressed, and that leads to a cyclical shift in sentiment. Wall Street tends to develop momentum that can last two to three years, and investors of all classes use these patterns to engage in the proverbial "buy low and sell high." The same goes for venture capitalists. The good news is that venture capital (VC) firms expect to nurture startups for up to five years, and that makes them somewhat less worried about short-term economic turbulence. However, a downturn in the economy means venture capitalists change course. Their strategy drastically shifts into what kind of upstart companies are safe to invest into, and others to be avoided. The key to understanding this shift is by poring over the most recent batch of industry data, and experts say this is paramount for anybody looking to join venture capital's ranks.

In good times, VC firms will sink billions of dollars into any business proposal that could become the next Google or Facebook. They are willing to take a gamble and pump money into ideas that could lead to a splashy initial public offering, and cash in by converting their investments into major stock holdings. That doesn't end entirely when the economy begins to slip. Instead, venture capitalists tend to entrench—picking deals at a slower and more targeted pace. VC firms, like investment banks and big private equity shops, are designed to make money in the midst of all kinds of economic conditions. A pullback in the U.S. might mean a surge of new deals overseas, one sector's glut could mirror the rise of another. Looking to secure a job as a VC analyst? Want to scout out the next blockbuster deal? Then bone up on the most recent data out there.

The first quarter of 2008 indicates that venture capitalists have scaled back their deal-making activity, but that doesn't mean the entire industry is locked up. Despite the slipping economy, VC firms sunk $7.1 billion into 922 deals during the first three months of the year, according to the *MoneyTree Report*. This is a decline from both the $7.8 billion raised during the fourth quarter and $7.5 billion raised in the same quarter last year. The drop wasn't unexpected considering the global credit crunch that has paralyzed global equity markets. And the industry hasn't been helped amid further anxiety from the worst housing slump in decades that has caused a wave of defaults in subprime mortgages. The biggest downside for venture capital is that the economic environment has drastically curbed the appetite for IPOs and mergers and acquisitions—two of the biggest ways VC firms cash in on their investments.

That doesn't mean deals aren't being done. To the contrary, insiders say investment activity remains high and that the industry is still faring better then it did after the last economic slowdown in 2001. John Taylor, vice president of research for the National Venture Capital Association, said the industry remains interested in new projects "albeit with a sense of caution." During the first quarter, 294 business plans were accepted among companies given funding for the first time. "The industry is still taking on new projects and it's consistent with what we've done in recent quarters," he said.

The Financial Industry and Venture Capital

The financial industry can be divided into two general segments: the buy-side and the sell-side. Venture capital firms are on the buy-side because they control a fund or pool of money to spend on buying an equity interest in, or assets of, operating companies. Investment banks, brokerages and commercial banks are on the sell-side because they offer such services as floating new companies on the stock exchange or issuing new debt.

For instance, when a large company wants to sell stock an investment bank's corporate finance department handles the legal, tax, advisory and accounting affairs of the transaction as well as the sale of those securities to institutional or individual investors. For providing these services, the investment bank receives a fee (between 2 percent and 10 percent of the money raised by selling stock). An investment banking firm's primary motivation is to sell such services, characterizing them as sell-siders. Meanwhile, major brokerages are paid a fee for the service of buying and selling stocks. Commercial banks get in

Visit Vault at **www.vault.com** for insider company profiles, expert advice, career message boards, expert resume reviews, the Vault Job Board and more.

VAULT CAREER LIBRARY 321

on the action for managing deposit accounts, making and then managing loans, etc. Again, they sell these services, so they are sell-side firms.

For the sake of this discussion, most buy-side venture capital firms have only one way to realize a return on their investment: selling their ownership stake to another private investor, a corporation (trade sale) or to the public markets for more money than they paid (often termed to be "in the money"). Private equity shops like Blackstone Group or Kohlberg, Kravis Roberts sink their money into later-stage companies with the hopes of cashing out in a public offering. Venture capital is about building young companies and finding an exit (liquidity event) on the back side for "x" times their original investment. Descriptions of each segment of the buy-side are included below. Keep in mind that these definitions are intended to be very general in nature and that many buy-side organizations cross organizational boundaries.

Friends and family

Sometimes referred to as "friends, family and fools," this is usually the first source of funding for startups at the idea stage of development. The amounts invested per individual are quite small, averaging $5,000 to $10,000. These people may not have an in-depth understanding of the business, product, technology or market, and are simply making an investment in someone they know. While this is probably the easiest money for an entrepreneur to find, it can also be bittersweet. If a startup fails, telling Aunt Edna that she's lost her nest egg could be the low point of one's career.

Angels

These are high-net-worth individuals who normally invest between $15,000 and $1 million in exchange for equity in a young company throughout the seed and early stage rounds, averaging $50,000 to $500,000. Angels prefer to invest within their immediate geographic area, and on average within one day of travel.

According to businessfinance.com, angels fund an estimated one-seventh of the 300,000 start-up/early growth firms in the U.S. They are often the first investor segment who have the opportunity to sit on the board of directors and contribute experience and contacts, guiding young companies through the difficult initial stages of growth. That said, most of the value added by angel investors occurs in the pre-institutional (or Series A) rounds of funding. As the professional investors come into play, venture capitalists take over board seats previously held by angels.

Angels can be doctors, lawyers, former investors, though increasingly they are former entrepreneurs who have had a lucrative exit in their chosen professional field. Microsoft co-founder and multi-billionaire Paul Allen has made headlines for his angel investing as well as his investments through his VC firm, Vulcan Ventures. Intel co-founder Andy Grove has made angel investments in numerous companies, including Oncology.com. Given the large number of new companies seeking funding as well as the rise in the number of wealthy individuals, in recent years the industry has seen the emergence of angel groups. These investor alliances create more structure for angel investors, and a more efficient conduit for moving startups along from seed funding to professional venture investors. Perhaps the best-known group of angels is Silicon Valley's "Band of Angels," a formal group of about 150 former and current high-tech entrepreneurs and executives who meet monthly to consider pleas from three startups for venture financing. This group has injected more than $100 million across some 150 startups.

Angels are often involved with hiring, strategy, the raising of additional capital, and fundamental operating decisions. These alliances also allow for better coordination of due diligence in "vetting" new deals. Angels are not without their own issues, however. Collectively, angel investors have been accused of being fair weather friends; one of the first sources of private equity to dry up when public markets fall or macroeconomic conditions deteriorate. With less money to invest across fewer deals than their VC brethren, many of these individuals have a lower tolerance for losses. This risk aversion is compounded by their generally lower position in the capital structure. While angel groups may be able to negotiate preferred stock instead of common, their equity rarely has the same level of preferences or security demanded by later stage investors. Though angels, of course, expect a significant return on their investment, they are also thrill-seekers of a sort—motivated by getting close to the excitement of a new venture.

High-net-worth private placements

Investment banks such as industry leader Goldman Sachs Group, Inc. that represent the sell-side of a deal may organize a group of very wealthy individuals, corporations, asset management firms, and/or pension funds to make a direct investment into a private company. These funds raise typically between $5 million and $50 million—sometimes in the billions for funds managed by some of Wall Street's biggest names. In essence, they enable a broad swath of institutional and wealthy private investors to put their money to work like major venture capital firms.

While these transactions may include a traditional venture fund as part of the round, in many cases they do not. As a whole, investment banks have historically been seen as having less perceived value in the early stages of the venture process. Since early-stage investing is not Wall Street's core competency, the downside is that the start-up company may not benefit from the expertise, operational savvy and rolodex of the venture capital firm. While there is a credible value proposition to using private placements and participation by investment banks in funding some types of deals, this is expensive money on several fronts.

Asset management firms and pension funds

These groups include a diverse collection of limited partnerships and corporations that manage between $5 million to $100+ billion. Most focus on diversified investment strategies, typically with public instruments including stocks, bonds, commodities, currencies, etc. They rarely invest in private companies, due to the large amount of time required to find and execute a private transaction, as well as the ongoing commitment of time to monitor such an investment. Instead of directly participating in individual startup fundings, many will allocate 5 percent to 7 percent of total funds to higher-risk alternative investments like VC partnerships, hedge funds, and distressed turnaround situations. The California Public Employees' Retirement System (CalPERS) is one of the largest players in this space. As of September 2007, their AIM (Alternative Investment Management) Program had total investment exposure of $42.6 billion. And, since its inception in 1990, the program has generated $12.5 billion in profit.

Private equity firms

Consider private equity firms to be the bigger, badder version of venture capital. They rarely involve themselves in upstart companies, but certainly have their eye on opportunity. Big PE firms like Blackstone and KKR have entire departments empowered to invest seed money into the next big Internet phenomenon. However, their main strategy is to buy vulnerable publicly traded companies that can hand them a huge profit. The strategy is to find an under-performing public company, take them private, and then reorganize them using loans. That's why it is called leveraged finance. And the big payoff for LBOs is when they make money bringing them public again. For instance, private-equity fund Cerberus Capital is now in the process of reorganizing Chrysler—an American icon it bought from German car titan Daimler AG (famous for its Mercedes brand). Once turned around, Chrysler will reap big financial rewards for Cerberus if the automaker goes public.

Hedge funds

These are entities that buy and sell public market instruments including stocks, bonds, commodities, currencies, etc. These firms take bets on market fluctuations to make money, and are often considered high risk/high return investors. The size of these funds ranges from a few million to several billion dollars. They care about making quick money.

Visit Vault at **www.vault.com** for insider company profiles, expert advice, career message boards, expert resume reviews, the Vault Job Board and more.

VAULT CAREER LIBRARY   323

Trading

Sell-side companies such as merchant banks, commercial banks and investment banks have trading departments that control and invest huge sums of money into public markets. These groups also take relatively risky bets on market fluctuations.

A Day in the Life: Venture Capitalist

7 a.m. Arrive at the office.

7:01 a.m. Read *The Wall Street Journal*, paying careful attention to the Marketplace section covering your industry focus.

7:20 a.m. Read trade press and notice four companies you haven't seen before. Check your firm's internal database to see if someone else on your team has contacted the companies. Search the Internet to find out more. Of the four companies you find, only one holds your interest. Send yourself an e-mail as a reminder to call them during business hours.

7:45 a.m. Clip out some interesting articles and put them in the inboxes of other associates or partners with a note explaining why you found the information interesting. The other members of your firm have more expertise in the areas covered by the articles. You stay and talk for a few minutes with each of the people in their offices, exchanging the latest word about the people and technology you follow.

8 a.m. Respond to e-mails or voicemails from the day before. People you are communicating with are primarily entrepreneurs, other VCs and personal acquaintances.

9 a.m. You attend a meeting with a group of entrepreneurs who want to make their pitch. You read the business plan for five minutes. One general partner (GP) sits in with you. The other GP, who planned to be there, cannot make it because he has a conference call with a portfolio company facing some challenges. The computer projecting the entrepreneur's presentation crashes, so you have to take their paper version of their presentation and work with your assistant to make four photocopies before the meeting can proceed.

During the 10-minute delay, the partner talks with the team informally, and learns more about the opportunity than he or she would in any one-hour presentation. You sit politely through the presentation, and identify the three critical issues facing the company. During the question and answer phase, you think of how to politely extract more information about those three issues, all the while evaluating whether you would want to work with this team or not.

In the end, you decide to make some calls to gather more information about the market, but you feel that there's a very low probability you would ever invest. You wish you could just kill the deal, but the management team is reasonable (though not great), the customer need they have identified may actually exist (you don't know firsthand, so you will need to call around), and you may learn something by taking it to the next step. Plus, in the back of your mind, you know the market for good deals is very competitive, and you don't want to reject a deal too quickly.

11 a.m. Phone the people who called during your meeting. These people include entrepreneurs, analysts, other VCs and your lunch appointment. You find out from another VC that the company you almost invested in two months ago was just funded by a competing firm. You wonder if you made a mistake. You find out from an entrepreneur you were hoping to back that he wants his son to be a co-founder and owner of the firm. You abandon all hope. You learn from an analyst that AT&T has decided to stop its trial of a new technology because it doesn't work, which creates an opportunity for companies with an alternative solution. You happen to know about two small companies, one in Boston, one in Denver, that have alternative solutions. You make a note to yourself to call them back to get a status report.

12:30 p.m. Lunch with an executive recruiter. This person is very experienced in finding management talent in your area of expertise. You have kept in touch with her over the years, and try to see her every quarter to hear the latest buzz and to make sure she will be available when you need her services quickly. It's a fun lunch, freely mixing personal and professional information.

2 p.m. Call new companies you have heard about over the last few days. Ideally, you could do this task a little bit every day, but you find you need to be in a friendly and upbeat mood to make these calls, so you batch them. Also, if you actually get in touch with the CEO, you may be on the phone for 90 minutes, so you need to have an open block of time. You leave the standard pitch about your firm on the voicemail of the CEOs of four other companies. You get through to one CEO, and although you can tell in the first five minutes that you won't be interested in investing, you talk for 30 minutes. You spend most of the 30 minutes probing about competitors who might be better than the company you're talking to and finding out more about his market space.

3 p.m. You and a partner meet with a portfolio company on a conference call. The company is facing some challenges and you offer to screen executive recruiters to help find a new CFO for it. The GP offers to talk to two M&A firms to get a first opinion about what might be done to sell the company over the next six months. At the end of the call, the GP gives you three names and numbers of recruiters, which you add to your own two contacts.

3:30 p.m. You call the recruiters, explaining the situation and asking about their recent experiences in similar searches. The critical element is whether the recruiters actually have time and interest in doing the search. You talk to two recruiters and leave voicemails for the other three.

4:30 p.m. You make due diligence calls for a potential investment you have been following for two months. Last week you called the company's customers, and they seemed happy for the most part. Today, you are calling the personal references of the management team. The idea is to get as much negative information as possible. You need to discover any potential character or personality flaws any member of the team may have. VC firms are "due diligence machines," doing the hard work of making sure a company is what it says it is.

5:30 p.m. You make calls to the West Coast. You also check your stocks and confirm dinner plans. You do some miscellaneous surfing on the Web to gather some articles about the technology areas you cover.

6:30 p.m. You stand around the halls talking with other members of your firm, brainstorming and filling each other in about what's happening in your area.

7 p.m. Dinner with two other young VCs downtown. You talk mostly about life, sports, travel and relationships, but also about the latest deals, cool business ideas and recent successes. You find out that a competing firm just made 30 times their money on a deal you never saw. You also find out that a company you turned down, which was invested in by someone else, is about to go bankrupt. A train missed; a bullet dodged.

VC Uppers and Downers

Uppers

- There is a reason that very few people ever willingly leave their VC careers. Where else can you have so much fun investing other people's money (plus some of your own), while being "in the middle of it all?"

- You often get to be the one making decisions because you have money.

- Over the long term, financial security will cease to be an issue, because the job is well paying and you should eventually get "carry" or equity in the firm.

- You have access to the best minds—the people you work with are typically some of the smartest and most interesting. Successful venture capitalists have interests and hobbies as diverse as mountain climbing to playing jazz in nightclubs.

Visit Vault at www.vault.com for insider company profiles, expert advice, career message boards, expert resume reviews, the Vault Job Board and more.

VAULT CAREER LIBRARY

325

- Your job is to absorb and enjoy the positive creative energy of entrepreneurs and direct it toward successful execution.

- You could suddenly become rich if one of your companies does extremely well and you were able to co-invest or you have carry.

- You have access to the best information systems.

Downers

Because so many think of the venture capital industry as "the hot job to have," people often forget to question whether it is the right job for them. Here is a list of some of the negatives we hear from those who have worked in the industry for a while.

- Unless you work with a hands-on, early-stage VC firm known for taking an active role in building successful companies, you don't have pride of ownership in anything. You're just an investor, not a builder.

- VC is a slow path to wealth compared with the immediate cash income you get in investment banking, hedge funds or even management consulting.

- It can be argued that venture capital is fundamentally a negative process. Because you reject 99 of every 100 plans, year after year, over time you focus on figuring out what is wrong with a company. You can then reject it and get on to the next deal. What is wrong with the management? The technology? The deal terms? The strategy? If you tend to have a contrarian disposition, after just a few years, that mentality may bleed into your life. What is wrong with my partners? What is wrong with my spouse? What is wrong with me? Oh, the angst! If this reaction hits too close to home, venture capital might not be for you. What fun is it to search through hundreds and thousands of business plans and ideas for that one rare gem, if you aren't an eternal optimist?

- Because you reject 99 of every 100 entrepreneurs, you can make some enemies, no matter how nice and helpful you try to be. No one likes rejection, and passionate entrepreneurs have long memories.

Employer Directory

Accel Partners
428 University Avenue
Palo Alto, CA 94301
Phone: (650) 614-4800
Fax: (650) 614-4880
www.accel.com

Apax Partners
153 East 53rd Street, 53rd Floor
New York, NY 10022
Phone: (212) 753-6300
Fax: (212) 319-6155
www.apax.com

ARCH Venture Partners
8725 West Higgins Road, Suite 290
Chicago, IL 60631
Phone: (773) 380-6600
Fax: (773) 380-6606
www.archventure.com

Austin Ventures
300 West 6th Street, Suite 2300
Austin, TX 78701
Phone: (512) 485-1900
Fax: (512) 476-3952
www.austinventures.com

Bain Capital
111 Huntington Avenue
Boston, MA 02199
Phone: (617) 516-2000
Fax: (617) 516-2010
www.baincapital.com

Benchmark Capital
2480 Sand Hill Road, Suite 200
Menlo Park, CA 94025
Phone: (650) 854-8180
Fax: (650) 854-8183
www.benchmark.com

Cerberus Capital Management, L.P.
299 Park Avenue
New York, NY 10171
Phone: (212) 891-2100
Fax: (212) 891-1540
www.cerberuscapital.com

Charles River Ventures
1000 Winter Street #3300
Waltham, MA 02451
Phone: (781) 487-7060
Fax: (781) 487-7065

Draper Fisher Jurvetson
2882 Sand Hill Road, Suite 150
Menlo Park, CA 94025
Phone: (650) 233-9000
Fax: (650) 233-9233
www.drapervc.com

Hummer Winblad Venture Partners
2 South Park, 2nd Floor
San Francisco, CA 94107
Phone: (415) 979-9600
Fax: (415) 979-9601
www.humwin.com

JAFCO America Ventures
505 Hamilton Avenue, Suite 310
Palo Alto, CA 94301
Phone: (650) 463-8800
Fax: (650) 463-8801
www.jafco.com

J.W. Childs Associates, L.P.
111 Huntington Avenue, Suite 2900
Boston, MA 02199
Phone: (617) 753-1100
Fax: (617) 753-1101
www.jwchilds.com

Jupiter Partners LLC
12 East 49th Street, 36th Floor
New York, NY 10017
Phone: (212) 300-1000
Fax: (212) 300-1001
www.jupiterpartners.com

Kleiner Perkins Caufield & Byers
2750 Sand Hill Road
Menlo Park, CA 94025
Phone: (650) 233-2750
Fax: (650) 233-0300
www.kpcb.com

Mayfield Fund
2800 Sand Hill Road, Suite 250
Menlo Park, CA 94025
Phone: (650) 854-5560
Fax: (650) 854-5712
www.mayfield.com

Menlo Ventures
3000 Sand Hill Road, Building 4
Suite 100
Menlo Park, CA 94025
Phone: (650) 854-8540
Fax: (650) 854-7059
www.menloventures.com

New Enterprise Associates
1119 St. Paul Street
Baltimore, MD 21202
Phone: (410) 244-0115
Fax: (410) 752-7721
www.nea.com

Norwest Venture Capital
525 University Avenue, Suite 800
Palo Alto, CA 94301
Phone: (650) 321-8000
Fax: (650) 321-8010
www.norwestvc.com

Sequoia Capital
3000 Sand Hill Road
Building 4, Suite 180
Menlo Park, CA 94025
Phone: (650) 854-3927
Fax: (650) 854-2977
www.sequoiacap.com

Split Rock Partners
10400 Viking Drive, Suite 550
Minneapolis, MN 55344
Phone: (952) 995-7474
Fax: (952) 995-7475
www.splitrock.com

TL Ventures
435 Devon Park Drive, 700 Building
Wayne, PA 19087
Phone: (610) 971-1515
Fax: (610) 975-9330
www.tlventures.com

Visit Vault at **www.vault.com** for insider company profiles, expert advice,
career message boards, expert resume reviews, the Vault Job Board and more.

VAULT CAREER LIBRARY   327

Employer Directory, cont.

U.S. Venture Partners
2735 Sand Hill Road
Menlo Park, CA 94025
Phone: (650) 854-9080
Fax: (650) 854-3018
www.usvp.com

Venrock Associates
30 Rockefeller Plaza, Room 5508
New York, NY 10112
Phone: (212) 649-5600
Fax: (212) 649-5788
www.venrock.com

Visit Vault at **www.vault.com** for insider company profiles, expert advice,
career message boards, expert resume reviews, the Vault Job Board and more.

VAULT CAREER LIBRARY   329

About the Editor

Vault Editors

Vault is the leading media company for career information. Our team of industry-focused editors takes a journalistic approach in covering news, employment trends and specific employers in their industries. We annually survey 10,000s of employees to bring readers the inside scoop on industries and specific employers.

Much of the material in *The MBA Career Bible* is excerpted from Vault titles for specific industries or career titles. Vault publishes more than 120 titles for job seekers and professionals. To see a complete list of Vault titles, go to www.vault.com.